The Practical Guide to Defect Prevention

Marc McDonald
Robert Musson
Ross Smith

PUBLISHED BY
Microsoft Press
A Division of Microsoft Corporation
One Microsoft Way
Redmond, Washington 98052-6399

Library of Congress Control Number: 2006931463

Printed and bound in the United States of America.

1 2 3 4 5 6 7 8 9 QWT 2 1 0 9 8 7

Distributed in Canada by H.B. Fenn and Company Ltd.

A CIP catalogue record for this book is available from the British Library.

Microsoft Press books are available through booksellers and distributors worldwide. For further information about international editions, contact your local Microsoft Corporation office or contact Microsoft Press International directly at fax (425) 936-7329. Visit our Web site at www.microsoft.com/mspress. Send comments to mspinput@microsoft.com.

Acquisitions Editor: Ben Ryan
Project Editor: Lynn Finnel
Editorial Production: Waypoint Press
Peer Reviewer: Ed Triou

Illustration by John Hersey

Body Part No. X12-41751

Contents at Glance

Table of Contents

Part I   Introduction to Defect Prevention

1   Defect Prevention

What do you think of this book? We want to hear from you!

Microsoft is interested in hearing your feedback so we can continually improve our books and learning resources for you. To participate in a brief online survey, please visit:

www.microsoft.com/learning/booksurvey

Part V   A Culture of Prevention

What do you think of this book? We want to hear from you!

Microsoft is interested in hearing your feedback so we can continually improve our books and learning resources for you. To participate in a brief online survey, please visit:

www.microsoft.com/learning/booksurvey/

Acknowledgments

After many years of studying how and why people make mistakes (and making plenty of them ourselves), we realize how common it is for humans to make errors of omission. It's our hope that we have successfully prevented any errors of omission in this section. This book stems primarily from the work of the Microsoft Windows Defect Prevention team, and therefore the first thanks must go to Darren Muir, General Manager of Windows Core Test, for having the vision and foresight to fund our efforts, and to his boss at the time of our inception, Brian Valentine, Vice President of Windows Core Operating System Division, for his confidence in this work, his faith in our ideas, and for our day jobs. None of this would be possible without these two people recognizing the long-term benefits of an investment in researching and developing these techniques.

This book is the work of many authors. Although only three of us are listed on the cover, we must thank each of the contributing authors for their work on their respective chapters, as well as for their time, effort, and contributions to the entire book, which also includes numerous reviews of other authors' chapters as well, providing valuable feedback and suggestions.

Dan Bean   Chapter 1, "Defect Prevention," and Chapter 13, "FMEA, FTA, and Failure Modeling"

David Catlett   Chapter 6, "Improving the Testability of Software," and Chapter 8, "Risk Analysis"

Lori Ada Kilty   Chapter 7, "Software Measurement and Metrics"

Joshua Williams   Introduction and Chapter 20, "Pulling It All Together"

We must also acknowledge the fantastic reviewing work of Ed Triou, Test Architect on the Microsoft SQL Server team. His careful study, review, and feedback on each chapter has improved this book immensely—trust us, you will enjoy it more as a result of Ed's efforts. We would like to thank Brendan Murphy from Microsoft Research in Cambridge for contributing lots of data to our cause, and Nachi Nagappan, Tom Ball, and Thirumalesh Bhat from Microsoft Research in Redmond for their help with the risk analysis work. Thanks to Patrick Wickline, another Microsoft researcher, and Chris Walker, Test Architect in the Secure Windows Initiative, for their help with our root cause analysis efforts. Thanks to Harry Emil, developer on the Defect Prevention team, for his help with the companion Web site *www.defectprevention.org*.

Thanks also to a long list of talented developers from the Windows Core Organization for creating a range of tools to support these techniques, including Harry, Jinu Joseph, Francie "Viva Piñata" Emory, Tim "Forza 2" Graves, Jeff "WFH" Forde, Guru "Black Friday" Vasisht, and James "Eat My Voltage" O'Rourke. Thanks to Jacqueline Richards, Program Manager for

Microsoft Windows Server Customer program, for help with scenario voting, and to William Rios, for his patience with us and the efforts on metrics and reporting. Thanks also to Ben Sawyer, founder of the Serious Games Initiative, for his inspiration and help with productivity games.

Additionally, thanks to the many teams, managers, mentors, friends, and colleagues we have worked with over the years who have helped us learn from our own mistakes. And, in no particular order, we would like to thank the Microsoft Test Architect Group, Klaas Langhout, MSDN Test Center, James Rodrigues, Angelika Kinneman for her work on games, Aseem Badshah of Scriptovia.com for his help with scenario voting, Monte Christensen for supporting and continuing the risk analysis work, the WinSE crew Junaid Ahmed, Alex Tarvo, and Koushik Rajaram for taking risk analysis to the next level, Craig Schertz, Kevin Burrows and the Coverage Tools Team, folks from XNA: Michele Coady, Aaron Stebner, and Dean Johnson, who took the time to review various chapters and provide much appreciated feedback.

Even with the help, support, and assistance of every one of the preceding people, you would not be reading this now if it weren't for the excellent team at Microsoft Press—the most amazing editor we've ever worked with, Lynn Finnel, who totally kept us on track (actually, we never were on track—she kept us from going too far off track), copy editor Christina Palaia, and Stephen Sagman, who worked on production, art, and proofs. Thanks to our editor Devon Musgrave for his help in getting things organized. Thanks also to Microsoft Press Commissioning Editor Ben Ryan.

And thank you, our readers.

We hope you enjoy the book and find it useful.

Please send along any feedback you have—we'd love to hear from you!

Introduction

Progress, far from consisting in change, depends on retentiveness. When change is absolute there remains no being to improve and no direction is set for possible improvement: and when experience is not retained, as among savages, infancy is perpetual. Those who cannot remember the past are condemned to repeat it.
—George Santayana, The Life of Reason (1905)

People have been making mistakes since the beginning of time. More important, people have been learning from their mistakes since the beginning of time.

Charles Darwin, on page 101 of Volume I of his epic *The Descent of Man* (1871), quotes Herbert Spencer: "*I believe that the experiences of utility organised and consolidated through all past generations of the human race, have been producing corresponding modifications, which, by continued transmission and accumulation, have become in us certain faculties of moral intuition—certain emotions responding to right and wrong conduct, which have no apparent basis in the individual experiences of utility.*"[1]

How many times do you lock your keys in your car before you get a Hide-A-Key or buy a car with a combination lock? How many checks do you have to bounce before you get overdraft protection or fudge the balance to prevent the twenty dollar fee? How often do cell phones go off in meetings? How many times are jail inmates accidentally released? There are thousands of simple, yet common errors that people make every day. Because some people are employed as software developers, it's only logical that errors appear in their work, too. For an assembly line worker in Detroit, a human error might result in a new vehicle with a loose bolt in the trunk. For a restaurant worker in New York City, a mistake might result in a burger without the requested extra pickles. For a software developer in Redmond, a human error might result in a user's inability to print driving directions downloaded from the Web.

The goal of this book is not to help you avoid locking your keys in your car. The goal of this book is to provide a set of techniques to help software developers, project managers, and testers prevent human errors, or defects, in their software.

 More Info   This book has an associated Web site at *www.defectprevention.org*. Some of the material in the book is available there, including examples, templates, and reader-generated content.

Following the introduction, this book is organized in five sections that follow the migration of defects through a project.

---

1 Letter to Mr. Mill in Bain's *Mental and Moral Science: A Compendium of Psychology and Ethics*, 722; London; Longmans, Green, and Company, 1868.

Part I, "Introduction to Defect Prevention," explains the goals behind the book and why you may want to implement many of these practices in your organization. These chapters introduce the concept of defect prevention, outline a number of prevention frameworks, and cover the economics of investments in prevention techniques.

Chapter 1, "Defect Prevention," provides an overview of and introduction to the topic of preventing defects. This includes describing what a software defect is, why defects occur, and what can be done to prevent them. This chapter also introduces the concept of defect detection, analysis, and prevention techniques and the factors to consider when determining the most appropriate defect prevention strategy for your organization.

Chapter 2, "Defect Prevention Frameworks," contains information on selecting a process improvement framework. The need for a framework is described and several popular frameworks are presented. The chapter is useful for those unfamiliar with such frameworks as the Capabilities Maturity Model or the Malcolm Baldrige Quality Framework.

Chapter 3, "The Economics of Defect Prevention," provides information on return on investment (ROI) calculations for software. The intent is to provide the reader with enough information to determine if a particular investment is worthwhile from a financial perspective. Additionally, an example calculation provides a rationale for process improvement in general. The information is useful for anyone seeking to invest in process improvements and also for those trying to estimate the value of existing processes.

Part II, "Defect Detection Techniques," focuses on techniques that are useful in improving product quality.

Chapter 4, "Quality and the Development Process," discusses what quality is for a software product and how the development method creates opportunities for defects. Software cannot be tested exhaustively, so it is important to make it rare for a customer to encounter a defect and to have zero tolerance for security defects. To a customer, there is no significant difference between a problem that is a "real" defect and a problem based on a design defect. These concerns affect the type of tests you write and how you measure quality. Writing software is a series of translations from one form to another, and, except for compilation, human review is involved. Errors in translation and loss of information typically occur.

Chapter 5, "Using Productivity Games to Prevent Defects," covers the use of games and competition to focus individual or team effort on defect prevention activity. The challenges of software development involve a variety of activities, and typical projects draw the focus toward immediate, short-term activities, whereas the payoff for defect prevention investments are often longer term. Productivity games and competition can help balance the time investments and draw attention to the longer-term investments.

Chapter 6, "Improving the Testability of Software," explains the importance of designing components and systems that can be tested easily so that defects are more readily discoverable throughout the product development life cycle. This chapter introduces the Simplicity,

Observability, Control, and Knowledge (SOCK) model of testability. Targeted at design engineers and testers, this chapter provides practical guidelines for improving testability.

Part III, "Defect Analysis Techniques," showcases several important techniques to analyze defects after they have been detected.

Chapter 7, "Software Measurement and Metrics," discusses the importance of building the right foundation before gathering and reporting metrics. Though this chapter may seem to apply only to managers or marketing personnel, it emphasizes the fact that everyone working on a project must understand what is being measured and why—how metrics are ultimately tied to the business. For example, what does measuring defect detection rates tell you? How will this either improve your process or the quality of the product? How does that improvement turn into dollars, and is the amount saved or earned worth making the change? Building a balanced scorecard for your business can help justify defect prevention techniques and show how programs can affect the bottom line.

Chapter 8, "Risk Analysis," defines risk and how it relates to the software development life cycle. Using a *Reader's Digest*, "Drama in Real Life" river rafting illustration, it provides a unique look at how important it is to understand and predict areas of risk as the software project moves downstream toward completion. This chapter provides a practical risk analysis model that you can apply to any software project. The model helps project decision makers and engineers understand the risk involved when changes are made during the software development life cycle.

Chapter 9, "Using Simulation and Modeling for Organizational Innovation," provides a statistical technique for process analysis that is useful for companies implementing Capability Maturity Model Integration (CMMI) level 4 practices. It provides a means to analyze process improvements, estimate schedules based on historical data, and analyze details of subprocesses as they relate to the organizational process. The chapter provides a process for modeling and develops an example from a simple model to a very detailed process that includes dependencies between different organizational groups. The chapter is useful for anyone planning process improvements and also for project managers looking to improve estimates of schedules and create estimates of quality.

Chapter 10, "Defect Taxonomies," discusses how to modify your defect reporting system to provide information for the prevention and reduction of defects as well as surface possible best (or worst) practices. Typical defect reporting systems track a defect through the correction process but provide little data-minable information to improve the development and testing processes. The learning from defect processes breaks down as a product becomes more complex or a development team grows larger.

Chapter 11, "Root Cause Analysis," covers the popular defect prevention technique that provides a structured methodology for analyzing the cause and effect relationships of an event or defect in pursuit of a corrective action that eliminates the cause(s) of problems. There are six phases to a typical root cause analysis study, and this chapter outlines how and when to apply this defect analysis technique and how to use it to learn from defects discovered in the development process.

Part IV, "Defect Prevention Techniques," begins to shift the focus to a longer-term view by covering techniques to prevent defects.

Chapter 12, "Adopting Processes," provides a view of several popular processes with respect to frameworks. It provides a brief discussion of problems associated with implementation and improvement opportunities in existing processes. The chapter is useful for those seeking to make a change or looking for change opportunities in an existing process.

Chapter 13, "FMEA, FTA, and Failure Modeling," introduces a couple standard defect prevention techniques: Failure modes and effects analysis (FMEA) and fault tree analysis (FTA). Both FMEA and FTA were originally introduced to improve reliability in such industries as the aerospace and automotive industries where the risk of defects and failures can be significant and life threatening. These same concepts can be applied to software development to help identify potential defects and proactively address them to improve software reliability and quality. FMEA and FTA are complementary techniques in that a failure mode identified by FMEA can become the top failure event analyzed in FTA. Combining the use of FMEA and FTA into a unified failure model has conceptual similarities to the threat models used in security threat modeling. The chapter concludes with a brief illustration of one possible approach.

Chapter 14, "Prevention Tab," provides a useful technique for gathering defect prevention data at the point of experience, when the knowledge is the richest. This technique can be implemented on any project, small or large, and offers development personnel an easy way to provide suggestions and input on how defects can be prevented.

Part V, "A Culture of Prevention," explains how long-term organizational and cultural changes are necessary to implement a successful defect prevention program.

Chapter 15, "Scenario Voting," discusses a technique you can use to integrate more tightly the voice of the customer in the development process. By using this customer feedback technique, software developers can take advantage of the wisdom of the crowd in assessing the viability and the quality of their software.

Chapter 16, "Creating a Quality Culture," discusses the typical impediments to creating a culture that values quality and methods to improve your culture. A quality culture can't be decreed; it is a value that everyone needs to accept and act on. Because quality and customer perception are intertwined, customer focus is a value that helps instill a culture of quality. Establishing a quality culture can be a long process, and it is often difficult to measure progress.

Chapter 17, "Moving Quality Upstream," discusses how improving quality at the start of development reduces defects downstream. Maintaining focus on the customer from the start is an important part of this, as is doing the due diligence during the predesign phases that minimizes design errors surfacing late in development. Customer focus is more than just scenarios; it is understanding a customer's mental model of the software's functionality. A development process that reduces defects and provides earlier customer verification is described as well as a future process oriented around both customer focus and reducing translation errors in progressing from vision to code.

Chapter 18, "Rewards, Motivation, and Incentives," outlines a variety of management techniques you can use to help motivate individuals and teams to focus their efforts away from the immediate short-term tasks and toward a bigger-picture quality view. Preventative actions require forward thinking and the ability to act on things before they happen. Showcasing mistakes as a learning opportunity is not a natural human behavior, and this chapter outlines a variety of techniques to help inspire efforts for long-term quality improvement through defect prevention activity.

Chapter 19, "Knowledge Management and Communication," covers how the flow of information can affect defects. As your product becomes more complex, the team grows, or the team becomes geographically dispersed, it is no longer possible for any one person to know everything about a product. Specialization—knowing about only a limited area rather than the entire product—is a typical approach to solving this problem. However, today's products often have intertwining dependencies that require broader knowledge. Methods to improve communication between fields of specialization are discussed as well as how to use size as an advantage rather than seeing it only as a problem.

Chapter 20, "Pulling It All Together," discusses turning your development process from a series of independent steps into an optimized workflow by analyzing each phase of the product and how it affects others. Each role plays a part in producing a quality product, and by coordinating quality practices throughout the development process, teams can create both the most efficient process and the highest quality output. Successful teams rely on effective communication, good workflows, and a mindset for continuous improvement. This chapter discusses these practices and provides personal experiences to demonstrate them. Although it was written primarily with the quality assurance staff in mind, project planners and managers can also benefit from a quick read of this chapter.

Much of this book stems from the experience of the Microsoft Windows Defect Prevention team, and although there are some specific Microsoft examples throughout the book, the goal is to describe the techniques in a way that is applicable to all software development efforts, large and small.

Many books have been written on the topics of software quality assurance, testing, agile development, and other related subjects. This book is meant to augment, not replace, those. Several successful quality assurance and defect detection and analysis techniques are not covered in this book because they are already well covered elsewhere. Where applicable, we've included references to other sources, and we maintain a list on the companion Web site at *www.defectprevention.org.*

Who This Book Is For

This book is for software developers, product planners, senior managers, project managers, and testers who want to learn practical ways to improve product quality by preventing defects in their software. This is a practical guide, written to be understandable and applicable regardless of organizational size, development language, or environment. Different chapters will make sense when you are at different phases of the development cycle; each chapter has a slightly different audience from the others. The introductory chapters provide a good overview and some context for how, why, and where the techniques can be applied. We suggest you read about techniques that may be applicable to you now, and then skim through the other chapters rather than trying to read the book cover to cover at first. Later, you can return to chapters that have become applicable as you move through the development process.

Support for This Book

Every effort has been made to ensure the accuracy of this book. As corrections or changes are collected, they will be added to a Microsoft Knowledge Base article.

Microsoft Press provides support for books at the following Web site:

http://www.microsoft.com/learning/support/books/

Questions and Comments

If you have comments, questions, or ideas regarding the book or the companion content, or questions that are not answered by visiting the preceding site, please send them to Microsoft Press by e-mail to

mspinput@microsoft.com

Or by postal mail to

Microsoft Press
Attn: *The Practical Guide to Defect Prevention* Editor
One Microsoft Way
Redmond, WA 98052-6399

Please note that Microsoft software product support is not offered through the preceding addresses.

Part I
Introduction to Defect Prevention

In this part:

Chapter 1

Defect Prevention

To make no mistakes is not in the power of man; but from their errors and mistakes the wise and good learn wisdom for the future.

—Plutarch, *Greek biographer and moralist (AD 46–120)*

You just opened this book and saw that the first page of the first chapter is printed upside down.

How did you react? Were you surprised? Annoyed? Angry? All of these emotions? Did the printing defect impact your initial impression of the book and its quality?

All products can have defects that impact the user, and some are more annoying than others. If this page only included minor spelling and grammar mistakes, you may have just noticed them, but moved on. However, for a major printing mistake you probably reacted much differently. Did you check the next page to see if it was printed correctly and then just turn the book over to read this page? Did this make you question whether to buy this book? If you had already purchased the book, did it make you think about exchanging if for a good copy or asking for a refund (please don't).

These are all normal reactions to finding a defect in any product, including software. Customers can choose to ignore the defect, accept it, consider a workaround, seek an exchange, or return the product for a refund. No matter which choice is made, their satisfaction with the product usually decreases. To make matters worse, customers experiencing product defects create additional product costs, such as direct costs from refunds and indirect costs from negative recommendations and lost sales. Ultimately, these are all costs of poor quality that will affect customer satisfaction and the bottom line of a business. To avoid these costs, the best option is to invest in defect prevention.

Figure 1-1 The 24-cent Inverted Jenny stamp at the Smithsonian National Postal Museum

Why should you and your software development team be concerned about defects? Because your goal is to produce high-quality software that provides value to users and meets their expectations. To accomplish this goal, your software, like a book with printed pages, must be as defect free as possible. Customers expect it to be so, and if you do not provide products that are defect free, your customers may not be your customers for long. Suffice it to say that any time there is a defect, it will eventually cost you something. In addition to money, it may also cost you a development team that is frustrated and worn out from continually fixing defects or a dissatisfied customer who switches to someone else's software product in the future. We wrote this book to help you avoid defects and their associated costs.

> **Tip**   If you are an experienced software engineer and thoroughly understand software defects and why they occur, you may want to skip directly to the section titled "What Can Be Done?" later in this chapter.

If you are reading this book, there is a pretty good chance you have experienced software problems and understand the impact they can have. Consider the last time you lost work because of an application crash, or a time when you could not figure out how to accomplish a task using the software. How did that make you feel? Do you want users to have these same kinds of experiences with your software? Use your personal experiences as motivation to learn how to prevent these types of defects in the future. Sometimes this is called "walking in your customer's shoes."

On the other hand, perhaps you believe that software will always have defects. After all, software is created by humans and "to err is human"; therefore, defects must be inevitable, right? Many people feel this way. Following this logic, should a software development team simply accept the inevitability of defects and the human errors that cause them? The answer must be an emphatic "*No!*" Defects can and must be prevented because users deserve better—they deserve high-quality software.

Improved software quality can be accomplished in a variety of ways, but the best approach is defect prevention because the benefits realized through prevention efforts can be reapplied in the future. Our goal for this book is to provide you with a high-level, practical guide covering defect prevention techniques that apply to all stages of software development and many different types of defects. Our hope is that the techniques outlined in this book will help software development teams improve their software over the long term to enhance the quality of the user experience. Although much has already been done and written about preventing defects in software, opportunities for improvement remain.

What Is a Software Defect?

A *software defect* is a deficiency in a software product that causes it to perform unexpectedly. From a software user's perspective, a defect is anything that causes the software not to meet their expectations. In this context, a *software user* can be either a person or another piece of software. A few examples are listed in Table 1-1. From a software developer's perspective, a defect is anything that must be corrected in a software work product.

Table 1-1   Software Defects from the User's Perspective

Typical Examples of Software Defects	
User Expectation	The software will help me accomplish a task
Software Defect	Desired software functionality is missing
User Expectation	Clicking on the button performs the task I want to do
Software Defect	Clicking on the button does nothing or not what I want it to do
User Expectation	A file can be successfully copied to another location
Software Defect	The file becomes corrupted during the copy process
User Expectation	Calling a method in the API will perform as documented
Software Defect	The API fails due to an undocumented change to the registry
Less Obvious Examples of Software Defects	
User Expectation	The software will hellp me avoid mistakes (for example, spelling errors)
Software Defect	A spelling error caused by using a valid word incorrectly is not detected
User Expectation	The software will respond quickly
Software Defect	The software responds too slowly from the user's perspective
User Expectation	The software is secure from hackers
Software Defect	Hackers are able to exploit vulnerability and attack the software
User Expectation	For a "fatal error," a return code will be received so impact can be mitigated
Software Defect	No fatal error return code is sent, and the software freezes

Defects can be introduced during any stage of the development cycle regardless of whether you are following the sequential requirements-design-implementation-verification-maintenance phases of the waterfall model or the rapid iterations of agile software development. The goal of this book is not to espouse any one development approach over another. However, it is important to have a context when referring to defects and the relative point in the development cycle when they can occur. Consequently, to provide a frame of reference the following product life cycle will be used:

Figure 1-2   Reference software product life cycle

In the Product Definition phase, the Value Proposition stage completes an analysis of what is happening in the marketplace. In the Product Development phase, the Requirements stage defines the scenario requirements and features of the product. The Design stage determines how the features will be built. The Implementation stage focuses on coding, documentation, and internal testing. The Verification stage focuses on customer beta testing of completed features in the product. The Release stage yields a completed product ready for customers. In the Product Servicing phase, the Maintenance stage provides ongoing maintenance for the product, including hotfixes, security updates, and service packs.

No matter how or when it occurs, the severity of a defect will vary based on the impact it has on a user. A software program that crashes or stops working has a major defect that prevents its use. A software program that presents an inconsistent user interface has a minor defect that may lessen its value or hinder user productivity, but doesn't actually prevent its use. Based on project schedules, available resources, and the impact and severity of the defects, you will need to prioritize some defects to be fixed before others. Although this prioritization can be the reality, the ultimate goal should still be to create and release software that is defect free.

Making High-Quality Software the Goal

To have a goal of high quality, you first need to understand what high-quality software means. Traditionally, high quality has meant a lack of defects found during inspection and testing. Unfortunately, as pointed out in Chapter 4, "Quality and Product Development," testing can only indicate a lack of quality and it is not possible to test software completely. Consequently, the number of defects found in test cannot be the only metric used to assess software quality. In many cases, quality is in the eye of the beholder, so you also need to evaluate subjective quality based on customer perceptions and expectations. (See Chapter 15, "Scenario Voting.") In terms of perceived quality, software defects caused by unmet customer expectations are just as important as defects related to broken functionality. Therefore, they both need to be taken into consideration. The cost of a problem found late in the development process can be significant. Repair costs rise as the development cycle progresses because of increased rework caused by design and coding changes, retesting, and impact on other dependent software. Industry studies have shown that a defect that costs 1x to fix in design could cost 100x to fix after the software is released.[1] Clearly, everyone—from product designers to product developers and product stakeholders—will benefit if the development team can *prevent* defects early rather than discovering and fixing them later.

Critical defects include issues such as lost data, data corruption, and inadequate security that prevent a user from having a reliable computing experience. A solid design helps mitigate the risk of critical defects. Fortunately, defect prevention techniques can be applied early in the design stage to improve the quality of the design and minimize risks.

---

1   B. Boehm and V. Basili, "Software Defect Reduction Top 10 List," *IEEE Computer Society* 34, no. 1 (January 2001): 135–137.

Over the years, many different defect prevention techniques have evolved to manage the "defect introduction" opportunities inherent in product development. Many of these techniques can be applied to software development. In the case of software development, the applicability and effectiveness of these techniques can vary dramatically across different projects. Therefore, it is important to consider which defect prevention techniques will be the most useful for your software project. The purpose of this book is to highlight practical and effective defect prevention techniques to help you make those choices and select the most beneficial techniques for your needs.

> *We have met the enemy and he is us.*
> *—Walt Kelly, Pogo comic strip*

Understanding Why Software Defects Occur

A defect in software results from some type of mistake. Usually these mistakes are a result of human error, but sometimes they are caused by systemic errors in the development process. Mistakes can also result from faulty development tools, a misunderstanding of customer requirements, or other issues that arise in the course of software development. Fortunately, not every mistake leads to a defect, but almost all defects can be traced back to some type of mistake (see Table 1-2).

Table 1-2   Mistakes and Resulting Software Defects

Typical Mistakes That Cause Software Defects	
Mistake	Communication difficulties between customers and software developers
Software Defect	Desired software functionality is missing
Mistake	Developer overlooks a logic error in the code
Software Defect	Clicking on the button does nothing
Mistake	Developer forgets error checking in the file copy code
Software Defect	A corrupted file is copied, and the software crashes
Mistake	Developer does not understand the customer scenario
Software Defect	The software does not meet the customer's needs
Mistake	Developer only tests the software using a fast computer and the performance seems fine
Software Defect	The software responds too slowly from the perspective of a user with an older and slower computer
Mistake	Developer does not review the code for software vulnerabilities
Software Defect	Hackers are able to exploit vulnerabilities and attack the software
Mistake	Developer does not recognize a fatal error condition, so no return code is sent
Software Defect	Software does not return a code indicating a fatal error condition

Although it may be easy, or even fashionable, to blame a computer for causing a software defect, in reality almost all defects can be attributed to some type of human error. Because computers are machines, there is a possibility that the computer hardware is to blame, but in most cases software defects result from mistakes made by people. Consequently, the study of human error offers a good framework for determining and understanding why software defects really occur.

Analyzing the Bases of Human Error

The science of human error is a fascinating subject, and some tremendous research into classification systems, causality models, and error reduction techniques has been done. Machine plant safety, disaster planning, and prevention of catastrophic accidents are all areas where human error studies have led to positive results. Investigation into human errors and their impact on software development was initiated during the 1970s. Since then, research has continued, first driven by interest in software safety and hazard analysis, and then more recently by interest in software quality and security.

The study of human error is a broad topic, and it helps to start with an initial foundation. One view of human errors draws its structure primarily from the work of James Reason.[1] In this view, there are three broad categories of errors that provide a framework for analysis: skill-based errors, knowledge-based errors, and rule-based errors.

Skill-based errors are usually the obvious mistakes that occur when a person knows what to do, has done it successfully in the past, and just "slipped up." *Knowledge-based errors* are mistakes made because a person doesn't know everything about a problem space and therefore didn't know what to do. *Rule-based errors* are mistakes made by following a rule; rule errors do not include mistakes made where a rule could exist, just those made by applying or misapplying an existing rule.

Applying human error research to software defects can yield interesting insights. In particular, a clear understanding of how and why people make mistakes can be useful in improving development processes, coding and check-in rules, compiler settings, design principles, user research, quality assurance efforts, and many other areas that require humans to do work. See Chapter 10, "Defect Taxonomies," for more information.

> *An ounce of prevention is worth a pound of cure.*
> —Henry de Bracton, De Legibus, AD 1240

What Can Be Done?

Mistakes can be made in many different areas of the software development effort. Coding defects are the most obvious, but mistakes can also occur in design, management, project planning, and other activities throughout the organization. It often seems that the only real

---

1 James Reason, *Human Error* (Cambridge, UK: Cambridge University Press, 1990).

guarantee is that mistakes will occur and some will cause software defects. Realizing this, most software development teams invest heavily in testing as their primary focus for eliminating defects before the defects can impact users.

Defect prevention requires investment with a different focus. An investment in defect prevention emphasizes a more proactive and cost-effective way to eliminate software defects. Rather than relying on testing to find software defects after they are introduced, defect prevention techniques focus on preventing the introduction of defects in the first place. The basic theme of this book is that defects can be prevented and that the software development process can be improved over time, using a variety of techniques, to reduce the number of defects in software.

Using Detection, Analysis, and Prevention Techniques

Software quality and defect rates can be addressed at three levels. The first level is *detection*. This is the most common approach to improving software quality. "Test quality into the software"—test the software until all the discoverable defects are found and fixed. (See Chapter 6, "Improving the Testability of Software" for more information.) Although this is a goal of all software development teams, it is not possible to completely test software. However, what is possible is to detect many of the defects, and there are many different ways to do that. Examples include static analysis tools, automated test cases, and user beta testing. These methods can identify defects where they exist but do little or nothing to prevent a similar defect from recurring elsewhere.

The next level of software quality improvement is achieved through *analysis*. At this level, time is spent analyzing previously discovered defects to look for trends and insights into how they occurred and why they were not detected earlier. See Chapter 11, "Root Cause Analysis," for more information. Analyzing defects takes time and expertise, but the effort can yield significant benefits when improvements are made based on the results.

Over the long term, the most effective level of quality improvement efforts is *prevention*. At this level, specific techniques are used to proactively identify and eliminate potential defects. Also, the findings from the detection and analysis levels can be used to modify processes and development practices to eliminate the root causes of defects. These findings may also be applied to earlier detection, thereby reducing repair and rework costs. Eliminating the defects and their root causes improves the effectiveness of future development efforts as well. The ultimate goal of any quality improvement effort should be to enable the development team to invest more time in defect prevention activity.

What Is Different in a Prevention Organization

Most software development teams recognize the need to prevent defects and try a variety of techniques to prevent them. However, most of these techniques focus on improved defect detection (testing) and not on defect prediction and prevention. Because of issues such as schedule pressures and insufficient resources, software teams are often constrained in their ability to invest in effective quality assurance and quality improvement processes. While they work hard to try different improvements and may even try some prediction and prevention techniques, the sustainable results they want are never fully achieved.

To help software development teams attain sustainable results, organizations such as the Carnegie Mellon Software Engineering Institute (SEI) have developed models like the Capability Maturity Model (CMM) to give teams a way to assess the capabilities of their development process and also provide a roadmap for improvement. See Chapter 2, "Defect Prevention Frameworks" for more information. In the CMM five levels of process maturity, level 4 organizations predict defects and manage quality using statistical process control techniques and level 5 organizations prevent defects by quantitatively improving processes through innovative process and technological improvements.[1] Because attaining this level of process maturity can help teams produce better, faster and cheaper products with higher quality and better customer satisfaction, this would seem to be a logical goal for all software development organizations. However, based on a 2006 profile of CMM appraisal results, SEI determined that only 137 (7.6%) of the 1804 organizations undergoing CMM appraisal were operating at level 4 and only 175 (9.8%) were operating at level 5.[2] The majority of the organizations were operating at a lower CMM maturity level with a focus on detection and reaction, the first level of defect prevention and not on prediction and prevention.

Why is this? It's primarily because a focus on analysis and prevention can initially require more time and resources, and although the return on investment is usually high, the costs can be significant. If a project is on a tight schedule or budget, the project manager must decide if it is more effective to ask senior engineers to invest their time in analyzing bugs and developing preventions or to have them write new features and fix existing bugs in the current product to accelerate the ship date. This creates a dilemma: make your boss happy by meeting a project deadline with some defects, or make the project stakeholders and users happy by preventing defects at the expense of missed deadlines and extra resource investments. Because software projects are typically rewarded upon completion, project managers usually choose the short-term view and opt for completing the current effort before investing in long-term quality improvement techniques. Although this can be a prudent decision for them to make, it can be shortsighted for their organization and company in the long run.

In contrast, a software development team that acknowledges and focuses on the potential of defect prevention is enlightened. As a "prevention organization," it understands that analyzing defects and applying the learning to drive continuous improvement can achieve high quality and significant economic benefits over the long term. Although a prevention organization still has the normal resource and scheduling challenges, it makes a conscious effort to invest in prevention activities. The biggest difference between a detection organization and a

---

1 CMMI Product Team, CMMI for Development, Version 1.2, (Pittsburg, PA, Carnegie Mellon Software Engineering Institute, August 2006)

2 CMMI Appraisal Program, *Process Maturity Profile, Software CMM 2005 End-Year Update*, (Pittsburgh, PA, Carnegie Mellon Software Engineering Institute, March 2006)

prevention organization is that a detection organization typically is in constant "fire drill" mode just trying to find and address all defects, whereas a prevention organization is typically more optimistic, focused on the future, and deliberate in its approach to improving quality.

We want to help you create your own prevention organization. There is an old adage that states, "If you always do what you've always done, you'll always get what you've always got." That will not happen in a prevention organization because a prevention organization concentrates on changing the processes and conditions that lead to mistakes in the first place. Stephen R. Covey in *The Seven Habits of Highly Effective People,*[1] talks about the importance of renewal and "sharpening the saw." He states, "Renewal is the principle—and the process—that empowers us to move on an upward spiral of growth and change, of continuous improvement." A prevention organization is focused on sharpening the saw—continued renewal through improved tools, processes, and people.

Using Defect Prevention Techniques

With all due respect to F. W. Taylor,[2] there is no "one best way" to prevent defects in software. Over the years, a variety of prevention techniques have been developed for use in different stages of the software development cycle. The purpose of all these techniques is to help predict, identify, detect, and ultimately prevent defects before they can affect users.

The techniques can be grouped into three categories based on their goals, testing focus, and how proactive or reactive they are within the software development process. The three categories are as follows:

- Defect detection techniques
- Defect analysis techniques
- Defect prevention techniques

(Please note that *defect prevention techniques,* as used here, is a subcategory of specific techniques in the overall category of *defect prevention.*)

Defect Detection Techniques

In terms of software development, a wide variety of testing techniques can be used to identify software defects. Functional testing, boundary testing, low-memory tests, code inspection, and end user beta testing are all effective techniques. Defect detection techniques such as these are used in most software development projects to discover defects and improve product quality. Software testing is an extensive topic and the subject of many excellent books,

---

1   Stephen R. Covey, *The Seven Habits of Highly Effective People* (New York: Free Press, 1989).

2   F.W. Taylor, also known as the "father of scientific management," advocated the analysis of work using time and motion studies to determine "the one best way" to do something.

such as *Hunting Security Bugs*[1] and the How to Break Software series,[2] so these testing techniques are not explicitly covered in this book.

However, a byproduct of software testing and subsequent error reporting is extensive information about defects and defect patterns that can be analyzed to identify root causes and how to eliminate or mitigate similar defects in the future. This information can feed directly into the defect analysis techniques.

Defect Analysis Techniques

The primary goal of defect analysis techniques is to learn from defects that have already been discovered and to use that learning to further improve the quality of software and even the productivity of those who build it. Defect analysis techniques help by applying the data gathered during traditional product development to ongoing personal and process improvements and defect prevention. The goal is to analyze defects, determine their root causes, and then develop ways to improve the development process to eliminate them. If the defects cannot be eliminated, the goal must be to create awareness of the defects, identify mitigation techniques, and then implement the mitigations to reduce the impact of these defects on users. Examples of defect analysis techniques are defect classification using defect taxonomies, root cause analysis (RCA), and stochastic modeling. (See Chapter 9, "Stochastic Modeling," and Chapter 11, "Root Cause Analysis," for more information).

Defect Prevention Techniques

The primary goal of defect prevention techniques is to anticipate and prevent defects proactively *before* they can occur and cause failures or confuse users. This is the best approach because a defect that does not occur is also a defect that need not be caught, fixed, and supported. The savings resulting from the successful application of defect prevention techniques can be reapplied elsewhere in the product cycle. Examples of defect prevention techniques are failure modes and effects analysis (FMEA), fault tree analysis (FTA) (see Chapter 13, "FMEA, FTA, and Failure Modeling," for more information), and use of the Prevention tab (see Chapter 14, "Prevention Tab," for more information).

Choosing Quality Improvement Techniques

Choosing quality improvement techniques requires careful consideration of project and organizational factors. Although each situation is different, the goal is to achieve the maximum benefit of defect prevention in an acceptable amount of time and using the available

---

1   Tom Gallagher, Lawrence Landauer, and Bryan Jeffries, *Hunting Security Bugs* (Redmond, WA: Microsoft Press, 2006).

2   James A. Whittaker, *How to Break Software* (Boston, MA: Addison-Wesley, 2003); James A. Whittaker and Herbert H. Thompson, *How to Break Software Security* (Boston, MA: Addison-Wesley, 2003); Mike Andrews and James A. Whittaker, *How to Break Web Software* (Boston, MA: Addison-Wesley, 2006).

resources. Figure 1-3 provides a general effort vs. benefit comparison of some commonly used defection prevention techniques.

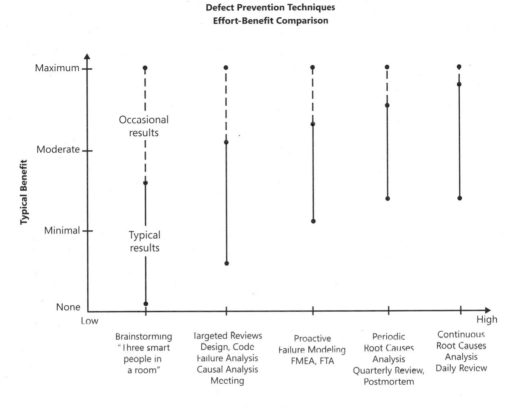

Figure 1-3   Effort vs. benefit comparison chart

In general, results improve as the investment in and rigor of the techniques increase. The downside is that formal and rigorous techniques also require more time and effort investment. As a result, with limited time and resources available, there is a tendency to use the less rigorous techniques, including brainstorming sessions and review meetings. Although these can be effective, the results are often highly dependent on the knowledge, skill, and experience of the participants.

Factors to Consider

No single technique can prevent all defects. A combination of techniques, requiring varying amounts of knowledge, experience, resources, time, and effort, can be employed to promote the design and development of high-quality software. Because time and resources must be determined and allocated up front, and because they are almost always in short supply, successful defect prevention programs require strong organizational commitment.

Be sure to consider the following factors when choosing among defect prevention techniques:

- **People resources**   Which people will be available to perform the defect prevention technique? Have they ever used this technique before? Do they have the right skills and knowledge, or will they need to be trained?

- **Tool resources**   Are the right technique-specific tools available to help guide people through the defect prevention effort? If the right tools are not available, how long will it take to obtain and implement them? Is tool-specific training available to the people who will be using the tools in a defect prevention technique?

- **Time resources**   How much time is available to the overall organization and key individuals in particular to complete the software development project? Are there conflicting priorities on how to allocate the time that is available? What stage of the product development life cycle is the project in, and how will that affect available time?

- **Organizational commitment**   Is management, in particular senior management, asking for the defect prevention results? Is defect prevention part of the standard engineering process in the organization? In product teams, how much support really exists for performing defect prevention techniques, especially those that are more involved and require more engineering rigor? When push comes to shove, will defect prevention efforts be always postponed or cut from the schedule?

Selecting a Strategy

Defect prevention techniques can be delineated by the resource or time investment required, by the short- or long-term effectiveness, and by the stages of the product cycle. Organizations should determine where their greatest needs lie, what their quality goals are, and the level of commitment to quality assurance versus ongoing quality improvement before deciding where and how to invest in defect prevention activity. As a result of this assessment exercise, organizations can set realistic goals for defect prevention investments and determine appropriate strategies to achieve them. Depending on the level of investment, here are some alternative strategies.

Best Strategy

Prevent future defects. Focus on techniques that help anticipate potential defects, and use these techniques to eliminate or mitigate possible failures proactively. In this strategy, the primary use of testing is to *confirm* software quality.

Good Strategy

Focus on the techniques that can help detect and analyze defects, and use analysis information to identify underlying causes. Implement improvements to eliminate those causes and mitigate the impact of defects before users are affected. In this strategy, the primary use of testing is to *ensure* software quality.

Bad Strategy

This strategy might represent the status quo based on how customers often perceive software quality today: Allow defects to escape, let users find them, and then react to the complaints. Use inadequate detection and prevention techniques or use adequate techniques half-heartedly. Allow indifferent organizational commitment to hinder the achievement of expected quality benefits.

Organizational Considerations

Organizations must realistically assess their level of commitment to and expectations of the defect prevention process. For example, many organizations want to achieve very low defect rates like those of the NASA Space Shuttle program and the airline industry but resist the investment, effort, and engineering rigor required to achieve such a high level of reliability and performance. Other organizations want to eliminate defects by just putting "three smart people in a room" to discuss an issue and quickly devise ways to resolve it. Unfortunately, although the brainstorming approach is quick, requires minimal effort, and can be moderately effective, it typically isn't very thorough.

At the other end of the spectrum are more robust defect prevention processes such as formal root cause analysis (RCA) and Six Sigma. These are more rigorous and typically based on gathering and analyzing objective data. These formal approaches can garner results that are significantly better but can also require much more time, effort, and organizational investment. Therefore, organizations must determine their real level of commitment to defect prevention and set their goals and expectations accordingly. In most cases, what organizations get out of defect prevention is determined by the effort and investment they put into it.

Moving Quality Upstream

In a typical software development project, the test team becomes involved late in the process to find defects and "test quality into the software." Unfortunately, as mentioned earlier in this chapter, the later a defect is discovered, the more expensive it is to repair and the greater the cost and impact on the overall project.

Consequently, if defects cannot be avoided altogether, a fundamental goal of a successful defect prevention effort is to move quality verification and improvement to an earlier stage in the software development cycle. Focusing on quality in the planning, design, and early development stages pays big dividends later in the cycle. By moving quality assessment and improvement "upstream" in the software development process, the test team can focus more on the end user experience and on integration-level testing, rather than finding design or functional errors. See Chapter 17, "Moving Quality Upstream," for more information.

Learning from Mistakes

It is important to implement a process that individuals and teams can use to learn from their mistakes. A fundamental aspect of this learning is the classification of defects using a logical defect taxonomy. With a structured taxonomy, an organization can analyze and learn about the types of defects that have been discovered and their relative frequencies. Focusing root cause analysis techniques on understanding why defects have occurred provides insight into what improvements are needed to prevent or mitigate those defects in the future.

On the other hand, without a feedback process in place to ensure that the team can benefit from the learning that takes place during defect detection, analysis, and repair, the likelihood of repetitive errors is high. Consequently, a goal should be that if a certain type of defect is going to occur, it should occur only once before safeguards are deployed to prevent it from recurring. See Chapter 10, "Defect Taxonomies," for more information.

Investing for the Future

It is important to reiterate that organizational commitment dictates which of these defect prevention techniques can be successful. An organization may desire to invest in rigorous defect prevention techniques that promise more complete and effective results, but the desire must be supported with a commitment to invest. If there is no willingness to allocate the necessary time and resources, or if the company culture resists using the more rigorous techniques, the likelihood of successful defect prevention efforts is reduced.

An important first step in securing organizational commitment and overcoming resistance is to clearly demonstrate the potential return on investment. Each defect prevention technique requires time and resources, and people will want to know how much benefit can be expected from the effort. See Chapter 3, "The Economics of Defect Prevention," for more information.

Conclusion

Consider this:

- A defect prevented will never need to be fixed, saving time, resources, and money for your organization.
- A defect prevented will improve the quality of your software and help increase customer satisfaction.
- A defect prevented will not impact customers and decrease their satisfaction with your software.

These simple statements represent why we wrote this book and the value we hope you receive from reading it.

Although the benefits can be significant, the effort often required to achieve high levels of defect prevention can be significant as well. Our hope is that the practical defect prevention techniques described in this book will help you minimize the effort, maximize the benefit, and more rapidly become a "prevention organization."

In this chapter, you were introduced to the topic of defect prevention including the concept of software defects, why they occur, and what can be done to prevent them. The other chapters in this section continue to lay a foundation for defect prevention by covering defect prevention frameworks, economics, and the concept of software quality. The remaining sections in the book focus on the practical detection, analysis, and prevention techniques to consider for your own organization.

Chapter 2
Defect Prevention Frameworks

It is theory that decides what can be observed.
—A. Einstein

He who loves practice without theory is like the sailor who boards ship without a rudder and compass and never knows where he may cast.
—Leonardo da Vinci

You may question why one of the opening chapters of a text targeted at practice would be about process theory. The best answer comes from W. Edwards Deming, who is often referred to as the father of process improvement. Deming stated that "experience alone, without theory, teaches . . . nothing about what to do to improve quality and competitive position, nor how to do it." Deming continued, "Experience will answer a question, and a question comes from theory."[1]

A framework, like a theory, provides a means to ask questions. A framework differs in that the incomplete portions are explicitly incomplete requiring each user to modify the underlying theory contained in the framework. A process framework provides the skeleton of a theory that can be filled in by the user of the framework. In 1830, Auguste Compte wrote "A Course in Positive Philosophy" and proposed a framework for learning and the progression of science, formalizing it into the Law of Three Stages.[2] The law proposes the following hierarchy of knowledge growth for a scientific discipline:

1. The theological stage, where belief and religion dominate
2. The metaphysical stage, where philosophy dominates
3. The positive stage, where scientific reasoning dominates

Compte points out that "facts cannot be observed without the guidance of some theory" and "no real observation of any phenomena is possible, except in so far as it is first directed, and finally interpreted, by some theory."

Much of the history of software development has relied on the first stage of learning, using belief as a means to determine the correct process. This is not surprising because D. N. Perkins found a positive correlation between intelligence and the ability to justify one's point of view, and a negative correlation between intelligence and the ability to consider others' points of view.[3] Thus, once a belief such as "increasing quality will increase cost" takes hold,

---

1 W. Edwards Deming, *Out of the Crisis* (Cambridge, MA: MIT Press, 1982).

2 Gertrud Lenzer, ed., *Auguste Comte and Positivism: The Essential Writings* (New York: Harper Press, 1975).

3 D.N. Perkins, *The Mind's Best Work* (Boston: Harvard University Press, 1981)

it is reinforced with each subsequent project, and the ability to consider other perspectives is reduced. Even highly intelligent software developers can find it difficult to alter such a belief.

Currently, there is a movement toward the second stage, the philosophical stage, with the so-called Agile processes leading the way. The philosophy is codified in the principles of the Agile manifesto.[1] The Agile manifesto attempts to organize the philosophy by which Agile processes such as Extreme Programming and Scrum operate. It defines principles such as "Continuous attention to technical excellence and good design enhance agility." This necessary second step in the evolution of software process provides the means for dissolution of old beliefs, but it does not result in measurable improvement to the engineering system. Thus, this is the rationale for Deming's statement that theory must be an integral part of experience to eliminate dogmatic beliefs and advance the engineering system. Without theory, there is superstition and philosophy, but no science.

Different frameworks tend to focus on different aspects of process improvement. This chapter provides guidance on choosing and then enhancing a framework that your organization can use to ask the right questions with respect to process improvement and defect prevention. Of course, the right questions are those that lead to measurable improvement and the dissolution of superstition. This chapter also describes some of the basic attributes of several popular frameworks. The purpose is to add scientific rigor to the practical application of theory.

Examining a Sample Framework

Theory need not be complex. In fact, the best theories are often deceptively simple. To illustrate the point, consider a simple theoretical framework for questions you may ask about a subject as described in the Introduction and used throughout this book. The questions fall into the categories shown in Figure 2-1. The theoretical framework provides a means to examine a subject area. For example, you may expect that a practical guide provides extensive knowledge in the How category. However, unless the topic is obvious or trivial, the model suggests that there must be a justification for the subject, so it seems natural that the book must cover Why to some extent. As was previously discussed, What is analogous to theory, and without it, there can be only belief, so even a practical guide must provide a theoretical basis. Therefore, according to this model, a practical guide to any subject must cover much more than simply a list of useful techniques.

Figure 2-1   Hierarchy of questions

1   See www.agilemanifesto.org/principles.html

Such a framework serves to assist in planning. Filling in the missing pieces of the framework provides a structure for the project much as a theory provides the basis for scientific inquiry. Notice also that it provides a means to question, that is, hypothesize, about the elements of the model. This simple three-question model is useful as a means to assess the coverage of a subject area. You may look at a variety of textbooks and gauge how well those books answer these questions. You also can use the model to categorize textbooks. A theoretical subject may include more material on What rather than How with little, if any, coverage of Why. On the other hand, a self-help book may include extensive coverage of Why. The model provides a means to categorize and plan research activities.

Notice that the example framework uses a subset of all possible questions. It is by no means all encompassing and provides only partial guidance for the subject material. Kuhn, in his examination of the structure of scientific theory, reports that a good paradigm actually *is not* complete.[1] The incomplete nature of the paradigm allows for scientific inquiry into the missing pieces.

For example, after using the simple three-question paradigm, you can enhance it to include a time-ordered progression of questions such as "Why, What, How" to provide more guidance while at the same time restricting content. You can further enhance the model by including more questions, such as "When" or "Who." However, enhancement occurs only after the base model is found to be insufficient through experiment.

If a researcher examines a number of textbooks and finds the need for more categorization, only then would another category be added. The model provides a basic theory by which a researcher can guide his or her thinking so that the decision to add more complexity is not based on only the researcher's beliefs. Model enhancement uses good science. Propose a model, test it, and then change it only after it is found to be lacking.

Proposing a Model

It is not always necessary to create a new framework because there often is no end to the number of models proposed by academia. Picking a reasonable process-improvement model requires understanding the content of the model. To determine What, a basic understanding of various existing models is required. Some models target software development, while others are general improvement paradigms. Often, the first model used for process improvement is a somewhat arbitrary choice to assist in the planning effort. After an organization gains a detailed understanding of the model, it is easier for the organization to enhance or change to another more suitable model. The next sections describe a few of the more popular models that can be used for process improvement.

---

1   T. Kuhn, *The Structure of Scientific Revolutions* (Chicago: University of Chicago Press, 1962).

Defect Prevention Model

The model used in this book considers the degrees to which a defect is detected versus prevented. Certainly, detection techniques prevent the customer from finding a defect, so they qualify as a rudimentary form of defect prevention. Figure 2-2 is the conceptual hierarchy and goals of each level. The three levels of defect activity contain a number of subactivities that satisfy the main category goals: defect detection, defect prediction, and defect prevention.

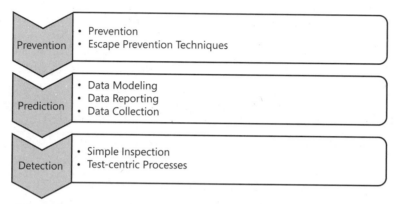

Figure 2-2   Defect prevention model

Defect detection has the goal of finding all defects before they are found by the next phase in the process. You may ask why such a practice is a prevention practice. In the strictest of terms, it is not, but most organizations begin with a practice of detection, so the model begins at this point, too. At this level, the organization is mostly reactive to defect reports. Practices focus on testing the product after defect creation. The two-step model presented in Chapter 9, "Stochastic Modeling" (see Figure 9-16), indicates such a culture. In some organizations, simple inspection techniques help to augment the test process. However, the focus is still reactive to defects, often resulting in inspections that occur after the test process completes.

From a culture of detection, the organization moves to one of analysis. The end goal of analysis is to predict areas that need attention either in the form of more removal processes or in the form of process improvement. This level requires good measurement techniques, which means the data is collected to answer specific questions associated with organizational goals (see the discussion of the Goal-Question-Metric approach in Chapter 7, "Software Measurement and Metrics"), and the reports are available to those who need them. Finally, this level makes use of prediction models, such as those made possible by stochastic modeling (Chapter 9). The models predict product and process quality.

The third level assumes a culture of prevention, where defects are not introduced in the first place and where existing defects are not allowed to escape the creation process, that is, the defects are not allowed to escape the engineer's office. Because human beings create code, it is not reasonable that it be perfect when written. It is, however, reasonable that the person creating the defect should also remove it. Practices at this level include prevention techniques such as formal design methods and escape prevention. An example escape prevention technique is a formalized inspection process that uses process controls such as review rate and predicts the number of escaped defects using a capture–recapture methodology (see Chapter 20, "Leveraging Good Processes").

Capability Maturity Model

One of the oldest and most thoroughly researched of all software models is the Capability Maturity Model (CMM), first described by Watts Humphrey (1989).[1] The original intent of the model was to assess the capabilities of an organization against a common set of necessary development processes. However, the model is also useful as a road map for improvement as a result of the arrangement of the practices. As the model's name implies, it describes the degree of process maturity an organization has with respect to required elements of the model. Here we describe the elements of the model. Literally thousands of companies use the model to assess organizational capabilities.

Model Structure

The CMM is an extremely rich, well-researched, and hence complex improvement model. However, conceptually, it is very simple. It consists of five levels of process maturity each of which has a purpose. Levels build on the capabilities mastered at previous levels. Each level has a number of key practice areas (KPAs) that together fulfill the purpose of the level. Each KPA has a set of goals. To have a disciplined process, an organization must show *commitment* to the process goals, have the *ability* to carry out a set of *activities*, and *measure* and *verify* adherence to the processes. The commitments, abilities, activities, measurements, and verifications form the What associated with each KPA.

As stated earlier, the model contains a wealth of information, but the downside is a temptation to implement the activities outlined in the KPAs directly as processes. Individual KPAs must not be thought of as processes but only as a way of assessing a process. In an attempt to implement the CMM as a How, organizations may become frustrated with the models, and the effort will likely fail. Figure 2-3 shows the level hierarchy and target process improvement areas for each level.

---

1 W. S. Humphrey, *Managing the Software Process* (Reading, MA: Addison-Wesley, 1989). For those readers not familiar with Humphrey, he joined Carnegie-Mellon's Software Engineering Institute after 27 years leading IBM's development organization and is a National Medal of Technology Laureate for his contributions to software development and production methodologies.

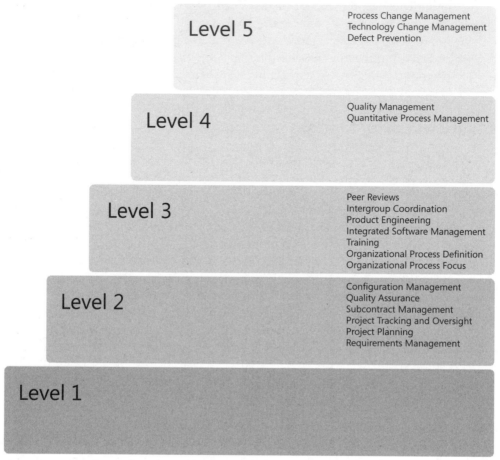

Figure 2-3   Capabilities Maturity Model hierarchy

Levels of Process Maturity

Level 1 is politely referred to as Initial, or sometimes Ad Hoc. An ad hoc process is one designed for a specific purpose and is typically intended for only one use. Once implemented, the exact rationale for the process may be forgotten, causing other projects to adhere to an unsuitable practice. The problem with level 1 organizations is obvious: they spend too much time inventing working processes or using unsuitable ones. Because most of the world's software is developed by level 1 organizations, the level does not indicate the ability to be successful in the market. However, the waste associated with using unfit processes means that most organizations could be much more profitable.

At level 2, an organization is said to have a Repeatable process. This means that skills mastered on one project are directly transferable to the next. At level 2, the skills are directed toward individual teams and the management of those teams. Figure 2-3 shows the practices associated with level 2 organizations and those associated with good project management. Organizations at level 2 establish basic project management processes "to track cost, schedule, and functionality" and provide the discipline "to repeat earlier success on projects with similar applications." The intent at this level is to understand the capabilities associated with the organization and the relationships in project planning. Important project management issues such as requirements management and configuration control are planned in advance, but a level 2 organization is still reactionary for most management issues. Although project management skills can reduce some costs, most of the benefit is realized through an understanding of each team's capabilities, hence the name Repeatable. An organization can repeat past successes and avoid known failures at the organizational level.

Level 3 is called the Defined level. Organizations at level 3 develop standardized processes that can be used organization-wide. By using standardized processes, level 3 organizations can take advantage of learning of each project team and spread it to other project teams. This does not mean that all teams use the same process but rather that all teams use a version of the standard process proven capable for the project of interest. A standard management process based on best practice coordinates multiple projects. The organization assesses its processes against standard models to determine capabilities. Notice that the need to first accomplish level 2 capabilities becomes obvious when reviewing the capabilities of level 3 organizations. Without the basic project management techniques of level 2, standardization of best practice is not possible.

At level 4, organizations Manage projects with statistical techniques using the data gathered by the standard organizational processes. As before, level 3 practices are prerequisite to achieving level 4. Unless organizations gather consistent data, the ability to use techniques such as statistical process control (SPC)[1] is not possible. Deming warns that statistical techniques are unusable on processes that are not "in-control," that is, processes with too many special cause variances.[2] Although level 4 does not require that an organization use SPC, it strongly implies that SPC is useful. Additionally, because using SPC requires processes to be in-control, the implication is that level 4 companies have controlled special cause variance. Again, the need for standardization at level 3 becomes obvious. Teams using ad hoc processes are less likely to have statistical control.

Finally, level 5 companies are known as Optimizing organizations. The practices at this level focus on improving the standard processes in a scientifically valid manner. The practices require the use of the information obtained at level 4 and a controlled introduction of new best practices. Once again, the progression to level 5 requires mastering the abilities of level 4. As a side note, the practices described in this book are useful for improving level 4 and level 5 capabilities.

---

1   SPC is a process of determining natural process variance and distinguishing variance inherent in the process from variance with special causes.

2   W. Edwards Deming, *Out of the Crisis* (Cambridge, MA: MIT Press, 1982).

Key Practices

We do not examine the key practice areas in detail. Instead, we describe the structure of a KPA so that you can understand the elements of building a process model. Table 2-1 provides a list of required practices and a brief description of the desired outcome of CMM KPAs.

Table 2-1   CMM Key Practices

Level	Description	Practice Area	Desired Outcomes
1	Ad-hoc - Processes are created on an as-needed basis and often outlive their usefulness.		None
2	Repeatable - Team processes are defined and past successes are repeatable	Requirements Management	Requirements are documented and changes are made known to everyone affected.
		Project Planning	Reasonable plans are made and plan assumptions documented. Changes find their way into all affected teams.
		Project Tracking and Oversight	The plans are used to control the work of the teams. Any changes will be made known and be agreed upon by those affected.
		Subcontract Management	Any work subcontracted to other organizations is managed in a repeatable manner.
		Quality Assurance	The quality of the process used to build the software is known. Quality assurance activities verify that products are built according to the planned standards.
		Configuration Management	Work products maintain version control. Products are baselined and can be rebuilt from the change control system.
3	Defined - Organization-wide best practices are defined and data are collected	Organization Process Focus	An organizational focus exists for improving process and sharing best practice.
		Organization Process Definition	A set of best practices are created and shared.
		Training	Engineers received necessary training to build products.

Table 2-1 CMM Key Practices

Level	Description	Practice Area	Desired Outcomes
		Integrated Software Management	The engineering activities and the management actvities are integrated into a single process.
		Software Product Engineering	Well-defined methods and tools are integrated into the process.
		Intergroup Coordination	All aspects of product engineering are participate to build a product to satisfy the customer needs.
		Peer Reviews	Peer reviews are used effectively to remove defects from the product.
4	Managed - Processes are controlled using the process data	Quantitative Process Management	The process is managed using statistical methods.
		Quality Management	The quality of the product is planned in much the same manner as the schedule.
5	Optimizing - Process are continuously improved	Defects Prevention	Defect prevention activities are planned. Root causes of defects are found and eliminated from the process.
		Technology Change Management	New tools are proactively identified and transitioned into the organization
		Process Change Management	The software process is continuously improved to reduce cost, improve quality, decrease cycle-time.

Figure 2-4 shows the CMM structure as defined by the model's authors.[1] Each KPA has a set of attributes known as *common features*, which define the structure of a KPA. As mentioned earlier, a KPA has five features: commitments, abilities, activities, measurements, and verifications. The activities clearly define the What of the process framework.

---

1 M. C. Paulk, C. V. Weber, B., Curtis, and M. B. Chrissis, *The Capability Maturity Model: Guidelines for Improving the Software Process* (Reading, MA: Addison-Wesley, 1994).

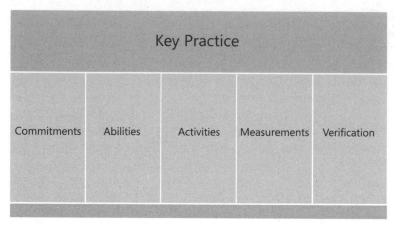

Figure 2-4 Key practices

Measurements may also fall into a What categorization, but an examination of the actual text leads to some doubt. The other three features clearly do not provide guidance for a software process. Their purpose is instead to provide organizational guidance for implementation of the process and assimilation into the organizational culture. If you are simply looking at process improvement, the implementation features do not define what must be done with the process.

The activities define elements of a process but not the process. The activities cannot be turned into a step-by-step procedure even with the help of the subactivities provided. For example, activity 7 under the Project Planning KPA has 10 steps that appear to indicate a process and may even appear to organizations at level 1 to be a reasonable process. However, you must not attempt to read it as a process because that would result in a very poor implementation.[1]

Capability Maturity Model Integration

The CMM was described first because it is a simple model that can be applied to the process of software development. One rationale for the more complicated Capability Maturity Model Integration (CMMI) model is to support organizations that are more complicated such as those with separate software and system engineering functions. The CMMI adds more information to the model as well as changes the maturity structure. Several names of levels change in an attempt to clarify terminology. For example, level 2 is renamed Managed, and level 4 is called Quantitatively Managed.

The CMMI renames the concept of levels as stages. In addition, there is a model representation known as Continuous that acknowledges that an organization may want to work on more than one level simultaneously. The price paid for the added flexibility is a need to understand the dependency between KPAs. Novice users may not fully grasp dependencies between

---

1 For a good implementation of the Project Planning KPA, see any of the books by Watts Humphrey referenced throughout this book.

various stages of process improvement. For example, you must have controlled processes before attempting to use techniques such as Statistical Process Control. Implementing in the wrong order can do more harm than good. The CMM controls the dependencies implicitly by assuming implementation of each level until the KPA goals are fulfilled. This makes for a simpler improvement road map.

The CMMI changes some of the KPAs to provide a more detailed business model. For example, the CMMI adds a KPA for decision analysis and one for causal analysis. Although such KPAs may be outside the scope of software development, they are highly desired elements of a software development organization.

Malcolm Baldrige Framework

The Malcolm Baldrige (MB) award provides another process model similar in some ways to the CMM but very different in others. The Malcolm Baldrige National Quality Improvement Act of 1987 provides for recognition of outstanding quality in goods and services by the president of the United States. The Malcolm Baldrige National Quality Award (MBNQA)[1] requires performance excellence along the following criteria categories:

- Leadership
- Strategic planning
- Customer and market focus
- Measurement, analysis, and knowledge management
- Workforce focus
- Process management
- Results

Figure 2-5 shows the model associated with the MBNQA. It contains seven categories and the associations between categories. Measurement forms a basis that all of the categories build upon, and the Organizational Profile is the overarching description under which the organization is assessed. Leadership, strategy, and customer focus affect the workforce and organizational practices that lead to results.

The seven criteria categories are broken down into *Items* and *Areas to Address,* much as the CMM levels are broken down into KPAs, and, coincidentally, there are 18 total *Items*, which is the number of KPAs that exist in the CMM. The assessment of an organization uses points for each of the *Items*, with a possible 1,000 total points available. The category of *Results* is nearly half the total (450 out of 1,000 available points), indicating the emphasis placed on seeing actual organizational benefits.

---

1   See *www.quality.nist.gov/PDF_files/2007_Business_Nonprofit Criteria.pdf.*

The goal of *Leadership* is to assess the means by which senior leaders guide and sustain the organization, the general governance process, but also the social responsibility of the organization. The organizational governance includes management accountability, fiscal accountability, operations transparency, independence of auditors, and protection of stakeholder interests. The social responsibility of the organization assesses the organization's ethical and legal behaviors as well as the relationship between the organization and key communities with which it interacts.

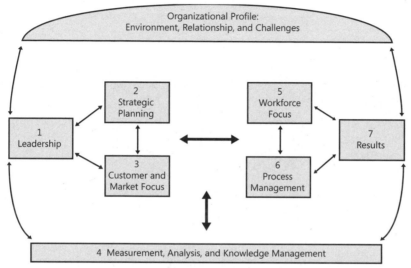

Figure 2-5   The Malcolm Baldrige framework

Strategic Planning assesses how the organization creates strategic objectives and their action plans. Included in the planning is the means by which plans are deployed and changed if necessary. The means by which information is gathered is also examined. The assessment explicitly examines the means for predicting performance from the data. Strategic planning may include both formal and informal means.

The category of *Customer and Market Focus* examines how the organization determines customer needs. Associated with this category is the customer relationship practice of the organization. The assessment includes market segment analysis and use of tools such as voice-of-the-customer. Customer relationships include the building of relationships and the assessment of customer satisfaction.

Measurement, Analysis, and Knowledge Management considers the means used by the organization to select data for gathering, the means used to gather the data, and the means used to analyze the data. Additionally, the means used to improve the measurements and the information management techniques are analyzed. The employee performance appraisal system falls into this category, as does the information technology used by the organization.

Workforce Focus examines the means used to manage the workforce, engage them in the business, and improve the workforce. Engaging the workforce refers to the means used to align people with the business mission and strategy. Workforce Focus includes the means used to develop new leaders.

Process Management refers to the means used to create core competencies. The assessment includes the means for designing, managing, and improving engineering systems such that the system delivers the required customer value and creates a sustained technology advantage for the organization. Also assessed are risk assessment and mitigation strategies.

The Baldrige model has a number of subpractices that the practices described in this book address. For example, in the area of *Strategic Planning*, business strategy requires the deployment of business goals. The Balanced Scorecard presented in Chapter 7 fulfills many of the needs. The CMM can fulfill the need for *Process Management*. Stochastic modeling provides a means for advanced analysis of measurements.

The final category, and by far most important in terms of the assessment points, is *Results*. Results are examined for products, services, customer activities, financial measures, workforce, processes, and leadership. The organization must indicate its position relative to the market and others in its market segment.

As described in Chapter 12, "Adopting Processes," many frameworks are not mutually exclusive. In a sense, the Malcolm Baldrige framework provides a meta-model for many other frameworks. Each of the categories could be considered its own framework. The difficulty arises from the relative complexity of the model. For example, the Balanced Scorecard fulfills some of the elements of Strategic Planning and some of the elements of Measurement, Analysis, and Knowledge Management. The CMM provides some of the elements of Process Management, some of Workforce Management, and some of Measurement. It is easiest to use this model as a check step to an overall goal rather than as a means of deploying processes. In addition, this model takes a systems approach relating causes, such as leadership, to the results. It acknowledges the relationships between organizational components, which many other models do not.

ISO Models

The International Organization for Standardization (ISO) publishes a wide variety of standards such as those for the threads on screws, telephony protocols, and quality management practices. ISO 9000 is broadly applied to any manufacturing process focusing on quality management practices. ISO 9001 is more often applied to software. It is more general than the CMM and provides general principles of quality management, not specifics. ISO 12207 may be a more applicable standard, but it is less well known.

ISO 15504, also known as SPICE, is a maturity model much like the CMM. SPICE stands for Software Process Improvement and Capability Determination. Processes are categorized according to the information in Table 2-2.

Table 2-2   SPICE Process Categories

Process Category	Description
Acquisition	Processes performed to acquire a product or service
Supply	Processes performed to propose and deliver a product or service
Engineering	Processes that elicit and manage the customer's requirements; specify, implement, and maintain the software product
Operation	Processes performed to provide for the correct operation and use of the software product or service
Supporting	Processes that may be used by other processes at various points in the software life cycle
Management	Processes that contain practices that may be used to manage a project or process in the software life cycle
Process improvement	Processes performed to improve the processes performed in the organizational unit
Resource and infrastructure	Processes performed to provide adequate human resources and IT infrastructure as required by any other process
Reuse	Processes performed to provide reuse opportunities in the organization

Table 2-3   SPICE Process Category Levels

5	Optimizing process
4	Predictable process
3	Established process
2	Managed process
1	Performed process
0	Incomplete process

SPICE provides six levels, as shown in Table 2-3, that begin with level 0, which is the equivalent of the CMM Initial level. The attainment of a level uses an assessment method similar to the continuous method of the CMMI. An organization receives a percentage score for its attainment of the maturity at each level. The assessment method attempts to quantify process capability along the following dimensions:

- Process performance
- Performance management
- Process definition
- Process deployment
- Process measurement
- Process control

- Process innovation
- Process optimization

A detailed examination of the model shows its similarity to the CMM. The most noticeable difference is an attempt to include many of the elements of the MBNQA and the ability to assess each process for a level.

Other Models

Many other models exist and are applicable to software development organization. SPICE and CMM are the most directly applicable because they were designed specifically for software. However, any a good framework meant to guide quality improvement practices is applicable to the software organization, with some modification. For example, Six Sigma methods use an improvement model called DMAIC, which stands for define, measure, analyze, improve, and control. The intent of the method is to provide the sequence of steps required to control any process. DMAIC is not so much a framework for improvement as a methodology for improvement and should not be confused with the CMM or SPICE frameworks.

Comparing the Models

The CMM is specifically targeted at software development organizations, as is ISO 15504. The CMMI adds some business processes to the CMM, and SPICE attempts to identify process dimensions not specific to software development. The Malcolm Baldrige criteria categories are more holistic and look to solve business problems across all functional disciplines. All models provide a means to assess competencies and compare the assessments across organizations.

Choosing and Using a Model

The first step in choosing a model is to understand the improvement goals for the organization. One obvious goal is business need. For example, if an organization must do business with the Department of Defense, it must use the CMMI and do periodic "assessments," which is a euphemism for process audits. The organization must get a certain rating from the assessment. An objective of receiving a positive rating is different from an objective of lasting process improvement.

After an organization understands its goals, choosing a model is a matter of understanding the questions a particular model is capable of answering. For example, the CMM provides a sequence of stages of process maturity. Each stage answers a set of questions. Level 2 answers the following questions:

- Do we have an established set of basic project management techniques?
- Do we know the cost of a project?
- Can we track schedule?
- Can we track functionality?
- Can we repeat past successes?

Using a model is much more difficult than choosing one. Using a model requires an organization to assess its capabilities, looking for both strengths and weaknesses in an honest, unbiased manner. This can be difficult for organizations new to process improvement because they may tend to overstate their strengths and understate their weaknesses. One primary reason for this is the lack of accurate data. Organizations that have practiced process improvement for a reasonable period may also have difficulty accurately assessing their capabilities against a model and may understate their strengths and overstate their weaknesses. The primary reason for this is the abundance of data. To remove the quandary caused by this double-edged sword of data, you must eliminate the emotional ties to the data and see it as just data. If a weakness is a side effect of a corresponding strength, you must consider it as such.

Organizational Considerations

As mentioned, models such as the CMM specify only what must be done and do not consider how or why. Additionally, the CMM provides only cursory organizational guidance. However, the process model is not independent of the organizational structure in which the process is used. H. Mintzberg provides a means of modeling the relationship between the environment in which a business operates and appropriate organizational structures.[1] Although the process framework does not depend on the environment, the implementation of the framework does. For this reason, it is important to consider the model provided by Mintzberg when implementing various processes.

Mintzberg writes that two environmental factors drive various organizational structures. The first factor is the stability of the environment, and the second is the complexity. Figure 2-6 shows a two-dimensional grid based on these attributes. The y-axis is the complexity of the environment, and the x-axis represents the stability of the environment. Mintzberg calls the stability attribute "dynamism" to show that the scale ranges from low to high. From this simple grid, several types of organizations can be described. For purposes of discussion, only the extreme points of each axis are considered.

When an environment is both stable and simple, the organization is known as a Machine Bureaucracy. The primary controlling mechanism is through standardization of work processes, which is enforced by a central authority. At first glance, the CMM seems to rely strictly on such coordination mechanisms leading to the misconception that it is applicable only in large, traditional bureaucracies. However, the framework is useful in all types of structures, as will be shown later in Chapter 12.

---

1 H. Mintzberg, "Structure in 5's: A Synthesis of the Research on Organizational Design," *Management Science* 26, no. 3 (1980): 322–341.

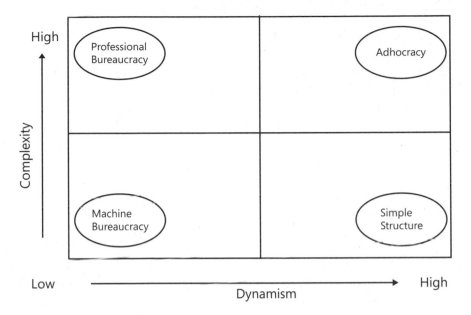

Figure 2-6   Mintzberg's model of environmental attributes

When the environment is complex but still relatively stable, the organization shifts to a state known as a Professional Bureaucracy. Professional standards replace centrally enforced rules and regulations. The standardization of skills causes standardized behaviors across the entire industry. The medical profession is an example of an industry with standardized skills. The key element of such an organization is the amount of training required to provide the standardization. The same processes used in the Machine Bureaucracy are useful in a Professional Bureaucracy, but responsibility for the processes rests with the individual, not with a central authority.

When the environment is simple but also dynamic, the organization forms a Simple Structure. A single individual provides the controlling mechanism and is involved in most, if not all, aspects of running the organization. Typically, processes are not formalized, and coordination is through direct supervision. This environment is the most challenging for use of a framework such as the CMM.

Finally, when the environment is both complex and dynamic, an organization forms what Mintzberg terms an "Adhocracy." The control mechanism is mutual adjustment, where individuals control their own processes much like in the Professional Bureaucracy. The difference rests with the ability to deploy many different types of specialties. The framework in such an organization must encompass the richness of different disciplines. An example of such a framework is the CMMI, which attempts to merge the systems and the software work. Adhocracies likely have many frameworks, one for each functional discipline.

When you decide to implement a framework, you must keep in mind the environment and the primary controlling mechanisms. It would be unreasonable to expect an organization with a simple structure to put into place practices more suitable for a professional bureaucracy. Although not strictly part of any of the models, the organizational structure may influence the choice of models and certainly the implementation. An organization must also take care to avoid the tendency of the tail wagging the dog. For example, putting into place a Machine Bureaucracy will not cause the environment to suddenly become less complex and less dynamic.

Conclusion

An organization must have a framework for improvement to build a plan for improving. Established frameworks are available to guide the process but require more effort to understand. Instead, an organization can begin with a simple model and add to it to provide a lower barrier to entry; this, however, limits the potential improvement opportunity. The software industry has a history of reinventing solutions to problems solved by other companies and other industries. Standard models provide for sharing practices and the ability to benchmark against other companies' efforts.

Theoretical models, such as the CMM, CMMI, and SPICE, provide the basis for asking such questions as the following:

- "Where is our organization as benchmarked against the industry?"
- "What capabilities are we lacking?"
- "Have others already solved a particular problem?"

Without a framework, such questions are meaningless. The frameworks provided in this chapter provide a starting point from which to build. Choosing a framework requires the organization to understand its business needs and desired outcomes. You can use the tools provided throughout the rest of this book to solve different problems using different frameworks. Be sure to understand the context of the process before attempting to use any of the tools. Context requires a model, even if that model is incomplete.

Einstein said, "Creating a new theory is not like destroying an old barn and erecting a skyscraper in its place. It is rather like climbing a mountain, gaining new and wider views, discovering unexpected connections between our starting points and its rich environment. But the point from which we started out still exists and can be seen, although it appears smaller and forms a tiny part of our broad view gained by the mastery of the obstacles on our adventurous way up." The point of a software framework is to create a view that incorporates the map of the process environment. The framework begins as the starting point on the improvement journey, incorporates lessons learned along the way, and provides a road map so that others can follow.

Chapter 3
The Economics of Defect Prevention

When a management team with a reputation for brilliance tackles a business with a reputation for bad economics, it is the reputation of the business that remains intact.
    —Warren Buffet

Religion and art spring from the same root and are close kin. Economics and art are strangers.
    —Nathaniel Hawthorne

In economics, the majority is always wrong.
    —John Kenneth Galbraith

Chapter 2, "Defect Prevention Frameworks," presented the idea that process improvement activities have three perspectives: What? How? and Why? This chapter discusses why organizations must prevent defects and presents a view on how to analyze the changes from a profitability perspective. This book provides you with a set of tools your software development team can use to improve the development process and prevent defects. When you make improvements, it is important to remain focused on the bottom line: defect prevention increases the organization's profitability. This chapter describes the economic benefits of defect prevention, which may be the single best investment that an organization can undertake. Every prevention activity reaps continual benefit. Once a defect is no longer possible in a process, all of the effort normally required to correct it is no longer necessary. Prevention effort pays off every time a defect does not occur. As long as an organization continues to develop software, the benefits will continue indefinitely.

Preventing Defects Is Good for Business

It is to an organization's advantage to measure and improve the software development process by using economic benefit as the means to gauge the efficacy of the engineering system. Comprehending the connection between the engineering system and the balance sheet is vital. Few organizations know the actual cost to develop and maintain software; organizations may go years without understanding the benefits and costs of various activities in the development process. For example, although a company may understand the concepts of budget and headcount, often it does not know the cost of repairing defects at various phases in the development process or the actual lifetime cost of a software feature. Some organizations measure the cost to produce a thousand lines of code, but such measurements are rarely able to capture the incremental value to the user. In fact, a feature's value to the end user is often unknown, unmeasured, and ill considered at design time. It is not surprising that the connection between engineering process and customer value is tenuous at best.

When an organization decides to make process changes or deploy a new tool to improve the software engineering process, management often uses experience, a.k.a. gut feeling, as the basis for making the decision. Sometimes the herd effect—a mentality that causes organizations to pick the latest well-marketed technology—determines which technology the company will implement, even though there is little or no scientifically valid research to determine whether the technology actually improves software engineering systems. (Sometimes creators of innovations can make a profit simply by consulting with companies on how to implement the new method.) In such cases, it is no wonder that new tools and new processes do little to improve a company's systems. In fact, it is to the consultant's advantage to provide only minimal value to the client, thus ensuring that clients require future process improvements and securing future consultancy business. Although such a view may seem overly cynical, it does explain how process change after process change results in little noticeable improvement in the quality of delivered software.

Because of a lack of process data, the value of improvement activities must be estimated. However, enough information exists to make a good estimate of the cost of various activities in the software development process. For example, in *Winning with Software*, the author, Humphrey concludes that testing consumes at least half of the total cost of the development process.[1] Further, according to a National Institute of Standards and Technology (NIST) report,[2] 80 percent of development costs are spent identifying and fixing defects, and the cost of inadequate testing, as defined by NIST, is estimated to be as high as $60 billion per year. The study concludes that half of the cost of defects found by the user is borne by users and half by the developing organizations. The NIST report estimates the direct costs incurred to test products using existing software development processes, which rely on defect *detection*, not defect *prevention*. Assuming the report is accurate, we can conclude that companies that implement defect prevention techniques can realize up to $30 billion in savings by preventing defects instead of spending resources detecting and fixing them, not including any savings associated with an improved development process.

So what are the true costs to organizations that do not practice defect prevention techniques? To answer this question, a brief background in cost–benefit analysis and economic costs is required. The next section describes one way of looking at the costs associated with the development process and provides a method of estimating the effect of defect prevention on the value of delivered software. The aim is to provide an economic argument for the value of defect prevention.

---

1 Humphrey, W. S. *Winning with Software. An Executive Strategy.* (Boston: Addison-Wesley, 2003).

2 RTI. "The Economic Impact of Inadequate Infrastructure for Software Testing." National Institute of Standards and Technology, Program Office Strategic Planning and Economic Analysis Group. (2002)

Economic Theory and the Value of Defect Prevention

Software companies are fortunate in that software is a very profitable product. Essentially, software lasts forever, never wearing out. A copy of DOS that ran a PC twenty-five years ago works as well today as it did when first shipped. Copies of existing software can be made for distribution at very low costs. So the nature of software and its development and distribution leads to high margins and occasionally the view that traditional cost accounting techniques do not apply. Although a strict adherence to traditional accounting measures do not always apply to the software industry, they can be modified so that techniques for conducting cost–benefit analyses and marginal cost analyses can work well to determine expected return on investment.

For purposes of this discussion, we must define a few terms and equations to provide a brief explanation of economic measures as they apply to the software industry. This section is meant to provide a quick introduction to the terminology of economic profitability as used in this chapter, which differs from its use in accounting. In addition, we do not consider subtle nuances of economic theory. This section illustrates how you can do a cost–benefit analysis, and you will likely need to modify it to apply to your specific organization.[1]

Profitability

It seems obvious that the primary purpose of a for-profit company is to make money. Although organizations generally also desire to contribute to the community, provide for the well-being of their employees, and improve their respective industries, these secondary attributes merely assist in the primary purpose. Milton Friedman[2] (1970) even went so far as to propose that profitability is really the only purpose of a publicly traded company and that long-term benefit to stockholders must drive all management decisions. Although many disagree with Friedman that profitability is a company's only concern, profitability certainly is a powerful driving force. Therefore, the decision to prevent defects must be supportable from the perspective of the balance sheet and corporate profits.

One model for maximizing profitability uses what is known as the marginal cost-marginal revenue method. The concept is simple and incorporates several well-known microeconomics concepts. *Marginal revenue* (MR) is the revenue realized from making one more sale. *Marginal costs* (MC) are those costs incurred to deliver to the marketplace one more unit of product. An organization's costs are all costs associated with production, and these fall into two categories. *Variable costs* are those associated with producing one more unit. For example, in manufacturing, the cost of raw material that makes up the product is an example of a variable cost. *Fixed costs* are those that are incurred regardless of the number of units produced. For example, in the software industry, engineers' salaries must be paid regardless of the number of copies of software sold. Likewise, rent paid for facilities and utility bills are also costs independent of

---

1   The estimates use data from a variety of sources to illustrate how to perform such an analysis and do not necessarily reflect data from the authors' organization.

2   Friedman, M. "The Social Responsibility of Business Is to Increase Its Profits." The New York Times Magazine (1970, September 13).

units sold. Because fixed costs are already spent, they are not part of the marginal analysis. Only the variable costs enter into the decision to produce one more unit of product.

Figure 3-1 shows profit maximization using the marginal cost–marginal revenue approach in a market with perfect competition. Notice that the cost curve drops as economies of scale allow for production efficiencies. At some point, however, the costs begin to increase as inefficiencies associated with large-scale production overwhelm the benefits. At the point where the marginal revenue (MR) line crosses the marginal cost (MC) curve, the price paid for the unit sold is exactly equal to its cost. Thus, marginal profit is zero. At this point, selling one more unit results in a net loss to the organization since the revenue received will be less than the cost to produce the item. Thus, the company maximizes its profit when it sells exactly quantity Q, occurring at the point MC = MR. Profit maximization using this theory is simple and intuitive. From the simple graph, the price for the software and the quantity sold are set. The total profit realized must exceed not only the variable costs but also the fixed costs in order for the product line to be profitable. The difficulty lies in determining marginal costs and revenues and relating the net profit to determine of they cover fixed costs.

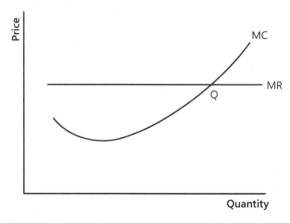

Figure 3-1 Maximum profit occurs when MR = MC

A key element of cost analysis is known as the *opportunity cost of capital*, or simply, *opportunity cost*. By investing in a particular product line, a company must forgo the opportunity to invest in some other area; the forgone profit of another alternative is the opportunity cost. Thus, when calculating potential profit, the profitability of a chosen product line must exceed the opportunity costs to determine the true economic profit; that is, the profits realized from an investment must exceed the profits expected from the next best alternative.

To satisfy stockholders, public companies must invest in a portfolio of products that returns a certain profit percentage. This risk–reward potential of an investment drives investment decisions at the senior management level and is reflected in the stock price of a company. That is, if the portfolio of products does not provide sufficient reward, investors sell their shares of stock, lowering the stock price. Therefore, the opportunity cost of capital and the profitability expectations of a company are directly contained in the price of the stock. Investments in lower-profit opportunities lower the stock price, whereas realizing profit in excess of the expected return, as measured by the opportunity cost, raises the stock price. This is the basis for justifying a defect prevention activity. If the cost of defect prevention can produce a return in excess of the expected opportunity cost, it benefits the stock price and is a good investment for the company to make.

Applying Marginal Cost Analysis to Software Development

Both software development organizations and traditional manufacturing organizations produce and distribute products. However, software companies differ from traditional manufacturing organizations in several important ways that require modification of the methods used to analyze cost and profit. For example, when a manufacturing organization builds, say, an appliance, the marginal costs include the costs of raw materials and labor to produce the appliance. To sell one more unit, more production work is required, which of course increases marginal costs. However, this is not the case with software. After a software application is created, to sell one more unit, a software company need only burn another CD or DVD copy. The marginal costs are the cost of the media plus the cost of salaries for those involved in the copying process, as well as any delivery costs—the total cost to produce one more unit is likely less than one U.S. dollar. And if the user downloads the software from the Internet, the only marginal cost for the software company is the cost of maintaining the communications network. This seems to suggest that the traditional economics of marginal costs cannot be applied to software companies.

However, from a slightly different perspective, traditional analysis can be applied to software companies. Marginal cost analysis focuses on production of the product. In the software industry, engineers produce the product when they create code. Therefore, it seems reasonable that marginal cost analysis for software should focus on the production of the final software product and not on the costs of literally selling one more unit, that is, shipping the media to one more user. In other words, it is more effective to analyze the creation of the code and consider the marginal cost as the cost of including one more feature in the software. From this perspective, *marginal costs* are those costs associated with adding one more unit of functionality to a software product.

The marginal cost–marginal revenue method described earlier can now be applied to software organizations. The cost associated with adding each feature to the software product is measured by using the scorecard methods described in Chapter 7, and then the benefit of each feature are measured using the scenario voting methods described in Chapter 15. This method is best suited to determining marginal benefits for every feature and is a viable means for organizations to maximize benefits to end users. However, evaluating the contribution to profitability for implementing a defect prevention technique is slightly more difficult because it applies to all features equally. This makes the analysis easier to conceptualize but harder to measure.

Estimating Costs

From an accounting standpoint, to calculate marginal costs, you must determine the cost of every feature, determine applicability to the feature of a particular defect prevention activity, and then calculate the associated benefits. Recall that the goal here is not to provide the business analysts with information; it is to determine the efficacy of a defect prevention method. To do so, you can use a proxy for the feature and perform an analysis based on the proxy. Because features are implemented with code, lines of code are a useful proxy for functionality. Although software products contain other functionality, for example, help documentation, the focus of the typical defect prevention activity is on the feature code. We can reasonably assume that an analysis focused only on feature code can provide an understanding of the benefits of defect prevention.

Some people argue that using lines of code as a proxy for functionality is not useful because not every developer codes alike, not all features are alike, different programming languages have different issues, and so on. However, all of these objections tend to focus on the difficulty of comparing features, languages, or possibly even engineers. In the marginal cost analysis case, two processes are compared with one another, not two features. Presumably, different processes would result in very similar implementations of a feature, with the only difference being the process used to create the feature. Lines of code would be a useful means to gauge the amount of work accomplished. In such a case, the cost of the activities associated with the process provides the means to judge the benefit of the defect prevention. That is, the time required to produce 1000 lines of code under process A is compared with the time required for process B. Using the techniques described in Chapter 7 of this book, you can gather data to make a reasonably accurate judgment for cost associated with the activities of different processes.

For discussion purposes, the method for comparing two processes is based on a simple model of the development process. The model has five major phases: Requirements (REQ), High-Level Design (HLD), Implementation (IMPL), Test (TEST), and Release (REL).[1] Each development phase includes more detailed activities. Table 3-1 provides phase breakdowns for two candidate processes. The first process primarily uses test to remove the defects and will be called a test-centric process (TCP). The second relies on defect prevention activities and inspections so will be called a defect prevention focused process (DP). The phases represent the work required of a software development project whether or not a process actually produces these products; that is, all systems have requirements, but not all processes produce them. In other words, many test-centric processes spend little time in the requirements phase and often do not produce a thorough work product. The phase exists, in that the product will have been implemented against some loosely defined requirements. The result is that very little time is spent in the requirements phase, and anyone trying to measure the phase may not even notice that it existed.

---

1 A worksheet of the detailed cost–benefit analysis is available on the Defect Prevention Web site at *www.defectprevention.org*.

The major activities require effort to produce the final software, even if no intermediate work product is produced. For example, a product manager may spend time considering various customer requirements and then verbally communicate the customer needs to the development team. The development team uses the verbal communication to produce the code. Additionally, the work is not necessarily carried out in the order listed, and some work may be done in parallel. The intent of this analysis is to consider the investment made in each work product and the associated benefit in the form of quality, that is, defects in the software.

The analysis requires every phase to have a cost probability distribution function (pdf) and an associated effect on quality pdf. The model of the development activities requires each step in the process to estimate costs in the form of effort and benefits in the form of quality. Chapter 9 provides effort estimates based on a process similar to that shown in Table 3-1. The numbers provided in this chapter are averages across the probability distribution functions.

Table 3-1   Process Comparisons

	Test-centric Process	**Defect Prevention-focused Process**
Phase	Detailed Process Step	Detailed Process Step
	Plan	Plan
Requirements	Write requirements	Write requirements
	Write system test plans	Write system test plans
	Inspection	Inspection
High-level design	High-level design	High-level design
	Write integration test plans	Write integration test plans
	Inspection	Inspection
Implementation	Detailed designs	Detailed designs
		Reviews
		Test case development
		Team design inspections
	Code	Code
		Reviews
	Compile	Compile
	Code inspections	Code inspections
	Unit tests	Unit tests
	Integration tests	Integration tests
Test	System tests	System tests

Every activity includes the possibility of introducing an error into the final product. Some activities have a tendency to create errors, whereas others have a tendency to find existing errors. For example, writing code creates coding defects, whereas inspecting code tends to remove existing defects without creating many new ones. As discussed in Chapter 9, it is possible to make changes in the process to minimize the defects that escape a product phase.

A change invariably requires some effort to implement and carries with it the potential of preventing defects from slipping to the customer release phase. Therefore, the effort required to prevent the defect is the cost of the investment, and the time saved in later phases is the benefit.

The next sections examine costs and benefits of two processes, a test-centric process and a defect prevention focused process. The technique is useful for any process change associated with defect prevention activities.

Process Cost Estimates

The primary driver of cost for software development is the salary of the engineer. The cost of the typical computer is very much less than the cost of engineers' salaries. Additionally, marginal cost analysis does not usually include the cost of capital equipment, only the cost of materials and labor. As was already stated, the cost of materials for the product is insignificant compared with the cost of labor. Determining the cost of defect prevention first requires an estimate of engineers' time spent in every development activity and their hourly rate. The problem is that most software organizations do not have this information available. In the examples used here, the data is gathered from various teams from a variety of organizations.

Table 3-2 contains a summary of the effort associated with each of the detailed activities for producing a thousand lines of code (KLOC) for one development organization using a test-centric process. This organization is a fairly typical example of a company that relies primarily on testing to find and fix problems. According to Humphrey, such an organization will deliver to the test phases on the order of 20 defects per thousand lines of code.[1] Davis and Mullaney[2] found that software released from a typical organization has 6 to 7 defects per KLOC when a reactive test-centric process is used.[3] In a very real sense, the engineer produces defects along with the code. Think of these defects as a form of warranty liability: there is a chance that they must be fixed at some future date, and a probability distribution determines the likely cost to do so.[4] As with warranty liability, the product may or may not be defective, which may or may not generate additional cost to fix the defective product.

From the data in Table 3-2, you can see that the average cost for producing a thousand lines of code is approximately 128 direct labor hours (DLHrs). This is an estimate of the direct effort associated with creating the work product (the thousand lines of code).

1 Humphrey, W. S.. Winning with Software. An Executive Strategy . (Boston: Addison-Wesley, 2003).

2 Davis, N., & Mullaney, J. The Team Software Process in practice: A summary of recent results. (Pittsburgh, PA.: Software Engineering Institute, Carnegie-Mellon University, 2003).

3 Davis and Mullaney related it to CMM level 1 organizations which tend to be test-centric.

4 Every engineer and every piece of code will have different liability curves. See chapter 9 for more on probability distribution functions.

Table 3-2   Process Effort Comparisons

Phase	% Total Effort	Detailed Process Step	% Total Effort	Total Hours
Test-centric Process				
	1%	Plan	1%	1.3
Requirements	4.20%	Write requirements	2.2%	2.9
		Write system test plans	0.9%	1.1
		Inspection	1.1%	1.4
High-level design	4.2%	High-level design	2.2%	2.9
		Write integration test plans	0.9%	1.1
		Inspection	1.1%	1.4
Implementation	24.6%	Detailed designs	2.2%	2.9
		Reviews		
		Test case development		
		Team design inspections		
		Code	11.7%	15
		Reviews		
		Compile	2.2%	2.9
		Code inspections	0.8%	1
		Unit tests	7.8%	10
		Integration tests	17.2%	22.1
Test	65.9%	System tests	48.8%	62.8
Total				**128.7**
Defect Prevention Focused Process				
	4.8%	Plan	4.8%	4.4
Requirements	19.9%	Write requirements	9.9%	9.3
		Write system test plans	5.0%	4.6
		Inspection	5.0%	4.6
High-level design	18.1%	High-level design	0%	8.4
		Write integration test plans	4.5%	4.2
		Inspection	4.5%	4.2
Implementation	41.3%	Detailed designs	8.2%	7.7
		Reviews	4.1%	3.8
		Test case development	4.1%	3.8
		Team design inspections	3.3%	3.1
		Code	7.4%	6.9
		Reviews	3.7%	3.5
		Compile	1.3%	1.2

Table 3-2   Process Effort Comparisons

Phase	% Total Effort	Detailed Process Step	% Total Effort	Total Hours
		Code inspections	3.3%	1
		Unit tests	5.9%	5.5
		Integration tests	7.2%	6.7
Test	16.1%	System tests	9%	8.3
Total				**93.3**

The cost for this code depends on the loaded cost of one labor hour. The *loaded cost* includes salary, benefits, and other overhead expenses associated with employing a software engineer, in this case. Most organizations calculate the loaded cost for every job title in the organization. For discussion purposes, assume a loaded cost of $156,000 per engineering year. This may seem high, but you must remember that it includes benefits, taxes, and so on, so the cost of an engineer earning $100,000 per year quickly reaches $156,000. Because there are 2080 hours in a work year, this yields a loaded cost of $75 per hour.

$$156,000 \div 2080 = \$75$$

Based on the number of hours required to build 1000 lines of code and the cost per hour, the direct cost of producing 1000 lines of code is $9600.

$$128 \text{ DLHrs} \times \$75 = \$9600 \text{ per 1000 lines of code}$$

However, this assumes that the engineer does nothing but develop code 8 hours a day, 5 days a week, 52 weeks a year, which is unlikely. Some time must be excepted for attending meetings, answering e-mail, taking vacations, observing holidays, and so forth. For purposes of this discussion, assume that half of an engineer's working time is spent developing and that other necessary organizational activities occupy the other half. Therefore, an engineer has roughly 1000 hours available a year for developing software, which means that a typical individual could produce just under 8000 lines of new code in a year. The cost becomes $19,500 to produce a thousand lines of code. This amortizes the unproductive time across all lines of code, that is. $156,000 per year divided by 8000 lines gives $19,500 per 1000 lines of code, or KLOC.

$$1000 \text{ hours a year} \div 128 \text{ DLHrs per unit of code} = 7.8125 \times 1000 \text{ lines} = 7812.5 \text{ lines of code per year}$$

But we must also consider that few engineers produce only new code. Most create new features while supporting existing features, typically manifested in the form of bug fixes. As discussed in Chapter 9 on stochastic modeling, an engineer who releases defective code has less time available to produce new code. As pointed out earlier, the maintenance work is much like a warranty on the work product. The probability of finding a defect in existing code is proportional to the number of defects in the product and to the product's usage.

This warranty cost must be added to the cost of software production. Every defect in the completed product is a potential liability for the engineer who created the software since the engineer may one day need to fix the defect. The software development test processes will find some defects, and users will find others. Calculating the liability—the cost—in hours of fixing every defect is necessary, and we use average values in this discussion. Assume that to fix the average defect detected by testing requires 1 day of an engineer's time, whereas customer-reported issues require 1 week to fix. This means a test-detected defect costs 4 hours of valuable development time, and a customer issue costs 20 hours.[1]

As stated earlier, the test team typically will find about 20 defects per KLOC. As reported by Davis and Mullaney (2003)[2], a typical company releases products with 6 to 7 defects in the final code, and the customer may find about 50 percent of those defects. This means that every 1000 lines of new code require about 14 to 14.5 test defect corrections and 3 to 3.5 user-reported defect corrections. The engineer will release 20 defects to the test process, and 6 or 7 will escape to the customer, meaning 14 are caught by test. Of the 6 or 7 that escape, about half will actually cause the customer a problem requiring correction.

At 4 and 20 hours per fix, respectively, the total cost for the life of the code is 254 hours, effectively cutting the engineer's productivity in half. The previous Table 3-2 process ended at the end of system test, so the defects that escaped to the customer were not counted. This shows up as a hidden cost to the organization that often goes unplanned. So the true rate of new code production in the organization is about 4000 lines of code per engineer, not 8000. Of course the numbers will vary for different types of code and different applications. The numbers here reflect typical application development organizations.

As an aside, this explains some of the debates on the lines of code that a typical engineer creates per year. Often, small organizations are credited with higher productivity rates. If an individual or an organization does not need to support existing code, or if the number of users is low, the warranty costs do not exist and engineers' productivity can double. The more an organization must support an existing code base and the higher the number of users, the lower an organization's effective productivity.

Direct Costs versus Opportunity Costs

The direct cost of quality in the example is $19,500 per thousand lines of code. The direct cost of quality is the difference between the maximum average lines of code and the lines of code with warranty costs added. The measurement time frame needs to be long enough to measure usage and factor in customer-reported defects. However, this represents only the cost of the engineer's time and not the impact on the entire organization. That is, it measures direct cost but not opportunity cost. To determine opportunity cost, the calculation must consider lost

---

1 Chapter 9 will include various other methods of finding the defect and calculate the effort savings when the developers detect their own bugs.

2 Davis, N., & Mullaney, J. The Team Software Process in practice: A summary of recent results. (Pittsburgh, PA.: Software Engineering Institute, Carnegie-Mellon University, 2003).

marginal revenue to determine actual impact. In other words, if the engineer were not fixing bugs, how much new valuable code would be produced?

As stated earlier, when making an investment decision, an organization must consider the next best use of the capital employed. In the case of defect prevention, simply comparing a new process with an existing process is all that is required. We can compare making a change to the development process with maintaining the status quo.

The test-centric development process incurs some investment costs in earlier development phases to create the code and the bulk of the costs later in the development process to test and fix the code. As discussed, a typical developer produces about 4000 lines of code per year. The assumption here is that new code carries the bulk of customer value. However, existing code must be maintained as a form of overhead, and the support costs result in even lower productivity rates than estimated. In the example, the defect prevention focused process results in more than double the amount of code supported and at least twice as much valuable new code.

The next step is to determine the effect on the business strategy of doubling the amount of valuable new code. As mentioned in the section titled "Economic Theory and the Value of Defect Prevention" earlier in the chapter, an organization's profit includes an opportunity cost, which is factored into the stock price by market forces. Therefore, changing the cost structure for producing software must have an effect on the stock price. Since software costs half as much to produce, it must somehow increase the value of the stock price by either increasing revenue or decreasing cost, or both. To determine the amount of the change, calculating the opportunity cost is necessary.

It is often difficult to determine the opportunity cost for an organization, but we can use a simple proxy. Organizations typically maintain a certain ratio of developers to non-developers. For example, Michael Cusumano writes of the Microsoft development process and describes the organization as consisting of product managers, developers, and testers.[1] The three disciplines work together in teams in a ratio maintained across the organization. In addition, organizations need managers, accountants, HR specialists and so on. Assuming that the functions other than development are staffed to support the development effort, adding 100 new developers requires some amount of support staff. This fact will be used to simplify the opportunity cost analysis. Because the number of personnel in other disciplines is a constant fixed against the total number of software developers, only the total number of developers is germane to the analysis. The organizational costs associated with areas outside development are some fixed ratio of the software development cost. This assumption will become important momentarily.

---

1   Cusumano, M. A., & Selby, R. W. *Microsoft Secrets*. (New York: Simon and Schuster, 1998).

Determining the Returns

The final step of the cost–benefit analysis is to determine the possible total organizational benefit of a process change. Assume an organization has $100 million per year in revenue. Further, assume that the organization requires 100 developers to produce and maintain its software. If the organization wishes to add one more developer, revenues must increase by $1 million. The increase in revenue must cover all costs to the organization that increase as the organization scales up to support one more developer. This includes such variable and fixed costs as salaries for employees added in other disciplines, office space, computers, benefits, utility bills, and so on. Of course some core operations such as HR and accounting require only a fractional increase and adding one more employee is not a problem. However, on average, the increase in revenue must be $1 million.

In a year, the new developer will produce 4000 lines of valuable code using the test-centric process. Therefore, each 1000 lines of code is valued at $250,000. The process improvement associated with defect prevention results in each developer creating about 10,000 lines of code per year, or $2.5 million worth of value. That is, a thousand lines of code required 93 hours, and 1000 hours of available time means just over 10,750 lines. Factor in post-release bug fixes, and the number is just over 10,000.

On the surface, this looks like more than double the profitability. However, the organization requires staffing at the old $1 million level. If the software company was making 30 percent net profit,[1] it was making $1 million on an investment of $700,000 for a net return of more than 40 percent. That is, the software produced under the test-centric process produced $1M in revenue, of which 30 percent was profit so $300,000 is profit, and $700,000 was required to generate the income.[2] Return on investment is $300m/$700m, or 42.9 percent.

With the same investment of $700,000 under the defect prevention focused process, the net profit increases to $1.9 million ($2.5 million worth of valuable code less the $700,000 required to generate it). The net return is then more than 270 percent ($1.9 million/ $700,000). The result is that the new process completely changes the return on every thousand lines of code.

Costs versus Stock Price

As stated earlier, the opportunity cost is tied closely to the current stock price. It is relatively easy to determine the effect that improving the process has on the stock price of a firm. Copeland, Koller, and Murrin propose discounted cash flows as a means to value a company.[3] For purposes of valuation, a company is considered to provide a set of yearly cash flows. To

---

1 Microsoft reported more than $16B of operating income on $44B in revenue, so 30% is reasonable if not low.

2 Remember the prior assumption that most of the cost of development was salary. To validate this assumption, one need only review the annual report of any large software company.

3 Koller, T., Goedhart, M., & Wessels, D. (1994). *Valuation: Measuring and Managing the Value of Companies.* Hoboken, New Jersey: John McKinsey & Company, Inc.

determine the value of the cash flows, subtract the net current assets of the firm from the current market capitalization. This provides the value of the expected future profits.

$$Cash\ Flows = Market\ Capitalization - Net\ Current\ Assets$$

Because the rate of cash flows changes by 2.7 times (from the prior profitability calculation, this company makes 270 percent profit per engineer), the new market cap of the company is

$$New\ Value = (Old\ Value - Current\ Assets) \times 2.7 + Current\ Assets$$

Divide the New Value by the existing shares outstanding to determine the new stock price.

For example, assume a company has $1 billion in market capitalization and 100 million shares of outstanding stock. The stock price is easily calculated to be $1 billion / 100 million, or $10 per share. Further, assume that the company has $250 million in cash and other assets, with $50 million in debt. The value of the discounted cash flows for this company is $800 million, or $8 per share. To get this, simply take the market value of the company and subtract its current assets. In this case, the net assets are $200 million ($250 million in cash less the current debt of $50 million). That leaves $800 million of residual value that must be the value of the cash flows as determined by the market.[1]

Now increase the cash flows by 2.7 times. The new value of the discounted cash flows is $2.16 billion. Add in the current net assets of $200 million, and the value of the company is $2.36 billion, or $23.60 per share. Defect prevention activities at this company more than double the stock price.

Of course it is unlikely that the company would convert all of the new productivity into revenue at the old value. Instead, it is likely that some of the new productivity would be used to enter riskier markets or accept projects that have lower returns. According to Clayton Christensen, disruptive technologies are often lower-return technologies when first discovered.[2] In fact, leading companies are often not able to create product lines with disruptive technologies because their stock prices prevent it.[3]

Conclusion

Nathaniel Hawthorne said that art and economics are strangers. He was probably correct in that view, which requires that software be turned into a science if economic analysis is to mean anything. As an organization gathers data and builds good process frameworks, the ability to directly connect software design activities to the balance sheet is possible. Using

---

1 Remember that the market is estimating future cash flows based on history. If the market values the company above its current assets, it must be valuing the future earning power.

2 Christensen, C. M. (1997). "The innovator's dilemma: When new technologies cause great firms to fail." Boston: Harvard Business School Press.

3 Using reasoning akin to that just described, although exactly the opposite because in this case the profitability is reduced.

traditional cost accounting and marginal cost methods, an organization can gain tremendous insight into processes and the ability to deliver customer value. Additionally, by changing the focus to defect prevention, additional business strategies are made available.

Christensen describes what he calls "The Innovator's Dilemma," which is the dilemma that occurs when a promising technology is dropped from consideration because of economic constraints.[1] A finding of Christensen's work is that innovation that disrupts an entire industry rarely, if ever, comes as a surprise to existing firms in the industry. In fact, many incumbent organizations have already dismissed the new technology as impractical for their existing customers. The reason for dismissing the new technology is simple: opportunity cost of capital. As explained earlier, investors require a specific rate of return on their investments, which in turn forces an organization to accept a very specific risk versus reward portfolio of projects. Company management can invest only in projects that yield more than the expected opportunity costs. As Christensen found, innovative technologies often do not provide the required rate of return, so are not considered. Innovation is the victim of the balance sheet.

However, defect prevention changes the cost of capital requirements, allowing an organization to accept a different mix of projects. By using defect prevention techniques, an organization can invest in a different technology mix, including disruptive technologies that might otherwise be valued at below the cost of capital. Therefore, defect prevention not only saves money in the short term, it allows for long-term innovation and enables a company to invest in disruptive technologies. Defect prevention helps to prevent the Innovator's Dilemma.

From a profitability perspective, defect prevention is possibly the single most valuable investment an organization can make. Few investments have the potential for 250 percent plus returns, and as demonstrated in this chapter, defect prevention activities can result in at least that amount. Additionally, no other activity short of massive reorganization can change the opportunity cost of capital, which has the potential to change the markets in which an organization can compete. Defect prevention allows for innovation in risky technologies and protects a firm's business strategy by opening completely different markets—no other activity provides the flexibility to innovate in existing markets while simultaneously opening new markets.

The natural question you may ask is, "If defect prevention is so valuable, why do so few companies focus formal activities on it?" The answer probably includes fear of the unknown, risk aversion, and perhaps even ignorance of the potential. Whatever the reason, the first company to get it right has a competitive advantage over every other company in every other software segment. Defect prevention itself becomes disruptive to every software segment simply based on the opportunity cost of capital. Economic profits, that is, profit in excess of the cost of capital, are rare in a mature field. As the software industry matures, the only advantage an organization can count on will be implementing defect prevention activities.

---

1 Christensen, C. M. "The innovator's dilemma: When new technologies cause great firms to fail." (Boston: Harvard Business School Press, 1997).

Part II
Defect Detection Techniques

Chapter 4
Quality and the Development Process

This chapter covers two issues: what software quality is and how the development process creates opportunities for defects to occur. All defects do not contribute equally to different levels of quality. Software development is a series of transformations from the original vision.

What Is Software Quality?

How do you define software quality? Do you think it's possible to test a sizable application completely? How do your processes consider quality? Do you implement and then enter a test-and-fix phase? As your application becomes larger or more complex, the answers to these questions can make a difference between success and failure of your product, particularly if your application is exposed to the Internet.

This section covers the typical model of achieving quality in software, which is based on a model used for making physical products before mass production was developed, and why this model doesn't work well. A model of quality that does apply to software is described as well as how your programming language allows for defects.

Development Methodology and Quality

Software development is unlike traditional manufacturing processes. In software development, only a single instance of the product is produced rather than a single product being mass-produced in traditional manufacturing. Improvements in modern manufacturing are applied to the system that produces the products, and when a defect is detected changes are made to reduce or eliminate the defect for future products. Software produces a single product that is then mass-duplicated.

Additionally, software has no equivalent of the laws of physics to provide continuity over different conditions, and the number of decisions made (hence, possible errors) is immense. For example, a metal beam can be depended on not to liquefy over a wide range of temperatures, whereas a software function can do anything depending on how it is coded. An error in a single decision could have an extreme effect. As a consumer of software, you may have wondered how seemingly random failures of software occur, and the simple answer is, "Software can do anything."

Physical manufacturing has evolved over time to use processes that improve productivity and quality. Originally, production consisted of making products that were shaped and modified until they worked (handcrafting). Then, in the early 1800s, using interchangeable parts in the manufacture of rifles began: the quality of components was such that they could be interchanged between rifles. Henry Ford used a moving assembly line process for mass production of the Model T (vastly outcompeting other manufacturers who still produced cars one at a time—an example of parallel versus serial assembly). The Japanese used Deming's insights into manufacturing and instituted quality processes.

Through history, manufacturing has been moving away from the handcraft model of banging each product into shape to achieve quality because correcting each produced product is inefficient compared with improving the production process to eliminate the defect in the first place (moving quality upstream). Additionally, the handcraft model depends on reasonably complete testing of all the important characteristics of the product.

In physical production, quality monitoring is used to verify that the processes that instill quality into the product are functioning correctly. If a product fails verification, it is rejected and the production process is improved to reduce that kind of defect.

In software, using multiple layers of verification, from reviews (spec, design, and code) to testing (unit, feature, scenario, system, stress, and customer), is one method of detecting defects to improve quality. This type of verification operates under the premise that defects not detected by one layer will be detected by a later layer in the gauntlet. Of course, large numbers of defects are still detected by customers after release. *You must accept the fact that it is not possible to test software completely.*

Physical products have far fewer opportunities for failure than even the simplest software applications do. Yet, in software, we primarily use this handcraft model of production that was supplanted back in the 1800s. But at least testing isn't completely manual. Static testing tools and process improvements are embodiments of the modern quality production methodology—that is, feedback flows back into the production process.

Best Practices   Software applications are incredibly more complex than any physical product is, yet typically for software we still use quality techniques that were abandoned in the 1800s for the testing of physical products that are many orders of magnitude less complex and far more testable than software is.

The Myth of Complete Testability

We can't completely test software. In fact, we can test only an infinitesimal percentage of software functionality, yet there are many processes that depend on this false assumption of testability and obsolete quality technique. For example, the assumption that a gauntlet of tests can catch defects that may escape a single test is based on the tests covering a high percentage of product functionality. Defects still escape and are discovered by customers. Such processes are inefficient and produced low quality decades ago when applications were smaller and defects were more acceptable. Consider how your development processes, roles, and organization reflect the myth of complete testing. Three aspects of the complete testing myth are widespread:

- Quality is a seasoning: fix bugs here and there until it *tastes* right.

- Quality is testing's job: testing *creates* quality.

- Quality is a tax on development: implementation is the *primary* goal; fixing defects is overhead.

Consider how your organization views quality. Do developers make the excuse, "A test should have caught this" or "The defect is fixed; who cares what caused it? Just get a new version." The first excuse implies that quality is not a developer's job. The second illustrates a lack of concern for the customer and learning why a defect occurred so that it can be prevented in the future.

The typical waterfall model of software development reflects the myth of testability—build it and then bang it into shape. Even when development processes do not follow the waterfall model, the separation of steps reinforces the attitude that testing is a tax on implementation; this is further reinforced by having separate development and testing staffs. A postmortem evaluation typically provides little learning because it is often viewed as another tax on implementation; it is performed after development, so many issues that occurred in the past may have been forgotten; and unless there is honesty, important issues won't surface. If the culture of your team is to assess blame rather than learn from mistakes, it is natural for people to understate issues.

How do you treat your customers during the development process? When are customers involved—before the design process or mainly for prerelease (beta) testing? Often, customers are used as an adjunct to the testing process to find scenario-oriented and configuration-based defects. Customers may report usability problems, but often by the time the customer is involved there is not enough time left in the schedule to make more than minor changes in response to customers.

Typical defect tracking systems reflect the handcraft model—they record all sorts of information about the processing of the defect through to resolution but really contain little information that could be used to learn from a defect to prevent or reduce similar defects in the future. The defect taxonomy (described in Chapter 10, "Defect Taxonomies") and the prevention tab (described in Chapter 14, "Prevention Tab") are examples of the kind of information to gather if you want to learn from defects; contrast it with your defect tracking system.

Current Testing Methods and Quality

There's a simple fact about testing: At best, all testing can do is indicate the lack of quality. Testing can never provide significant coverage of an application's functionality. If few defects are found, it can be the result of testing areas that have already been repeatedly tested or of testing using tests that are incomplete rather than an indication that the product has no defects. It is not possible to tell the difference between high-quality code and poor testing.

If No One Exploits It, Is It Secure?

Security is a great example of this. Before widespread use of the Internet, software developers were not very concerned about security exploits because the means of exploitation were limited (such as running a program you got from someone else). Because computers were isolated, there was little value to be gained in terms of exploitation. The attitude was that if a defect was hard to encounter, it wasn't as important to fix as an easily encountered defect. Security wasn't an important issue.

Then the Internet arrived, Web sites proliferated, and computers became interconnected. Suddenly, a multitude of means to exploit vulnerabilities existed, and the value in terms of exploits affecting other systems and theft of information such as identities or financial information increased. Malicious people actively began to try to find security defects, so *hard to encounter* was no longer a valid excuse for not fixing a security defect. Many defects, such as null pointer references, division by zero, or memory leaks, can become a denial of service attack if they can be triggered remotely, so they must be addressed.

There wasn't a lot of testing for security defects before the widespread acceptance of the Internet, hence few such defects were found—but does that mean quality was high? No, in fact this is an example of a deceptive indicator of quality.

Deceptive Indicators of Quality

Code is inherently nonlinear: a function may work correctly for a large number of parameter values and combinations, but a certain combination may cause a failure. Every decision in a function is an opportunity to do something different based on a parameter or external state. The external state can create dependencies on the execution of different bodies of code—one function may affect external state so that another function that uses that state fails.

You really can't determine the number of potential defects in an application from the defects that have already been detected—even though many sampling techniques assume a reasonable coverage of the functional space. Even if you analyze code coverage of tests, you have verified only that a section of code worked for the parameter values tested, not that it will perform correctly with different parameters, configuration, or state.

So, if you have no reliable estimate of the total number of defects, how can you determine when a product can be shipped? A slump in defects reported (a *zero bug bounce*) can occur for many reasons besides actual quality (and typically does, considering defects in released products). How many times have you had indications that quality has been achieved only for this to be proved false when the test team changes focus?

Tests have two purposes: preventing regressions and discovering new defects. After a test discovers a defect, you hope the defect won't occur again after it is fixed, but a small percentage of regressions (defects reappearing because of changes made in correcting another defect) do occur. Typically, the trend is that after an initial shakeout phase, regression failures become relatively rare. If your testing staff restarts testing of a new version, you can expect initially low defect reports because they are testing what they just tested in the previous version unless regressions are degrading the code.

A test pass is typically a combination of automated and manual tests, and it is not instantaneous for large software applications. This can be because of the sheer amount of automated tests or because some testing is manual. Automated tests are preferable to manual tests for consistency's sake, increased rate of testing, and portability (anyone can run these tests). Manual tests can be script-based, in which case they are similar to automated tests, only slower and less portable because a person must be involved in execution. Manual testing can also be more freeform and ad hoc, which after the shakeout phase tends to discover most of the new defects because manual tests may be testing areas not tested by the automated tests. Often, after ad hoc testing discovers a defect, an automated test is added to detect any future regression.

There are two other forms of manual testing: self-hosting inside the company and external self-hosting such as beta testing (see Chapter 20, "Pulling it All Together"). Any period of testing is a mix of regression (automated or script-based manual) tests and ad hoc tests, where most new defects will be discovered. The rate of defect reporting will correlate with this mix, and without knowledge of the mix over a time period a false zero bug bounce may occur.

For example, if a regression pass takes two weeks, involves a manual portion, and there is an overlap of people doing the manual portion with ad hoc testing, you could expect low defect reporting for that first week and a rise once ad hoc testing ramps up again. If your defect counts are low, you could hit zero defects during this first week and falsely believe you've turned the corner on defects. Even the ad hoc testing may have a delay in reporting because time is involved in installing the new version, testers may not immediately switch to the new version, and people will tend to repeat a significant amount of their previous operations before trying new ones.

A better approach is to continue a test cycle from where it left off in the previous version rather than starting over because it is less likely that what had been tested will fail in the new version as opposed to what hadn't been tested in the previous version. Ad hoc testing needs to start as soon as possible after some level of regression testing has verified a basic level of quality. The goal is to find defects sooner rather than to look for regressions. More negative feedback must be given to developers for introducing and testers for not detecting regressions rather than for introducing new bugs—regressions are far more costly.

You Can't Test Everything

Effective testing is not impossible but requires you to embrace the fact that significant test coverage is not possible. So how can you effectively test and know the level of quality you are providing to your customers? Accept the idea that the basis of current testing is a myth and think about what quality is from the customer's point of view.

Subjective Quality: Customer Perception

To customers, quality is a subjective measure. If customers do not encounter a defect, they may perceive quality as high, even though a defect exists. So, for software development organizations, the quality goal is for customers not to encounter any defects.

Scenario testing, or performing tasks your customers do, is a good way to improve customer-perceived quality. Because it is not possible to test even an insignificant portion of functionality, you should focus testing on what your customers may encounter. Customer-perceived quality is measured by mean time between failure (MTBF). This is a quality metric that is meaningful.

Ensuring that perceived quality is high means that organizations must reverse the typical attitude that considers fit and finish defects to be less important than other defects are. Fit and finish defects are important contributors to a customer's perceived quality of a product. With software, customers make the same assumption that they do with physical products: if the manufacturer of the product showed little concern for surface issues, that lack of concern is assumed to follow into less apparent aspects of the product. For example, car manufacturers have known this for decades—sloppy paint jobs, badly fitting doors, noises, and lack of ergonomic design can lose a sale no matter how great the technology in the engine is. Do you give fit and finish bugs a lower priority?

Instead of primarily concentrating on low-level tests, such as unit and feature tests, which are useful initial shakeout and regression tests, run tests that mirror typical customer scenarios. This pays a double dividend because determining customer usage scenarios should be an important input into feature design. Such scenario testing does cover a wide range of perceived functionality, so a value such as MTBF in testing scenarios is a directly meaningful measure of quality.

The likelihood of encountering a defect can be used to determine where you look for defects. Areas where code has been changed, for instance, are likely places to find new defects. A combination of analysis of code coverage of scenario tests and code churn can prioritize scenario testing on likely sources of new defects (see Chapter 8, "Risk Analysis").

Scenario voting, as described in Chapter 15, "Scenario Voting," gives customers a way to describe the satisfaction and importance of scenarios as well as report defects. The satisfaction and importance information can be used to determine a scenario testing mix. Current testing methodology can include stress testing (see Chapter 20, "Pulling It All Together") where a set of tests is repeated in parallel over a long period of time to uncover defects. By focusing such stress testing on scenarios with a wide variety of configurations and cases, MTBF values can be generated and used as a target for release quality.

Even better than using the scenarios that have been defined by scenario voting and voting results is actually to know what your customers are doing. Rather than your depending on scenario voting, a special version of an application can be metered to describe the operations that a user is performing to generate scenarios and their frequency. Of course, there can be confidentiality issues with this data. However, major customers may be quite interested because such testing can ensure that when the product is delivered it will have a high MTBF for their common scenarios. General beta testing could be transformed from an adjunct to internal testing to include defining common usage patterns for scenario testing.

Objective Quality: Security

Security is an objective measure. Malicious parties are actively seeking security defects to exploit. You can't ignore a defect because it is unlikely to be encountered if it can be a valuable exploit to a malicious user. You need to have a zero tolerance policy for security defects. Security defects need to be made—as much as possible—impossible rather than unlikely. A zero tolerance policy means implementing automatic verification of any human process and verification that isn't based on execution.

Catastrophic failures are important liability issues. In software, these revolve around security and data loss. The defects targeted by scenario stress testing are those encountered in typical operation, so such testing will not necessarily uncover many security exploits because such exploits are usually atypical operations.

In trying to achieve zero security defects, it should be obvious that any dynamic (actual execution of the code) testing is ineffective—you can't test everything under all conditions. (Such testing is useful for regression testing, not ensuring that no security defects exist.) Zero tolerance implies static testing—validation involving scanning the source code rather than executing it. Modern compilers are examples of static testing, such as detecting uninitialized variables, dead code branches, and branches that don't return a value.

Product Development as Transformations

Simply put, software developers make dreams into reality. A less colorful description of what we in the software industry do is, we satisfy customer needs with our products. Meeting or exceeding customer expectations is our goal. Our products consist of two parts: The software and the documentation. Customers expect a product we build to have the following characteristics:

- **Functionality**   Product improves accomplishment of user scenarios.
- **Reliability**   Product provides consistent results and does not lose or interrupt work.

- **High quality**   Minimal errors are encountered by the user.
- **Consistency**   A consistency of concepts and interfaces across product and between product and documentation exists.

A customer evaluates these aspects in determining the value of a product.

A software *defect* is a discrepancy between implementation and expectations. At the highest level, a defect is a difference between customer expectations and the product, not merely between the product and its manual. Consider a product and customer expectations to be two independent expressions of customer needs; unfavorable discrepancies lower the perceived value of the product.

The stages of the product cycle typically consist of many transformations (translations) and verifications such as reviews of written documents and testing of code. The final result delivered to a customer is the code and the documentation. During development, an additional result is verification (tests). All three of these results can be considered translations, and they are verified against each other. Tests verify that the code is consistent with the specification (although the test may also be in error). Customers may report discrepancies between the code and the documentation. A stage in the product cycle often consists of a combination of the basic transformations:

- **Translation**   A transformation of form without loss of detail or meaning
- **Aggregation**   Collecting information from multiple sources into a single representation
- **Distillation**   Reducing information through abstraction, simplification, and/or filtering
- **Elaboration**   Expanding information through supplying or creating more detail

When transformations are done by humans, a possibility of error naturally exists. Context can be lost, nuance can be lost, simplifications can be made, parts can be forgotten, and myriad other types of error can be committed.

For example, when Coca-Cola was first sold in China, its erstwhile slogan "Coke adds life" was translated into Chinese. The Chinese ideograms, when translated back into English, read, "Coke brings your ancestors back from the dead"—the result of using reasonable synonyms in the translation if you don't know the context.

Adding Verification Steps to the Product Cycle

To address this possibility of transformation error, verification gates (or steps) typically are added between stages of the product cycle, as shown in Figure 4-1. A development process usually has a typical set of document and code review steps—feature, scenario, architecture, design, and code. Because the reviews are also human processes, they too may contain errors.

Adding a verification gate for every manual step could continue indefinitely because every added gate is a manual step and hence may also contain errors. But this rapidly reaches a point of diminishing returns.

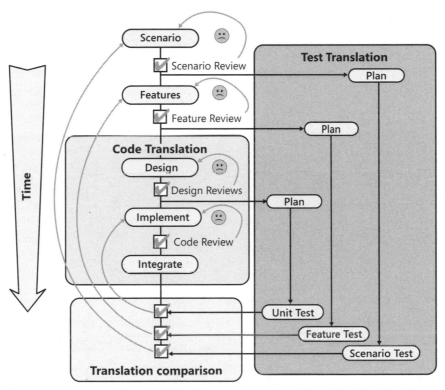

Figure 4-1   Stages of a typical development process and associated verification steps

So, what is done instead to detect the defects that escape a single review of a manual step? Additional translations independent of the code and comparison. Tests are an example of independent translation—a tester reads a specification of the expected behavior and translates that into tests that determine whether the translations match. The assumption is that the two different translations, code and test, have different errors—that each blocks a different class of error and in combination they block more errors (the Swiss cheese model). But there is no guarantee that the combination spans all possible defects; the complexity of software makes it impossible to test any application completely. Additionally, because code and test are based on an earlier translation, an error in the earlier translation tends to be reflected in both translations. Finally, a large amount of time passes (and a sizable implementation effort is invested) before many defects in the earlier translation are discovered.

At the end of testing, defects may still exist, as shown in Figure 4-2. Scenarios represent the expectations of the customer, what the product is expected to do. The product may not completely cover each scenario, and it may provide functionality beyond the scenarios. The product tests may not test every scenario, and they may not test all of the code's functionality. The area where there is higher confidence that the product will meet customer expectations is the area where there is code for the scenarios and there are tests for that code. There can still be defects because the scenarios may not completely represent customer expectations, and even if a test covers an area, it is very difficult to test it completely.

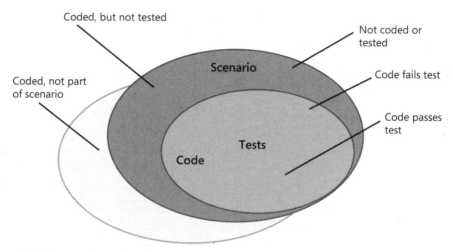

Figure 4-2   Intersections of code, tests, and scenarios and their relation to defects

The problem is the lack of independence of the translations, code and test, from each other. Specifications often are out of date or not detailed enough, so the code is usually considered the more accurate translation for the purpose of designing tests. The purpose of independence is to reduce propagated translation errors in code by catching them with a parallel translation in the form of tests. When tests use code as one of their sources for translation, as does white box testing, both translations may have the same errors and the test can let defects pass. (see Figure 4-3, and read the sidebar titled "White box versus black box testing," which follows.) Because of this lack of independence, an error in the implementation may be reflected in the test, which can mean that an implementation error will go undetected.

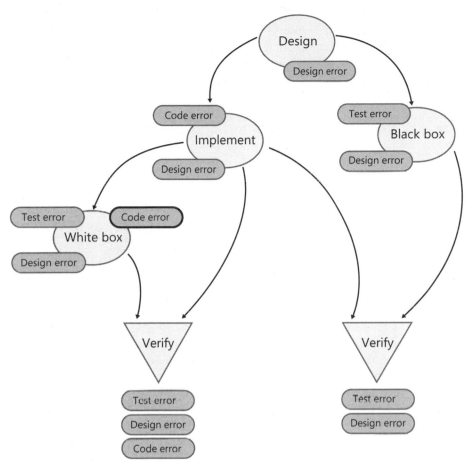

Figure 4-3   White box testing can miss coding errors that would be detected by black box testing.

White box versus black box testing

Typically, *white box testing* (when tests are written with knowledge of the implementation) is considered better than *black box testing* (when only the specification is used) because it can test edge conditions that are not necessarily known from the specification. However, there are drawbacks when you consider these types of testing from the viewpoint of translation.

White box testing is best used to verify compatibility from version to version. A white box test written on an initial version can detect incompatible changes in a later version. White box testing is a case of self-referential testing—testing an implementation using itself as a guide. Many output values tests are also self-referential when they test against last known good values. All of this reflects one basic problem: our chief artifact for specification is the code because often documents are out of date and not executable.

So, what is done to reduce translation errors? Multiple levels of test translation are included in the product cycle—function, interface, scenario, performance, stress, end-to-end scenarios, and system testing, for example. Then there is internal self-hosting, prerelease version to customers, and compatibility testing. Again, the assumption is that a combination of methods can cover more usage scenarios and that there are relatively independent verifications at each level.

But after all these verification steps are completed, customers still detect defects.

This is because, in this whole process, there is an unstated assumption in play: once translated, the original doesn't change. This is rarely true. Discovery of defects in later stages of the product cycle often uncovers defects in the original scenarios or design. This isn't a fault of the translation; the original wasn't complete or correct. And the inaccuracy of the original isn't an unexpected fault because providing adequate detail for complex scenarios is a complicated process.

Acknowledging Defects in the Original Specification

We recognize the possibility of error by providing multiple review steps as code progresses from scenarios to implementation, but we really don't provide for error in our original specifications. In practice, a review step focuses mainly on comparing against the immediately pevious step rather than against the original steps (far more corrections are made to the immediately previous result).

New information tends to be reflected in code and less likely in previous stage artifacts such as scenario or design documents. If the original isn't changed to reflect corrections, any parallel transformations may become out of sync. For example, documentation may not agree with the code and tests may be incorrect.

There is an underlying assumption that errors in a much earlier stage can be corrected locally, that is, by correcting the last result rather than doing a new translation from the stage of the error. For example, a design flaw may be discovered, and instead of correcting the design and its document, local changes that complicate the code and that don't completely resolve the defect are made. This can result in repeated updates being made to a flawed design. Because of the delay inherent in defect detection, considerable time and effort may be invested in the current design and a new design may have defects, too. Other code may be dependent on a design, which increases the cost of a design change. Schedule pressure may manifest as a result of the late discovery of design defects. A culture of defect prevention makes a greater effort in preventing defects in the early stages of development and more often avoids short-term tradeoffs. (See Chapter 17, "Moving Quality Upstream.")

The nature of software development, as a human endeavor, includes the possibility of error. Each stage typically involves translating the results of the previous stage, so any errors tend to propagate forward. Tests are also a human endeavor and are based on the results of a previous stage common with the code. Until tests are run against code, multiple manual reviews may have been done, but they can't be guaranteed to be error-free. In a large product, everything tends to be on a large scale—the number of developers, the number of bugs, the size of the code, and its complexity. On this scale, you can't afford to correct each defect in isolation; you must learn from defects to improve development processes and tools to reduce similar defects in the future.

Transforming Design into Code

The language you write your code in provides opportunities for error. Design concepts that are definitional at the design level often become referential in code: rather than a single expression of the concept, the concept is expressed everywhere it is used. The abstraction level of programming languages is close to the underlying processor, which provides powerful expression, including incorrect expression (for instance, unverified casting, no units enabling byte vs. character confusion, modifying persistent state, and buffer overruns) and multiple or complex ways of writing a particular section of code that makes the recognition of good or bad patterns by code analysis tools more difficult and error prone.

Counterintuitive Syntax

One very simple coding error in the C family of languages is mistakenly to use an equal sign (=) in an *if* rather than the equality operator (==). This mistake results in an assignment being done rather than a comparison, and if the left-hand side is not zero, the *if* succeeds. Some typical examples include not using a return value and, as mentioned, using the assignment operator (=) instead of the equality operator (==) in a C/C++ *if* statement. (See the code listing that follows.)

Simple Error Patterns Involving *If*

```
if (a == 2)     // A valid comparison with 2
if (a = 2)      // Likely semantic error, assigns a to 2
if (2 == a)     // Coding convention to cause error if = used
if (2 = a)      // Syntax error, reversing operands causes error
```

The idiom of reversing the *if* causes the compiler to generate an error when the left-hand side is a constant (as in the preceding code), but of course reversing $a == b$ will not cause an error when both terms are variables.

The designers of C could have used another symbol for assignment, but there wasn't an obvious one on the keyboards of the day (the Pascal language used := for assignment). They could have not allowed assignments in *if* statements, in which case the equal sign (=) would mean equality in an *if* statement, but assigning a variable to a logical expression (such as a <assignment> b <equality> c) would expose the ambiguity again. The designers of C decided multiple assignments would be allowed, so $a = b = c$ assigns a and b to the value of c.

This example is interesting from the point of view of human error.[1] For at least a decade of mathematics in school, you were taught that the equal sign (=) means equality, not assignment. The designers of C changed the meaning of the equal sign, so the long-learned habit of writing equals for equality is semantically incorrect but syntactically correct. To code correctly, you must break a long-held habit, turning an automatic habitual action into a conscious, directed one. James Reason has a term for this error, *strong habit intrusion*. This syntax choice created this whole class of likely error. In the Pascal syntax, the error can't happen.

Lost in Translation

It is difficult to infer higher-level design from code for both validation and manual code review because there is quite a translation distance between a design and code. Compilation to machine code is deterministic, yet the reverse translation is difficult and loses information. And compilation is based on fixed code generation and optimization rules, unlike a developer translating a design into code. The expansion factor of translating a design into code also tends to be large, which makes it harder for a reviewer to validate that code matches a design.

Another major source of errors is that, in translating design to code, concepts that are definitional (defined in one place) in the design become referential (code added for each usage) in the code. This turns a 1:1 mapping into a 1:N mapping, which increases the possibility of errors of omission (forgetting to add code for a reference) and transcription (making a mistake in expression). The per reference instantiation of a design definitional concept is not necessarily identical in each reference; it may need to be transposed in various ways for the context in which it is used. This can make it hard to verify that the implementation is present and correct (manually or automatically) and obscure the design. If the design changes, finding and changing these instances can be error prone and difficult.

Class libraries are used to represent design-level concepts, but nothing forces a developer to use them, and as a result of the restrictions of a class developers may need to write their own different implementation. Developers may "roll their own," which potentially can introduce many kinds of error. Not only does such duplication increase the size of code, but there is also the possibility of making a mistake in the individual instantiation, and if a change in the concept is made in the future, it can be difficult to find all of the duplicates. The following examples of how language-level concepts can contribute to errors are described in the following subsections:

- Type systems
- Buffer overruns
- Memory allocation
- Non-null object references
- Use of signed rather than unsigned integers
- Integer overflow

---

1 James Reason, *Human Error* (Cambridge, England: Cambridge University Press, 1990).

Example 1: Type Systems   In physics and other sciences, units are a method to verify the validity of a formula (the operations on the units result in the units of the result) and also suggest which formulaic transformations can be used to solve a problem or what additional data is needed. For instance, given a speed in miles per hour, it is obvious that multiplying by time will give distance.

The type systems of languages such as C/C++, Java, and C# are weak for scalar types. There are no numeric units, and everything is folded into integers and floats. In some of the languages, even Booleans are folded into integers, and all three languages fold enumerations into integers. Casting—particularly unsafe casting—provides all sorts of opportunities for errors. You can't even declare a variable is a pointer that is not allowed to be null. Many defects are the result of unit conversion such as string length (excludes the terminating 0), memory length (which, for a string, includes the 0 and is measured in bytes), character length (which is half of string length for double byte characters), pixels, points, and others. This weakness contributes to the loss of information in translating a design into code.

Example 2: Buffer Overruns   Consider buffer overruns caused by the use of unsafe string functions, such as copying a string into a fixed-size buffer. Because of historical compatibility, unsafe C functions such as *strcpy* are in every C runtime library. You may define a safe version of *strcpy* that doesn't allow copying a string beyond the buffer size and add a static validation that the unsafe function is not used. But why not just remove these dangerous functions and make the error inexpressible to even the compiler?

Even when you restrict the use of the unsafe function, you cannot prevent an inline iteration from copying a string unsafely or getting the string length and using *memcpy* to copy the string unsafely. Languages provide all sorts of means of expressing unsafe operations, and it can be difficult to detect all the variations. The original cause of buffer overruns was a performance consideration: Passing a buffer, typically allocated on the stack, with the size to be filled in rather than allowing the called function to allocate the memory and return it.

Example 3: Memory Allocation   Consider memory allocation. There are typically only a couple of patterns of memory management: An object is owned by another object and is created when that object is created and deallocated with it; stack allocation, which is deallocated when the function is exited; and everything else is "roll your own." Everything except the first two become individual expressions that can be miscoded, so is it any wonder that memory leakage and dangling pointers happen?

Managed memory models with garbage collection provide another model that eliminates dangling pointers but only reduces but does not eliminate memory leakage. The managed version of memory leakage is the accidental retained reference to obsolete data; a single reference may indirectly retain a large number of objects through indirect references. All that garbage collection does is eliminate the unreferenced objects, not the accidentally still-referenced objects.

An analysis of the memory models used in an application could be abstracted into a set of library classes that would reduce errors both because there is only one version of the model rather than multiple inline expressions of the model and validation could be aware of these classes and detect more errors.

Life span is a key concept for allocated objects, so why not provide classes to implement the various kinds of life spans objects have? For instance, a common life span is a set of objects may live until a function that called the functions that allocated the objects returns. For example, a class could be created and an instance passed in to the called functions that is used to allocate any objects and retains the set of objects allocated. Freeing that object would free all objects allocated through it.

Example 4: Non-Null Object References   The limits of what can be defined about a type can change what is conceptually associated with the type into added code for each reference to an instance of the type. This is a case of a 1:N mapping from concept to implementation (as shown in the following code listing).

Types Don't Include Null Constraint

```
public void PlaceOrder(Product product, int quantity)
    {
    if (product == null)
    {
        throw new ArgumentException("Product must not be null");
    }
    …
```

You can't define *NonNullProduct*, so instead everywhere you use *Product*, the body of the method needs to have a check for a null value. An error is possible in inserting all of these parameter checks or forgetting to do it at all in a method. In addition, a compiler or validation tool doesn't recognize the pattern, so it can't detect a call such as *PlaceOrder(null, 4)* as an error or detect the absence of the *null* check. The error can be detected by visual inspection or execution, which assumes you test all methods with such invalid parameters. Explicitly writing tests that use invalid values and adding annotations to describe a non-null type for static tools are two means of addressing this issue.

Example 5: Using Signed Integers Rather than Unsigned Integers   If you look at the preceding example, you will see another type of common error: *Quantity* is defined as a signed integer, which implies that ordering a negative number of items is permitted. That may certainly be reasonable for returning items but really shouldn't be in an order placement method. Imagine a Web site that allowed you to order negative quantities—you may end up with money refunded to your credit card even if you never bought anything. Careful review looking for improper use of signed integers can address this issue. The use of *size_t* for counts rather than *int* is also an example.

Adding a Check for Negative Quantities

```
public void PlaceOrder(Product product, int quantity)
{
    if (product == null)
    {
        throw new ArgumentException("Product must not be null");
    }
    if (quantity < 0)
    {
        throw new ArgumentException("Quantity must not be negative");
    }
    …
```

But why add this check? The *quantity* parameter should have been declared as an unsigned integer. There are many reasons for using signed integers instead of unsigned integers, including history, habit, and sloppiness. The original C language[1] did not have an unsigned integer type or exceptions; they were added in later versions of C. The single return type of C family languages (and for habit reasons even now where output parameters are allowed) often overloaded an unsigned integer return value with negative values for an error indication or other reasons. For example, the C# *String.IndexOf* function returns the character index of the first occurrence of a string and −1 if the string isn't present.

Overloading an Index with an Error Value

```
public string AppendAfter(string sourceString, string subString, string appendString)
{
    int    index = sourceString.IndexOf(subString);

    return    sourceString.Substring(0, index) + subString + appendString
              + sourceString.Substring(index + substring.Length);
}
```

The preceding code will throw an exception if the *subString* is not present in the *sourceString* because *IndexOf* will return negative one (−1) and *Substring(−1)* will throw an exception—all because of overloading the return value with an error. A better solution for this issue depends on whether the caller is supposed to ensure that the substring is present or not. In the first case, the preceding implementation is merely misleading because the exception thrown doesn't clearly indicate that the problem in the substring isn't in the source string but instead that you specified an invalid character offset. In the second case, it would be better to use an exception or separate error return value, as shown in the next code listing.

1 B. W. Kernighan and D. M. Ritchie, *The C Programming Language* (Englewood Cliffs, NJ: Prentice Hall, 1978).

Alternate Definition of *IndexOf*

```
public uint IndexOf{String sourceString, string subString)
{
    int    index = sourceString.IndexOf(subString);

    if     (index < 0)
    {
        throw new OperationException("Substring not found");
    }
    else
    {
        return     (uint)index;
    }
}
public string AppendAfterIfPresent(string sourceString, string subString, string
appendString)
{
    try
    {
        uint    index = IndexOf(sourceString, subString);
        return     sourceString.Substring(0, index) + subString +
                        appendString + sourceString.Substring(index +
                        substring.Length);
    }
    catch (OperationException)
    {
        return     sourceString;
    }
}
```

You can argue that using an exception is too expensive in terms of execution time, that it is really a matter for improving code optimization, providing a different error model (see the sidebar titled "Prolog error model," which follows), or some other construct. Using a separate error return value does not guarantee that the caller will check it first, so the issue of what to assign the return value to exists.

Prolog error model

Prolog has an interesting model of errors and variables. Failure is an innate concept. Any equivalent of a function call has two means of returning control to its caller:

- Success, which calls the return address
- Failure, which returns to the last point where there was a choice and unbinds all variables

It's quite a different model and has some interesting characteristics after you understand Prolog's concepts. It is one of the few languages where failure (error) is an innate part of the language's concept.

You could reverse the index and the error indication by returning a value that indicates whether the *IndexOf* succeeded and changing the output parameter to a reference as follows.

Definition of *IndexOf* Not Using Exceptions

```
public bool IndexOf{String sourceString, string subString, ref uint index)
{
    int     strIndex = sourceString.IndexOf(subString);

    if (strIndex < 0)
    {
        return   false;
    }
    else
    {
        ndex = (uint)strIndex;
        return    true;
    }
}
public string AppendAfterIfPresent(string sourceString, string subString, string
appendString)
{
    bool    notFound;
    unit    index;

        notFound = IndexOf(sourceString, subString, ref index);
        if (notFound)
        {
            return    sourceString;
        }
        else
        {
        return    sourceString.Substring(0, index) + subString +
                appendString + sourceString.Substring(index +
                substring.Length);
        }
    }
}
```

The preceding example won't compile because reference parameters—unlike output parameters—are not guaranteed to be set. There is no valid index if the substring is not found, and supplying one just allows for the error of using it without checking if *notFound* is false. The compiler doesn't know that the *index* variable would be set only if *notFound* were false. You could initialize the index to 0, but that would open up the possibility of using *index* when *notFound* is true. That's why an exception is a better method to use for semantic reasons, even though it may be slower.

Note that the name of the preceding function has been changed to *AppendAfterIfPresent*. The assumption of what happens when the *subString* isn't present should be explicit in the name of the method rather than requiring the developer to look up the behavior of the method to see what happens if the string is not present. Both *AppendAfter*, which throws an exception if the *subString* isn't present, and *AppendAfterIfPresent*, which does nothing if *subString* isn't present, may be useful methods for different callers. If the design is such that *subString* should be present, *AppendAfter* should be used so that if some other defect causes it not to be present an exception is thrown and the issue can be diagnosed rather than invisibly not appending. Serious defects can be hidden by such *helpful* defaulting in error conditions.

Example 6: Integer Overflow   Interfaces that use signed rather than unsigned parameters are open to security attacks using negative numbers, as in the previous example of using negative quantities to get refunds. In addition, even correctly used unsigned numbers can be used in an attack through overflow wrapping. If two numbers are multiplied together, choosing large enough values will cause the result to exceed the resolution of the integer, resulting in a vastly smaller result than expected or even a negative result.

By default, runtime systems at best detect errors such as divide by zero but not integer overflow. Specific code needs to be added for each instance of a possible overflow operation (another definitional concept changed into per reference).

C# provides a checked construct that throws an exception on integer overflow. You could sprinkle your code with checked constructs around integer operations, but just as with the previous example, errors can be made and places missed. Instead, at least in C#, you can detect integer overflow centrally in a type definition. However, it is quite a few lines of code, as follows.

Overflow Safe Positive Integers

```csharp
struct PosInt
{
    private    uint        Value;

    public PosInt(uint value)
    {
        this.Value = value;
    }

    public override bool Equals(object obj)
    {
        return this == (PosInt)obj;
    }

    public override int GetHashCode()
    {
        return Value.GetHashCode();
    }

    public override string ToString()
    {
        return Value.ToString();
    }
```

```csharp
public static PosInt operator +(PosInt a, PosInt b)
{
    return new PosInt(checked(a.Value + b.Value));
}

public static PosInt operator *(PosInt a, PosInt b)
{
    return new PosInt(checked(a.Value * b.Value));
}

public static PosInt operator -(PosInt a, PosInt b)
{
    return new PosInt(checked(a.Value - b.Value));
}

public static PosInt operator /(PosInt a, PosInt b)
{
    return new PosInt(checked(a.Value / b.Value));
}

public static PosInt operator %(PosInt a, PosInt b)
{
    return new PosInt(checked(a.Value % b.Value));
}

public static bool operator ==(PosInt a, PosInt b)
{
    return a.Value == b.Value;
}

public static bool operator !=(PosInt a, PosInt b)
{
    return a.Value != b.Value;
}

public static bool operator >(PosInt a, PosInt b)
{
    return a.Value > b.Value;
}

public static bool operator >=(PosInt a, PosInt b)
{
    return a.Value >= b.Value;
}

public static bool operator <(PosInt a, PosInt b)
{
    return a.Value < b.Value;
}

public static bool operator <=(PosInt a, PosInt b)
{
    return a.Value <= b.Value;
}
```

```
    public static PosInt operator +(PosInt a)
    {
        return a;
    }

    public static PosInt operator ++(PosInt a)
    {
        return new PosInt(a.Value + 1);
    }

    public static PosInt operator --(PosInt a)
    {
        return new PosInt(a.Value - 1);
    }

    public static bool operator !(PosInt a)
    {
        return a.Value != 0;
    }

    public static implicit operator uint(PosInt a)
    {
        returna.Value;
    }

    public static implicit operator PosInt(uint a)
    {
        return new PosInt(a);
    }

    public static implicit operator PosInt(int a)
    {
        return new PosInt(checked((uint)a));
    }
}
```

Using Overflow Safe and Unsafe Integers

```
static void Main(string[] args)
{
    int      i,j,k;
    Pos      IntiPosInt, jPosInt, kPosInt;

    i = 2000000000;
    j = 2000000000;
    k = i * j;                              // latent overflow -1651507200
    Trace.WriteLine(string.Format("{0} = {1} * {2}", k, i, j));

    iPosInt = 100;
    jPosInt = 200;
    kPosInt = iPosInt * jPosInt;
    Trace.WriteLine(string.Format("{0} = {1} * {2}", kPosInt, iPosInt,
                jPosInt));
```

```
    iPosInt = 2000000000;
    jPosInt = 2000000000;
    kPosInt = iPosInt * jPosInt;              // Throws exception
    Trace.WriteLine(string.Format("{0} = {1} * {2}", kPosInt, iPosInt,
               jPosInt));

    iPosInt = -1;                             // Throws exception
    }
Output:
-1651507200 = 2000000000 * 2000000000
20000 = 100 * 200
A first chance exception of type 'System.OverflowException' occurred
```

Conclusion

Software quality is a combination of perceived quality based on the likelihood of a customer encountering a defect and security defects, which are maliciously sought. You can't test a significant percentage of the functionality of a software product, so processes based on that assumption can give a deceptive sense of quality.

The process of software development consists of a multitude of transformations from the original vision into the final product. Many of the steps in this process have manual artifacts that can't be automatically verified; software development depends a lot on human verification processes (reviews). Because any human process includes a possibility of error, verification must be against something—another translation.

Each transformation is also into a different language of description. The first few are typically written documents, but finally code and tests are written. The step of writing code often loses a lot of information because some concepts can't be completely expressed in code or a definitional concept is turned into a referential concept as a result of limitations of the language.

Chapter 5
Using Productivity Games to Prevent Defects

In every job that must be done, there is an element of fun. You find the fun and–SNAP–the job's a game!
　　　　　　　　　　　　　　–Mary Poppins

Most people think of games as a leisure activity and not part of their daily work. Merriam-Webster defines *game* as an activity engaged in for diversion or amusement.[1] In the case of defect prevention, you are trying to engage people for diversion–to divert or distract them from their day-to-day tasks and encourage them to exert some effort on preventing defects.

Plenty of books and resources on game design are available. This chapter does not cover game design in detail but shows how and why competition is a good technique to use to encourage defect prevention effort. Most organizations do not use games and competition in the workplace as motivational techniques, which is unfortunate because they can be incredibly effective ways to get people to do things. Consider Frederick Winslow Taylor and his "one best way" in the famous *Principles of Scientific Management*. Taylor put a lot of work into studying workers and work processes to find the optimal output rate, and then analyzing behavior to move the median productivity rate toward the optimal rate. It's interesting to ponder if using games or competitions may have been a more effective approach to motivating workers. See the sidebar titled "Using the carrot, not the stick," which follows.

> ## Using the carrot, not the stick
>
> "This man we will call Schmidt. The task before us, then, narrowed itself down to getting Schmidt to handle 47 tons of pig iron per day and making him glad to do it. This was done as follows. Schmidt was called out from among the gang of pig-iron handlers and talked to somewhat in this way:
>
> " '... Well, if you are a high-priced man, you will do exactly as this man tells you tomorrow, from morning till night. When he tells you to pick up a pig and walk, you pick it up and you walk, and when he tells you to sit down and rest, you sit down. You do that right straight through the day. And what's more, no back talk. Now a high-priced man does

---

1　Merriam-Webster Online, "Game," *http://m-w.com/dictionary/game.*

just what he's told to do, and no back talk. Do you understand that? When this man tells you to walk, you walk; when he tells you to sit down, you sit down, and you don't talk back at him. Now you come on to work here tomorrow morning and I'll know before night whether you are really a high-priced man or not.' "[1]

Now, if Schmidt were presented with a "pig iron per day" game to play, he may have been as productive, perhaps even more so, without the "rather rough talk," as Taylor labels it. The question for this chapter is whether a "high score" may have challenged Schmidt and his cohorts to "beat the high score" and made them even more productive. Would the "second class workman" (Taylor's term) be motivated enough to show up the "first class workman" in a competition that he could handle 50 tons of pig iron instead of 47? Would Schmidt be *glad to do it* because he won that day's competition? Use the carrot, not the stick.

What Is Game Theory?

Game theory is a branch of applied mathematics and economics that studies situations where players choose different actions in an attempt to maximize their returns. John von Neumann was the first to expand on early mathematical analysis of probability and chance into game theory in the 1920's. His work was used by the military during World War II, and then later by the RAND Corporation to explore nuclear strategy. In the 1950s, John Nash, popularized in the film *A Beautiful Mind,* was an early contributor to game theory. His "Nash Equilibrium," which helps to evaluate player strategies in non-cooperative games. Game theory is now used in many diverse academic fields, ranging from biology and psychology to sociology and philosophy.[2]

Game theory outlines how and why people play games. Games have players, rules, strategies, outcomes, and a reward. Games are things people do, following a set of rules, developing strategies to create a certain outcome to receive a reward or prize. The players in the game must make certain "moves" to determine their reward. The players must follow certain rules while making these moves. Each player is supposed to behave rationally, which means trying to maximize personal reward, regardless of what the other players are doing. They are trying to "win." Each player pursues a set of moves, within the rules, to maximize his or her reward. See the following sidebar titled "Prisoner's Dilemma" for a discussion of how this classic dilemma can illuminate aspects of player strategies and motivation.

---

1   Frederick W. Taylor, *The Principles of Scientific Management* (New York: Harper and Brothers Publishers, 1911).

2   Wikipedia, "Game Theory," *http://en.wikipedia.org/wiki/Game_theory.*

Prisoner's Dilemma

The creation of the Prisoner's Dilemma is attributed to Merrill Flood and Melvin Dresher, who described it in their investigations of game theory as a nuclear strategy at RAND in 1950. The Prisoner's Dilemma is about two criminal suspects, questioned separately about a crime. If one suspect testifies against the other, and the other is silent, the silent suspect gets the full sentence, while the testifier goes free. If both are silent, both get minor but nonzero sentences. If both testify, they get partial—more than minor—less-than-full sentences. Each suspect must choose whether to testify or remain silent. However, neither suspect knows what the other will do. The dilemma arises when you assume that the suspects care only about themselves and do not know what the other will do—and yet the outcome for each depends on the choice of the other.

Much has been written on the Prisoner's Dilemma and its role in game theory. Since the use of games can have a dramatic impact on defect prevention efforts, it is useful to consider some of these fundamentals of game theory in the design of games to understand player strategies and encourage participation in defect prevention activity.

Games in History

Games have been around for centuries. For example, the game of Go was played in ancient China in 500 B.C. and is for sale along most toy aisles and in game stores, as well as online. (See the Free Go Programs Web site at *www.gnu.org/software/gnugo/free_go_software.html.*) The royal game of Ur was played in the fourth century B.C. You can play it online today on the British Museum Web site at *www.thebritishmuseum.ac.uk/explore/families_and_children/ online_tours/games/the_royal_game_of_ur.aspx.* Evidence even seems to indicate that games were used to motivate workers to build the pyramids of Egypt. (See the sidebar titled "Productivity Games Helped Build the Pyramids," which follows.)

Productivity games helped build the pyramids

One of the greatest testimonies to work and productivity is the ancient pyramids. There are many theories on how these great structures were built—everything from slave labor to aliens. What motivated the workers to accomplish these tremendous feats of engineering?

The Great Pyramid of Giza is the largest of the pyramids and has approximately 2.3 million stone blocks, weighing an average of 2.3 metric tons each. The estimate is that 35,000 workers built this great structure. Originally, the theory was that slave labor was used for construction, but archaeologists now think the building of the pyramids was accomplished predominantly as a volunteer effort—farmers, masons, carpenters, and metalworkers all contributing for the sake of national pride.

Most of the pyramids in Egypt each took decades to build. Former President Jimmy Carter once quipped, "I'm surprised that a government organization could do it that quickly." So the relevant question is, How did the workers stay motivated to complete the projects? Were productivity games used?

The answer is yes. (Otherwise, we wouldn't have included this example here!)

Workers were organized into teams, or phyles (tribes)—"Friends of Khufu" and "Drunkards of Menkaure," left and right, green and red, and so on. The evidence seems to indicate that these teams competed with one another to improve productivity. For example, stones were tagged with color to indicate the team that placed them.[1]

Phyles were subdivided into divisions. And divisions were identified by names represented by single hieroglyphs with meanings like endurance, perfection, strong (see Figure 5-1). So how do we know this? When you visit the pyramids, you come to a block of stone in the relieving chambers above the Great Pyramid. First, you see the cartouche of a king and then some scrawls in red paint—the gang's name—after it. In the Old Kingdom in the time of the Pyramids of Giza, the gangs were named after kings. So, for example, you may have a name, compounded with the name of Menkaure (a pharaoh), and it seems to translate as "the drunks or the drunkards of Menkaure."

It gets even more intriguing. In certain monuments, you can find the name of one gang on one side of the monument and the name of another gang, we assume a competing gang, on the other side of the monument. It's as though these gangs were pitted against each other. From this evidence, we can deduce that a labor force was assigned to respective crew gang phyles and divisions.[2]

1 Virginia Morell, "The Pyramid Builders," *www7.nationalgeographic.com/ngm/data/2001/11/01/html/ ft_20011101.5.fulltext.html.*

2 PBS Online, Nova Online Adventures, "Who Built the Pyramids?" *www.pbs.org/wgbh/nova/pyramid/explore/ builders.html*; Alan Winston, "The Labors of Pyramid Building," *www.touregypt.net/featurestories/pyramidwork- force.htm*; Joyce Tyldesley, "The Private Lives of the Pyramid-Builders," Bbc.co.uk Web site, *www.bbc.co.uk/ history/ancient/egyptians/pyramid_builders_07.shtml.*

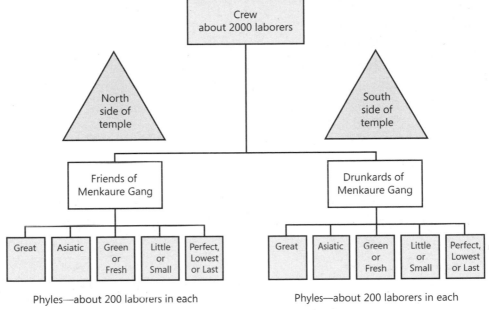

Figure 5-1   The pyramid builders' teams

The Gamer Generation

Although the current generation of electronic games has its roots in the 1950s and 1960s, with Spacewar and PONG, computer and game console developments over the last few decades have taken gaming to a new level. Perhaps it is unfair to attribute the start of a generation to a single game, but in 1981, Nintendo published Donkey Kong, which really was a defining moment in mainstream gaming. The popularity of video games far exceeds that of other historical game types. According to the Entertainment Software Association (ESA), the sales of gaming units alone have grown from 2.6 million units in 1996 to 228 million in 2005.[1] Contrast those figures with the game of Monopoly, which has sold more than 200 million units in its 65-year history.[2]

The point of this very brief overview of the history of electronic games is to emphasize the fact that the workforce today is composed of people who have grown up in a world of video games. The ESA says that the average gamer is a person who is 33 years old and has been playing for 12 years.[3] For example, any recent college computer science graduate employed in

1   Entertainment Software Association, "Facts and Research: Sales and Genre Data," *http://theesa.com/facts/ sales_genre_data.php.*

2   Hasbro, "History," *www.hasbro.com/monopoly/default.cfm?page=history.*

3   Entertainment Software Association, "Facts and Research: Game Player Data," *http://theesa.com/facts/ gamer_data.php.*

software development grew up playing video games. The rise in popularity of fantasy sports games, tribal casinos, televised poker, and gaming consoles (Xbox, PS3, and Wii) is no coincidence. This is a generation that thrives on games and competition.

What does that mean for defect prevention?

It comes down to "know your customer." In their book *The Kids Are Alright*, John Beck and Mitchell Wade enumerate the basic principles that video games have taught this generation:[1]

- If you get there first, you win.

- There is a limited set of tools, and it is certain that some combination will work. If you choose the right combination, the game will reward you.

- Trial and error is the best strategy and the fastest way to learn.

- Elders and their received wisdom can't help; they don't understand even the basics of this new world.

- You will confront surprises and difficulties that you are not prepared for. But the sum of those risks and dangers, by definition, cannot make the quest foolish.

- Once you collect the right "objects" (business plan, prototype, customers, maybe even profits), you'll get an infusion of gold to tide you over.

- Although there may be momentary setbacks, overall the trend will be up.

It is important to pay attention to these principles when designing games to motivate the workforce to invest time in defect prevention activities. The people closest to the work—the individual developers working with the code—know the most about defects. Because they are so familiar with the defects, they have the knowledge of how to prevent defects. Typically, the majority of the individual coders are recent college graduates or those newer to the workforce. Coincidentally, these same people grew up with video games as a significant part of their daily environment and were taught the preceding basic principles through their heavy interaction with video games. The result is that they identify with and will respond to the idea of using games in their work activities.

Why Games Change Behavior

Games are compelling. Human nature has always responded to competition. Darwin's theory of natural selection touches on the need for members of a species to compete with one another for food or living space or some limited resource to survive. It is well within human

---

1   John C. Beck and Mitchell Wade, *The Kids Are Alright: How the Gamer Generation Is Changing the Workplace* (Cambridge, MA: Harvard Business School Press, 2006), 43.

nature for people to compete with one another, so creating a contest to drive behavioral change targets survival instincts that are core to everyone. As Darwin says,

> The struggle will generally be more severe between them [members of a species], if they come into competition with each other.
> —Microsoft Encarta, 2007.

NCAA Tournament Games

Every year, March Madness descends when the National Collegiate Athletic Association (NCAA) hosts a basketball tournament for men's and women's teams. Sixty five college basketball teams are seeded and compete against one another until one team wins the tournament. Many spectators set up brackets that list the teams competing and try to predict which teams will win their matchups and move forward in the tournament to the final competition. Often, employees in companies host office pools in which they compete against one another to see who can predict the basketball team winners most accurately. The NCAA tournament is usually preceded by a host of news articles on the loss of employee productivity brought on by office betting pools.

According to many articles, the cost of lost productivity is more than a billion dollars. Several articles suggest that employers suffer the losses and are happy with the "morale benefits," saying that office pools build camaraderie and foster closer relationships between staff members.

Perhaps the answer is to integrate work tasks into the pool. According to one survey, employees spend more than 13 minutes a day during the tournament checking basketball scores. Why not put this out in the open and attach "real work" to the pool? For example, an insurance company can hold a contest to allow claims processors to fill out one bracket per 10 claim forms processed. Or highway patrol officers can get a Final Four pick for every five speeding tickets they write—just kidding!

The point of productivity games is to align the game with the goals of the organization, and if people are spending their work time checking NCAA results, companies should integrate that behavior into the task at hand.

Types of Games

Game theory offers a categorization of types of games that is helpful in designing productivity games for defect prevention. As management or the "game designers" think about how to use games to encourage defect prevention activity, an understanding of the different types of games is tremendously helpful in making the games more fun and more effective at attracting players to defect prevention work.

Following is a general categorization of the types of games that exist:

- **Noncooperative**   Players work independently without concern for the other players. These are typically the best type of games for work-related competitions.

- **Cooperative**   Players may cooperate with one another. This can lead to tricky issues when used as a motivator for defect prevention activity.

- **Zero Sum**   The sum of all rewards for all players is zero. Zero-sum games are not recommended for defect prevention competition because people can do work, perform tasks, and lose ground.

- **Constant Sum**   The sum of all rewards for all players is constant. However, a variable reward is a more exciting and motivational incentive for defect prevention work.

- **Aligned Games**   Productivity games that are played to help achieve the goals of the task at hand are called *aligned games*. For example, a janitor may see how many garbage cans can be emptied in an hour. NCAA tournament picks that are awarded as a result of doing a task in line with company goals can be considered aligned games.

- **Incidental Games**   *Incidental games* are played during the course of work and do not contribute or directly affect the outcome or accomplishment of the task. Incidental games probably will help improve morale, will keep people from straying too far off task, and may foster community. However, they do not directly relate to the goals of the job. An example might be a hotel maid who lines up pillows in certain patterns from room to room, or a truck driver who waves to Volvo wagons for the fun of it. These incidental games keep people thinking and keep their minds working but do not necessarily improve output. NCAA tournament watching—as it is done today—is a great example of an incidental game.

Games of Chance vs. Games of Skill

Games and competition used for defect prevention work can be games of either chance or skill. The nature of the scoring and reward mechanisms determines the type of game. If the rewards are random, these competitions are considered games of chance. On the other hand, the competition can, for example, be about finding the most buffer overrun bugs—making it a game of skill. It is worth noting, however, that games of skill may tend to discourage competition unless the players are all of roughly equal competence. If one or two players are far more skilled than the rest are, they will stand out and the rest of the players may become discouraged. A game of chance gives more players an opportunity to earn rewards, thereby encouraging participation.

Mini Games

One fascinating possibility of productivity games is to make the game take the place of the work. There are many examples in the real world where mini games alter behavior or focus attention on a specific issue. A simple example is the "days without an accident" sign posted at many construction sites.

Two distinct categories of mini games can be created and played within the task: games that are aligned with the goal of the task—call these *challenges*—and games that are not aligned—call these *incidental mini games*. Here is an example to illustrate the difference between the two. The task is to drive a truck from New York to Seattle. The goal is to travel coast to coast in the least amount of time. An aligned challenge can be created in which points are awarded to the driver whenever the second hand on a watch passes the 12 at exactly the same time that the truck passes the physical milepost, assuming the driver follows the legal speed limit, road conditions are favorable, and so forth. The score is increased for each successful "hit"; that is, for each time the second hand clicks to 12 at the exact milepost location. This game is aligned with the overall goal of driving to Seattle, and "winning" this game contributes positively to the goal of driving to Seattle. Most video games include mini games that are aligned with the overall goal of the game—players can get new tools or weapons, build strength, and so forth.

An unaligned, or incidental, mini game in the truck driving scenario may a point awarded every time the driver honks the horn at a silver SUV. The scoring for the incidental game does not contribute positively to the overall goal of driving to Seattle. There is a third, rarely occurring type, where winning the mini game penalizes the player in progress toward the overall goal. For a truck driver, this adverse game may be to get off the highway at every even-numbered exit, turn around, and get back on. Winning this game is detrimental to the goal of driving to Seattle in the least amount of time.

During the design of mini games, be sure to consider existing work and the repercussions of overlaying a game on work that's already being done. For example, if one person is employed full time to find defects in the code, starting a game to encourage others to do that work may have an adverse effect on that person. Simply starting a game to score others on the "regular" work of another is not a good idea. Perhaps involving that person in the design of the game, with a careful explanation and understanding of the goals, will help, but even those efforts may not overcome the negative implications of inviting, encouraging, or rewarding others for doing his or her job.

Prediction Markets

A prediction market is a type of betting, where the payoff is based on the outcome of some future event. In software development, prediction markets built around product release dates are one of the more common uses of the genre. Prediction markets can be established around defect prevention techniques as well, and they can provide a useful alternative to common productivity games. Again, the design and reward structure are imperative for prediction markets, so as to discourage people from doing the wrong type of work in order to win the game.

More information on prediction markets:

- Prediction Markets: Wolfers and Zitzewitz - Journal of Economic Perspectives—Volume 18, Number 2—Spring 2004—Pages 107–126

- Hollywood Stock Exchange - *http://www.hsx.com/*

- *http://www.ideosphere.com/*

- *http://en.wikipedia.org/wiki/Prediction_market*

Alternate Reality Games

An alternate reality game is a storyline that weaves real-life elements into the game. These "games" involve creative writing, role playing, and puzzle solving around a common story. Alternate reality games can be extremely useful in tying together various other productivity games for defect prevention work. As with other types of games, significant effort must be put into the design and the rewards to ensure that the right behavior is reinforced. The design of an alternate reality game is significantly different from a simple productivity game, but the storyline can sit on top to help connect various productivity games around a common theme.

For more information on alternate reality games, see

- *http://www.argn.com*

- *http://www.unfiction.com*

Practical Guide to Defect Prevention Games

There are some simple steps you can follow to create games for defect prevention. The goal is to take advantage of the natural attraction of games and competition and use it to encourage people to invest time and effort in defect prevention activities.

Start with a Leader Board

The easiest way to create a competition is to start to keep score. As Peter Drucker says, "What gets measured gets done," and this applies directly to the use of games and competition to encourage investment in defect prevention. As soon as you start keeping score, people sit up and take notice. If, for example, the project could benefit from a higher defect discovery rate, posting a running total number of defects discovered by each developer will compel people to compete to increase their score. However, as soon as you start to keep score, people will start to optimize their behavior for a higher score—to "game" the system—that is, the player may enter artificial or dubious defect discovery reports just to win the game. A well-designed game does not have this problem, but if there are holes in the scoring mechanism, it can cause huge problems.

Keep It Simple

It is easy to overthink a game. The game should be simple enough that people can play easily and score points. Simple games attract players. People tend to overanalyze and overdesign the games at the cost of results. A simple game is easy to administer and can get people playing immediately. There is always time to refine it as you go.

Think Through Scoring

People will quickly find any holes or improprieties in the scoring system. The famous Dilbert response to a "bug bounty"—a competition to find the most bugs—illustrates this point exactly by leading to completely unexpected results. It is critical to think through the scoring and rewards to make sure they drive the right behavior. Scoring system design is a skill that improves with practice. The best way to find and fix scoring problems is by using a small pilot program. People are creative and will find holes immediately.

DILBERT: © Scott Adams/Dist. By United Feature Syndicate, Inc.

After participants hear the game rules, spend some time with them to understand their playing strategies; this can help flush out any scoring inconsistencies. Scoring is not something to take lightly—the success of the game depends on an equitable scoring system. Even the best intentions can end up being misconstrued.

Reward the Right Behavior

A game will entice people to do things. The design of the scoring system and rules of the game can encourage people to change what they do. The rewards for the game should go to those who perform the intended actions. This may sound simple and obvious, but many times, subtle nuances of the scoring system are missed until it is too late.

For example, an initial goal may be set to find bugs. A team can host a "bug bash" for an evening and give a prize to the person who finds the most bugs during the event. However, reviewing those bugs a week later may reveal that the winner actually entered a high number of duplicate, insignificant, or invalid bugs and didn't do quite as well as it looked when prizes were distributed. In the design of the scoring system, it is important to consider the game's goals and the desired behavior necessary to achieve those goals. The goal may not be to find a sheer number of bugs, but to find high-quality bugs or bugs that must be fixed. Be as clear as possible on the exact behavior change desired when designing the scoring and rewards.

Use Scoring to Encourage Participation

This is another reminder to consider the goals of the game carefully. If the goal is to get the entire team to perform an activity, the scoring system should account for the fact that one or two people may jump way ahead, or people may prioritize the activity differently and fall way behind. An example is a "consecutive days" reward when scoring is based on consecutive days of performing the desired activity. If a team member is out of the office for the first three days of the competition, he or she can never catch up and therefore likely will not participate for the rest of the game. In such cases, the scoring system should allow people to catch up or offer alternative ways to compete.

Design the scoring to encourage, not discourage, participation. Perhaps there are bonus points to earn or alternative activities that people can do to get themselves "back in the game." Also, consider leaders: If one person works hard to get a big lead and that person's effort results in a big gain for the project, he or she should be acknowledged and rewarded for the effort, not discouraged by being penalized and brought back to the pack through rule changes and bonus point distribution.

Using scoring to encourage participation is harder than it looks.

Keep the Players Coming Back to Check Their Score

A good game keeps the players' attention. The idea is to encourage players to monitor and improve their scores. If the players are regularly checking their scores, it is more likely they are trying to improve their scores and performing the tasks that earn them rewards. Anything that the game designers can do to bring people back to the game helps maintain interest and keeps people playing. Following are some activities people do when they are engaged by a game:

- Check scores
- Read about winners
- Look up friends' and co-workers' scores
- Learn about new games
- Challenge others to one-off competitions

All these behaviors keep the interest alive and get people thinking about performing the tasks to earn a place in the game.

You'd Be Surprised at What People Will Compete For

As mentioned, people are naturally competitive. From birth, we are taught to compete for survival—for food, attention; competition is a natural part of life. Implementing a simple game to perform an action and receive a point can result in behavioral change. A competition to spell a word or click a button will attract participants. At first, you may tend to think big, elaborate games are necessary, but simple competitions are a great way to start. Model some of the games after popular "analog" games, such as card games or board games. Games like Chinese Checkers, Othello, Scrabble, Hangman, and popular board games are all based on very simple concepts.

Allow Room for Adjustment—Set a Time Frame

A game or competition will be more successful, especially at first, if it exists for a set length of time. If the scores are tallied daily or weekly, adjustments can be made periodically to fine-tune the competition. When starting a game, schedule an update in a short amount of time to allow for adjustments. If it is impossible to shorten the length of the competition—for example, the game follows the football season—host a pilot version prior to the start of the game period so that you can make any scoring adjustments before deployment.

Stratify to Maintain Interest

In most games, there will be serious or hardcore players and casual players. The existence and participation of hardcore players should not discourage casual players. The scoring system should accommodate and motivate both types of players to compete, even if they are not competing with each other.

Retain a Player's History

As games evolve or new games begin, try to avoid starting over. Players have earned some value and prestige, and it is useful to retain these attributes. Players who finish second or third, for instance, might lose interest if they are forced to start over from zero in a new game. However, a player who finishes last wants a fresh start, so analyze the playing field and develop the scoring and historical retention policies accordingly.

Start with a Small Pilot

By using a pilot program, the product team can monitor participation more closely. A pilot provides the opportunity to monitor the game play and keep track of scoring rewards. With a pilot, the product team can interview players and get a full understanding of how the game will be played and how the players perceive the rules and rewards.

Let People Play at Their Own Pace

People work at different rates—some are slow and steady, and some work in bursts. The game should allow players to participate at their own pace. Scoring and participation should reflect the need for people to play at a rate that is comfortable for them.

Augment Interest by Using Cash and Prizes

To sustain interest, add cash and prize rewards. It's probably best not to do this at the start, but add them as the contest continues to keep interest levels high.

Use Random Drawings

When determining prizes, random drawings are sometimes a more effective way to distribute rewards. Sometimes leaders are so far ahead of the others that the rest of the pack loses interest. In this case, a random drawing can help to keep interest in the game while you are still acknowledging the leaders.

Examples of Using Games for Defect Prevention

During the development of the Windows Vista operating system, the Microsoft product team developed and hosted a number of different games to drive productivity. The size of the project and corresponding length of the development cycle led to a repetitive set of activities, and as the team entered the beta phases, the use of games was successful in injecting new energy into the development effort. In some cases, there were productivity gains of as much as 300 percent using competition as a basis for encouraging task completion. As shown in Figure 5-2, the beta 1 game asked team members to perform various tasks to "earn a letter" and spell *beta1*.

See if you can spell...

Vista Internal Beta 1 Game

Install Vista, vote on quality Complete challenges to earn letters that spell **b e t a 1**.

b - Install a beta 1 build
e - Vote on a beta 1 build
t - Run overnight
a - Install 3 consecutive beta 1 builds
1 - Run overnight 3 times

Check out the **Leaderboard** and the list of current beta1 **Winners**

New! Check out the **Beta1 Game FAQ**

Figure 5-2   Windows Vista beta 1 game

The beta 2 game (Figure 5-3) expanded on the concept and awarded points for test activity. There were multiple levels of prizes and random drawings, and players could earn wristbands based on participation. In some cases, the wristband became a symbol at meetings and in hallways that spurred competition.

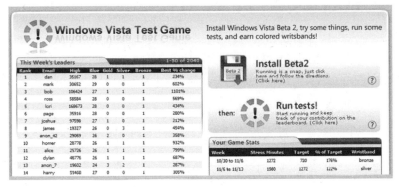

Figure 5-3   Windows Vista beta 2 game

These games culminated in a release game that was distributed company-wide. Prizes were based on random drawings for those who completed installation and certain test activities. Once again, the results were phenomenal, with the majority of the company participating in the final days of testing Windows Vista.

Tips on Game Design

It is easy to spot the similarities in simple games that work well. Noncooperative games, where each player is responsible for his or her own scoring, usually work best.

- Simple leader board—do something, earn a point
- Spell a word or phrase—earn letters
- Hangman—earn a guess
- Pick a number—earn a guess
- Guess a word—earn a letter guess
- Graffiti—earn letters to spell a phrase
- Guess the mystery celebrity (or mystery *whatever*)—earn clues to guess
- Scavenger hunt
- Clue

Game Design Checklist

Any productivity game should accomplish the following:

- Get players to be more productive (and have data to prove it)
- Be easy for people to play and compete

- Have well-thought-out rules and scoring

- Be competitive and/or fun

- Keep players engaged and looking at their scores

- Keep a history of player activity

- Let players play at their own pace

- Let players compete against themselves

- Be tested with a small group first

- Evolve and be refined over time

- Be careful with games that overlap existing work.

A great resource on the use of games for productivity and to change behavior is the Serious Games Initiative (*www.seriousgames.org*). This organization helps to connect game designers and organizations using games for health care, social change, education, and productivity.

Conclusion

Productivity games are an effective way to encourage investment in defect prevention techniques. Games can attract interested players and motivate people to make investments in prevention activities on their own. There have been many scientific studies around the use of games in various situations. Game theory, pioneered in the 1920s by John von Neumann, is a useful foundation to aid in the design of productivity games. There are a wide variety of games that can be applied to help change people's behavior. In the daily regimen of the software development cycle, there's usually very little thought about the "big picture" and preventing defects. The focus is on the immediate problems, and simple competition and games can add some fun and excitement to defect prevention work. The success of the game in improving productivity is dependent on game and reward design. There are several key factors that can make or break the use of games as a successful defect prevention technique. Games can be simple or elaborate but must consider the behavioral impact on the players—games should encourage the desired effort. Reward design is critical to a successful program. Smaller rewards and smaller game programs are usually better because they provide an opportunity for frequent design and reward adjustments. Productivity games provide a tremendous opportunity to attract effort toward defect prevention in a fun and exciting way.

Suggested Reading

GameTheory.net. Home page. *www.gametheory.net.*

IEEE Computer Society Task Force on Game Technologies (TFGT). "IEEE-CS Task Force on Game Technology: Publications." *www.ucalgary.ca/~jparker/TFGT/publications.html.*

"Kids Games." *www.gameskidsplay.net/.*

Marks, Robert. "Strategic Game Theory for Managers." *www.agsm.edu.au/~bobm/teaching/SGTM.html.*

Serious Games Initiative. Home page. *www.seriousgames.org.*

"Game Theory: Types of Games," *http://library.thinkquest.org/26408/math/ gametypes.shtml.*

ThinkQuest. "Game Theory: An Example game." *library.thinkquest.org/26408/math/prisoner.shtml.*

Walpole, Stuart. "Designing Games for the Wage Slave." GameDev.net. *www.gamedev.net/reference/articles/article2121.asp.*

Chapter 6
Improving the Testability of Software

A fundamental part of defect prevention is to discover defects as efficiently as possible even after they are introduced into software. Architecting, designing, and implementing software that is relatively easy to test increase the efficiency of the testing process and make defects more discoverable. *Testability* is the degree to which components and systems are designed and implemented for test automation to achieve complete code path coverage and simulate all usage situations in a cost-efficient manner. This chapter introduces the Simplicity, Observability, Control, and Knowledge (SOCK) model of testability and provides practical guidelines for improving testability.

Realizing the Benefits of Testability

Testing can be one of the most expensive parts of the product life cycle. Anything that can be done to reduce the cost of testing is obviously a huge benefit. Architecting and designing testability into a product from the start go a long way toward reducing the cost of testing and making maintenance of the software easier (that is, more cost effective).

Software that is highly testable also tends to be well designed. In the Net Objectives Design Patterns[1] curriculum based on the book *Design Patterns Explained: A New Perspective on Object-Oriented Design,*[2] by Alan Shalloway and James R. Trott, the authors state that there is an important link between testability and good design: "Easy testability is tightly correlated to loose coupling and strong cohesion [two main pillars of good design]." In the context of unit testing, they also assert the following:

Code that is difficult to unit test is often:

- Tightly coupled: "I cannot test this without instantiating half the system."

- Weakly cohesive: "This class does so much, the test will be enormous and complex!"

- Redundant: "I'll have to test this in multiple places to ensure that it works everywhere."

By keeping testability in mind during the architecture, design, and implementation phases, software becomes better designed and more easily diagnosed when problems arise, which can lead to lower maintenance costs.

---

1 Net Objectives, "Design Patterns Training," *www.netobjectives.com/courses/c_design_patterns.htm*.

2 Alan Shalloway and James Trott, *Design Patterns Explained: A New Perspective on Object-Oriented Design*, 2nd ed. (Boston: Addison-Wesley Professional, 2004).

The same methods used to make the software more testable can also be used to make the software more manageable, for example, making it easier to control remotely or to script common actions or detect and centrally report bad behavior or significant events. The same tenets of testability also provide the foundation for *self-healing software*: Software that has the ability to observe its own state, know if the state is operationally valid, and if not, take an action to return the software to a correct state or at the very least report on the observed operational failure.

Testability doesn't come free, but a good balance of testability features can reduce the overall cost of developing, supporting, and servicing the software. Early thinking about "how are we going to test this?" starts the discussion on testability features, which in turn leads to good design and allows for efficient creation of test automation that fully exercises the software under test. The same testability features can also be used to improve the diagnosability, manageability, and supportability of the software, which then continue to benefit the software throughout its support and servicing lifetime.

Implementing Testability

Testability is tied to test automation and its ability to programmatically verify whether software is working the way it should and whether the actions of the software under test are having the expected effect on the system on which it is running. In their 1992 paper *How to Automate Testing–the Big Picture,*[1] Keith Stobie and Mark Bergman describe effective test automation in terms of the acronym SEARCH: Setup, Execution, Analysis, Reporting, Cleanup, and Help. Every automated test must include each of these elements to be a true and effective test. *Setup* is the effort it takes to bring the software up to the point where the actual test operation is ready to be executed. *Execution* of the test is then followed by an *analysis* of whether the software did what it was supposed to do and didn't have any unintended side effects on the system as a whole. *Reporting* the results of the analysis is then followed by a *cleanup* phase that returns the software to a known state so that the next test can proceed. For the test to be runnable and maintainable by more than just the person who wrote it, a decent *help* system should be in place as well to describe the three basics of test documentation: How to set up the tests, how to run the tests, and how to interpret the results.

The goal of creating more testable software is to help facilitate effective test automation by making it easier to set up, execute, analyze, clean up, and provide straightforward help for the tests. Software can be designed from the start to allow for efficient test automation. The key tenets of testability described by Microsoft Test Architect David Catlett are Simplicity, Observability, Control, and Knowledge of expected results, or SOCK.

---

1 *http://www.keithstobie.net/Documents/TestAuto_The_BigPict.PDF*

Simplicity: Creating Noncomplex Software

Obviously, the more complex software is, the harder it is to test. Software that has a large number of interrelated or stateful operations is inherently more difficult to test than are systems that have only a handful of tasks with a limited number of options.

Adhering to the basic pillars of good design of high cohesion, loose coupling, and low redundancy is a great way to decrease complexity, which in turn increases testability. For example, software that is designed with high cohesion—meaning each method or function in the software accomplishes one and only one task—simplifies the test matrix. Not having to go through a complicated series of operations using a specific set of parameters just to get the software to the point where the test can actually be executed is a huge testability win.

Similarly, methods that have a minimal amount of coupling, or a low number of dependencies, are much easier to test. For example, using something like a SQL database instead of a simple text file for configuration storage causes the testing to be much more complicated. Reading and writing information over the network increase the possibility of encountering errors, and learning how to set up and maintain a computer running Microsoft SQL Server can greatly increase the complexity of the test matrix as well as the cost of testing. Testing code in only one place instead of having redundant code that must be tested in many places also simplifies testing.

Simplifying the software design to reduce the test matrix and reduce the time it takes to set up and clean up the tests is a big win for testability. For example, if the only way to clean up the test pass is to restart the computer, testing will become very expensive in terms of time. One way to reduce the cost of setup to improve testability is something that many people probably take for granted: The TCP/IP loopback functionality present in operating systems such as Microsoft Windows. Setting up a client and server on the same computer and being able to exercise a majority of the code paths using this simple one-computer configuration goes a long way toward making network applications more testable. Anything that can be done to simplify the process of getting the computer into a certain state bodes well for testability. Another example of simplifying testing is the capability of installing multiple configurations of the same software package on the same computer.

Componentization

Componentization, the ability to break up functionality into logical groups as separate libraries that can easily be swapped out, is an important part of making software more testable. For example, a contract developer working on the networking portion of a tax software package was required to build the entire client package including his changes and install the entire client package before he could test his changes. The process took 40 minutes. Not only that, there were three separate types of software packages, and they could not be installed at the same time on the same computer. So, to verify a single fix or feature addition, the developer had at minimum two hours of setup, not including how long it took to remove the software and restart his test computer. Needless to say, he admitted that most of the time when he made changes he tested only one client package instead of all three.

If, however, the software had been componentized, the developer could have swapped in and out the networking components he was working on without having to spend 40 minutes building and reinstalling. Also, if the three client configurations could have all been installed on the same computer, he could have easily tested all three configurations with only the cost of the initial setup.

The other important testability feature that componentization affords is the ability to insert test components in place of the real components. This is sometimes called *fault injection* and is used to make better use of *mock objects*, modules that can simulate usage and error conditions without implementing the entire dependent infrastructure. Separating logical tasks into modules, such as the networking library from the tax software, makes it easier to test these components separately, which reduces the complexity of setting up the tests, which increases testability.

Using complexity metrics, one can also get a feeling for how testable software may be. Complexity is also defined in terms of not only the specific methods or modules in the software under test but also the system in which the software operates, its direct and indirect dependencies. The more complex the software and the systems in which it interacts, the less testable. Stephen Kan in the second edition of his book *Metrics and Models in Software Quality Engineering*[1] specifically mentions the usefulness of complexity metrics "To estimate programming and service effort, identify troublesome code, and *estimate testing effort*" (p. 318, emphasis added). Although there is some debate about using specific metrics such as McCabe's Cyclomatic Complexity for estimating test effort, most agree it is a good starting point for identifying the absolute minimum number of test cases needed to completely cover a function or module. In practical terms, agreeing on a threshold for complexity metrics that have been proven to be predictors of defects is important not only in reducing the number of defects but also in maintaining the testability of software.

Another way of reducing the complexity of software is by using established design patterns. With the use of design patterns comes predictable and inherently more testable software. The canonical example of a design pattern that greatly improves testability is the Model-View-Controller (MVC) pattern of user interface (UI) design. A UI becomes more testable when the business logic is separated from the UI or the view of the model through a controller. This is because the business logic can then be tested separately from the UI, and if (and when) the UI changes, the core business logic tests will not have to change. For example, when the interaction with a database or file system is intertwined in the UI code itself, it makes it very difficult to automate validation of the behavior of both the UI and the business logic, and if (and when) the UI ever changes, the tests have to be completely rewritten.

---

1   Kan, Stephen H., *Metrics and Models in Software Quality Engineering,* 2nd ed. (Addison-Wesley, 2003).

Here's a simple example of how to make a Microsoft .NET console application written in C# more testable. This application outputs a list of customers from a database.

```
static void Main1()
{
    SqlConnection conn = new SqlConnection(Settings.SqlDatabaseConn);
    conn.Open();
    SqlCommand command = new SqlCommand(Settings.GetCustomersQuery, conn);
    SqlDataReader reader = command.ExecuteReader();
    while (reader.Read())
    {
        Console.WriteLine(reader.GetString(0));
    }
    reader.Close();
    conn.Close();
}
```

This code seems simple enough until it comes time to automate the validation of the results. In Windows, this would typically mean writing a complicated batch file to run the application, capture the standard output, parse it, sort it, and compare it against some known list in a text file. Then, when the customer decides they want a graphical user interface instead of a console interface, all the tests have to be rewritten. Instead, if the developer had followed (at least loosely) the MVC pattern, tests could be written to validate the data directly from the database along with separate tests to validate the actual displaying of the data. In this case, by componentizing the interaction with the database into a different library, the application becomes more testable. This also simplifies the *Main1* program quite a bit:

```
static void Main2()
{
    ArrayList results = CustomerList.GetCustomers();
    foreach (String result in results)
    {
        Console.WriteLine(result);
    }

}
```

The *CustomerList.GetCustomers* method is then in a separate library that the tester could call directly to validate the results from the database. Then, even if the UI changes, these tests are still valid.

This type of design for testability also enables a key aspect of testing: fault injection. *Fault injection* is the ability to force error conditions on software. The best candidates for fault injection are at the boundaries of any external dependencies. In this example, it is the interaction with the SQL database. We're sure many a programmer is cringing at both the *Main1* and *Main2* code because it does not handle *any* error conditions. There are bugs aplenty waiting to be uncovered when this poor defenseless application gets put into the real world. In *Main1*, it would be very difficult to induce error conditions to force the code to deal with the various exceptions that could be thrown by the interaction with the SQL database. It would be relatively expensive to set up a testing environment that forced, for example, a connection timeout or login failure or query timeout. In *Main2*, it is much easier to force these conditions and ensure that the UI code handles them properly. The tester could easily replace the *CustomerList* library with his or her own fault injection test library that returns every possible error condition the UI should handle without needing to set up a complicated test bed. Enabling fault injection is a key part of designing testable software, and following the key design principle of loose coupling as well as using design patterns such as the Model-View-Controller pattern help improve the design as well as the testability of software.

As discussed, testability is greatly improved by following good principles of design, componentization, monitoring complexity, and using established design patterns such as the Model-View-Controller pattern. After software is designed, other steps can be taken to improve testability further.

Observability: Making Software Observable

During the analysis phase of a test, to determine whether a test passes or fails, the test automation must be able to observe the results of the software under test and its effect on the system as a whole. The ability to do this in a cost-efficient manner is the degree to which the software is observable.

Observability is a very important part of testability because it allows for efficient and accurate test automation. The more easily the automation can observe the test execution action, the more accurately it can judge whether the test passes or fails. Sometimes the important information required for accurately analyzing test results is not exposed to test automation. This is especially true in cases where an action may result in more than one reaction that may or may not be valid based on environmental variables or a particular configuration setting.

For example, a small business version of a server application may accept only 10 connections, but an enterprise version may accept a thousand connections. If a test application tries making 11 connections, it will pass or fail depending on whether the small business or enterprise version of the software is installed. Either the test suite could duplicate test connection code and check for the boundary conditions for each server version, increasing the cost of setup, test automation, and maintenance of the tests, or, if a method were implemented in the server software that simply returned the version of the software, the test code could query that method and make pass/fail decisions based on that observable piece of information. Separate test suites would not have to be run on each version of the software because the test would be able to automatically adjust its expectations of when a connection is refused based on querying the software under test for its version.

Even better, if the queried method returns the threshold value, if the thresholds are changed later (for example, say, the small business server version increases its acceptable client load to 20), the tests do not have to be changed because they maintain themselves, keying off the threshold value exposed by all versions of the server application. Additionally, if a new "medium-sized business" version of the software that supported a maximum of 200 clients were released, the same tests could be run against the new version with no modifications. In each of these cases, the test simply scales up connections until receiving a connection refusal, queries to see whether the actual connections match the threshold value returned by the software under test, and passes or fails the test accordingly.

When test automation can query for threshold values, it makes the software more observable and thus more testable. Other examples of making software more observable include the following:

- Understand any configuration option that changes the behavior of the software under test. By making these configuration values programmatically observable, you eliminate the need to hard-code values in the test code, which helps reduce maintenance of the test code, especially when the software under test changes.

- Know timeout values or any "magic" number that influences the observed behavior of the software. Knowing what these values are ahead of time and how they influence the observed behavior is important during the analysis phase of a test. For example, a media-streaming server may reduce or increase the quality of a video stream based on a heuristic calculated from current networking conditions. To validate that the media-streaming server algorithm is working as expected according to specification, the results of the heuristic formula must be programmatically observable to the test software.

- Discern decision formulas. Knowing which path is taken after a branch statement (such as an *if* or *case* statement) helps make the determination of pass/fail more accurate. For example, the XPath query language parser has a "fast path" that is activated only if the Extensible Markup Language (XML) the query is to be run against is in a particular format. In a specific test, because the results from the XPath query were identical regardless of whether the fast path was taken, to verify whether the code took this fast path on qualified XML input, the test team had to look at an internal variable as well as the actual XPath query results. Having programmatic access to that internal variable increased the observability of the software.

- Examine internal resource usage to find memory and handle leaks. Beaconing when memory is allocated and subsequently deallocated or when an external resource is used and then disposed of can be an important test and diagnostic tool. In testing for memory leaks, the software under test can simply beacon when memory or handles are allocated and deallocated. Then the test software can validate these claims against the actual observed memory usage recorded by the operating system and can determine whether there are any resource leaks. This technique can be extended to any type of interaction with a resource that should be freed after it has been used. For example, a temporary file that is created should be deleted after it has been used, and a network connection should be torn down after a transaction is completed. When software exposes its internal state to test software in an easily observable manner, this increases the testability of the software.

- Expose errors or warnings the software encounters as it goes through its operations. This allows test software to have its own self-checking mechanism. For example, a test may seem to pass (perhaps a method was called and it returns ERROR_SUCCESS, one of the classic Windows error codes), but the method may have actually encountered some internal problem, logged an error or warning somewhere else, and returned the wrong error code, which is unfortunately very common. If there is some programmatic way of accessing the error log file, such as through the Windows Event Log APIs, the test will not be fooled by the bogus ERROR_SUCCESS return code.

- Beacon major state changes in the software, for example, system initialization or shut-down, establishment of a connection, or any other change a test automation program could consume to understand the current state of the software.

- Observe what happens after the software completes a task. This is particularly crucial for certain testing methods, such as Model-Based Testing, which relies on the ability of the test harness to programmatically evaluate the state of the software under test and compare it with the "model" state, or test oracle. The more observable the software is, the more accurate the comparison between the model and the actual state can be, thus enabling a very powerful test methodology. Even if Model-Based Testing is not used, it is very important to have multiple data points that the test automation can use to make an accurate and complete analysis of whether the software is behaving correctly. For more on Model-Based Testing, see *Practical Model-Based Testing: A Tools Approach*[1].

Control: Increasing Control over Software Under Test

A very important aspect of testability is the capability of efficiently and reliably exercising the software under test through all usage situations. This is considered the main pillar of testability: Can test code easily manipulate the software in a way that is more efficient than having a human sit down and manually put the software through its paces? Increasing the control of both setup and execution of a test is critically important in improving testability. The more controllable a component, the more deterministic and predictable the behavior, which increases confidence in the results of the analysis phase.

Similar to being able to observe thresholds and timeouts, it can be equally important to control configurable options at run time. When a configuration option for an application can be programmatically changed and does not require a system restart, testing can realize a huge efficiency gain. Another important aspect of control is the ability to control external factors that cause the system to behave differently. The best technique for controlling external factors

1   Mark Utting and Bruno Legeard, *Practical Model-Based Testing: A Tools Approach.* (Elsevier Science & Technology Books, 2006).

is to wrap any external calls, such as system calls, which allows the calls to be overridden by test modules, sometimes called fault injection. Controlling external factors helps increase determinism in testing a specific scenario. For example, it is much less expensive to wrap a file system Write call and simulate a Disk Full error than it is to actually try and fill up the disk and force the system to cough up a Disk Full error.

Testing Windows Vista

In the Windows Vista operating system, one of the biggest test matrices was in the upgrade and migration engine. Here's what one of the test developers said about how the team made the migration engine more controllable:

One thing we did was in the migration engine add a "system abstraction layer" that all migration engine calls must go through to touch the actual machine. With this support, it becomes really easy to do smart fault injection, unit test the engine, and create a harness for system simulation. The system simulation step allows us to simulate any migration (win9x, win2k, xp, etc.) in a single machine without having to set up all of the different environments. This improves the number of test variations we can run in a fixed time, and improves the configurability of those variations because they don't have to correspond to a real system.

This was a huge efficiency gain and allowed the team to run an enormous number of test cases over and over, ensuring that users would have a smooth migration experience with Windows Vista. With the addition of the abstraction layer, the team created deterministic behavior without having to go through the expense of actually installing an earlier operating system (some of which could only be done manually), upgrading, wiping the upgrade, and reinstalling the old operating system. They still had a set of core scenarios they ran on "real" down-level clients, but they didn't have to run those scenarios every day, and the scenarios weren't required to do a quick unit or regression test pass.

In some cases, having a controllable configuration option is the only practical way to get testing accomplished. For example, if a developer wrote code to handle a certificate expiration error and by default certificates expired only after six months, it would be difficult to run a quick unit test to verify that the error code is handled correctly. But if the certificate timeout value could be changed to six seconds, the code suddenly would become testable. Forcing determinism and predictability or forcing a particular code path or being able to change a threshold value such as a timeout without having to reinstall the software or restart the computer is an important way of increasing control and thus testability.

Knowledge: Knowing What the Expected Results Are

OK, so the software is easily exercised in an automated fashion, and the results are efficiently observable. How does one know if the observed behavior is actually the correct behavior? Knowing what the right behavior is and communicating that effectively to the human tester who is writing the tests is another important aspect of testability. Testers have to know what the expected results are based on a specific set of inputs. This can be classified as predictability and is very important in simplifying test development.

During the analysis phase of a test, there must be some authority, sometimes referred to as the *test oracle*, against which the actual observed results of the software under test are compared. When software isn't predictable, it makes programming the oracle nigh on impossible—at least not without causing the tester to write extensive interpretive code to deal with the ambiguities. For example, if a method returns an unsorted list of data, the tester has to sort the data before validating the list of data. If the data is returned sorted, the code to validate the data is much simpler because the data is more predictable. This information is sometimes left out of specifications, and often the project documentation does not contain all the information a tester needs to know to program the test oracle accurately.

One practical way to improve the documentation is to create a specification inspection checklist specifically for testability to ensure that the key pieces of information a tester needs to implement the test oracle accurately and fully are included in the documentation. Creating such a list and then reviewing product specifications and even filing bugs against the specification if the information is missing will greatly improve testability. The following are some pieces of information that directly affect knowledge of expected results and should be part of the project definition and design documentation:

- Anytime lists of data are returned or stored or displayed, the order should be established to enhance predictability.

- Computer or data flow diagrams describing the interactions between components in the software, both normal conditions and how the software behaves for each possible error condition.

- Details about major methods or functions used that determine the state of the system. These may include conditions under which the method is called (those old assertions from Computer Science 101) and the expected results, including error codes or exceptions that can be thrown and under what circumstances.

- Expected memory usage at start and at various points in the component lifetime.

- Security implications and restrictions, which are particularly important if behavior is changed based on the user rights of a particular user account.

- Usage logging or tracing that the developer may use for diagnostic and debugging purposes, but that often proves helpful for testers as well.

- Complete list of source files and locations and where the resulting built binaries are in an installed system. This helps create a map of where components are and where they go to improve setup automation.

- List of dependencies that are external to the software.

- Configuration options, threshold values, timeouts, any heuristics that influence the behavior of the software under test.

- Any information that can help the tester understand what can be observed and controlled in an automated fashion. Oftentimes, for their own diagnostic purposes, developers put in hooks that can also be reused by test automation to improve the setup, execution, or analysis phase.

Having extensive knowledge of expected results is important to create a test oracle or model of the software under test such that the analysis phase of the test can be accurate and complete in judging whether the test passes or fails. This knowledge must be transferred to testers to increase testability and make the whole test automation more accurate and efficient.

Avoiding the Risks of Implementing Testability

Anything can be overdesigned, including testability. Unless there's a clear plan to use a specific testability feature, it's a waste of time to implement such a feature. Sometimes testability features can also be security risks. Bret Pettichord related an incident in his seminal paper *Design for Testability:*[1] "A security flaw in the Palm OS that allowed anyone to access password-protected information took advantage of a test interface."

Logging output that was designed to unveil the inner workings of software to improve testability can end up revealing too much information, for example, a customer password in clear text or other information disclosures. Without a plan to ensure that security and privacy concerns are being mitigated, testability can end up being more costly by creating a maintenance and public relations nightmare and possibly a security hole that can be used to exploit customers.

Conclusion

To improve overall testability of software, improve in each area of SOCK: Simplicity, Observability, Control, and Knowledge of expected results. A project that is only as complex as it needs to be, is observable, is controllable, and provides knowledge transfer and predictability to test developers about expected behavior is a testable project. Along with testability comes an increase in the ability to diagnose problems quickly. Improved testability reduces the cost of test automation and increases the reliability and accuracy of the tests in proving whether the software is meeting the requirements. The most practical way of ensuring that software is highly testable is through the specification inspection process, whereby a testability checklist is used to ensure that the software from the beginning is architected and designed to be testable.

---

1 Bret Pettichord, *Design for Testability* (2002), p. 24, *www.io.com/~wazmo/papers/ design_for_testability_PNSQC.pdf*.

Part III
Defect Analysis Techniques

Chapter 7
Software Measurement and Metrics

To identify the defect prevention metrics and other metrics that are right for your business, you must start with a strategic overview. The balanced scorecard is a good way to realize this. Only with a strong understanding of your business can you tie defect prevention metrics to your goals. An effective scorecarding effort ensures that you know the impact of what you are measuring. For example, many software teams find code coverage[1] an important defect prevention metric. Unfortunately, there is no correlation between higher code coverage and higher-quality code. In fact, it is quite the opposite, although this in not intuitively obvious. There are many explanations for this—one of which is that higher code coverage numbers reflect more test breadth and not test depth. If the Pareto principle[2] tells us that 80 percent of the defects customers care about are likely in 20 percent of the code, higher code coverage numbers correlating to lower quality makes sense.

Even though code coverage is a widely collected metric and thought necessary, many people think that this metric tells them more than it actually does. It certainly sounds like an important metric. The challenge here is to tie the metric data back to a business goal. Basically, why do you want to know this number? We recommend that rather than mapping metrics back to a business goal, start with an understanding of your business goals to establish which metrics you should track. Look to the remaining chapters in this section of the book to learn more about the metrics associated with specific defect prevention techniques.

This chapter discusses mission, goals, and metrics, the keys to implementing an overall scorecard that can help you identify the most important parts of your business strategies and improve alignment between your strategies and business performance, eventually leading to the metrics you should really care about. The primary focus of this chapter is how to build an effective scorecard. The focus is not on specific defect prevention metrics but rather on methods of getting to the right set of metrics for your business. Although it seems everyone wants to know what the ideal metrics needed for optimal effectiveness are, there is no magic set. The metrics you need to collect and employ truly depend on what you are trying to do and what your business is about.

---

1 Wikipedia, "Code Coverage," *http://en.wikipedia.org/wiki/Code_coverage*.
2 Kerri Simon, "80/20 Rule," iSixSigma, *www.isixsigma.com/library/content/c010527d.asp*.

Understanding the Keys to Building a Successful Scorecard

Any discussion of metrics must start with clear identification of the organization's mission and goals. By identifying these first, you can track and course-correct as necessary during the life cycle of your project. Without knowing the mission and goals, you will have an extremely difficult time choosing metrics that will give you a good picture of your business. Also, you will not have a strong understanding of any metric dependencies and the behavior that will be driven by the metrics.

It may sound easy to write goals, and it can be, but it does take time and effort to think through what you, your business, and your organization need and want to accomplish. A common mistake organizations make is to spend their effort planning what the scorecard will look like and deciding which metrics they should track, and setting their goals afterward. This frequently leads to driving for the wrong results. By setting your goals first, you can ensure that the metrics you track drive the behavior, performance, and results you want to achieve. Also, by setting good goals you will know when your project is completed.

There are many organizations that either do not take the time to set their goals appropriately or do not effectively communicate their goals throughout the organization. This leads to management interrupting when they want information (data) because the data is either not collected or is not reported. Mad scrambles to collect and report the necessary data required to make effective business decisions disrupt productivity.

In one instance during the development of a popular product, the executive staff wanted a set of specific information pulled together from across multiple teams. Thankfully, each team already knew the data they needed to report and had previously set up disparate systems to do this. Unfortunately, there was no one pulling this together in one place. Separately, the data was interesting, but together, the data was vital. Although this ended up as a fire drill for a small set of individuals, because goals had been set and the data was already being collected, it was simply a matter of pulling everything together. It would have seriously affected productivity and the overall product if the teams had not taken the time first to understand their goals from the beginning of the project.

Setting good goals is all predicated on the knowledge that you understand your processes and their capabilities. Without such understanding, goal setting makes little sense: How can you set a goal if you don't know whether your process is actually capable of achieving it? After the business processes are defined,[1] you will be able to ascertain how they can be optimized for the system. This knowledge leads you toward goals that will truly make a difference in the resultant internal efficiencies and product quality.

---

1 For more information about process capability, see W. Edwards Deming, *Out of the Crisis* (Cambridge, MA: MIT Press, 2000).

To establish a scorecard for your business, you must first identify the purpose of what you want to accomplish. For example, the purpose could be to refocus the organization on the company's strategy or to improve alignment between strategy and business performance. As long as you understand the purpose, you will be able to tie your vision, strategy, goals, and metrics together into a usable and effective scorecard.

By implementing the following four keys,[1] you can build a successful scorecard:

- Create clear definitions of strategic objectives and business result metrics.
- Create clear definitions of business, process, and improvement objectives.
- Communicate defined goals to all levels of management.
- Gain broad acceptance of the defined goals.

Each key is described in more detail in the following sections.

Creating Clear Definitions of Strategic Objectives

In the software business, the vision and mission of most organizations boil down to *sell more and spend less to develop or create the end product*. Depending on the size of your business, *selling more* is often left up to sales and marketing forces and *spending less to develop or create the end product* is left up to product development teams. Clear definition of strategic objectives and business result metrics ensures that the product teams and sales teams are accountable to each other. As we saw in Chapter 3, the high initial cost and the low marginal cost of software development really drive toward these goals.

First, you must identify your business strategies. Whether you are doing this for a small or large business, you will need to engage the appropriate leaders. The four categories of business strategies or perspectives are as follows:

- **Customer**   How do customers see your business results?
- **Internal business**   What things must you excel at?
- **Financial**   How does your business look to shareholders?
- **Innovation**   Can you continue to improve and create value?

Defining a Customer Strategy

At the start of a software development cycle, you need to identify your target customers and why they would want to buy your product. For whom are you building this product? You also need to ensure that your product is scoped appropriately for your customer. For example, if

---

1 Internal CPE training developed by Lori Ada Kilty, based on BI Apps Balanced Scorecard documentation taken from Kaplan/Norton and Robert B. Grady, *Practical Software Metrics for Project Management and Process Improvement* (Upper Saddle River, NJ: Prentice Hall, 1992), and internal Six Sigma training.

your product is targeted only to accountants who have specific hardware requirements, scope your product for that audience. You need to make sure that you truly understand your customers' needs and acceptable limitations.

If you have a marketing department or personnel, they should be well versed in performing Kano[1] analysis outlining needs and wants. In a Kano model, customer needs are called "must-haves" and customer wants are considered "delighters." The caveat with delighters is that past delighters may now be current must-haves, so you should ensure that needs and wants are categorized appropriately. For example, having different levels of software security is a must-have for some customers, and for others, it is a delighter. There are certain needs businesses must have with respect to security that other customers do not necessarily need but do appreciate. One example is parental controls. Mostly, parents want this level of security, and for them it has gone from being a delighter to a must-have. Other advanced security features may unfortunately affect the usability for some customers, turning security features into detractors. To mitigate this business must-have, we give the customer choices in setting their security level. This is important when dealing with a a broad customer base.

A simple nonsoftware example is traveling by air in coach versus business or first class. Coach will get you to your destination, which is the must-have. However, traveling in business or first class would be a delighter if you were unexpectedly upgraded from coach. Keep in mind that unexpected amenities could be delighters or detractors, depending on what is provided. It is important to understand what a delighter is and what is noise or a detractor. This brings up another benefit of Kano analysis—it allows you to understand what doesn't matter. In other words, you can discern areas in which making improvements or innovations won't result in higher customer satisfaction or more sales, so spending effort in those areas doesn't make sense. Southwest Airlines has used analysis techniques to recognize that advance seat assignment is not a must-have for all passengers and is not enough of a delighter to justify slowing the boarding time by providing this service.[2] However, when sitting together is a must-have for certain clients (parents with children, for example), these clients are allowed to seat themselves first. With this strategy, the airline can guarantee quicker boarding times overall while still ensuring that parties who must sit together do so. As the airline grows and expands, so do their requirements. They are now undertaking new studies to determine whether a seat assignment is indeed a must-have in the future.[3] After you understand customer needs and wants, you will have your top customer scenarios. At this point, you can use a tool like Scenario Voting, as described in Chapter 15, to monitor and assess scenario value.

---

1 iSixSigma, "Kano Analysis," *www.isixsigma.com/tt/kano/*.

2 Wikipedia, "Southwest Airlines," *http://en.wikipedia.org/wiki/Southwest_Airlines*.

3 Dan Reed, "Southwest Closer to Assigned Seating," USAToday.com, June 21, 2006, *www.usatoday.com/money/biztravel/2006-06-21-southwest-usat_x.htm*.

Defining an Internal Business Strategy

Of the four categories of business strategies, this one can be considered the toughest to define because it focuses on how you operate your business. Software metrics for productivity are frequently the most sought after and most difficult to implement and maintain. The Personal Software Process and Team Software Process (see Chapter 12, "Adopting Processes") advocate size, time, and defects as the three areas of productivity metrics. This is a good way to frame the strategies you need to achieve internally.

Although it may seem an oversimplification, these three areas really cover it all. Another way to think about this is that any productivity metrics you measure can be bucketed by size, time, and defects. Lines of code, though controversial, can be an effective (not perfect) measure of size. Both size and time help you understand effort: How long did a project or task take? (estimates versus actual times, and so forth). Combining effort data with defect data (found rates, fixed rates, and so on) helps you understand process capability. Again, this is covered in more detail in Chapter 12.

Defining a Financial Strategy

This is by far the most important area to focus on because a business cannot survive without a sound financial plan. This strategy focuses on both revenue and the dollars behind how you run your business. How you run your business can be the most tricky to understand in monetary terms. If you are in one of many organizations in a large business, it may be more difficult to tie your profit and loss to the overall financials of the company. Still, you must identify the right measurements to make to drive the right behaviors in your organization and ensure that the business makes money.

Businesses often focus on cost cutting and trying to improve an area's efficiency. The questions you need to answer are, *Is your business focusing on the right things and are you sure?* If you answer yes, think about what makes you sure and if it is justified. If you answer no, you need to identify what you should be focusing on and why. In businesses other than software, investment decisions follow a rigorous method for approval. In software, decisions often are less precise due to the low needs for capital expenditures and the difficulty of measuring costs. Further, high margins mask executive mistakes and erode fiscal discipline for anything not tied directly to a budget. The focus on the bottom line along with a strategy that measures only budget leads to ignoring high-return improvement projects. The risk versus reward measurements need to provide an accurate view of investment opportunities. The goals of the organization need the correct measures to guide investment.

Defining an Innovation Strategy

Innovation is about identifying ways to grow your business beyond what you do today. It may mean creating new product lines or innovating features in current products. It could also mean driving processes to foster innovation internally. This strategy may seem to overlap with the others, but it truly is worth calling out separately to ensure that your business focuses not only on the bottom line today but what you would like to achieve long term. Strategies in this area can help you stay on track for advancement.

After you have established your business strategies, review them. If you are satisfied that your business can achieve the strategies laid out and in the appropriate time frame, you can move on to identifying goals. Otherwise, you will need to prioritize the strategies so that you can focus on the most important ones first. For some, it may simply be obvious where you want to focus based on financial data. For others, it may not be as clear. You can prioritize in many ways. One good way to prioritize is by using a prioritization matrix. Table 7-2 later in this chapter is an example of a simple prioritization matrix.

Table 7-1 shows an example of how to map your business strategies to goals. The customer goals are used throughout the rest of this chapter as an example of how to set goals and determine the right set of metrics to track.

Table 7-1   Business Strategy Mapping

Vision	Strategy	Perspective	Goal
Improve customer satisfaction	Ensure that top customer issues are addressed	Financial	Increase number of very satisfied customers at same or lower cost.
			Reduce cost per incident.
		Internal business	Reduce time to solution for reported bugs.
		Innovation	Introduce automatic updating to solve issues before reported.
			Create Tool X to collect data on customer issues automatically.
		Customer	X percent of top customer problems included in service pack.
			Use Tool X data to prioritize service pack work.
			X percent of technical staff respond to newsgroups weekly (hourly).

Creating Clear Definitions of Business, Process, and Improvement Objectives

Although this topic may sound daunting, this is really about identifying your goals. To get started, you need to determine the type of goal you are trying to achieve, how you will measure completion, and how you will measure success.

Understanding Goal Types

There are three types of goals: business, process, and process improvement.

- *Business goals*, also considered strategic goals, are what the organization needs to do to stay in business. To set these goals, use results of market analysis and constraints from the larger organization (such as mandatory compliance with an overall corporate policy).

- *Process goals* are based on your past performance and serve as a barometer for current process stability. You can use schedule, cost, quality, and productivity history to set these goals appropriately.

- *Process improvement goals* are intended to alter the steady state of your process goals after they have been reached. You can then transition process improvement goals into standard process goals. It is within this goal type that defect prevention techniques play the largest role.

After you understand the different types of goal, you can more easily create the right goals for your needs. Understanding which type a goal is helps you formulate the goal properly and assess where the primary focus needs to be or whether an area is being neglected. Ensure that you include the three different types of goals in your scorecard.

Identifying Goals

Now that you have identified your strategic objectives and understand the goal categories, the next step is to identify the goal. Determine which actions (goals) you need to take to execute your strategies. You can use the following questions in this process:

- What are you seeking to accomplish?

- How will your success be measured (leading and lagging indicators)?

- What are the deliverables?

- When will you need to deliver the results?

For example, for Microsoft's business and employee goals, we ensure that our goals are specific, measurable, achievable, results oriented, and time-bound (SMART). (SMART goals are discussed in more detail at the end of this section.) A great way of getting to SMART goals is by using a technique Victor R. Basili developed and coined the Goal Question Metric approach, or GQM.[1] The GQM model has three levels:

- Conceptual level—Goal

- Operational level—Question

- Quantitative level—Metric

---

1 Victor R. Basili, "Establishing a Measurement Program" (College Park: University of Maryland, 2006), *www.cs.umd.edu/~basili/presentations/2006%20WiproTalk.pdf*.

GQM is a great model to follow because it forces you to ask the questions to ensure that you are measuring the right things. In other words, it helps you tie your metrics to your goals.

Determining Metrics

It is easy to say that you need to establish how your success will be measured, but to sit down and plan it is not so easy. However, taking the time to do this will lead to the creation of useful metrics and release you from relying on postmortem perceptions or gut-feel checks.

If you are having trouble determining the right metrics for your goal, you can derive a set of metrics from the answers to the following questions:

- How will you know you have met your goal?
- What questions do you need answered to show success?

Example: I want to use Tool X (which gathers quantifiable feedback from customers on shipped product) results to affect prioritization of future service pack (SP) work. To derive metrics for this goal, answer the following questions:

- How are Tool X results being analyzed?
- Have Tool X results been prioritized based on impact?
- Does the SP include fixes addressing top Tool X issues?

After you know the answers, you can brainstorm potential in-process metrics (also known as *leading indicators* or *predictors*). Be sure to focus on predictive measures and not reactive measures. Also, choose actionable information to course-correct appropriately throughout the product development life cycle. Finally, ensure that your information source is consistent with itself.

Example: Potential Tool X In-Process Metrics

- How are Tool X results being analyzed?
  - ❏ % of results sorted in buckets (categories)
  - ❏ Elapsed time between results and sorting
- Have Tool X results been prioritized based on impact?
  - ❏ % of prioritization complete
- Does the SP include fixes addressing top Tool X issues?
  - ❏ % of high-impact problems fixed and included in SP

Prioritizing Metrics

When you have identified a set of metrics, you need to prioritize them. First, you must validate any assumptions about the metric. For example: Are you getting representative feedback from all customers? Are there types of failure where Tool X will not collect data? Does prioritization correctly take into account customer needs? Also, you must provide any additional detail or taxonomy information, if necessary. This helps you remember exactly how the metric is being defined and will allow for easier weighting. For more information on representative feedback, see Chapter 15.

Weighting Metrics

After you have defined the metric and provided necessary detail, you need to identify an appropriate weighting method. The following method was established internally at Microsoft to weight metrics across several different product teams, including Windows, Visual Studio, and Exchange.

- **Ease of Startup**   How easy is this metric to get initially?
- **Ease of Maintenance**   How easy is this metric to track continually?
- **Usefulness**   How useful is this metric to you?
- **Collected Today**   Is this metric collected today?
- **Trust Level**   Do you trust the data this metric provides?

The multiplier for each weight is as follows:

- Ease of Startup = 3. Although setting up a metric to be tracked may entail difficulty or work, it is not the limiting factor on whether the work should be undertaken.

- Ease of Maintenance = 3. Again, difficulty or work that definitely affects our abilities may be involved in collecting and tracking a metric but is not the limiting factor on whether the work should be undertaken.

- Usefulness = 9. If the metric is not useful even if it is related or seems as though it might be useful, there is no point in collecting and tracking it.

- Collected Today = 1. This is a yes or no question, and although it should not have a huge impact, an edge could be given to a metric that is currently being collected.

- Trust Level = 9. If a metric has no Usefulness and Trust Level rating, there is no value in monitoring and using that metric; therefore, these two factors should carry the most weight.

The rating system is based on high = 9, medium = 3, and low = 1. In some cases, you may want to use additional granularity between medium and high (such as medium-high = 6), but if you can avoid this, do so. The prioritization numbers are generally far more interesting and accurate when your granularity is not too tight. This may seem illogical until you go through the exercise of prioritizing the ratings. However, some individuals find it extremely difficult to rate appropriately without a finer granularity. To avoid this issue, use letters such as h = high, m = medium, or l = low instead of numbers when rating in a group setting and apply the numbers in the background afterward or in an unexposed formula. The only rating this will not apply to is Collected Today. For Collected Today, use "Yes" or "No" with values of 1 and 0, respectively.

The formula for prioritization is the following:

(Ease of Startup × 3) + (Ease of Maintenance × 3) + (Usefulness × 9) + (Collected Today × 1) + (Trust Level × 9) = Prioritization Value

Table 7-2 shows an example prioritization matrix.

Table 7-2   **Metrics Prioritization Matrix**

Improvement Target: Tool X								
Weight Values			**3**	**3**	**9**	**1**	**9**	
Goal	**Goal Priority**	**Metric**	**Ease of Startup**	**Ease of Maintaining**	**Usefulness**	**Collect Today**	**Trust Level**	**Priority**
Tool X used to prioritize SP work	h	% of results sorted in buckets	m	m	m	No	h	136
Tool X used to prioritize SP work	h	Elapsed time between results and sorting	h	m	h	No	m	154
Tool X used to prioritize SP work	h	% of prioritiz- ation complete	m	l	m	No	m	100
Tool X used to prioritize SP work	h	% of high- impact fixes included in SP	m	m	h	No	h	190

From Table 7-2, you can see that the percentage of high-impact bug fixes is definitely the metric that carries the highest priority. This example does not take into account the goal priority. Prioritizing goals is discussed later in this chapter. When setting up your formula, determine whether goal priority should have an impact on the metrics and adjust your formula accordingly.

For conducting a group rating exercise, you need to define how to rate. For example, where ease of startup is most difficult, the rating will be 1 or d for difficult (where d = 1) or h for high difficulty (where h = 1). Use a lettering system that makes sense to you and that you can define and explain to others. Although numbers may be simpler to explain, as mentioned earlier, using numbers could affect the granularity of the ratings, and thus, the outcome would be less distinguishable.

Avoiding Metric Manipulation

One other important thing to keep in mind is that metrics are easy to manipulate or game if people think they are being rated on the outcomes. And you must be careful to ensure that what you are measuring will result in the behaviors you want to encourage. To avoid metric manipulation, you will likely need to rely on a combination of metrics so that the manipulation of one will not cause invalid data. This means understanding metric dependencies.

For example, you want to decrease the turnaround time on bugs, so you start tracking how long it takes developers to fix bugs. When the developers realize that fix time is being tracked and possibly used as a performance metric against them, they will surely find a way to game the metric to make themselves look better. One way to do so would be to report a false resolution. By the time the bug is reactivated, the developer may have a real fix and the turnaround time recorded for the developer would be much less than if he or she had left the bug unfixed while coding the fix. Measuring turnaround time alone is definitely driving the wrong behavior because the metric has a dependency.

To counter this sort of metric manipulation, you can monitor the reactivation rate of bugs along with turnaround time to ensure that false resolutions are not being used to buy time. Use the GQM methodology to help you uncover metric dependencies. Also, DeMarco's book *Controlling Software Projects*[1] delves into metric modeling and can help you map out and understand the underlying dependencies.

Scoping Goals Appropriately

After you have completed the prioritization exercise, you should have a set of defined metrics that map to your goals. In other words, you should know how your goals will be measured— both in-process goals and final results (success). Now that you have measurable goals, you need to scope each goal appropriately so that you can actually meet the goal in a reasonable or specified time frame.

Consider also if your project is broken down into milestones or modules. If so, you need to set goals for each milestone as well as set overall project goals. To do this, you will need to estimate when your deliverables will be completed. Most estimates are based on previous experience, thoughtful planning (if previous experience cannot be relied upon), or total guesses. Tom DeMarco has put a lot of thought into what makes estimates valid, so we do not go into that here. Suffice it to say that referencing his material is well worth the effort so that you can

---

1   Tom DeMarco, *Controlling Software Projects: Management, Measurement, and Estimates* (Upper Saddle River, NJ: Prentice Hall, 1986).

plan your software development projects using valid estimates. An accurate schedule is an effective defect prevention technique.

Prioritizing Goals

The final step is to prioritize your goals. After you have set goals and prioritized metrics, you may realize that you have too many or too few goals. If too few, you need to identify the gaps in your goals. The best way is to do this is by ensuring that you have goals mapped to all four categories of business strategies (customer, internal business, financial, and innovation) and that the goals are an appropriate mixture of goal types (business, process, and process improvement).

More likely, you will have too many goals. If this is the case, you need to prioritize them. To do this, focus on the critical goals first and then establish a time frame to focus on the next set of goals. For example, what are the must-haves for final release or beta release but not essential for the next milestone? Keep in mind that prioritization does not need to be done by committee and may come from senior leadership. Otherwise, you can weight goals by overall strategy, customer impact, need, feasibility, current performance, and other factors important to your business.

Creating SMART Goals

What are SMART goals? As stated earlier, goals that are **s**pecific, **m**easurable, **a**chievable, **r**esults oriented, and **t**ime-bound. Microsoft's business and employee personal goals (each employee sets up formal professional goals annually) must meet the following criteria.

- **Specific**   Does it address a real business problem? Is it exact? Is it mapped to a business strategy? Is it scoped appropriately? The project scope defines the boundaries of the business opportunity. What are the boundaries, the starting and ending steps of a process, of the initiative? What parts of the business are included? What parts of the business are not included? What, if anything, is outside the team's boundaries?

- **Measurable**   Are you able to measure the problem, establish a baseline, and set targets for improvement? How do you know you are on track to complete the goal successfully? How do you know you have completed the goal successfully? Have you identified in-process and result metrics? (Remember, if you are having trouble making your goals measurable, try using the GQM method to help identify the right set of metrics.)

- **Achievable**   Have you scoped your goal to be challenging but not unrealistic? Can you actually complete what you have defined? Is this goal in the control of the organization, team, or individual? What are the system dependencies? How much control does the organization, team, or individual have over the dependencies? Ensure that you are not setting up an individual or group for failure by setting a goal they have no realistic ability to meet as a result of forces beyond their control.

- **Results oriented**   Have you outlined your deliverables (and success metrics for your deliverables) and not just the steps you need to take?
- **Time-bound**   Have you identified milestones, checkpoints, and a completion date? This step often is omitted initially because this information is unknown and then, unfortunately, forgotten about. It is critical to ensure that you actually achieve your goals when they still matter.

Communicating Defined Goals to All Levels of Management

Now that you know how to create SMART goals that are important to your business, the next step is to determine how to collect the data to track and measure the goals as well as how this information will be effectively communicated to the right parties.

Although it is sometimes useful to track metrics in separate places, aggregating the information in one location allows for easier tracking of overall progress and dependency analysis. This process is best done by a group separate from the software development group to keep from degrading the metric. Even if a team has the best of intentions, it is human nature to optimize for the metric rather than for the intended purpose of collecting the metric. A third party can help to alleviate that. It is also best to make data collection automatic when possible to help with data integrity.

Collecting and Presenting Data

For each goal and metric, you need to identify the data source and measure current performance to establish baselines. It is helpful to have the metric definition available as well. If history is available, you can review this data and use it as a potential predictor. If this data is not available, you need to decide whether maintaining history is important and, if so, how that data will be stored and maintained. If you have the ability to store it, you should. Historical data can be invaluable for planning your next project, learning what went right and wrong with your last project, keeping tabs on what is going on with your current project, and identifying trends in and between product cycles.

By understanding trends, you can more easily set your own release criteria. Release criteria must include the minimum acceptable targets and stretch goals. Basically, what is acceptable for shipping versus the ideal goal? It is often difficult to differentiate between what is acceptable and what is ideal because, of course, you want to ship the best-quality product you can. Unfortunately, this is not often realistic because you do not have all the time in the world to release a perfect product. If ship dates are missed, opportunities are missed and the technology becomes stale. To be ready when a window of opportunity is open, sometimes tradeoffs must be made. This is why understanding the must-haves and delighters is so important—you need this knowledge to make the right decisions for your customers.

Armed with minimum and stretch targets, you next need to identify the interval for data collection. Should you collect data hourly? Daily? Weekly? Or should the data be real time? If not in real time, what time of day or week is the data updated? This leads to questions of how often the data needs to be reported and in what format.

After you have collected metric data, you must determine the best way to present it. Do you want to present by goal? By strategy? By metric? One of the ways the Microsoft Windows team centralizes data and presents it internally is by using a *heatmap* that shows release criteria. The release criteria are a set of goals with related metrics that must be reached to ship the product. The Windows team sets release criteria around a number of areas such as performance and security. The heatmap reflects if any of these areas are not on track. The heatmap shown in Figure 7-1 is an example of an in-process one that could be used to drive goals toward a specific milestone. You would track each of the blocks to ensure that they are green by a specified date before considering entering the next milestone. (Note: The data reflected in Figure 7-1 has been randomly created to demonstrate chart use and is not an accurate representation of Windows metric values.)

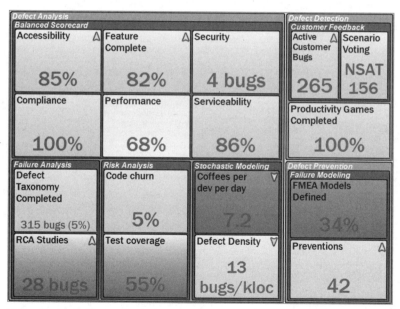

Figure 7-1   Release criteria heatmap

Regardless of what medium you use to reflect your data, the most important thing is to get the data published in a way that is available, appropriate, and consumable by various audiences. We have found that executives like the heatmap view, but midlevel managers want to be able to focus on the details. For large and small organizations, you need to provide both overview and detail perspectives. One way to do this is to have click-through data that gives more detailed information for each block. Also, mouse-over information can provide specific targets and other pertinent information that is not too detailed.

Automating the Data Collection and Reporting Processes

Automating data collection and reporting is frequently the focus of a metrics program. Unfortunately, all the activities that lead up to this point should really be the focus. In all the metrics programs in which we have been involved internally, the only successful ones have been those for which the teams took the time to set their goals, tie goals to their business objectives, and determine the best set of metrics to track their success. Teams that spent time focusing primarily on the technology of automating and reporting the data ended up not having any metrics story or having to start over again. Many teams across Microsoft have focused first on establishing goals and ensuring that the goals were tied to the team's business objectives.

For example, in 2002, one team started by mapping their business strategy to technical goals and eventually developed a detailed scorecard that they were able to automate. This team recognized that there were holes in their mapping and identified the six areas that were highly important for their business and universal to each feature team, such as performance. They then created a program with central reporting to provide visibility into each of those metrics. They had monitors all over the building advertising these central defect prevention metrics, updated daily. This gave visibility to the areas they felt were vital to quality but were not getting enough attention.

Another team started by defining what quality meant for their business and then identified the areas most important for quality, such as reliability. From there, they were able to prioritize the metrics they thought would give them the most insight into reliability: Average/mean/median response time and response time variation. They were also able to identify metrics they would like to track in the future but that they were not going to tackle for their first-generation scorecard. This was a good plan because it allowed the team to acknowledge the importance of additional metrics while ensuring that they were focused on the critical few to start.

The key takeaway from each of these efforts is that each team started with goals that were mapped to business objectives, which is crucial to having a successfully adopted metrics program. That said, automation and reporting are not areas that can be ignored, but we want to emphasize that you must not jump ahead to this point before establishing useful goals. Having an automated reporting system with no knowledge of what data to collect is not terribly useful.

When you are ready, you need to spend some time figuring out how you will automate the data streams you have identified. For some streams, this may be fairly straightforward: for example, defect data, if it is already being collected. As long as the defect data is in a tracking system, it should be easy to query the data for trending purposes. Most systems use a database or data warehouse to store data for reporting and some sort of Web front end for viewing the data. Several systems available for purchase provide this functionality, or if you have the resources internally, you can certainly build such a system yourself.

Before you can determine the frequency with which the streams need to be updated and what the actual report looks like, you need to understand how the data will be viewed and by whom. As mentioned in the preceding section, you will likely need to provide different views for different audiences. Do you need to provide a daily, monthly, or quarterly report? Does the report need to be broken down by milestone? Do your metrics need to be separated as in-process and results? How much drill-down capability should be available? Is the report live or static and updated hourly, daily, and so forth? If live, consider performance issues depending on the amount of data being accessed.

After you understand your audience's needs, you can hook up the data streams and generate the appropriate reports. The heatmap in Figure 7-1 is an example of a daily report with at-a-glance information for managers and drill-down capability for more detail as necessary.

Review

This chapter so far has provided instruction on how to create a scorecard. Key points to remember:

- Identify the data source for each metric.
- Get baselines (current performance).
- Set release criteria.
- Set minimum acceptable targets.
- Set stretch goals.
- Set frequency of measurement.
- Determine how measurement will be automated.
- Determine how data will be stored historically.
- Set frequency and mode of reporting.
- Determine how often you need to report each metric—once per milestone, weekly, daily, and so forth.
- Determine how metrics will be reported—scorecard on Web, release criteria through release management team, daily status meetings, or some other way.

Gaining Widespread Acceptance of the Defined Goals

For any scorecard and metrics program to be successful, the established goals must be accepted by the population at large. Teams being measured that don't believe in the goals or metrics being used are not likely to take the results seriously. Executives who don't understand how the goals you are tracking align with their objectives will not pay attention.

Although it may seem simpler to skip creating a metrics program if you do not believe that the organization will support it, not having one will ultimately destroy your business. A business cannot survive without understanding what it is doing—through goals and measurements. Even if they resist initially, people are ultimately happier when they know what they are working toward, why, and how they will be rated. Although it may seem counterintuitive while the program is being implemented, morale invariably improves when people know what is expected of them.

Yes, it can be difficult to get a metrics program off the ground, but it is certainly not impossible. To get started, you must ensure that you are using metrics as incentives and not using them against individuals as a performance evaluation tool. Especially in the early stages, using metrics as a performance stick practically guarantees lack of support and ultimate failure of the program.

To create and establish a metrics program, whether company-wide or for a small team, you need to identify the key players. First, you must know the type of team members needed. Are you planning on having a separate metrics group? Or will the effort be driven from project management, release team, or testing? Will metrics team membership be taken from across functional areas? Or must team membership consist of key leaders in the organization? Ideally, you incorporate team members who have credibility and the ability to influence others because they will be the most helpful in driving adoption and acceptance of the metrics program.

Further, you must define at what stage each member will be needed and who is accountable to whom and for what. As mentioned earlier in the chapter, you need to be able to answer the questions of how and how often the team reports the metrics. Can they use an automated system that has been set up centrally, or will they need to supplement an existing system or provide the data for it?

One key point is understanding who the executive sponsor is and defining this individual's responsibility to the team. Depending on the culture of your organization, a good executive sponsor brought into the effort can make or break adoption of a metrics program.

After you have the team in place, goals established, metrics identified, the reporting mechanism set up, and reporting protocols defined, you need to ensure that a continual feedback loop validates the metrics being tracked. There is no point in tracking metrics that either do not reflect what you thought they would or drive the wrong behavior. It is important to evaluate your metrics continually to ensure that they are painting an accurate picture.

For example, on one team a situation arose in which a product unit tracked a particular stress metric for many months before someone on the defect prevention team discovered that the formula in use did not reflect the actual status. The biggest problem in correcting this situation was in changing the mindset of the audience to accept a different set of numbers than they had been accustomed to seeing. Because of that, the team chose not to correct the formula until the next milestone. Although wrong for the remainder of the milestone, the metric in use was consistent, and by understanding how it was wrong, the team was able to use the metric data appropriately. It was clear that changing this metric mid-milestone would not be accepted. Indeed, the team predicted that too much time would be spent by team members arguing against the correction because of people's natural resistance to change and the perception that they would be held responsible for presenting misleading data.

As with any cross-group effort, a widespread metrics program needs to be implemented with a system of continuous improvement. You can validate and police your goals and metrics using a feedback loop to ensure that your program continues to reflect the ever-changing realities of your business and customer landscape. As long as you are tracking metrics against goals that make sense to the organization and support driving the right behaviors, you will be able to garner broad-based support for the effort.

Conclusion

Dozens of books have been written on software metrics, and yet teams across the industry are continually stumped about what to measure. Designing a scorecard program is seemingly simple logic that is difficult to materialize because we are engineers and like numbers, logic, and predictability, so we tend to focus on metrics and not on goals. If you start by conceptualizing goals that are tied to your business objectives, you will measure the things that matter for your business, which could include code coverage, lines of code, inspection rates, defect densities, code churn, complexity, and so forth. Measuring these factors matters only if you can show how they are tied to your goals and objectives—how measuring them will improve your business.

To be valuable, your scorecard must help answer the following questions:

- What is your strategy?
- When your strategy succeeds, how will your organization be different?
- What are the critical business results (success factors)?
- What are the critical progress (in-process) measurements?

With these questions answered, the process of setting up a scorecard and metrics program becomes achievable and will be a valuable tool in building success in your overall business.

One final caveat: A metrics program should be used to understand the process your team or organization uses to create software and determine process capability to make appropriate predictions. This data should not be used to manage the process itself. In other words, if you understand your process capability, you know what is realistically achievable, and setting that as a goal is redundant. Setting goals that are tied to your business objectives, that focus on improving the entire system, and that are achievable and in the control of the organization is what will make a difference in your business.

Chapter 8
Risk Analysis

A prudent person foresees the danger ahead and takes precautions. The simpleton goes blindly on and suffers the consequences.

—Proverbs 27:12 (New Living Translation)

What Is Risk?

Risk has been simply defined as "the possibility that an undesirable event occurs."[1] Brendan Murphy, researcher at the Microsoft Research Center in Cambridge, UK, defines software-related risk as "the likelihood of software containing bugs [defects]." NASA says, "Risk involves the likelihood that an undesirable event will occur, and the severity of the consequences of the event, should it occur."[2] Defined this way, it is clearly important to understand the risk level of a software project. In particular, when you know the areas of code that have the highest risk, you can detect the areas with the highest potential for defects so that you can mitigate that risk by uncovering those defects as quickly and efficiently as possible.

This chapter focuses on identifying the risk incurred each time code is added, changed, or deleted. This *churn* is the primary source of risk in the implementation, verification, and maintenance phases of software development. Several other chapters in this book provide insights and practical tips to ensure that the overall goals and requirements of the software are being achieved. For example, scenario voting is a powerful mechanism used to let a product's judges, the customers, vote early and often to ensure that the right dance routine with the right partners is being performed in the right way. (See Chapter 15, "Scenario Voting.") This chapter gives practical steps on how to do historical and current risk analyses during the implementation, verification, and maintenance phases. It steps through creating a risk prediction model and then applying that risk prediction model to software as it is being changed. Doing a risk analysis as soon as the code changes provides a mechanism to focus validation efforts where the highest potential for defects exists.

---

1 BeAnActuary Web Site, "What Is an Actuary?" *www.beanactuary.com/about/whatis.cfm.*

2 Linda H. Rosenberg, Theodore Hammer, and Albert Gallo, "Continuous Risk Management at NASA," NASA Software Assurance Technology Center. Paper presented at the Applied Software Measurement/Software Management Conference, February 1999, San Jose, California. *http://satc.gsfc.nasa.gov/support/ASM_FFR99/crm_at_nasa.html.*

What Is Risk Analysis?

Broadly speaking, risk analysis is made up of two separate but related activities. One is the creation and maintenance of a risk prediction model based on historical data surrounding an activity. This is *historical risk analysis*. The other is the application of the risk prediction model to a current activity. This is *current risk analysis*. The goal of historical and current risk analyses is to understand areas of risk *with the intention of mitigating those risks*.

During the final few months of 2006 before the Windows Vista operating system shipped, a risk assessment was done on every fix that was made. In each case, a detailed risk analysis was completed by a senior test architect. The initial risk analysis report was sent to the Windows Vista project management leadership, who then ensured that the teams responsible for the late churn and the teams that were affected by the late churn had accomplished all their risk mitigation activities before allowing the change to be accepted into the final product.

In one case, a change was made in one commonly used C run-time library function, which potentially affected hundreds of binaries that called the function. With that many binaries potentially affected, the product release could have been delayed by two weeks because almost every team in Windows Vista would be required to reset its test efforts. The Windows Vista leadership team focused on the details of the changes and quickly determined that the fix was actually in a code path that was run only in earlier versions of the Microsoft Windows operating system and the code that all the Windows Vista binaries were using was actually unchanged. So, instead of having to raise an alarm that would have caused dozens of teams to reset their testing efforts, only a few teams needed to verify the fix, saving a great deal of time and money over what could have been a huge fire drill.

In another case, the opposite occurred. A fix was made in a source file for a specific Control Panel application's Edit dialog box. The team that needed the fix made the change and tested their fix in their Control Panel program. What they apparently didn't know was that the source file they changed was shared by several other applications. The risk assessment was able to detect the impact of the change in a dozen other binaries and notify the owners of those binaries that they needed to run the subset of their tests that hit the changed dialog box. In this case, the risk assessment did create more work, but it was focused on the teams that were affected and gave them direction on what tests to rerun to mitigate the risk of a regression occurring.

The sweet spot with risk analysis is knowing when to raise an alarm and to whom. Sometimes a silent alarm is best: it notifies a few senior people, and they in turn ask a few pointed questions to ensure that the elevated level of risk is being properly mitigated.

The result of a historical risk analysis is a risk prediction model that accurately unveils proven areas of risk in a particular version of software. The result of a current risk analysis is to take the historical risk prediction model and apply it to interim versions of the software, tracking the relative risk of each new version as a project progresses. In the Windows Vista examples, that the historical risk prediction model was based on a study by Microsoft Research[1] that showed the number of dependencies that a binary has is an important factor in calculating risk. The current risk analysis was done by monitoring the dependencies of the code that was changing and ensuring that all affected binaries and the teams that owned them were notified of a change in one of their dependencies so that they could run regression tests to ensure that dependencies were still compatible with the new code.

It's also important to learn from the current analysis and use it to maintain and improve the accuracy and applicability of the risk prediction model. The historical and current analyses of the risk involved in certain activities are at the heart of risk analysis. Many industries as well as individuals engage in risk analysis all the time.

Applying Risk Analysis to River Rafting

River rafting guide companies analyze the risk of someone getting injured on a rafting expedition and establish risk mitigation protocols based on historical data associated with the industry. They take that knowledge and combine it with their knowledge of a particular stretch of water. They may even balance the difficulty of a trip with how much they charge or with safety precautions that they require for their customers. For example, the company may have a graduated pricing scale based on the length of the trip and white-water rapid classifications, such as the one shown in Table 8-1.

Table 8-1   **Graduated Pricing Scale for River Trips**

Rapids	Half-Day	Full-Day	3-Day
Class I, II	$75	$150	$500
Class III+	$250	$500	$1,200

A guide company may also require certain safety equipment to be used based on the type of trip, such as helmets for Class III or higher rapids, and a mandatory 30-minute safety orientation for new customers. Although the company is certainly concerned about the welfare of its customers, it is also aware that implementing these types of safety protocols goes a long way in protecting the company from monetary damages and legal actions.

In the case of a river rafting guide company, a historical risk analysis yields an understanding of areas that will likely cause problems and provides an opportunity to put preventive mitigation strategies in place before a boat goes in the water. Current risk analysis is used as events unfold to make course corrections or, if a problem arises, to limit the severity of the adverse event. Guides on the river use their past experience and knowledge to get the raft oriented correctly as they approach a riffle or potentially dangerous section so that they won't flip their raft, damage the boat, or worse, get a customer tossed into the water. Unfortunately, not everyone has a guide in their boat, as explained in a true story told by Microsoft test architect David Catlett.

---

1   Nachi Nagappan and Tom Ball, "Explaining Failures Using Software Dependences and Churn Metrics," *ftp://ftp.research.microsoft.com/pub/tr/TR-2006-03.pdf.*

Rafting the Rogue River

When I was young, some friends had told our family about a section of the Rogue River in southern Oregon that was supposed to be a relaxing afternoon run. They mentioned that there were a few snags in the water to avoid, but otherwise it was a straightforward float. They failed to mention exactly where the snags were located, but it was more of a side comment anyway, and because we'd already successfully navigated the Class II Dunn Riffle in Hell Gate Canyon many times, we figured the trip would be nice and easy.

After about 30 minutes, we rounded a bend and got caught up in a swiftly moving section of water. Our relaxing afternoon ended as we realized we were lined up on the wrong side of the river coming out of the bend and were headed straight toward a six-inch log that was jutting three feet out of the water. Our raft was being pulled toward it like so many doomed spaceships that get sucked into black holes in B-rated movies. My dad desperately tried to paddle us around the projecting tree trunk, but it was too late. The current was too strong, turning the raft sideways and causing it to be bisected by the log. Being a rubber raft, it buckled, the rapidly moving river bending it around the solidly placed log. Being a well-inflated rubber raft, it bent for a few seconds and then violently returned to its original shape, catapulting me and my entire family out and into the cold water. Somehow my brother ended up in knee-deep water and was able to hold his own, keeping the raft in place while my dad clambered back aboard.

Unfortunately for me, the holding of the raft had unintended consequences. My mother and I had taken the brunt of the rubber-band effect, being tossed buns-over-teakettle, landing in the water upstream from the raft and immediately being pulled downstream underwater. My mom was immediately swept around the raft and continued downstream. I was not so fortunate and, not having a life jacket, I was sucked directly under the raft and up against the log. Underwater, I was so disoriented from being tumbled by the current, I didn't know whether to scratch my watch or wind my bottom. I tried to surface, but the top of my head hit the underside of the raft. After a few agonizing moments, my 10-year-old brain finally figured out I was stuck under the raft, and in a panic-induced feat of super strength, I fought my way back upstream, finally breaking to the surface.

Despite being caught off guard, we weren't totally unprepared. Before we put the raft in the water, my dad had reminded us that, although we didn't have life jackets for this trip (remember, this was supposed to be an easy float, plus this was before life jackets were required), we did have flotation pads, just in case. He also imparted some words of wisdom in case anyone fell out of the raft. As I surfaced, I grabbed a flotation pad that was fortuitously floating within arm's reach. I also happened to grab the plastic bag that held our dry clothes and more important my dad's wallet. The current quickly pulled me downstream away from the raft. I started to try and fight my way back to the raft, but then recalled my father's instructions for unplanned departures from the rubber boat: Relax, point your shoes downstream, bend your legs to fend off any rocks and trees in the river, and let the river take you down to a calm spot where you can be recovered without having to fight against the water and riverbed.

After being knocked around a bit when the Rogue took me under the branches of a half-submerged snag-of-a-tree, I was reunited with my dad and brother. Alas, as I was pulled up into the raft, the plastic bag I had managed to hold onto, even after being battered by the tree, slipped from my grasp and immediately disappeared. My thoughts of being deemed a hero were dashed. Further down, we rescued my mother, who had flawlessly executed the risk mitigation instructions doled out by dad. We survived, albeit with a few bumps and bruises and a missing wallet. In the future, we decided that regardless of how easy someone said a stretch of river was, we'd always wear life jackets and put our valuables into a waterproof and floatable container.

Identifying Risk Analysis Phases

The Rogue River rafting trip experience goes through all the phases of risk analysis.

- *Historical risk analysis* was done as previous experiences as well as wisdom received by supposed experts, which were taken into account as the family prepared for the trip. Before they even put the boat in the water, they had a certain amount of risk mitigated, which was enough that they felt comfortable putting the boat in the water. If they had gotten to the launch site and had seen a waterfall downstream, they probably would have skipped the whole thing and gotten hamburgers and a milkshake at the local drive-in.

- *Current* (no pun intended) *risk analysis* was done as the family floated down the river. As soon as they were flipped out of the boat, they recognized the risk they were in, some at a higher level than others. Each person initiated a risk mitigation strategy commensurate with the situation they were in and in the end survived, except for the wallet, which probably became barnacle food in the Pacific Ocean near Gold Beach, Oregon.

- Afterward, they also *evaluated* their historical risk analysis model and, finding it lacking, made adjustments that lowered the risk. They reduced the likelihood and severity of future adverse events by planning on always donning life jackets and bringing along a dry bag for future river runs.

As soon as developers commit code to the compiler, it's like putting the raft into the river: risk is incurred and off they go, inexorably drawn downstream to their final destination. Just as with the tree trunk in the river, you often come upon snags during software development.

Good river rafters know the dangers of rafting in general. They know the river they are on and its specific dangers, and they know what to do when bad things happen. They also know when not to repeat a mistake. Water safety tip of the day: always wear a life jacket on a river, no matter how calm its reputation. Good software engineers similarly know the risks that are part of any software project, how to mitigate those risks as the project life cycle proceeds, how to handle snags in the development process, and how to learn from their mistakes. At least that's the hope. The reality is that new engineers come on board and veterans move on, so capturing the collective knowledge of an engineering staff for posterity is crucial. Documenting this information is discussed further in Chapter 14, "Prevention Tab," and a good risk analysis system incorporates wisdom gleaned by using such techniques and ensures that similar mistakes are not made as changes are made to the software during the implementation, verification, and maintenance phases.

Understanding the Artifacts of Churn

As developers make changes, the artifacts of these changes are what can be used to determine risk. Continuing the archaeology metaphor, Microsoft test architect David Catlett describes these artifacts of churn using the acronym CAIRO, which stands for characteristics, amount, impact, reason, and ownership. These are the data points that need to be dug up to understand the type of risk incurred with churn.

- **Characteristics**   These are code characteristics that are proven indicators of risk associated with the location of the code that is changing. Some typical metrics are size, complexity, number of dependencies, historical failure proneness of the module or similar modules if it's new code, and current number of discovered defects.

- **Amount**   This is the amount of change in any characteristic of the code. Usually this is the number of lines of code that have been added, changed, or deleted and the amount of change relative to the size of the source file, function, or binary. It also includes changes in any other code characteristic, for example, in the number of dependencies or in the amount of complexity compared with the version of the software before the changes were made.

- **Impact**   It is also important to understand the impact of the changes. For example, looking at which functions and external applications call into the changing code, how the changing code fits into end-to-end user scenarios, how many existing tests (if any) hit the churning code, and how the changes affect quality attributes such as security, performance, or internal library usage policies. These are all important measurements of impact.

- **Reason**   Knowing the reason why the code is changing is important in determining risk. The reason for change should be considered differently according to how far along the project has progressed. For example, early on in a product's development, the addition of features or code redesign work should be the main reason for code churn. As the product gets closer to being completed, the reason for churn should shift exclusively to defect fixes.

- **Ownership**   Knowing who is making a change is important in determining risk. For example, it is critical to know when a junior developer is making code changes in order to instigate more extensive mitigation strategies, such as having a code inspection with more senior developers. Ownership also includes the test owners and specialty owners, for example, a localization owner. Ownership extends to anyone who is signing off on the changes and has responsibility for the quality of the change.

Having a system in place that automatically compares current risk levels against historical levels goes a long way in digging up the artifacts of churn, which in turn helps show where the project is headed and when it has arrived at the final destination. Going through the exercise of identifying risk and coming up with risk mitigation strategies to reduce the risk is an important aspect of project management. It is also important to adjust the risk level when the risk mitigation strategies have been executed. For example, a highly complex module may indicate risk, but when the engineering team does a full-scale code inspection and all the tests for the module are passed, the risk has been significantly lowered. The final risk ranking should reflect the mitigated risk.

In software development, risk analysis is an exercise in understanding the past to prevent defects in the future. It helps to focus the risk mitigation activities in areas of highest risk to find defects before the customer finds them after release.

Benefits of Risk Analysis

Knowing the risk level at any given point in the product life cycle provides critical information to engineers and project managers alike. It helps them focus resources on the most risky areas of the software in ways unique to each role.

Benefits for Engineers

For developers, knowing which areas of code are at the highest risk helps focus code review efforts and aids in refactoring or redesign decisions to help reduce the likelihood of defects occurring. For testers, knowing what changed and the risk level incurred by the change can help prioritize test efforts. If testers must run through only a small number of tests to test the changing code, they've just saved an enormous amount of time over the course of the project.

For example, one maintenance engineering team at Microsoft would take two full weeks to do test passes each time code changed. This was a very expensive process, but because they weren't sure of the impact of the changes on the system as a whole, they had to retest the entire system, just to be safe. They implemented a risk evaluation system based on historical risk analysis to help them prioritize their test efforts. Initially, they took a very conservative approach by ranking all the binaries in their software package from riskiest to least risky based on the CAIRO model of risk evaluation. Then, instead of retesting all of the binaries, they dropped the bottom 30 percent "least risky" binaries from their test pass and focused their efforts on the remaining binaries.

They also put in place a program to continually tune their risk prediction tools so that if they guessed wrong and one of the binaries they didn't test had a customer-reported regression, their risk prediction formula learned from that and kept improving over time. This helped their engineering efforts be much more efficient, significantly reducing the cost of a full regression test pass.

Benefits for Project Managers

For project managers, a risk management system that reports risk level before the software is distributed is very helpful. By knowing the risk level of each change, decision makers can ensure that the right mitigations have occurred. This can be as formal or informal as the team needs.

Another important example of assisting project managers is in the area of partner notification. When an interim build of software is analyzed for risk using the CAIRO model, its potential impact on key partners is assessed. The most affected partners can then be given a prerelease copy of the software to ensure that it still works with the partner software. Oftentimes, project managers simply make the build available to all partners, but those partners often don't take the time to test the software because they aren't informed as to the level of risk to their own software. When a custom risk analysis is created for each partner, the partner can then better manage their own time and resources for integration testing. It also helps project managers specify from whom they need to gather feedback, focusing on the most affected partners instead of all the partners.

Similarly, if customer scenarios have been profiled and tied to specific functions in the software, when those functions change, a list of potentially affected customers can be generated and the project managers can target specific customers for feedback on prerelease copies of the software so that the customer can ensure that the scenarios they care about are working as expected.

Understanding the current risk of a project as changes are being made is very beneficial to both engineers and project managers. It provides data to support the decision-making process and helps everyone focus limited resources on the riskiest areas of software.

Understanding Risks

In the end, data is just data. The data must be analyzed intelligently to determine the correct course of action. One of the biggest risks in a risk analysis system is in producing data that no one knows what to do with. Metrics must answer a specific set of questions that are focused on achieving a specific goal. Collecting data for data's sake can cause confusion and often leads to long debates about veracity (the data is just wrong) and applicability (everyone wants an exemption at some point and often they have good reasons for this). Too much data muddies the waters and does not provide the clear answer to a clear question that is tied to a clear goal.

Having what Steve McConnell calls a "Risk Officer" in his book *Rapid Development*[1] or what the financial and insurance worlds call an actuary is crucial to the correct interpretation of the data. A software actuary needs to be a senior member of the staff, and although this person may have other roles, to be successful the software actuary must have the full support of all

---

1   Steve McConnell, *Rapid Development* (Redmond, WA: Microsoft Press, 1996).

decision makers. The actuary's job is to interpret the data correctly, make accurate predictions, and continually modify and reanalyze risk indicators so that the data and the predictions become even more accurate. Without proper interpretation of data as well as knowledge of how to prove or disprove which data points are good indicators of risk, the risk analysis can point to more boogiemen than bugs, setting off fire drills that frustrate and sending up red flags that turn into red herrings.

Implementing Risk Analysis

Risk analysis involves collecting and analyzing the artifacts of churn: CAIRO. It can be broken into two phases: (1) creating and maintaining the risk prediction model based on historical data and (2) applying the risk prediction model during a project. The following sections briefly discuss proving which code characteristics or metrics are good indicators of risk and then how to use them along with the amount, impact, reason, and ownership information to create a risk prediction model that can then be used as part of a risk analysis or assessment tool set. This type of tool can then be used during the implementation, stabilization, and maintenance phases of a software project to analyze the risk involved with changes as they occur.

Creating a Risk Prediction Model

Creating a risk prediction model starts with identifying artifacts from each area of the CAIRO model that may be good indicators of risk. Then you must determine whether those chosen metrics are really true in a code base that is similar to the code base that will be created as part of an upcoming software project. Typically, the most recent version of software is used as the historical data for the next version of the product. In cases where the software has no previous version, the following subsections contain some standard industry metrics as well as some practical suggestions on good starting points for creating a risk prediction model.

Characteristics: Identifying Code Characteristics

When trying to uncover which code characteristics are going to be good indicators of risk for a software project, it is important to remember that one size does *not* fit all. Various studies have shown a number of existing size and complexity metrics to be good indicators of risk. What's important to note is that many of those studies were done on a certain kind of code, for example, telecommunications software written in C, which may vary wildly from the environment and purpose of your software project.

For example, researchers at Microsoft examined the Microsoft Windows XP and Windows Server 2003 code bases using some traditional size and complexity metrics and found that the largest functions actually had fewer defects per thousand lines of code (defects/KLOC) than did medium-size functions. In the case of a popular complexity metric, the most complex functions also had less defects/KLOC than did their medium-size counterparts. The researchers also found that binaries that were fixed the most in service packs were ones that had the most calls into and out of the binary, what is referred as *fan in* and *fan out*. Another metric that positively correlated to a high number of defects was what Microsoft Researchers Brendan Murphy and Nachi Nagappan called "late churn," when binaries were changed close to when the operating system was shipped. Their research showed that code that was changed at the last minute had to be updated afterward.

In general, a good place to start is with some of the standard size and complexity metrics. Certainly, if it is easy to predict which modules are going to be fault prone with these metrics, use them. Other metrics that may prove useful are fan in and fan out metrics, which functions are called the most, functions used in key customer scenarios, and functions related to key quality attributes such as security and performance.

Proving Metrics

Establishing which metrics are good indicators of risk means defining exactly how risk is measured in a specific context. Traditionally, defects/KLOC, or the number of defects per one thousand lines of code, has been used as a measure for indicating fault proneness in a single source file or a group of source files that together are built into a single binary. At this level, you can predict risk at the source file or binary level, but not at the function level. Oftentimes, it is more useful to understand risk at the function level instead of the source file or binary level. The ability to predict risk at this lower level is important because this is where real action can be taken. For example, by being able to rank the functions in a binary by risk, code reviews can be focused on the riskiest functions first and testers can ensure that their tests cover these riskiest functions. Many times, these riskier functions are the most complex, which can lead to testability issues. By identifying these functions early on, testability can be improved earlier as well. (See Chapter 6, "Improving the Testability of Software.")

By studying the characteristics of the functions that contained the highest defect density (or defects per lines of code, or LOC, because hopefully most functions aren't thousands of lines of code) and doing the risk analysis at a more granular level, you can predict risks at a more granular level. As it stands, most risk analysis systems usually measure defect density associated with all the source files in a single binary and study the characteristics of the binary as a whole instead of individual functions inside the binary. In any case, the point is to first find out where the defects are coming from and then search for correlations with metrics in the code that have high defect densities compared with modules that have low defect densities. Correlations should be "meaningful," as Norman Fenton and Shari Pfleeger describe in the second edition of their book *Software Metrics: A Rigorous & Practical Approach*,[1] or "causal," as Stephen Kan describes in the second edition of his book *Metrics and Models in Software Quality Engineering*.[2]

---

1 Norman E. Fenton and Shari Lawrence Pfleeger, *Software Metrics: A Rigorous and Practical Approach*, 2nd ed. (Boston: PWS Publishing, 1997).

2 Stephen H. Kan, *Metrics and Models in Software Quality Engineering*, 2nd ed. (Boston: Addison-Wesley, 2003).

Several approaches can provide accurate and revealing information about whether a particular metric or combination of metrics correlates with a higher defect density. Entire books are written about this subject, including the two just mentioned. Kan provides some practical advice on proving metrics in his book:

> *It is important to have empirical validity established before the team decides on an action plan. By empirical validity we mean a good correlation exists between the selected metrics and defect rate...and a causality can be inferred. To establish a correlation, data gathering and analysis are needed. In the case that statistical expertise is not readily available to perform complex analysis, simple techniques...coupled with good brainstorming by team members will be just as effective. Causality can also be established by individual defect causal analysis.*[1]

The simple techniques that Kan describes are tools like scatter diagrams and simple tables. Figure 8-1 and Figure 8-2 are two examples of scatter diagrams.

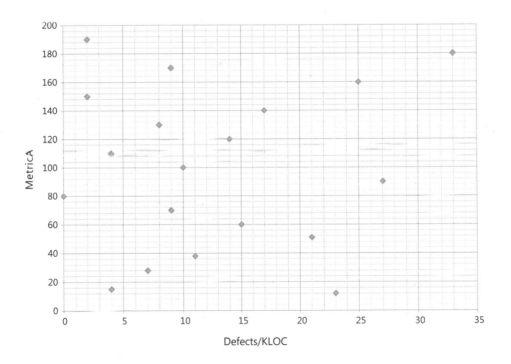

Figure 8-1   Scatter diagram with no correlation between metric and defects/KLOC

---

1 Stephen H. Kan, *Metrics and Models in Software Quality Engineering*, 2nd ed. (Boston: Addison-Wesley, 2003), 329.

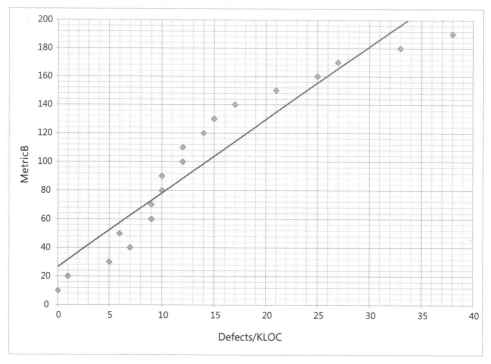

MetricB

Defects/KLOC

Figure 8-2   Scatter diagram with strong correlation between metric and defects/KLOC

In comparing Figures 8-1 and 8-2, it is clear by simply looking at the data that there is no correlation between MetricA and defects in Figure 8-1, but a strong correlation between MetricB and defects in Figure 8-2. As the value of MetricB goes up, so do the number of defects. This establishes a high correlation.

The next step is to use a causality discovery technique such as described in Chapter 11, "Root Cause Analysis," to determine how meaningful this correlation is: whether the reason the defect density is high for a particular binary or function is really that the metric is high. For example, a function may be measured as complex, for example, by using McCabe's Cyclomatic Complexity[1] metric, and it may have an unusually high defect density, but a root cause analysis may show that the reason for the high defect density is actually that the function has a large number of external dependencies and the high complexity value may be a coincidence. The only way to know this would be to understand the true cause of the defects and use that as a way to avoid noncausal, nonmeaningful, coincidental correlations between defects and a particular metric.

After a code characteristic or series of characteristics proves to provide a nicely diverse portfolio of risk indicators, it can then be used to monitor the risk of new and changing code as the project progresses.

---

1   Wikipedia, "Cyclomatic Complexity," *http://en.wikipedia.org/wiki/Cyclomatic_complexity.*

Amount: Tracking Churn

Tracking the amount of churn is straightforward and should be done in terms of the lines of code added, changed, and deleted. Separating the churn into these categories helps in understanding the type of development activity happening. Generally speaking, new code has a higher risk than changed code does, and changed code has a higher risk than deleted code does. The only time these relative risk weightings change is if there are dependencies on the changed or deleted code.

Code churn relative to the size of its binary or source file is important in understanding the scope of the changes that are happening. This is particularly important to note at the beginning of a project. Depending on the project, at the beginning it should have more new code than changed or deleted code. If the project is primarily a refactoring of existing code, changed and deleted code churn activity is more common.

By looking at the size of the changes relative to the total size of the project, one can judge the scope of effort. In Windows Vista, if an existing code base that was moved forward from Windows XP was changed more than 30 percent, the effort was considered to be equivalent to a new feature and was subject to the same requirements as new code.

As the amount of churn winds down toward the end of a project, it's important to track the total amount because relative amounts are much harder to understand. For example, it's easier for most people to understand a three-line code change versus a 0.0045 percent change. At the end, because any change can be risky, tracking the total amount is important because it provides much more clarity, which in turn makes the risk easier to interpret. It's also important not only to understand how much the code is changing, but what kind of potential impact the churn may have on the software as a whole.

Impact: Understanding the Effect of Changes

Code characteristics are just one way to predict risk. Knowing not only what changed but the impact of the changes is an important part of assessing risk. Viewing impact from function, scenario, test, and quality viewpoints, as described in this section, gives a diverse portfolio of risk factors that helps the overall risk assessment be more accurate.

It's important to look at how the software components interact in the entire project. This is particularly important if library or utility functions or modules are commonly reused, or if functionality is layered and reused. For example, in an operating system, low-level calls that interact with hardware are wrapped in library functions that are then called by higher-level services and applications (see Figure 8-3). Often, functions are wrapped again and then exposed to even higher-level services and applications, up and up many layers, until a word processor or spreadsheet application or Internet browser sits at the top, consuming these functions to provide a useful experience for the user. Clearly, a low-level change could potentially have an impact all the way up through the layers for anyone that made a function call whose call graph eventually called the changing function.

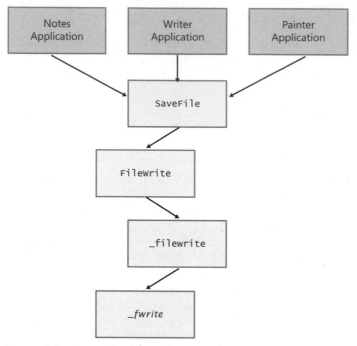

Figure 8-3   Dependency graph

Something as simple as adding or changing a return code can wreak havoc on a poor, unsuspecting application that sits at the top of the stack. For example, say a developer discovers a defect in a low-level function. The function incorrectly returns error code 5 when a file the function writes to is in use by another user, as in the _fwrite_ function in Figure 8-3. Being a good developer, the developer switches the error code to the correct value of 32, writes some quick tests to make sure it works, and then moves on. Meanwhile, the poor, unsuspecting application that uses a high-level function that calls another function that calls another function that eventually calls the changed function (see Figure 8-3) now shows this entirely unhelpful message: "An unknown error (32) occurred. We have no idea what this means. Cry in your coffee until one of your cubicle mates consoles you, and then press Abort, Retry, or Fail to continue."

If the developer had just left well enough alone or, at a minimum, had known to contact the high-level application that relied on the low-level disk function, the user may instead see this infinitely better and proscriptive error message: "A known error (5) occurred. This means another person, logged in as 'Joe,' has the same file open. Feel free to shout over your cubicle wall and ask 'Joe' to please close file 'meeting notes' so that you can get some work done. Thank you and have a nice day." Tracking those kinds of dependencies is how functional or call graph impact can be calculated.

Identifying Function-Level Dependencies

Usually, call graph or profiling tools are used for performance optimization analysis or refactoring, but they can also be used to get function-level dependencies that can then be placed into a database. A simple table that has every function in a binary along with a list of both internal and external functions that it calls (its fan out list) provides a data source that can then be used to determine the functional impact of a change (see Table 8-2). It can also be used to calculate the fan in counts of a function.

Table 8-2   Function Fan Out List

Binary	Function	Binary Fan Out	Function Fan Out
binary1.exe	*main*	binary1.dll	*functionB*
binary1.exe	*functionB*	binary2.dll	*function1*
binary2.dll	*function1*	system.dll	*sysfunctionX*
binary2.dll	*function2*	system.dll	*sysfunctionY*

By doing a simple reverse lookup, searching for any instance of a function in another function's fan out list, both functional impact and fan in counts can be garnered for use in risk assessment. For example, if *sysfunctionX* were to be changed, *function1* in binary2.dll, *functionB* in binary1.exe, and the *main* function in binary1.exe are all potentially affected by the change in *sysfunctionX*. This would be a riskier change than, for example, changing *functionB* in binary1.exe, which is only called internally by the *main* function. In the case of *functionB*, there is only one binary that is affected and most likely only one developer and test team. In the case of *sysfunctionX*, potentially many teams are involved in ensuring that the change has been validated. Other types of impact are also important to note: *customer scenario, test,* and *quality attribute* impact.

Identifying Customer Scenario Impact

Customer scenario impact can be an outgrowth of the functional impact. Because scenarios boil down to a series of function calls, it's straightforward to associate a scenario with a group of functions that are used to complete the scenario.

For example, in Table 8-3, a series of functions and scenarios are linked together in a mapping table. Anytime one of the functions in the function table changes, it is a simple lookup to see which scenarios are affected. Depending on the priority of the customer scenario, the risk level may be lowered or raised. Depending on the number of scenarios and customers that are affected, the risk level may also be lowered or raised. For example, if the binary1.dll *function2* were changed, it would potentially affect two high-priority scenarios (Scenario1 and Scenario3) and two separate customers. In this case, a change to *function2* would be a relatively higher risk than a change to *function1* would be because it affects more high-priority scenarios and customers than if *function1* were to be changed.

Table 8-3   Scenario-to-Function Mapping

FunctionTable

ID	Binary	Function
1	binary1.dll	function1
2	binary1.dll	function2
3	binary2.exe	functionA
4	binary2.exe	functionB

FunctionScenarioMapping

ID	FunctionID	ScenarioID
1	1	2
2	2	1
3	2	3
4	3	3
5	4	3

ScenarioTable

ID	Name	Customer	Priority
1	Scenario1	Customer1	1
2	Scenario2	Customer1	2
3	Scenario3	Customer2	1

Mapping which functions are associated with which scenarios can be accomplished by augmenting the call graph database described previously. Lists of functions are associated with a scenario like the fan out list for a function. This makes it easy to query the database to find a list of scenarios that are affected by a change. Matching scenarios with the functions they call can be done through code coverage or other operational profiling tools, or by simply having the code beacon that information to a log file as the scenario is being run. The log file can then be the basis for the customer scenario database.

After the mapping is made between a customer scenario and the functions that are called to complete the scenario (as in Table 8-3's FunctionScenarioMapping table), every time a function changes, the database can be queried to see which scenarios are potentially affected by the change. This is one important way to help predict risk because it brings in the customer perspective. It also further assists in focusing test efforts, ensuring that the affected user scenarios are well tested.

Identifying Test Impact

Another way of judging risk through impact is by looking at how many tests have to be rerun when a change is made. By profiling the functions that a test hits, test impact can be gauged in a way that is similar to customer scenario impact. However, it is better to know not only which functions are being called, but *how much* of a function is being called down to the exact lines of code that a test hits, to get an accurate risk assessment.

This type of detailed understanding of how effective a test is in exercising code can be obtained through a code coverage analysis tool. This will tell not only if a function is hit, but how much of the function in terms of line coverage.

By knowing exactly which lines of code a test traverses, one can know if a particular change in a function will be hit by an existing test. Assuming a reference database is created that documents exactly which functions and lines a specific test hits, it is again a simple query to get a list of tests that hit the changing code, if any.

There are two key risk analysis points with test impact. The first is how many tests hit the changing code. This is a good judge of impact because it will quickly be apparent how extensive the changes are from a test perspective. The second is how much of the changing code does not have any existing tests. If there is new code, there may not be an existing tests that hit the code. This code is at a higher risk than code that has hundreds of tests that hit it because there's no verification present. Allowing untested code to be integrated with the rest of the project is one of the highest-risk activities a developer can do. It must be watched for carefully. By using a code coverage system, the team can be automatically alerted to this kind of behavior.

Identifying Quality Attribute Impact

There are often quality ramifications when changes are made. Most of these are mitigated by the testing that follows the integration of changes into a project. However, there is an opportunity to flag potential issues with specific quality attributes such as security, performance, localization impact, or even usage of the correct dependent function calls. For example, during the development of Windows Vista, there was a big push to convert all code in Windows to use a new set of "safe string" related functions instead of older string functions that had proven to have security defects. After all code was converted, in order to ensure no new piece of code accidentally called any of the banned functions, a "quality gate" was put in place to scan code changes and ensure it did not call any of the banned functions. This is a great example of a practical application of analyzing the impact on quality, specifically security, that changes can make. Used in combination with the call graph and scenario impact, one can tag certain sets of functions as either positively or negatively affecting some quality attribute such as security, performance, or localization. Similarly, changes can be scanned for use of incorrect or old methods. Sometimes old dogs need to be taught new tricks whether they like it or not, and this is a great way to verify those old dogs don't revert back to their old ways and use library function calls that shouldn't be used. Understanding how changes affect the quality attributes of software is an important part of a complete risk analysis and can prevent a lot grief by detecting any potential problems right after the code is changed and before it gets integrated with the rest of the software project.

Aside from the characteristics, amount of churn, and impact of a change, knowing why a change is happening is also an import part of the risk prediction model.

Reason: Understanding Why a Change Is Made

There are typically three reasons for project code churn: New code, defect fix, or redesign. Early in a project, the main reason for churn should be to add new code or redesign legacy code. As the project proceeds, changes should be more and more in the defect-fixing camp, until ultimately, the only changes being made at the very end of a project should be defect fixes.

The horror stories of feature creep are all too common: those last-minute features that get jammed into a project, wreaking havoc for months on end until finally being canceled, the only memory being a slipped ship date and maybe a few pink slips. By tracking the reason for the churn, you can potentially eliminate or at least unveil feature creep late in the project.

One way to track the reason for changes is to have a count of the number of defect fixes that are part of a particular churn payload. By looking at the ratio of defects fixed to how many lines of code have changed versus how many new lines were added, you can usually quickly discover if a new feature is being added or if defects are being fixed. For example, in Table 8-4, it's easy to see that *binary3* has clearly had a new feature added because there's no associated defect with the code churn and the churn is all newly added code.

Table 8-4   **Number of Defect Fixes for Churned Code**

Binary	LOC Changed	LOC Added	LOC Deleted	Defects Fixed
binary1	50	5	2	2
binary2	50	200	0	1
binary3	0	500	0	0
binary4	0	200	150	35

On the other hand, *binary1* can be categorized as being a defect fix. Even though there is some new code being added to *binary1*, it is a relatively small amount and the churn has two associated defects.

Sometimes it's hard to tell if churn is related to either a new feature or strictly a defect fix. In the case of *binary2*, although there is a defect associated with the churn in the binary, there is a lot of new code. In this case, it's important to query the owner of *binary2* to uncover the mystery. It could be that to be truly fixed one of the defects required a code redesign, hence the new code, or it could be a case of trying to sneak a new feature in under the guise of fixing a different defect.

With *binary4*, it's clear that a portion of code was completely redesigned, perhaps because the previous method in the binary was so defect ridden that there was nothing left to do except rewrite it.

Having access to the data in these cases makes it easier to start asking questions and brings greater transparency to the project. Note that although it could actually be OK for both defect fixes and new features to be added at the same time, it does increase the risk and should be taken into account when evaluating the overall risk of a particular software release. Knowing the reason for the change is important, and although there can be some level of discernment based on the type of churn (changed versus added or deleted), it's also important to get the reason straight from the horse's mouth: the owner.

Ownership: Knowing Who Owns a Change

The owner of churn can be the developer who made the actual code change or the tester who is responsible for testing the change or anyone who has some burden of responsibility for ensuring the quality of the change. Clearly, risk varies depending on the experience and talent of individuals. The usual way of mitigating risk is to make sure that people who either are less experienced or have a poor track record have a more senior person or persons review the work being done. Having subject matter expert review owners goes a long way in mitigating this kind of risk. For example, in Windows Vista, any change made late in the ship cycle was reviewed by the core architecture team and then by the project management team. By making sure both the technical and project-related requirements were being met by designated reviewers, the quality of the code changes was very high.

Having a report that can quickly tell the owners of the churn who they have affected goes a long way in fostering better cross-group communications, which is particularly important in large projects. This type of report, such as the one shown in Table 8-5, is important to have as part of any risk analysis tool set because it makes it easier to take the next step and contact the affected owners to ensure that they have mitigated the risk incurred by the churn.

Table 8-5   **Owners Affected by Churn Report**

Churned	Owner
binary1	Tim
binary2	Tim
Impacted	**Owner**
binary3	Francie
binary4	Josh

The CAIRO model provides a good background for understanding what the indicators of risk related to code churn are. It also highlights the need to account for not only code characteristics that provide historical failure proneness but the amount, impact, reason, and owners of those changes. Each area is important in getting a broad set of risk factors that then helps make the risk prediction more accurate. Like a diverse portfolio of investments that brings stable and predictable returns over the long haul, a diverse set of risk factors also provides a solid risk prediction model that can be counted on to help drive better decisions and mitigate risk in the right areas and in the right way.

Applying a Risk Prediction Model

After a set of risk indicators is identified and proven to be good predictors and to draw from all parts of the CAIRO model, data for each indicator must be collected in an automated fashion on a regular basis, for example, evaluating all changes that have occurred since the previous day or the previous week. Data collection can be a complicated process and depends heavily on how source code is stored, compiled and built, and distributed. It also depends on having tools that can extract the CAIRO data from a variety of data sources on a regular basis and then present the data in a format that generates useful reports. Table 8-6 is one example of a high-level report that gives a good sampling of CAIRO artifacts from which to do a risk assessment. In this example, the highest-risk binary is binary2.dll, which has high risk indicators across all rows.

Table 8-6 High-Level CAIRO Report

Binary compared to previous week	binary1.dll	binary2.dll	notes.exe
Total size	500	10,000	250
Complexity	22	54	8
Historical fault proneness	0.45	0.84	0.24
LOC Changed	10	500	2
LOC Added	2	950	0
LOC Deleted	1	100	0
% Churn	2%	15%	1%
Function Impact	3	128	0
Scenario Impact	2	25	1
Test Impact	10	234	1
Defect Fix count	2	18	1
Dev owner	Sue	Tomika	Erik
Test owner	Aramis	Alan	Jan
Senior Reviewer	Bill	Bill	Bill

Data for each row, with the exception of the calculated % Churn row, must be gathered, preferably automatically when changes are made. Part of the issue with some existing tools used for risk assessment is that they gather only a fixed set of code characteristics. This provides only a subset of CAIRO data and makes such tools insufficient for a robust risk prediction model. The other challenge is that some artifacts such as ownership information are sometimes never stored in a format that is programmatically accessible.

In practical terms, to get a risk prediction model working requires some development work. Even if every piece of data is stored somewhere in a programmatically accessible location, you still must use a tool that gathers that information into a single place to generate reports and for analysis to take place.

The Windows Vista Risk Analysis team created a tool that quickly aggregated data into a single place and then extracted, transformed, and loaded (ETL) the information needed for the risk assessment into a Risk Analysis Microsoft SQL Server database. Depending on the audience, charts, e-mail, and Web-based reports were then generated using the stored artifacts of churn for each set of daily changes made in Windows Vista. See Figure 8-4.

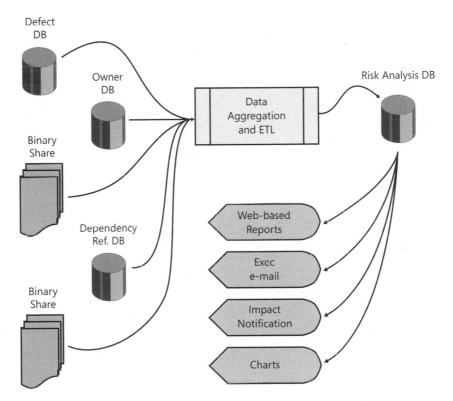

Figure 8-4   Risk Analysis system

Each time a new build of Windows Vista was completed, the resulting binaries were copied to a file share. A series of tools was then run against the binaries to extract the CAIRO artifacts of churn. Some of the information was contained in the binaries themselves, such as specific code characteristics and the amount of churn compared with the previous build. Other information, such as the impact of the changes, reason, and owner, was gathered by looking up the information in separately maintained databases. For example, the owner of a binary was stored in one SQL Server database and the defect fix information that described the reason for the churn was kept in another database. The end result was the ability to see all the risk indicators in a single place and be able to make informed decisions from that data.

It is also important to store the details that make up the reports and not just the high-level CAIRO information as shown in Table 8-6 because different users of the data require different levels of detail. For example, a project manager may want to know only the overall churn trends to get an idea of whether progress is being made on the project as a whole, whereas testers may want to know precise details down to the function level on which functions are changed and which tests are affected by the changes so that they can go run the tests. Developers may need to know precisely who is the affected owner of a change they are making so that they can send an e-mail message to coordinate their efforts.

For example, Table 8-7 includes a more detailed report on the changes that occurred in the binary1.dll binary from Table 8-6. The detail is down to the function level, specifying the functions that were changed and how much they changed. Additionally, there is information on the affected functions, including which functions were affected and the owners of the affected functions. Test and scenario impact details are also available along with the names of the test owners and the actual customer associated with the affected scenarios.

Table 8-7 CAIRO Impact Detail Example

Binary	Function	Size	Complexity	LOC Changed	LOC New	LOC Deleted	Functions Impacted	Tests Impacted	Scenarios Impacted
binary1.dll	function1	250	6	5	1	1	2	2	0
binary1.dll	function2	250	10	5	0	1	0	1	1

Binary Impacted	Function Impacted	Impacted By	Impacted Owner
binary2.exe	FunctionA	binary1.dll:function1	ken
binary2.exe	FunctionB	binary1.dll:function1	ken

Binary Changed	Function Changed	Impacted Test	Test Owner
binary1.dll	function1	Test1	connor
binary1.dll	function1	Test2	marissa
binary1.dll	function2	Test2	marissa

Binary Changed	Function Changed	Impacted Scenario	Customer
binary1.dll	function2	Printing Sales Report	Acme Watering Cans

This level of detail is needed to make the information truly actionable. Providing actionable data as part of a risk assessment is critical to its success. Some actions that can be taken from this data are for the testers to run tests on the affected scenarios and ensure that they are passing. The developer who has code that calls into the changing code should verify that his or her own code doesn't also have to be changed to accommodate the changing code, for example, if the change is in a function parameter, to make sure any function calls are changed to match the new function's signature. It should be verified that the customer scenario that is potentially affected still works according to the customer's expectations. It may even be useful to give the customer a prerelease version of the build to ensure that the scenario continues to work in the customer environment. Getting customer feedback early and often, particularly when a change in the software potentially affects customers directly, goes a long way in mitigating risk before the software has officially shipped.

Having information about where to focus test efforts, which scenarios to verify, and which partners to consult is much of what can come out of a risk assessment. A more advanced risk assessment system can provide information about areas of risk and what has been done, up to the current point in time, to mitigate the risk. With each artifact of churn, there should be an associated mitigation activity. Ideally, after the mitigation activity is completed, the results are entered side by side with the risk factors. After both the risks and mitigations are lined up, it becomes clear what part of the risk remains unmitigated.

Conclusion

Risk analysis of software is broken up into two activities: historical and current risk analyses. Performing historical risk analysis results in a risk prediction model that can be applied to a software project. Risk prediction models should contain a variety of measures that can produce an accurate risk assessment. Current risk analysis uses the proven risk prediction model during the software development life cycle to assess risk as changes are being made to the code.

During software development, the risk prediction model should take into account not only code characteristics such as size, complexity, and historical failure proneness but also the amount of churn, the impact in terms of function call graph, tests, and customer scenarios. The reason for the churn, whether it is a defect fix, a new feature, or redesign, and who has ownership of the churn are also important risk factors to consider. These CAIRO artifacts of churn should be measured with each new interim version of the software and used to assess the overall risk.

High-risk areas should have targeted testing applied. When changes affect other code, tests, or customer scenarios, the result should be better communication between affected developers, testers, and customers. Mitigation strategies such as more stringent code reviews should go into effect when less senior developers are making changes in high-risk code. The result of any risk analysis should be that project decision makers are able to make data-driven decisions, asking pointed questions on how the risk that comes with writing software has been mitigated so that it's clear when the project is ready to ship.

Chapter 9
Using Simulation and Modeling for Organizational Innovation

> All models are wrong but some are useful.
> *—George E. F. Box*

> Men's courses will foreshadow certain ends, to which, if persevered in, they must lead. But if the courses be departed from, the ends will change. Say it is thus with what you show me.
> *—Ebenezer Scrooge*

Modeling is the process of building a representation of how the world works. A model of the software development process can help to explain a portion of the process, but by its nature a model is incomplete and therefore incorrect. However, this does not mean that the model is not useful. It is sometimes difficult to focus on the usefulness of the model rather than its limitations. Nevertheless, the aversion that most software engineers feel to partial solutions must be overcome to make use of the uncertain information inherent in software development.

Simulation is the process of using a model to predict what is likely to happen. It is the natural extension of modeling, and like modeling, it is not a perfect solution. The future cannot be known with certainty, and some software developers feel it is a waste of time to simulate, while others may not want to hear bad news should the model predict schedule slips. However, as this chapter shows, the effect of a decision can be predicted by using a useful model. By using simulation techniques, an organization can build contingencies based on a range of possible outcomes rather than expecting a single outcome associated with conventional black-and-white thinking. An organization can use modeling to think in new ways not necessarily intuitively obvious. Think of modeling as "the shadows of things that may be only" and not the things that will be. The intent is to find those things that can alter the course of development and lead to the desired ends.

Modeling and simulation make possible a view of the world and an understanding of what is possible. By using stochastic modeling, schedule, cost, and quality of the work product are predictable. Additionally, you can gain an understanding of the sources of variance in a process and the expected results of a process improvement technique. This chapter explains how to model a process and then use the model to simulate the development process as it is and as it may be. It provides several examples of how to build models from a limited understanding of a process and how to use validation techniques to enhance the model. Finally, this chapter shows how to use the model as a management tool to determine the process changes in which to invest and the reasons an improvement project did not deliver the expected results.

Understanding Stochastic Modeling

The basis of simulation and modeling rests with an understanding of systems and the relationships between variables of interest. From an early age, most people learn to break down problems into their fundamental building blocks and then reconstruct the system from the composite knowledge. This deconstructionist view is helpful when first attempting to understand a system, but it begins to create a misunderstanding of "the Big Picture" view of the world.

Ludwig Von Bertalanffy, considered by many as the creator of systems theory, points out that "to understand an organized whole we must know both the parts and the relations between them."[1] Traditional science provides a means to understand the parts through deconstruction of the problem. It is systems thinking that allows for the combination of the individual parts into an organized whole. Regardless of how you break down the problem of software engineering, the pieces must recombine in a way that re-creates the original system, or at least a reasonable facsimile. Stochastic modeling is one means to garner an understanding of the whole.

Because this is a practical guide to stochastic modeling, we do not define the exact mathematics. Additionally, we take some liberties with terminology. Our intent from this point on is to provide you enough understanding to create workable models that will be wrong but useful.

When analyzing data, you can perform regression analysis to produce an equation that somehow relates two or more measured variables. The equation is often referred to as a model of the data. For example, a relationship exists between a person's height, weight, and body mass index (BMI). The following equation relates the three variables in a model for calculating BMI:

*BMI = .1517 * Weight − 0.78 * Height*

From this equation, you can calculate BMI using the mathematical model expressed in the equation. The preceding model produces a discrete answer for every height and weight pair of variables; for example, a person of height 68.5 inches and of weight 159 pounds has a BMI of 23.7. This mathematical model produces a single answer for BMI from the variables of weight and height.

A *statistical model* adds to the basic mathematical model by introducing a degree of uncertainty. In analyzing the data, the modeler also reports the standard error of the coefficients for both the height and weight variables to represent the uncertainty of the calculation. An indication of the significance of the variables is reported along with the importance of each variable. For example, the BMI for someone of height 68.5 inches and of weight 159 pounds is 23.7 plus or minus 0.8 with a confidence of 95 percent and a standard error of prediction of 81 percent.[2] The result provides an indication of the expected amount of variance one would

---

1 L. Von Bertalanffy, *General System Theory: Foundations, Development, Applications* (New York: George Braziller, 1976).

2 The exact meaning of the elements of a statistical model is not important. You need only understand that this type of model produces a measure of uncertainty along with a single result.

see in a population of people 68.5 inches tall. There is more information available to the user of the data.

Stochastic modeling, also known as Monte Carlo analysis, is a technique used to solve equations that are too difficult to solve using traditional numerical techniques. Stochastic modeling differs from traditional statistical modeling in that a system of equations is not solved for an exact solution but rather for a distribution function of possible solutions. According to the *American Heritage Dictionary*, the word *stochastic* means "of, relating to, or characterized by conjecture; conjectural" and is an excellent description of the result of the models that you can create. The process is one of continual "what-if" conjecture. As such, the output of the modeling effort often involves more questions than answers. However, when used correctly, you can gain an understanding of the greater whole. In the BMI example, a stochastic model would likely add variables for gender, age, general health, nationality, and so on, producing a system of equations that may or may not be solvable by numerical analysis. Additionally, interactions between variables are easily modeled stochastically; for example, if the BMI increases with age except when the general heath is exceptionally good. Exceptions in the equation are difficult to handle but are a natural part of a stochastic model.

In statistics, *stochastic* means involving probabilities or containing random variables. Although the previous regression model for BMI uses random variables as well, the variables are given a discrete value and the model is solved for a single solution with a range of expectation, such as 23.7 plus or minus 0.8. There is no indication of how the population is distributed in the range. A stochastic model provides a probability curve that indicates exactly how the population is distributed. The primary unit of analysis that a stochastic model uses is the probability density function (pdf) if the distribution is a continuous curve, or the probability mass function (pmf) if the output uses discrete values.[1] A *stochastic process* is one that involves probability equations that contain random variables and a level of uncertainty in the outcome.

The output of a model typically is a probability curve indicating the range of possibilities. In some cases, it may be a set of possible outputs and the probabilities for each member of the set. The inputs to the model will be one or more pdfs along with any known actual values. The input pdfs are known as *stochastic variables*, indicating that a simulation of the model will replace the stochastic variable with some form of a probability function. The model is a set of equations indicating how the input data is transformed into the possible outputs.

To understand the elements of a model, consider the following equation:

*Cups of coffee consumed = Demand per hour * time*

The equation models the demand for coffee using the stochastic variable *Demand per hour* along with an actual value for time. To simulate this model, a pdf for *Demand per hour* is necessary. To develop the pdf, the modeler can measure the actual cups of coffee consumed in various time periods, creating the pdf. Alternatively, the data may already exist (perhaps

---

1 A pmf gives the probability for discrete random variables, whereas the pdf must be integrated over a range to determine the probability for a continuous random variable. The difference will become apparent shortly.

through sales receipts), and the modeler can mine for the data. Finally, data may exist in other companies or in similar domains, and the modeler can adapt this data to his or her domain. Adapting data from other domains requires the extra step of verifying the predications of the simulation. It also introduces a greater risk but does allow building the model even when little or no organizational data exists.

The model is only as useful as the data used to create the pdfs. The degree to which the data is similar to future data determines the degree to which the model predicts future events. In the coffee example, assume that sales receipts allow for building the pdf shown in Figure 9-1. The tool used in this and other examples is called Crystal Ball by Decisioneering.[1] Most simulation software produces similar information.

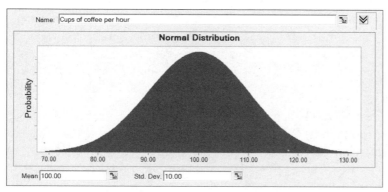

Figure 9-1   Example pdf

The range of expected cups of coffee sold in an hour is shown in Figure 9-1. The stochastic variables are often called *model assumptions*. This particular assumption has a shape that follows a normal distribution. It shows a mean of 100 cups with a standard deviation of 10 cups.

There are many possible distribution shapes (see the sidebar titled "Probability function basics," which follows), but two of the most common are the normal distribution and the log-normal distribution. With a good simulation software package, you can input a data set and have the software generate the appropriate curve. Although the exact shape of the curve is important in fine-tuning the model, the slight error introduced by differences in the pdf shape are not a problem. Often, the errors in the data set exceed the error introduced as a result of slight differences in the distributions. The modeler should strive to be as accurate as possible but need not agonize over the choice. The graphs are presented here to provide an understanding of the type of shape appropriate for various process variables, such as time between events versus size of the product.

---

1 See *www.decisioneering.com* for more information about Crystal Ball.

Probability function basics

The probability density function can have a variety of shapes. It is important to know a little about the pros and cons of using different distributions. Beginners need not be too concerned with the subtle differences, which become important only for very complex models. It is important to realize that a good simulation tool provides flexibility in the choices for pdfs and pmfs.

Normal Distribution

A *normal distribution* (see Figure 9-2), also known as a Gaussian distribution or bell curve, is useful for representing many natural phenomena, for example, people's heights, weights, intellects. This curve is probably the most familiar to people. The curve is symmetric about the mean so that the mean, median, and mode are all the same value. In theory, the distribution ranges from plus to minus infinity, so care must taken when using this distribution because it may result in impossible values generated by a simulation. The normal distribution is a good place to begin working with models and is easily generated in spreadsheet software such as Microsoft Office Excel without the need for specialized simulation tools.

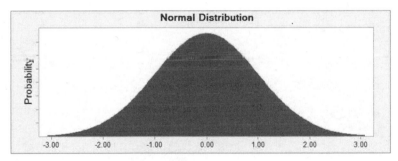

Figure 9-2   Normal distribution

Log-Normal Distribution

The log-normal distribution is skewed to either the right or the left. It is termed log-normal because the logarithm of the random variable is normally distributed. It is often used in reliability analysis to model failure times. Note that the median and the mean are not the same value. If the distribution is skewed to the left, as shown in Figure 9-3, the median is less than the mean.[1] Like the normal distribution, the log-normal distribution ranges to infinity. Also like the normal distribution, it is easy to generate in spreadsheet software such as Excel. The curve is often used when many of the values occur near some

---

1   The skewness becomes important in the example developed in this chapter.

minimum value. For example, in stock prices there is a natural lower limit, zero, but there is no upper limit.

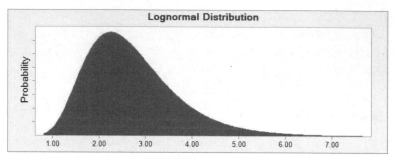

Figure 9-3   Log-normal distribution

Beta Distribution

The beta distribution (see Figure 9-4) is actually a family of different shapes continuous over an interval. The difference between it and the normal or log-normal distribution is that it can be constrained to have minimum and maximum values. It is often used in project management to describe the time required to complete a task, for example, the time required to brew a pot of coffee. It is the distribution function most commonly used for the examples in this book.

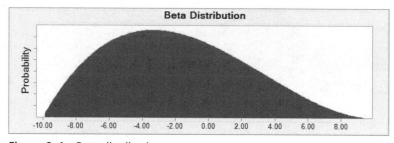

Figure 9-4   Beta distribution

Gamma Distribution

Like the beta distribution, the gamma distribution (Figure 9-5) forms a family of continuous functions. It is useful in modeling the time between events, for example, the time between subsequent customers. It is also useful for modeling the time between releases of components to the test process, time between defect reports, and so on.

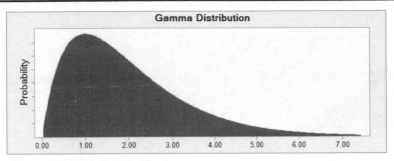

Figure 9-5   Gamma distribution

Wiebull Distribution

The Wiebull distribution (Figure 9-6) is one of the most commonly used because it can closely approximate distributions such as the normal and exponential distributions. It is often used in failure rate analysis, to represent manufacturing or project time, or to represent delivery times, for example, time required to receive a cup of coffee after ordering it (assuming the coffee was already brewed).

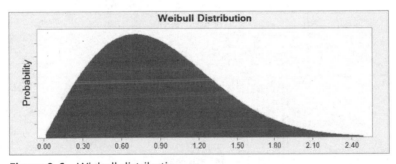

Figure 9-6   Wiebull distribution

Exponential Distribution

Exponential distribution (Figure 9-7) is useful for any variable that decreases at a rate proportional to its value; for example, the temperature of the coffee in a cup follows an exponential decay curve. The exponential distribution is also used to model the time between independent events happening at a constant average rate. Defect density per software development phase can often be modeled using an exponential distribution, as can the time between system crashes.

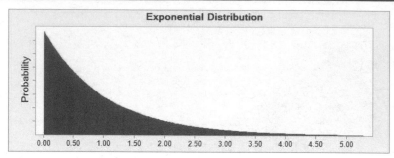

Figure 9-7   Exponential distribution

Poisson Distribution

The Poisson distribution (Figure 9-8) is a discrete probability function, making it a probability mass function. For simplicity's sake, continuous random variables are used for the functions used in this chapter, but all of the models could be improved by using the Poisson distribution. It is useful for modeling such things as the number of spelling mistakes in this book or the number of customers per day in a coffee shop. The probability is read directly from the y-axis; for example, the probability that 100 customers will order coffee per day is 4 percent.

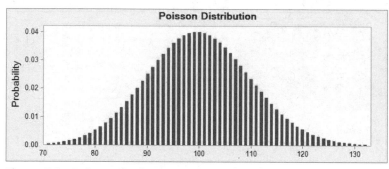

Figure 9-8   Poisson distribution

If a simulation is run with a time input of 1 hour, the cups of coffee demanded should exactly mirror the probability density function, as shown in Figure 9-9. The difference is that this chart contains the descriptive statistics along the right edge and appears as a histogram rather than a smooth density function.[1]

---

1 Note: All future pdfs actually show this style of chart to highlight the values for mean and standard deviation without requiring you to understand the exact distribution function values. In some cases, values are rounded off.

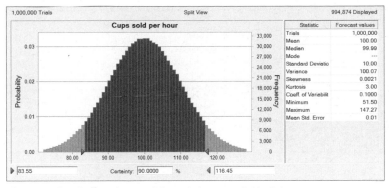

Figure 9-9   Coffee demand for a 1-hour period of time

The chart indicates the value for mean and standard deviation in the area along the right, along with minimum value, maximum value, and so forth. Also, the number of trials in the simulation is shown as the first number in the statistics. This particular model was run one million times. The minimum number of cups was 51.5, and the maximum was 147.27.

It is often desirable to include a measure of risk along with the simulation. In this case, the *Certainty* percentage shown below the histogram provides such a measure. In the diagram, the central area represents the outcome for 90 percent of the trials. This means that 5 percent is in each of the tail areas of the curve. In other words, 95 percent of the time, the coffee demand will be in excess of 83.55, and 95 percent of the time, the demand will be less than 116.45. Most organizations use 95 percent as an acceptable level of risk.

If the trials of the previous model are increased to 10 million, the statistics change, as shown in Figure 9-10. Notice that the minimum and maximum values change significantly, but the values at the 90 percent certainty level are not noticeably affected. The simulation would conclude that sales will be between 83 and 117 cups of coffee with greater than 90 percent certainty (the values were rounded down and up, respectively, because cups are sold in discrete units) after as few as 10,000 trials (see Figure 9-11).

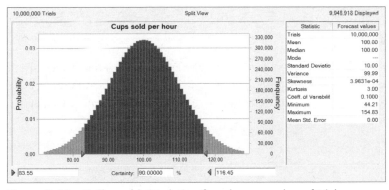

Figure 9-10   Coffee sold simulation for a large number of trials

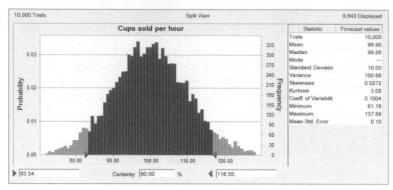

Figure 9-11   Coffee sold simulation for a small number of trials

Using the Modeling Process

We described the basic attributes of a model first so that you can understand the desired outcome of the process. This section describes a process for creating a model to run a simulation. You should realize that modeling is actually a thought experiment, so the process is more important than the outcome. The trial-and-error nature of the process is where the learning occurs. The purpose of this section is to provide a process for building a model and understanding how to improve a model. The process described is as follows:

1. Define the goals.

2. Identify the initial process.

3. Determine process inputs and outputs.

4. Build the espoused process.

5. Compare process results with organizational results.

6. Develop the actual process.

7. Repeat if necessary.

Defining the Goals

The first step is to determine the questions that the model is to answer, as mentioned in Chapter 7, "Software Measurement and Metrics," the Goal Question Metric (GQM) paradigm by Vic Basili.

Victor R. Basili, "Establishing a Measurement Program" (College Park: University of Maryland, 2006),[1] is useful in determining organizational metrics. Because one use of a stochastic model is to model the organization's metrics, it is necessary to determine the questions that the model is capable of answering. To determine the questions you will ask of the model, you must understand the goals of the model.

---

1 *www.cs.umd.edu/~basili/presentations/2006%20WiproTalk.pdf.*

Humphrey (1989) categorizes data as either predictive or explanatory.[1] This categorization provides an initial point for thinking about the goals of the model as either explanatory or predictive. For example, a model of development presented later in this chapter was created for the purpose of explaining why a highly efficient test organization was not capable of increasing the total software throughput. In fact, on the surface, the organization seemed to be less capable irrespective of the scorecard metrics. Upon modeling the situation, it became obvious that the problem was one of an overall system—not simply one process—requiring improvement. Had a predictive model, such as the one presented in this chapter, first been created, it would have been obvious that improving one element of a tightly bound system would hurt overall throughput.

Identifying the Initial Process

Chris Argryis describes a model of decision making and uses the phrase "espoused theories of action" to describe the situation in which an individual's or organization's stated ideas are incongruent with that person's or organization's behaviors.[2] Often, the inconsistency goes unnoticed. The concepts of espoused process and process-in-use are viable as a means to explain actual development. Often, an organization's stated process does not match its actual process. The purpose of this step is to define the process that everyone believes is used.

The espoused process may be documented but often is not. Even if a documented process exists, the developers may still have a very different espoused process. It is best to begin by modeling without critique or modification the process that the developers think they use. A team of software developers may truly believe that they develop software using the espoused process. By using the espoused process as the basis for understanding, it becomes easier to develop organizational buy-in for the model produced.

Determining Process Input and Outputs

The next step is to determine the inputs and outputs of the espoused process. Associated with each input and output is a set of data that should already be known to the organization or else is readily available through data mining. For example, the most typical output of the software development process is a working product or products. In other words, the output is code. The lines of code (LOC), or thousand lines of code (KLOC), can be counted. The defects produced can be counted, assuming they are tracked in a database. Each input and output needs to be countable in some fashion so that probability density functions can be built.

Often, an organization just beginning in process improvement will not have data in a directly consumable form but instead must mine for it. One of the benefits of an organizational scorecard is to have a common definition of data that is directly applicable to modeling. If such data is not available, estimates must be made. The estimates can come from either the organization

---

1   W. S. Humphrey, *Managing the Software Process* (Reading, MA: Addison-Wesley, 1989).

2   C. Argryis, "Single-Loop and Double-Loop Models in Research on Decision Making," *Administrative Science Quarterly* 21, no. 3 (1976): 363–375.

or the industry. Industry data is available in reports such as those produced by Davis and Mullaney.[1] Reports from researchers will provide the process used to collect the data, which can then determine the applicability of the data to other organizations. At a minimum, industry reports provide average values that are usable as comparisons.

To find a value such as lines of code per requirement, the organization will likely need to provide a best guess estimate using a combination of average data and industry research. For example, using information in the sidebar titled "Probability function basics" earlier in this chapter, the modeler can estimate the general shape for a type of data. In this case, it is known that the size of a requirement cannot be less than zero, but it can increase without bound. From the descriptions of the curves, it seems reasonable that the log-normal distribution is a good starting curve shape for the distribution function. To create such a curve, you need the mean value and the standard deviation.[2]

It is likely that teams have not gathered information on lines of code per requirement directly. Instead, each team will know the total requirements created and the total new lines of code. As an aside, most correlations are true only for new and changed lines of code, that is, defects found in the product correlate to new and changed LOC but not necessarily to total LOC. (See Humphrey[3] for detailed information on this point.) If a team knows the requirements produced in a release and can count the total new and changed LOC, the average LOC per requirement is calculable for the team. Measuring this across many teams provides enough information to determine the average LOC/requirement and a standard deviation. Table 9-1 provides an example.

Table 9-1   Lines of Code per Requirement Calculations

Team	Requirements	Lines of Code	LOC per Requirement
1	16	19,040	1,190
2	14	62,092	4,435
3	11	12,199	1,109
4	7	31,900	4,557
5	20	140,060	7,003
6	28	79,128	2,826
7	21	124,866	5,946
8	25	21,375	855
9	18	37,728	2,096
Average LOC per Requirement			3,335
Standard Deviation			2,249

---

1 N. Davis and J. Mullaney, *The Team Software Process in Practice: A Summary of Recent Results* (Pittsburgh, PA: Software Engineering Institute, Carnegie-Mellon University, 2003).

2 A good modeling tool such as Crystal Ball can indicate the required information for every curve type.

3 W. S. Humphrey, *PSP: A Self-Improvement Process for Software Engineers* (Upper Saddle River, NJ: Addison-Wesley, 2005).

Each team is treated like a sample of the organizational average. The average LOC per requirement is calculated for each team, and then all of the averages are averaged together to get the final number for the pdf. The standard deviation of the averages is calculated, and enough information is known to provide a reasonable value for LOC/requirement for these teams.

Building the Espoused Process

The most important aspect of building the initial model is the understanding of the relationship between inputs and outputs. The desired goals determine one or more outputs of interest. At this point, it is not important that the espoused model accurately reflect the actual development process, only that the outputs are properly chosen and that individuals reviewing the model will believe it is the process they actually use. To build the model, a system of equations is created. Each equation solves some part of the system, and when the solutions are all assembled, a view of the process emerges.

In the coffee example described earlier, a very simple equation related consumption to a random variable for demand per unit of time. The model could be queried for an estimate of the number of cups required for any time period. Typically, each step in a sequential process can be nearly as simple as the coffee example.

Comparing Process Results to Organizational Results

After the initial set of data is available and the equations are entered into a simulation tool, the model is ready for testing. If the model has a goal that is explanatory in nature, the output of the model must be compared with actual organizational data. Often, explanatory models are used in an attempt to determine qualitative results. For example, later in this chapter a model is developed that attempts to explain the failure to see the expected results of a process improvement effort. The known fact was that little or no throughput was visible to an organization, and yet one step in a process was significantly improved. The goal of the model was to explain the apparent failure of a defect prevention activity.

In the case of predictive models, the proof of viability is in use. If the model accurately predicts the outcome of development, it is a viable model. Often, subtle differences between predicted and actual results are seen. If the model is developed in enough detail, intermediate results, such as defects per class, can be predicted. This adds credibility to the model as well as provides useful information for shorter-term projects.

Developing the Actual Process

Begin modifying elements of the model based on many runs of the model. Look for subprocesses that produce discrepancies in the data elements or that have wide variances. Use industry data as a check against a process. For example, Davis and Mullaney indicate that a Capability Maturity Model (CMM) level 1 organization will have about 7.5 defects per thousand lines of code discovered after release.[1] (The Capability Maturity Model is discussed in more detail in Chapter 2, "Defect Prevention Frameworks.") A level 2 organization is not much better, at about 6 defects per KLOC. It is reasonable to assume that most organizations will be somewhere near this number.

Make sure that the data and the model produce an output somewhere in the expected range. If the output data is significantly different from the predicted results, more detail is needed to pinpoint the cause of the discrepancy. The easiest place to begin looking for discrepancies is to check the PDFs. If they are correct, it may be that a hidden process step exists.

Repeating If Necessary

Continue to run the model and look for discrepancies building the process-in-use; iterate until the process-in-use produces the actual output. Eventually, the data elements that do not seem to make sense should appear in the model. For example, as code reviews become more and more effective, the time required to fix defects in unit test should actually increase. This is a result of the fact that a minimum amount of testing is required even when no defects are actually discovered. Because the probability of finding a defect in unit test decreases, the time spent testing defect-free software must be amortized over a smaller and smaller pool of defects that are found.

A naive conclusion would be that the process is becoming less effective. When such discrepancies appear, new opportunities for process improvement occur. In our example, the high degree of stability in the inspection process makes possible the use of statistical sampling techniques for the test process. Rather than attempting to do thorough code cover of all functionality, a quick sample can be used to ensure the quality of the inspection and reduce the time spent testing high-quality code.

Baseline Process Model Example

In this section, we build a model that provides a baseline for organizational improvement. The model begins with a simple representation of software development and illustrates how to improve the model over time. The baseline model is then used to predict the results of a defect prevention activity. Finally, a complex representation of the entire development process is provided to illustrate modeling dynamic aspects of software process. The data used in these models is based on data gathered from many organizations and is used for illustrative purposes only.[2] You should realize that actual implementation of these models requires using data mined from the actual organization where the model is to be used.

---

1 N. Davis and J. Mullaney, *The Team Software Process in Practice: A Summary of Recent Results* (Pittsburgh, PA: Software Engineering Institute, Carnegie-Mellon University, 2003).

2 For purposes of confidentiality, the exact organizations cannot be named. However, the data agrees strongly with the results described by Davis and Mullaney mentioned earlier.

Simple Planning Model

This model can be used during the planning process, so its goal is to predict several aspects of the development process accurately, for example, the likely size of the product and its approximate cost. Consider the simple process shown in Figure 9-12. This is just about the simplest representation possible for a software organization. Requirements are provided to the software engineers, and after some time delay, working code is produced. The equation

*Lines of code = Requirements * LOC per Requirement*

is used by the development process to translate from requirements to lines of code. The *LOC per requirement* variable is the stochastic variable in this equation. A corresponding stochastic model requires a pdf for the number of lines of code per requirement and an input count of the anticipated software requirements. Figure 9-13 contains a pdf for the model relating requirements to lines of code developed using a method similar to that described earlier. Notice that this pdf has a slightly different mean and standard deviation than that calculated earlier because it uses many more teams, and yet the data produced by the relatively small sample of nine teams agrees strikingly well with the larger organization. The data from a small fraction of the organization would have produced a reasonable result.

The *x*-axis in Figure 9-13 indicates the lines of code per requirement, and the *y*-axis indicates the probability of occurrence. With 95 percent certainty, a requirement contains more than 780 lines of code.[1] Also with 95 percent certainty, a requirement contains less than 7,343 lines of code. Also available are the descriptive statistics for this pdf, that is, mean, median, standard deviation, and so on.

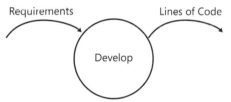

Figure 9-12   Simple development model

---

[1] Note that each of the tails contains 5 percent of the probability function, so the area in Figure 9-12 with less than 780 LOC is 5 percent of the total.

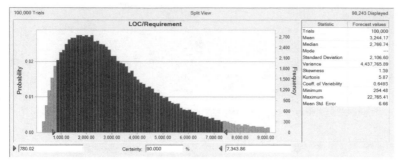

Figure 9-13 Probability density function for LOC per requirement

You may think a pdf that contains a range as large as that in Figure 9-13 would not be very useful. Certainly, attempting to predict the product size for any individual requirement will lead to a large range of possible outcomes. However, very few products with an interesting amount of functionality will have only one requirement; most will contain hundreds if not thousands. Assume that the example product contains 100 requirements. The pdf in Figure 9-13 is sampled once for each requirement, and the total combined estimate of code size indicates the likely outcome for a single simulation. As mentioned previously, modeling requires simulating the outcome over and over until a trend is noticed. Figure 9-14 contains the output probability curve for a product consisting of 100 requirements simulated 100,000 times.

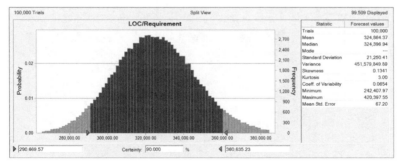

Figure 9-14 Probable product size for 100 requirements

From the descriptive statistics to the right in the figure, the product will have an approximate size of 325 KLOC plus or minus 21 KLOC and will be no larger than 420 KLOC. This information is useful in determining resources for the project. Assuming the organization codes at an average rate of 10 lines of code per hour, the project can plan for between 29,000 and 36,000 engineering-hours of effort.

This estimate uses a size estimate of between 290,669 and 360,635 lines of code for the product. In a model such as this, the value at the 95th percentile is used, giving 36,000 hours as the expected effort. The reason for using this value is that it is 95 percent likely that the project will be smaller than 360 KLOC, and 5 percent is typically considered an acceptable risk level. At a $90 per hour loaded engineering rate, the project will cost between $2.6 million and $3.2 million.

Notice that the model has produced a fair cost estimate with relatively imprecise data. One weakness of this technique is that it requires that the new system requirements match the requirements used to generate the *LOC per requirement* pdf in approximate size. A well-established requirement-gathering process is likely to produce fairly consistent requirements. However, to mitigate this risk, the model must be improved and the explicit and implicit assumptions removed.

Notice that the cost estimation produced by the simple planning model makes three assumptions. To convert from lines of code to engineering effort, the explicit assumption of 10 LOC per hour for the productivity rate is used. Of course, every hour of effort does not produce 10 lines of code, so one improvement is to determine a pdf for productivity. The second assumption is that 100 requirements will be produced. It is likely that past projects had a range of planned versus actual performance. The third assumption is that every requirement entering the development process in Figure 9-12 uses exactly the same process to develop the code.

The first two assumptions are easy to model with additional random variables. For example, Figure 9-15 models the planned versus actual requirements from past projects.[1] This example shows that the team delivers only about 9 of every 10 requirements planned. There is a chance, albeit a small one, that the team will deliver more than the planned amount of work. However, 95 percent of the time the team will not make the committed amount of functionality.

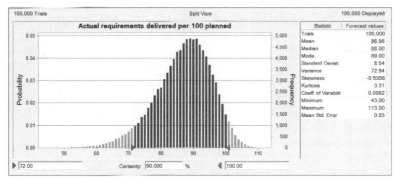

Figure 9-15   Actual requirements delivered per 100 planned

The improved model associated with the pdf in Figure 9-15 includes a new stochastic equation. The equation set becomes the following:

*Requirements = Planned Requirements * Completion Rate per requirement*

*Lines of code = Requirements * LOC per Requirement*

---

1 Because the distribution shows discrete values, it is more properly termed a probability mass function. The probability of delivering N requirements for every 100 planned is read directly from the scale at the left edge; for example, the probability of delivering 90 requirements is just under 5 percent.

For the remainder of the examples, the focus is the process used to develop software. For simplicity, the system assumes a fixed number of requirements. You should realize that the addition of a planned versus actual completion equation allows the model to eliminate the assumption. Also, a more complex model would include the possibility of requirements being developed but never shipped as well as new requirements added after the start of development.[1]

Improved Planning Model

The assumption that every requirement goes through exactly the same process is actually more problematic than the assumed rate of lines of code produced per hour. It requires that all productivity rates are equal, all defect densities produced are equal, and so on. To prevent defects, the team must understand normal process variance, and the process must somehow make the variance explicit. To predict the variance, a better process model is needed. After the simple model of Figure 9-12 is found to compare well with the actual organizational performance, it can be broken down into more steps for more thorough analysis. It is recommended that each model be compared with actual performance to verify that the data collection is producing usable information.

To improve the model, the single step called development must be decomposed into its aggregate parts and the relationship between those parts must be examined. A two-step process consisting of writing the code and then testing the code, or what can be thought of as creating the defects and fixing the defects, provides a reasonable improvement as a starting point for more understanding. Future models then build upon the concept of one process injecting defects while another tries to prevent the defects. Processes with steps that are in opposition often model the system better because a positive change in one process results in a negative change in another process. The model will have a step that determines the number of lines of code and the total defects created, followed by a step that removes the defects from the product (see Figure 9-16).

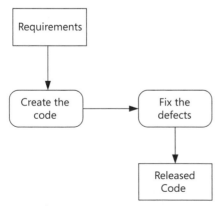

Figure 9-16   Two-step process model

---

1   Changes in requirements can also be modeled as a type of defect.

The stochastic equations associated with this model are as follows:

Classes = Requirements * Classes per Requirement

Lines of code = Classes * LOC per Class

Total Defects = (Lines of Code/1000) * Defects per KLOC

Code Effort = Lines of code/LOC per hour

Discovered Defects = Total Defects * test yield

Testing Effort = Discovered Defects * Effort to find and fix a defect

Total Effort = Code Effort + Test Effort

This system of equations must be solved using the stochastic variables shown in Table 9-2. The simplicity of Figure 9-12 has increased dramatically with the addition of just one more process step and the associated variables.

Table 9-2   Process Data for Two-Step Process Model

Process Step	Inputs	Outputs	Stochastic Variables
Create the code	Requirements	Lines of code	LOC per Hour
		Count of classes	Defects per KLOC
		Defects	Classes per Requirement
		Effort	LOC per Class
Fix the defects	Defects	Released LOC	Yield
		Discovered defects	Effort to Find and Fix Defects
		Effort	

Notice that the model was built with the measurement system in mind. All of the required probability data is obtainable by mining organizational databases.[1] Typically, a team is assigned a requirement or set of requirements and produces the product from the assigned requirements. The total number of classes for the team is easily determined. The lines associated with each class are also countable, as are defects per class, defects discovered by testing versus other sources, and so on. The only difficult item is the effort required to produce a set of requirements. A suitable proxy for effort is a count of engineers on the project and the actual elapsed time for the project. Assume a 40-hour week, and a reasonable effort measure is obtained. Of course, a more detailed effort measure is preferable—the more detailed the measurement, the better the model and the more granular the prediction. Detailed data obtained through a process such as the Personal Software Process allows prediction at the individual level, whereas the proxy effort estimation just described may allow for modeling only at the organizational level, that is, hundreds of requirements across multiple teams.

---

1   Assuming that the organization tracks its defects, has project plans, and uses some form of source code repository.

Building the Model

For each requirement, sample the pdf for *Classes per requirement* and the pdf for *LOC per class*, multiplying the two values to determine the probable lines of code for the requirement. Totaling the LOC for the planned number of requirements and ignoring that the team typically delivers less than planned, the total project LOC is obtained as shown in Figure 9-17.

Notice that the simple model previously discussed and this model produce about the same mean number of lines of code. However, the more detailed model produces a smaller standard deviation. Often, the more detailed the model, the more precise the estimate because extreme values occurring simultaneously on two pdfs are more unlikely to occur.[1] The exception to this general principle occurs when two processes produce variances that have a high probability of canceling each other out, which is rarely the case in software development. However, if the model does produce such a result, additional detail is not beneficial.

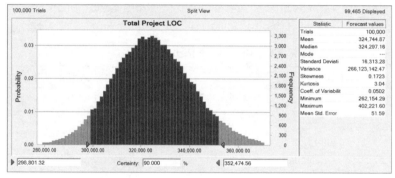

Figure 9-17   Estimated LOC for the more detailed project model

The estimate is now 325 KLOC plus or minus 16 KLOC, reducing the range on the cost estimates as well as reducing worst-case estimates (based on the original assumption of 10 LOC per hour). However, the cost estimate can also be improved by creating estimates for individual tasks rather than total LOC. To improve cost estimates, the effort estimates for creating the code must be separated from estimates for fixing the defects. This will model the natural variability of the test process much more realistically.

An estimate for the number of classes was just created when projecting the total LOC. Also, an estimate for lines of code per class was created. By using the effort probability density functions for hours per class and hours per LOC, an estimate for total effort to design the classes and create the code is obtained. This is an estimate for the effort to create the code as well as creating the defects.

---

1   This effect shows up in the actual product development. You may get unlucky during the design phase, spending more than the planned effort, which then allows the coding phase to proceed more quickly. Breaking up the process into many steps more accurately reflects the real-world interactions in the process.

The next step in modeling the defect removal process is to estimate the total product defects. Because the lines of code for each class are known, the model estimates the class defects by sampling the pdf for defects per KLOC, once for each class. Multiply the lines of code in the class by the sampled value for defects per KLOC. This simulates the defect creation process and provides an estimate for the total defects in each class. The process is repeated for each simulated class to estimate the total defects in the product.

When managing the actual project, the estimated total defects is as important, if not more so, than the total project cost. It becomes a means to track the progress of the defect removal process and determine the estimated code quality. Without it, the team can never determine the probable product quality.

At this point, the simulation has a defect per class estimate, but the defects must be found and fixed. For each class created in the *Create the Code* phase, estimate the defects removed by sampling the yield pdf. Multiply the total defects by the yield to determine the number of defects that will be found and fixed. The effort to find and fix each defect is estimated, and the total cost to fix the defects in the product is determined. Summing the total effort to create the code for each class and the total effort to fix the defects provides the total effort to build the class. At this point, all of the equations for the model have been solved. As before, the simulation is run multiple times to determine predicted defect densities, size, effort, and so on.

After the model of the process flow is complete, you can determine how much effort is required to create the code and fix the code. The defects removed during various development phases are known as well as the likely defect density of the product at release. Using expected cost per development hour, the total project cost is known. All of this data is determined based on historical organizational performance and expected system functionality. The model is a useful tool for project planning and a necessary first step to defect prevention. If an organization cannot reasonably predict the product quality, it will be unable to predict the benefits of particular improvement activities, making process improvement a hit-or-miss proposition.

At this point, you may think that two types of processes exist. The first process creates work product, for example, code, increasing the total count of defects in the product. The second type of process removes defects and perhaps changes the code size moderately. In fact, there exists only one type of process. It takes as input the size of the product and current defect count and produces as output a new size and modified defect count. Each phase builds product with some productivity rate, reduces defects at some yield rate, increases defects at a defect injection rate, and calculates the effort required to execute the process.

Abstracting the processes in such a manner allows the modeler to build a simple yet powerful data model. The model requires only size, cost, and quality metrics for each step. Humphrey provides more information on determining proper measures for size and quality for the development process, but the principles described are easily translated into test and requirements analysis processes.[1] With a pattern for a process step, the modeler can build complex sequential processes.

Detailed Quality Model

The simple two-step process produces reasonable accuracy for estimating size. However, many engineers object to the fact that all defects are considered equal in the two-step model. As stated earlier, more detail in a process typically reduces variance, and the range for defect fix times is significantly different depending on the type of test activity used to find the defect. Therefore, breaking the fix process into the component pieces allows for more refined probability density functions. Additionally, the process must have enough detail to determine activities that prevent defects from slipping to the test process.

Assume the development process consists of the process phases shown in Table 9-3. The process is fairly typical of traditional development organizations and is a simplified version of the process used in Chapter 2. You can think of each phase as an instantiation of the simple process in Figure 9-12, that is, each phase inputs data, processes the input, and produces an output.

As shown in Table 9-3, each step takes as input the size of the output from the prior phase and the expected defects in the product. Each step then produces a new size, effort, and quality estimate.

Table 9-3 Detailed Development Process

Phase	Inputs	Outputs
Design	Number of requirements	Number of design classes
		Number of design defects created
		Design effort
Code	Number of design classes	Number of lines of code
	Number of defects	Number of code defects
		Number of total defects
		Effort

---

1 W. S. Humphrey, *PSP: A Self-Improvement Process for Software Engineers* (Upper Saddle River, NJ: Addison-Wesley, 2005).

Table 9-3   Detailed Development Process

Phase	Inputs	Outputs
Compile	Lines of code Number of code defects	Lines of code Effort Number of total defects Code defects discovered
Unit Test	Lines of code Number of remaining defects	Lines of code Code defects discovered Design defects discovered Number of remaining defects Effort
Integration Test	Lines of code Number of defects	Lines of code Code defects discovered Design defects discovered Number of remaining defects Effort
System Test	Lines of code Number of defects	Lines of code Code defects discovered Design defects discovered Number of remaining defects Effort

There are many ways to build the model, with each providing a slightly different view. It does not matter how you begin creating additional detail. The easiest method from the perspective of initial data gathering is to expand the sequential process beginning with the inputting of the planned requirements and completing with released software, as shown in Figure 9-18. Each process step requires several pdfs to simulate the process. The model is drawn to highlight the fact that each step executes as a separate process.

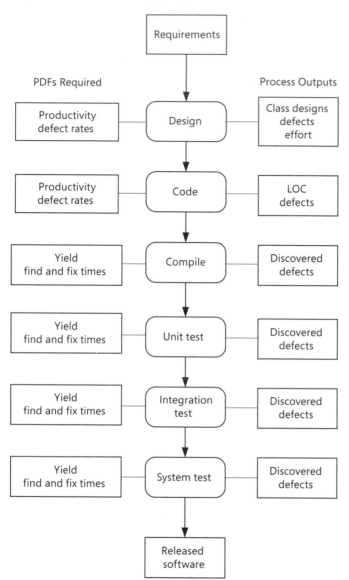

Figure 9-18   Sequential process model

The model solves the following system of equations:

1. *Classes = Requirements * Classes per Requirement*

2. *Design Defects = Classes * Defects per class*

3. *Design Effort = Class * Hours per class*

4. *Lines of code = Classes * LOC per Class*

5. *Code Defects = (Lines of Code/1000) * Defects per KLOC*

6. *Coding Effort = Lines of code/LOC per hour*

7. *Lines of code added in compile = Code Defects * Code churned per defect*

8. *Defects removed in compile = Code Defects * Compile Yield*

9. *Defects escaping to UnitTest = Design Defects + Code Defects − defects removed in compile*

10. *Compile Effort = Defects removed in compile * Defects per hour removed in compile*

11. *Lines of code added in unit test = Defects entering Unit Test * Code churned per defect*

12. *Defects escaping to Integration Test = Defects escaping to Unit Test − defects removed in Unit test*

13. *Unit test Effort = Defects removed in Unit test * Defects per hour removed in Unit Test*

14. *Lines of code added in Integration Test = Defects entering Integration Test * Code churned per defect*

15. *Defects removed in Integration Test = Defects escaping to Integration Test * Integration test Yield*

16. *Defects escaping to System Test = Defects escaping to Integration Test − Defects removed in Integration Test*

17. *Integration Test Effort = Defects removed in Integration Test * Defects per hour removed in Integration Test*

18. *Lines of code added in System Test = Defects removed in System Test * Code churned per defect*

19. *Defects removed in System test = Defects escaping to System Test * Compile Yield*

20. *Defects escaping to the customer = Defects escaping to System Test − defects removed in System Test*

21. *System Test Effort = Defects removed in System Test * Defects per hour removed in System Test*

22. *Total effort = Design Effort + Code Effort + Compile Effort + Unit Test Effort + Integration Test Effort + System Test Effort*

23. *Total Defects Remove = Design Defects + Code Defects − defects escaping to the customer*

24. *Total product size = Lines of code + lines of code added in compile + lines of code added in unit test + lines of code added in integration test + lines of code added in system test*

The PDFs required for the process are as follows:

1. Classes per requirement

2. Lines of code per class

3. Hours per class

4. Hours per thousand lines of code

5. Defects per hour removed in compile

6. Design defects per class

7. Code defects per KLOC

8. Yield in compile

9. Yield in unit test

10. Yield in integration

11. Yield in system testing

12. Defects per KLOC

13. Hours per defect removed in unit test

14. Hours per defect removed in integration test

15. Hours per defect removed in system test

16. Total LOC per hour

All of the data items can be measured directly in a typical development organization and do not require that an entire development cycle be completed to get a representative pdf. Because project cycles are iterative, early estimates are easily verified after a small sample of the total classes are designed, coded, and tested. Also notice that the cost of quality is directly determined in this model. Because the defects discovered in a phase of development are directly measured and because the effort to find and fix the defects is measured, the total cost per defect per phase is a derived measurement.

As shown in Figure 9-19, the mean productivity for this enhanced model is still approximately 10 LOC per hour for each requirement. If the various teams in this organization measure their average productivity, they would average about 10 LOC per hour, which is the value used earlier. However, the total project effort is estimated at about 37,700 hours plus or minus 2,350 hours, as shown in Figure 9-20. The average total project productivity is closer to the median value rather than the mean value. The effort range is about the same as the previous model using only the size, but the total effort is greater by almost 3,000 hours. In fact, the effort falls outside the prediction interval of the simple model.

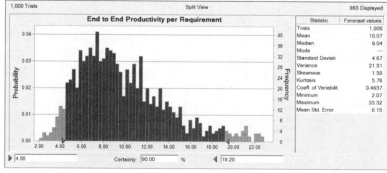

Figure 9-19   Project productivity predication for detailed software process

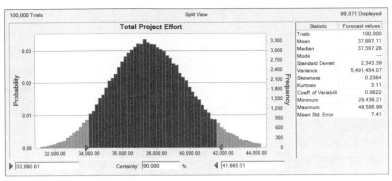

Figure 9-20   Estimated project effort for detailed process and 100 requirements

A detailed examination of the data indicates that the higher effort is a result almost entirely of the high variance of activities in the testing phases of the project, specifically the system testing process. The tail on the effort required for test is very long, indicating a significant chance that system test will require much more than average effort. In a project of this scope, it is virtually certain that several of the requirements will end up performing on the elongated tail, thereby causing the project to slip by about 15 percent over the simple model. In fact, each of the defect removal phases has the possibility of an extended duration, that is, the effort appears to have a log-normal distribution. System test has the longest duration and therefore appears to be the cause for schedule slips. However, each of the test phases contributes to the slip, but problems seen in integration test are masked by the problems seen in system test hiding the problem in the other test phases.

These results correspond well with the subjective data. Many projects are held up by one or two features that seem to take forever to complete. This model suggests that less than 5 percent of the code will be cause for continual rework and never-ending bug reports. In fact, industry studies from IBM confirm such a finding. Humphrey reports an internal IBM study that showed half of the total customer-reported defects occur in just 4 percent of the code.[1] It turns out that the model predicts that more than half of the defects remaining in the product are in about 5 percent of the code, thus proving the old adage: the only way to get a quality product out of the test process is to have one going in.

The model also predicts a defect density of between 6.4 and 7.4 defects per KLOC (see Figure 9-24). According to Davis and Mullaney,[2] typical release quality for software is 7.5 defects per KLOC for CMM level 1 companies and 6.24 for CMM level 2 companies.[3] Since most companies are at levels 1 and 2, the range of 6.4 to 7.4 defects per KLOC predicted by the model agrees with industry studies.

---

1 W. S. Humphrey, *PSP: A Self-Improvement Process for Software Engineers* (Upper Saddle River, NJ: Addison-Wesley, 2005).

2 N. Davis and J. Mullaney, *The Team Software Process in Practice: A Summary of Recent Results* (Pittsburgh, PA: Software Engineering Institute, Carnegie-Mellon University, 2003).

3 See Chapter 2 for a description of the CMM process framework.

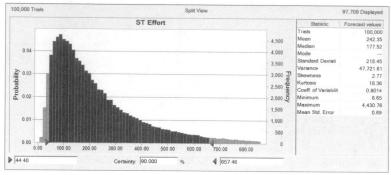

Figure 9-21   System test effort for detailed process

This data is enough to build a fairly comprehensive model, but note that improvement is still possible. For example, design and code defects can each have their own pdf for discovery and for churning the code. Effort for design defects is likely to be different from effort for code defects. Additionally, the compiler will be highly effective at finding code defects but relatively poor at finding design defects. After a working model implements the basic pattern for a phase, changes are easier done than said.

Some data can be used to cross-check the model. Previous models determine the total defect density in the product. The new model should produce results similar to the previous models. If it does not, it may indicate an error in the model, or it may indicate a worst-case outcome never actually experienced. With models that evolve over time, the modeler can more thoroughly explain the development process, as is the case in the differences noted in the effort estimate in the preceding examples.

Although additional detail in the sequential model is possible, more detail is not necessary for purposes of this example. There is enough richness in the combinations of data already described to determine the effects of proposed prevention activities. As will be shown in the next example, the model just developed provides useful information on the interactions of defect creation and discovery activities.

Process Improvement Model

An organization gathering the type of data necessary for the baseline models just developed is capable of examining the effects of a variety of proposed improvement activities. This example shows how to add a new process to an existing model and examine the effects. To simplify the example somewhat, the process is limited to the design, code, compile, and unit test phases. For the most part, this eliminates the need to model more than one organization. Although the method for integrating product components and then system testing the entire product may differ significantly across the industry, organizations often have a single individual design, code, compile, and unit test his or her own work. The example defect prevention activity simulates the effects of formalized inspections on the development process.

Assume that an organization is using a process as described earlier. The sequential process of Figure 9-18 works well in predicting the product size, total cost,[1] and quality of the final product. However, the organization desires quicker time to market, reduced costs, and improved quality, as do most organizations. Faster, better, cheaper is the desired outcome of all process improvement activities.

From the data, the organization determines that defects found earlier in the process cost less than those found during system test. Additionally, the effort expended in system test is the highest for any of the process phases. In fact, the cost for test is roughly equal to the combined costs of the other phases. Thus, system test is a bottleneck resource for the process. Eli Goldratt and Jeff Cox write that one way to reduce pressure on a bottleneck resource is to inspect all of the work product before it enters the bottleneck.[2] However, formal code inspections require effort. It is desirable to understand the effect a process change will have on schedule, cost, and quality before undertaking an expensive training program.

Because the target of this effort is to reduce the defects escaping the engineers' office, the new phase called Code Inspection can be placed in one of three locations, as shown in Figure 9-22. The inspection can take place after the code is written, after it is compiled, or after it is unit tested.

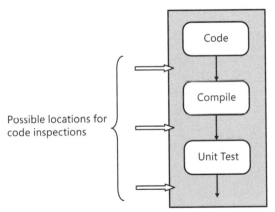

Figure 9-22   Development process with possible code inspection points

To determine the optimal point in the inspection process, it is necessary to model the process. Using the input-processing-output pattern developed earlier, the process requires an input size and the estimated defects discoverable by inspection. The output is the effort required and an estimate of the defects found (or those escaped). The equations to be solved are as follows:

*Inspection effort = LOC inspected * effort per KLOC*

---

1   *Cost* is simply the total effort in hours times the loaded engineering rate per hour, in this case, $90 per hour.

2   E. Goldratt and J. Cox, *The Goal: A Process of Ongoing Improvement* (Great Barrington, MA: North River Press, 1992).

*Defects escaped = Defects entering inspection * Yield*

Defects found = Defects at start of inspection − Defects escaped

*Correction effort = Defects Found * Effort per defect*

Notice that the equation for defects escaped uses a probability density function from either the coding, compiling, or unit test phase. This will likely affect the pdf for possible yield. Also notice that the effort to inspect is calculated from the size of the lines of code. It could also use a defect per hour rate similar to the other defect discovery phases, but product size is easier to measure and gives a more accurate relationship in extreme situations.[1] For example, if the code has no defects in it, the defect per hour model gives an incorrect time of 0. Because it requires almost as much effort to inspect high-quality product as low-quality product, LOC is a better predictor of effort. A better model is one that separates the effort to find the defects from the effort to fix them.[2] Then the effort to inspect is proportional to both lines of code and quality of the code. For code of reasonable quality, the differences will not be significant for purposes of this example.

To determine the correct placement in the process, three different models must be created with the new simulated process phase, and the effects on the remaining processes must be calculated. For simplicity, only the net effects are described, that is, the total project cost and the total defects escaping the process. It is unlikely that the inspection process will have a noticeable impact on the code size because the product is assumed to be already coded. The effort to review the code assumes three or four reviewers for every portion of code and that the review rate will vary from 100 LOC per hour to as high as 300 LOC per hour. The yields range from 25 percent to as high as 55 percent. Of course, in a real development process, there is an impact of learning and continuous improvement in the inspection process, so the yield starts out low and gradually increases.

Figures 9-23 and 9-24 show the charts with no inspection process. Figures 9-25 and 9-26 show the inspection before compile charts, Figures 9-27 and 9-28 show the inspection just after compile, and Figures 9-29 and 9-30 show the results for the inspection after unit test. From the charts, expected improvement in cost and quality can be determined.

---

1 Assuming that effort per KLOC is controlled during the inspection process, which it should be, given the assumption of a formal code inspection method.

2 You may argue that the test phase should also separate the find and fix times. In fact, a complete model would do just that in addition to separating out defect types and possibly defect report sources.

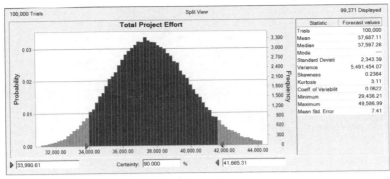

Figure 9-23   Total effort with no inspection process

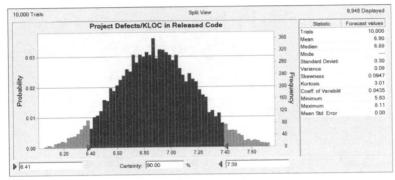

Figure 9-24   Defect density with no inspection process

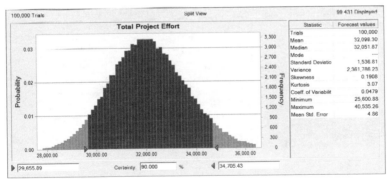

Figure 9-25   Total effort when inspection occurs before compile

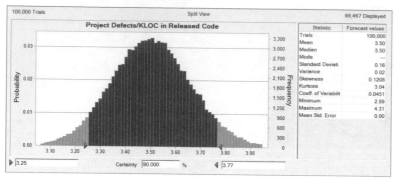

Figure 9-26   Predicted released defect density when inspection occurs before compile

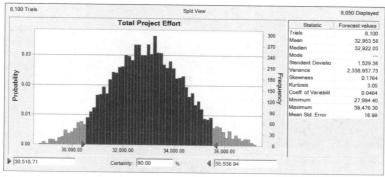

Figure 9-27   Project effort when inspection is after compile

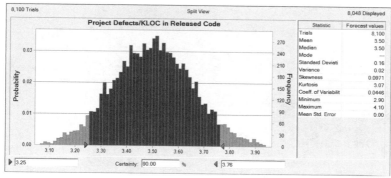

Figure 9-28   Predicted defect density when inspection is after compile

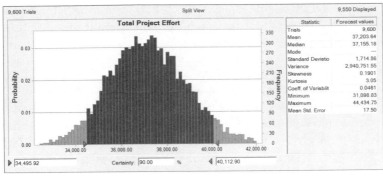

Figure 9-29   Total effort when inspection is after unit test

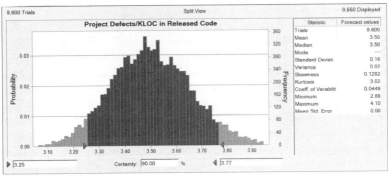

Figure 9-30   Defect density when inspection is after unit test

When the inspection is placed before compilation, the total effort drops to about 32,100 hours plus or minus 1,540 hours, with an average predicted release defect density of 3.2 defects per KLOC. Although the productivity has improved, it has done so by an average increase of less than 10 percent. The marked improvement in cost is caused almost entirely by eliminating the wide variances associated with system test. Without inspections, a few of the simulated requirements spent seven times longer in test than they did in development. The new process step reduces the excessively long tail on the output distribution and cuts the variance by more than a factor of 3.

When the inspection process occurs after compile, the quality is not significantly affected, but the cost is. The total project cost increases to 32,900 hours, with a defect density of 3.5 defects per KLOC. There is actually a slight drop in inspection yield because the compiler is finding bugs that were found previously during inspection, but the combined phase yields are approximately the same. Notice that this results in a counterintuitive decrease in productivity. The reason for the drop is that the cost for inspection is about the same in either case because it is the number of lines of code that determines the cost. In compile, it is the number of defects that drives cost. A cleaner product submitted into the compile phase reduces the cost of compile without changing the cost to fix the defects.

Finally, when the inspection is done after unit test, the cost is slightly less than it is without inspections, although not significantly different. The reason is that much of the benefit to the project effort is lost. The compile and unit test phases have already found many of the defects. However, as was already mentioned, it is the size of the code that determines cost, not the quality. In this scenario, the project incurs all of the cost with only a fraction of the benefit. However, the quality is affected in a manner similar to the other two inspection process models.

Unfortunately, the defect density is not usually measured in the development process, which may lead the development team to the mistaken conclusion that inspections negatively affect project cost. Additionally, the cost variance increases, which may lead to the belief that inspections are actually counterproductive. One positive benefit of inspections regardless of the placement is the reduction in variability in system test. A team experiencing exceptionally poor quality will likely benefit no matter when inspections are done. Finally, the difference in defect density is very large for no cost penalty, proving Phil Crosby's point that "quality is free."[1]

The conclusion for this process improvement effort would be that to minimize cost the inspections must be done before the compile phase. However, quality is increased regardless of the process phase. This likely seems odd to most developers because the logic is that the compiler removes defects faster than an inspection does. However, the effort of the inspection process is mostly affected by the size of the work product, not by the defect density. The compiler, however, is gated by the quality of the product. Therefore, from a cost perspective, the minimal cost occurs when the highest-quality product is compiled and then tested. This agrees with the conclusions Eli Goldratt reaches in *The Goal*.[2] Goldratt's advice is to optimize product flow by having only the highest-quality product possible submitted to the bottleneck resources.

---

1   P. Crosby, *Quality Is Free* (New York: McGraw-Hill, 1979).

2   E. Goldratt and J. Cox, *The Goal: A Process of Ongoing Improvement* (Great Barrington, MA: North River Press, 1992).

The conclusion on the optimal placement for the inspection process also agrees with the one reached by Steve McConnell, who presents an elegant argument for reviewing the code mentally before compiling it.[1] McConnell's argument is that the rush to get the code to work may cause errors and that inspection before compilation is one sign of a professional programmer. Another sign of professionalism, according to McConnell, is the move from superstition to understanding. The improvement model presented here eliminates gut feeling and replaces it with data and process understanding.

Development Throughput Model

Needless to say, the example models presented thus far are much simpler than the actual process of software development. The most glaring omission is the fact that teams produce products and rarely is the process as neatly contained as the models suggest. A team may begin work on one requirement, and then move to a second requirement for a period of time, and then return to the first requirement, and so on. A large team moves from area to area at various levels of abstraction, producing partial products rather than a sequence of complete requirements. Leaping from area to area may continue for the majority of the product development and is necessary to provide testable units for the integration and system test processes. Some code is under development while other code is being tested.

The iterative and chaotic nature of development is well known by most practitioners. As a result, a realistic process contains feedback loops. For example, one team may be testing a portion of the project, finding defects in the code that require another team to stop code development to fix the existing product. This section examines a model that acknowledges such feedback processes.

Model Overview

For simplicity's sake, the model in Figure 9-31 examines the interactions between the development and test processes without considering feature changes. The assumption is that a separate team exists to system test the software to highlight the interactions between groups. This assumption can be eliminated by simply splitting time among all four processes rather than just the two.

---

1   S. McConnell, *Code Complete: A Practical Handbook of Software Construction* (Redmond, WA: Microsoft Press, 1993).

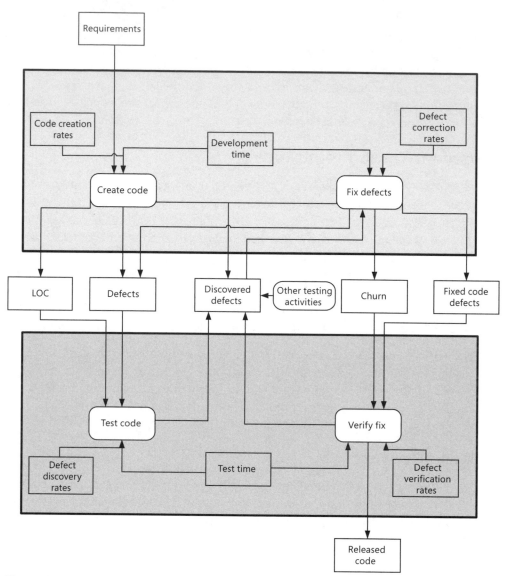

Figure 9-31   Model of separate development and testing efforts

To examine the flow of information, assume that a set of known product requirements is available from which to begin development. This is shown as the input to the development cycle in the *Requirements* data store. After the handoff of a requirement to the development process, the *Create Code* process begins. The creation of the code is modeled using the process previously outlined with class size and LOC per class.

Developers create at a rate as determined by the *Code Creation Rates* using available *Development Time*. Notice that developers must split their time between the *Create Code* and *Fix Defects* processes. This is the first change from the simple model outlined earlier. Effort is split among two processes rather than dedicated to a single task, thereby creating a dependency between requirements, that is, requirement 2 is under development while requirement 1 is being fixed. It is now likely that a developer may simultaneously be creating a new class while fixing a defect in an existing one.

The output of the coding process is lines of code (*LOC*) and *Defects*. During the creation of code, the developer may find defects in the existing product, and this information is stored in the *Discovered Defects* database, creating yet another dependency between product features. *Discovered Defects* form the input to the *Fix Defects* process.

After the creation of enough code, the testers can also begin to discover defects, and the active defect count begins to rise. Discovering defects through test occurs at the rate defined by *Defect Discovery Rates* and requires *Test Time*. The reason that developers must split their time between the *Create Code* process and the *Fix Defects* process is to reduce the active defect count stored in the *Discovered Defect* data store. If the defect count grows without an upper bound, a reasonably sized product would not even compile. Often, teams implement some form of a maximum defect count whose purpose it is to guarantee that the product will be of sufficient quality to compile and allow the test team to work in parallel with the development team.

The *Fix Defects* process requires *Development Time*, taking away from the ability to *Create Code*. A change to the new code created in the *Create Code* process causes *Churn* and results in *Fixed Code Defects*. These fixes require testers to take time away from testing to *Verify Fixes* at a rate defined by *Defect Verification Rates*. Once verified, the code is available for release and integration back into future requirements. Notice that there is another process called *Other Testing Activities*, which models defects discovered by sources outside the development cycle, such as through customer reports.

With this model, you can simulate multiple activities per engineer. The dynamic nature of development is contained in the simultaneous nature of the four main activities of creating code, discovering defects, fixing defects, and verifying the fixes. Each of the four main processes could be further broken down using methods described previously. However, even at this level, the dynamic nature of the model adds significantly to the previous model. It also requires considerably more code than do the sequential models described earlier.

Model Analysis

Running the model provides interesting insights into the delicate balance of a large development team. Begin by assuming that enough feature requirements exist to occupy completely all of the available *Development Time*. For the most part, this is a valid assumption because product planning and marketing are working in parallel. Further, assume that the development team must operate under a maximum defect count, or bug cap. That is, at some point the developers must stop creating new code or, more flippantly, must stop creating new defects after the product reaches a certain predefined discovered defect density. Again, this is probably a valid assumption to have a product capable of at least some useful work. The development team begins the process by creating code and the associated defects. After enough code is created to have a testable unit, the test team begins finding defects, and at some point, discovered defects reach the bug cap, which probably occurs long before running out of features for a product of any substantial size.

After developers reach bug cap, they must stop creating new code and fix existing code. With no new code coming into the test process, the defect discovery rate begins to decrease, and the only source of new defects is the *Verify Fix* process. Because this rate is very much less than the initial creation rate, the developers eventually reduce the backlog of defects and start to code new features. After this happens, testers have a new source of defects and once again reach bug cap, causing the cycle to repeat.

In a typical organization, the rate of code creation balances the rate of defect discovery based on the size of the various teams, the effort expended on each process, the efficiency of the test process, and the quality of the code. Now imagine that the test team increases its efficiency independent of the development team, that is, the development team production rates remain constant while bug discovery rates increase. Developers reach bug cap sooner, which requires them to stop coding as many features and thereby reduces the source of defects as before.

Reducing the number of features reduces the source of defects, meaning test will report fewer new defects, so developers can go back to coding requirements. Increasing the efficiency of test pulls developers away from coding new features sooner, thus reducing the available defect count, which reduces the total defects found by test.

If you assume that most, if not all, of the features must be coded before release, the total throughput of the system remains nearly constant. Individual components are released sooner, but the entire product throughput remains mostly unchanged. This is an example of a principle espoused by Peter Senge, namely, that the harder one pushes on a system, the harder the system pushes back.[1]

This development process is capable of a known throughput constrained almost entirely by the total defects contained in the *Defects* data store. A change in any of the processes that use *Defects* without consideration of the other processes causes a variation in the system that eventually stabilizes at the prechange rates. Of course, this assumes that each process is stable to begin with.

From this model, and the previous detailed development model, the optimal process improvement is to implement code inspections but use effort that would have gone into testing the product. If two different teams exist, use the testers rather than developers to inspect the code.

---

1   P. Senge, *The Fifth Discipline: The Art and Practice of the Learning Organization* (New York: Currency Doubleday, 1990).

Although it may not be possible to have 100 percent of the inspection effort come from the test team, at least 50 percent and closer to 70 percent or 80 percent is possible. The inspection model assumes 3 to 4 people inspect the code, so 2 or 3 of those can be members of the test team. Of course, this assumes that the test team is composed of software engineers. If not, more extensive training is required to implement this process change. However, the net effect of such a change is a fundamental change in the relationship between quality and effort, which changes the system throughput. Only such a fundamental change keeps the system from stabilizing at or near prechange throughput levels.

This model was created to explicitly explore the system impact when a separate test group exists. The two different forms of the model, namely, the sequential nature of the detailed quality model versus the parallel nature of the development throughput model, provide differing views into many organizational forms. As was said earlier, Microsoft uses separate development and test teams. Many organizations use a single team, with members splitting their time across functions. The models created apply to both types of organizations. The difference lies only in how the pdfs are applied. For example, at a company like Microsoft, separate effort pdfs exist for development and test functions, whereas an organization with a single engineering function would have a single pdf split across code creation and defect detection activities. The model does not attempt to differentiate across organizational forms, but it would be a logical progression for the modeler.

Relationship to the CMM Framework

The CMM has a level 4 capability known as Quantitative Process Management. The CMMI has a KPA also, known as Quantitative Project Management, but with more detail about the expected use of statistics to manage the process. The purpose of these practices is self-explanatory, that is, to use quantitative methods for managing the processes used by the team. The practice in the CMMI uses terms such as statistically managed and special causes, which seems to imply statistical process control (SPC), as defined by Shewhart and as described extensively by Deming.[1] SPC is used for prediction and has no signs of special cause variations. Such a process is said to be in statistical control.

Using SPC requires processes that are well controlled. Unfortunately, in software engineering the sources of special cause variance are numerous, so much so that SPC may not be possible. Deming cautions about the use of control charts for processes that are not in control. Management decisions made about such processes are likely hit or miss. The inability to use SPC reliably often leads to the creation of target values with little relationship to process capabilities. A desired target value with some equally arbitrary range, based on a percentage of the target, is used to create a pseudo process control chart. The target and range are then used to evaluate process changes. Unfortunately, this often results in the chart changing based on a single data

---

1 W. Edwards Deming (1982). *Out of the Crisis* (Cambridge, MA: MIT Center for Advanced Educational Services.)

point. A process change may be thought to cause variations in the data when, in fact, the discrepancy was simple process variance. Stringent adherence to valid statistical methods is required if the desired result is a good decision. Using ad-hoc statistics results in poor-quality management decisions.

Humphrey describes how the use of process is most appropriate at the individual level, and how many elements of data cannot be compared among engineers. Additionally, processes, such as the PSP described in Chapter 12, require that the individual take ownership of his or her process. If that is the case, each individual will have a different process. Unless a team remains together for an extended duration, the individual processes will change as team members change. Thus, the individual processes that constitute the team's control charts will no longer be valid. SPC, at a team level, will be ineffective under such circumstances and may actually be counterproductive, leading to incorrect decisions.

If the variance between individuals is significant, SPC is not a valid technique for CMM and CMMI level 4 capabilities. The control chart will have too large a range to provide any useful information. Fortunately, stochastic models are another means of statistically managing the process. As shown in Figure 9-20, the expected effort, and therefore the cost for the product, was estimated with a confidence interval. If the process is broken down by phases, and each is estimated with such an interval, the sub-processes are statistically managed. Additionally, the breakdown can be by product or by engineer, providing additional insight into the process. A stochastic model will provide more information and will not be susceptible to the problems associated with control charts. Schedule, quality, and cost can all be predicted and controlled using the information provided by the model.

Another aspect of statistical management is determining the process improvement efforts in which the organization will invest. As with the inspection example, it is quite easy to model estimates of the effects of a change and simulate the results. Management can then determine which process change will meet organizational needs on a project-by-project basis. In fact, it is unlikely that traditional SPC will provide the same wealth of information as modeling because it does not provide the ability to model the system as a whole. It is unable to explain the complex dependencies between the development of the code and its testing.

Conclusion

Modeling the product quality and the process attributes provides a powerful means to estimate the effects of defect prevention activities. Simple models provide information useful in project management and in predicting the largest return on investment for process improvement. Additionally, simple models can provide valuable insight into development, but you must not forget the effect of the entire system.

Sequential models do not contain the richness necessary to evaluate system effects associated with process change. Defect prevention activities may appear ineffective unless the dynamic aspects of change are considered. Improving one practice often has unanticipated side effects. Therefore, a skilled modeler uses a combination of simulation tools and a detailed understanding of the process dynamics to determine the optimal defect prevention activity.

Although it is no trouble to create powerful simulations quickly and easily to determine predicted outcomes, using the information developed by the model is much more difficult. The hardest part of modeling is getting others in the organization to use the information. Those familiar with Greek mythology may remember the story of Cassandra, who was given the gift of prescience and subsequently cursed with disbelief by all those who heard the predictions. In many ways, those who use stochastic modeling have the same gift and associated curse. Knowing the future requires the courage to change it. As Scrooge remarks, "Ghost of the Future! I fear you more than any spectre I have seen."

Chapter 10
Defect Taxonomies

A defect taxonomy provides a low-overhead means to learn about the kinds of errors being made in the product development process so that they can be analyzed to improve the process to reduce or eliminate the likelihood of the same kind of error being made in the future (in the current version of the product under development as well as in future versions of the product and other products). A defect taxonomy is a method of gathering indications of problem areas.

The general goal of a defect taxonomy is to reduce the number of product defects that reach customers. Although this goal could be accomplished by implementing excessively long beta and internal testing using certain sets of customers as "permanent" beta sites, this kind of solution wouldn't necessarily do anything to improve the quality of code produced—it would simply detect and correct more defects before they reach the customer. Little learning may occur in correcting defects in isolation and may not improve quality during development or for future products. The learning that occurs resides in the minds of the developers, and as teams become larger it becomes more difficult to share the accumulated learning.

Prevention of defects is intimately tied to the product cycle and the development processes used. Defect prevention either moves detection of defects closer to their introduction in the product cycle or reduces their introduction through prevention or immediate detection. The construction of a defect taxonomy is based on the processes used in development and human error models, so we begin this chapter with the background before discussing defect taxonomies.

Learning from Defects in Large Software Projects

After a software project grows beyond the scope of a few people, learning from defects becomes more difficult. Not everyone knows everything about the code. Not everyone knows about or fixes every bug. Distribution of effort in the development process can weaken shared knowledge. So how do you recover accumulated learning about defects when defect correction is distributed?

Root cause analysis (RCA) is one method the product team can use to learn from defects (see Chapter 11, "Root Cause Analysis"), but it can be a time-consuming process involving interviews with the developers who fix the defects. In large projects, typically there are a large number of defects—studies have shown that the number of defects is related to number of lines of code, so a large number of defects should not be surprising. With a large number of defects, it is untenable to perform an RCA study on every bug. There must be either a lower-overhead method of getting the results of an RCA study or a means to focus RCA efforts on a subset of defects that may have the greatest payoff. The prevention tab, discussed in Chapter 14, is a lower-overhead technique to gather some salient root cause information.

However, to learn from every defect on a large scale, the effort of classifying the defect needs to be distributed to the developers who correct the defects. IBM developed a technique called Orthogonal Defect Classification (ODC), as described in the sidebar titled "Orthogonal Defect Classification," which follows. ODC uses a statistical method to learn from the type of defects that occur. When they correct a defect, it takes very little effort for developers to fill out the classification forms, and the classification produces useful, albeit limited, global information. In some cases, it can directly indicate a root cause, but more often it identifies subsets of defects that could profit from more in-depth analysis such as RCA.

A defect taxonomy extends the idea of statistical classification of defects to one that provides classification *and* actionable global information. A defect taxonomy uses more categories to describe a defect than ODC does. In so doing, a taxonomy can indicate a much broader set of hot spots and even the kind of correction needed. It does require more effort to fill out than ODC but vastly less than an RCA study.

A taxonomy can be used by developers during the development process to discover problem areas that could profit from deeper analysis, such as RCA studies. The highlighting of problem areas allows more expensive techniques such as RCA to be focused because such techniques can't be applied to each defect on a large scale. Some indications from a defect taxonomy directly imply the cause of the defect without resorting to an RCA study. A taxonomy can also help determine means to detect, reduce, or eliminate causes of defects.

In small development teams, there is typically ad hoc learning about defects, but in large products often too many people are involved and too many defects are detected for such learning to occur. The key aspects of defect taxonomies are that they concern learning from defects rather than just correcting defects and they scale for large projects where the numbers are overwhelming.

Orthogonal Defect Classification

ODC was developed at IBM[1] by Ram Chillarege and is used to flag problem areas and the state of code not matching the schedule. In ODC, you collect a few categories of information about defects. It is a low-overhead method that provides immediate (no extensive root cause analysis) indication of problem areas.

ODC taxonomies have three requirements. An ODC taxonomy should be

- Orthogonal so that choices are clear and categories don't overlap.

1   IBM Research, *www.research.ibm.com/softeng/ODC/ODC.HTM*; Chillarege, *www.chillarege.com/odc/odcbackground.html*.

- Consistent across phases in the product cycle because defects are often detected well after they are introduced.

- Uniform across products (and versions) so that resulting analysis can improve future products and revisions.

A main attribute used in ODC is the defect type, which can be Function, Interface, Checking, Assignment, Timing/Serialization, Build/Package, Documentation, Algorithm, or Design. Many of these attributes purposefully reflect the phase in the product cycle that produced them. The defect type category should span (include all possibilities) and relate to product life cycle phases.

Classified defects can sometimes directly indicate a root cause without requiring a deeper analysis. For example, function defects found late in the development cycle directly indicate that there was a problem in the design phase—the design had functional holes. Additionally, information on the distribution of defect types and trends indicating which defect type occurs most often in specific product phases highlights problem areas.

Specifying the Goals of a Defect Taxonomy

It's important to define the goals of a defect prevention project more clearly so that a taxonomy can be created to highlight defect areas. The more specific goals are as follows:

- Detect defects earlier in the cycle.

- Reduce the introduction of defects.

- Prevent the introduction of defects. (It is better to make something impossible rather than merely unlikely.)

- Improve efficiency as an indirect goal. (If developers are more efficient, they have more time to fix defects and perhaps think more about root causes or other causes of defects. If testers are more efficient, they can write more complete tests and reusable test code.)

Everyone has ideas about how to accomplish these goals. The problem is that the union of these ideas is huge and the payback for a particular idea is not necessarily clear. A defect taxonomy provides frequency information so that the product team can judge the payback on implementing an idea. It may also, through lack of hits, indicate areas where the team is doing well or perhaps where one group or component is doing better in a class of defect than others are. This can drive discovery of best practices.

A defect taxonomy makes no assumption about what needs to be changed to improve quality. It simply provides metrics so that you can discover areas that need attention and further analysis, which can then suggest changes.

Understanding the Organizing Principles of Defect Taxonomies

A defect taxonomy is constructed using a few organizing principles that lead to the taxonomy's major categories and subcategories:

- Describe the entire product life cycle from scenarios to maintenance.

- Avoid repetition of the same item in different categories or subcategories when possible.

- Make items in a category clearly different (orthogonal) to avoid confusion.

- Describe the defect correction process, including items for detecting/reducing/ preventing future occurrences.

- Work backward from the kinds of changes that may be made to items that indicate need for those types of changes.

These principles shouldn't be controversial. Often, software development concentrates on testing and correcting customer-reported defects. Many times, missing scenarios, missing functionality, design defects, build problems, and other issues aren't recorded. A typical defect-handling process is mostly ad hoc; that is, information about why a defect wasn't caught by testing, what contributed to the defect, how the defect could be detected, or how the defect could be reduced or prevented is not provided except perhaps in the text field of some defect correction reports. A defect taxonomy gathers this information in a data-minable form.

Clarifying the Assumptions Made in a Defect Taxonomy

We can change only things we can control, so it makes little sense to detect issues we can't affect. For example, it makes little sense to determine whether there is a relationship between defects and the weather. A defect taxonomy is designed to cast a wide net and see what it catches. The nature of the net determines the areas the taxonomy can highlight, so it is important to use a wide net to catch not only what you think may be issues but the rest of the spectrum as well.

A taxonomy is colored by the assumptions made in creating it. Assumptions made in a taxonomy affect the data gathered and the conclusions that can be reached. You can use a few techniques to limit the effect of these assumptions in coloring the results:

- Include the entire range in classifications to avoid focusing on a particular subsection and missing the rest.

- Use different viewpoints on the process.

- Collect low-level and high-level information.

- Use viewpoints that reflect well-accepted methodologies of error analysis (ODC, Reason's cognitive error modeling, and others).

In this chapter, we can most easily show you how to apply these techniques in the example defect taxonomy we create later. But first, we discuss several assumptions commonly made in defect taxonomy creation.

To make sure your net actually is wide, you can describe the assumptions (hypotheses of possible failures) you are making in determining the attributes you choose for your taxonomy. For example, you may suspect from experience that certain types of errors are being made, and adding attributes to identify them can provide validation of your hypothesis from actual defect data. This validation can provide concrete justification for the effort involved in developing a new tool or changing a process. However, you need to make the attributes you choose provide for a wide variety of answers beyond the answer you are looking for.

For example, if you suspect that you will have significant design defects in the latter part of product development, you may add attributes describing the scope of a code change. The attributes describe more than if the change is a design change; they describe the whole range of corrections from a single line to a scenario change. (See correction phase in the example taxonomy that follows.) Given this data for defects, you will be able to see if a significant number of late-term design defects occur. If you didn't include these attributes, you wouldn't be able to tell. Significant numbers of these types of defects can justify spending more time in the design phase and more rigorous verification. You can also verify the results of such changes by seeing a subsequent reduction in the occurrence of late-term design errors.

The following assumptions are made in constructing the example defect taxonomy later in this chapter. The assumptions are typical for a development process, but your taxonomy may or may not include them. They show examples of how to map a concern about a type of failure to attributes in a defect taxonomy.

Assumption: We Can Make Only Certain Kinds of Changes

The taxonomy should reflect the kinds of change that are possible, and it should not focus on only a narrow set of possible changes. Here's a sampling of possible changes that can be made:

- **People**   Change the processes of hiring, staffing, or training
- **Culture**   Change the team's mindset, what we reward or discourage
- **Process**   Change the stages of production
- **Guidelines and procedures**   Use tools for detection, reduction, and prevention
- **Automation of manual steps**   Correct error-prone or unreliable procedures/processes
- **Communication of best practices**   Improve organization and access to systemic knowledge (domain, guidelines, procedures)

Assumption: People Will Make Errors

One very important thing to realize is that you can't change human nature (cognitive nature of human error): people will make mistakes of various kinds.

The tendency to find the immediate cause of a bug and to blame it on human error because some rule wasn't followed does not scale to large or complex applications. Of the hundreds (conservatively speaking) of rules and arcane pieces of information involved in a project or process, which ones are the most important? Ask 10 people and you'll get 10 different answers. Defining the most important rules and procedures is a problem that checklists in the team software process (TSP) try to address, but the working set of rules tends to be too large to include in a checklist. Hindsight is 20-20, but reducing or preventing defects requires foresight.

You have to look beyond the immediate fault to determine how external factors contribute to failure. Automated verification tools are a prime example of addressing a human weakness—they efficiently detect a rule violation so that it can be corrected. Compiler warnings about uninitialized variables or dead code are a simple example. Gathering cognitive failure information and global knowledge access issues in the taxonomy can help you discover how common such problems are.

Assumption: Defects Are Discovered Late in the Cycle

Defects tend to be detected by testing or customers, and bug-tracking systems are organized around this assumption. The cost to correct a defect at introduction is far less than the cost of correcting it if it reaches the testing phase, much less reaches a customer or other teams with dependent code.

To determine performance in this dimension, gather data on the phase of the product cycle where a defect is detected, where the defect was introduced, and where it could have been detected earlier.

Assumption: Defects Escape Their Phase of Creation in the Product Cycle

Prevention is making a defect inexpressible or implementing a verification method that detects all instances of the defect in the same phase of the product cycle as the defect was introduced. Better error detection in compilers is an example of a prevention tool: the code can be written, but the defects are detected, and you can't proceed without resolving them.

Classes of defects that aren't detected become more expensive to fix, both in effort and in time (in terms of schedule), as the product life cycle moves forward. For example, a missing scenario detected in test may cause an area to be redesigned after weeks of work have gone into the flawed design, and this can disrupt the schedule as a result of dependencies and a false indication of design maturity.

Assumption: Testing May Be Unbalanced

With any sizable or complex application and the wide range of configurations possible, there is no way to test everything. Customer testing often becomes a significant part of testing and extends the release cycle.

Typically tests aren't classified by how you determine validity, so you may not be testing areas as thoroughly as you should. A large percentage of tests may be testing using valid values and to see if errors occur. In the realm of security, testing using invalid or extreme values (for example, a 20-megabyte [MB] path string) as well as error path testing is very important. You may not be able to test for some problems because you can't measure their presence. Common measures you can test for include heap validity and some cases of memory leakage.

Some defects have complex conditions that make them hard to reproduce, let alone discover using a written test. This can be because of the complex conditions or because previous actions create invisible damage[1] (damage not detectable by any test) that then indirectly causes a visible defect. Undiagnosed crashes are an example. The visible defect is so far removed from the original problem that determining the cause is difficult.

Assumption: You May Have Outgrown Your Tools and Processes

Often, tools are designed and processes are implemented when a product is small and less complex. As the product grows, improvements may have been made, but they may not be adequate to the increased size or complexity of the product.

As conditions change (particularly when they change radically), assumptions and designs should be revisited. Piling correction on top of correction eventually produces a system that is fragile and collapses under its own weight.

Assumption: You May Be Doing Late-Phase Design Correction

How much of your defect correction effort is spent correcting deficiencies in design? Conditions may change from when the design is created to when the product is released, particularly for legacy designs. Are usage scenarios being missed? When real usage is attempted, are dead ends reached as a result of missing functionality? If you design before the details of scenarios or interactions with other code are known, the design may create omissions.

Late-phase design changes are inherently dangerous because they indicate an oversight in the original formulation of the solution. It is natural to expect that you will know about the details of a scenario when you have written code to implement it and it has been tested. It is also natural to expect that you may know better how the product should have been designed at this

---

1   Invisible damage often takes the form of the typical hard-to-reproduce defect caused by some previous action that causes a change in persistent state that makes the failure possible.

point. (See Chapter 17, "Moving Quality Upstream.") The knowledge of the side effects of a design change may not be as well known later in the product cycle, and the people who did the initial design may no longer be accessible. Schedule pressures can result in needed design changes being avoided in favor of ad hoc corrections because of risk and time to correct.

Building the Example Defect Taxonomy

The defect taxonomy we use as an example in this chapter is organized around the five stages of a defect:

- **Occurrence stage**   What kind of failure occurred? Where was it discovered in the product cycle? How widespread is its effect?

- **Contributing cause(s) stage**   What human error or systemic knowledge problem contributed to the defect? In which phase was the defect introduced?

- **Change stage**   What was the type and extent of the change made to correct the defect? How widespread is the effect of the change? Where in the product cycle was the change made?

- **Detection stage**   Was the defect detected by an existing test? If so, why wasn't it caught then? If not, why wasn't there a test to catch it? What kind of test would catch it? Where in the product cycle should it be caught?

- **Mitigation stage**   How can this type of defect be reduced or eliminated in the future? In which phase in the product cycle would the change be made? What type of change would it be?

The product cycle for each of the stages is useful for describing the delay between discovery of a defect (occurrence stage) and when it was actually introduced (cause stage). The stage where the change was made that caused the defect is not necessarily the same as the stage in which corrective action is taken. Detection should move the discovery of the problem closer to the cause; for example, if a defect was detected by external testing, an automated test could be added to detect it in the tests run to verify a source change. The goal is to detect defects as soon as possible after their creation rather than allowing them to escape to later phases of development and testing.

The description of the phases of a defect taxonomy is quite long, so an outline of the complete example taxonomy follows to provide some context.

The complete example taxonomy

Occurrence stage
    Discovery product phase
    Defect area
    Defect type
        Reliability
        Performance
        Corruption
        Disclosure
        Functionality
        Documentation
        Localization
        Geopolitical/legal
    Attack surface area
    Damage extent

Contributing causes stage
    Cause product phase
    Human factors
        Selection
        Analysis
        Solutions
        Execution
    Systemic factors
        Rules (procedures and guidelines)
            Conditions
            Action
        Domain information
        Organization
    Quality

Change stage
    Correction phase
    Correction area
        Method code
            Change branch
            Change part
        Private class structure
        Nonprivate class structure

New classes/structures
Design change
Specification change
Process
Rule
Domain knowledge
Knowledge organization
Change type
Change extent

Detection stage
Detection product phase
Test result
Test process
Test type
Parameters
Measurement

Mitigation stage
Mitigation product phase
Extent
Type

The basic goals of a taxonomy are to prevent further instances of a particular class of defect from escaping (that is, make sure a test detects the problem) and to reduce or prevent future occurrences of that type of defect. Because mitigation may not be perfect, detection is used as the backstop. Also, if mitigation can't be implemented immediately, detection can prevent further instances of the error from reaching the customer, albeit at a higher cost (because defects are detected at a later phase). Detection is the backstop, but mitigation is the preferable solution.

For all stages of a defect, there is a corresponding phase in the product cycle. The product cycle phase indicates when the defect is detected, where in the cycle the contributing causes are located, where the immediate fix was made, and where detection and mitigation should occur. In a perfect world, defects are detected or prevented in the same product life cycle phase in which they are introduced. The more separated detection or prevention is from introduction, the higher the cost of correction.

Most of the phases of the product cycle, as shown in Figure 10-1, should be familiar. Testing is broken into the type of test (unit, feature, scenario, system). *Dependent use* occurs when another team is using code that has not reached the internal use level. *Internal use* is general use by nondevelopers, such as use of an internal beta version.

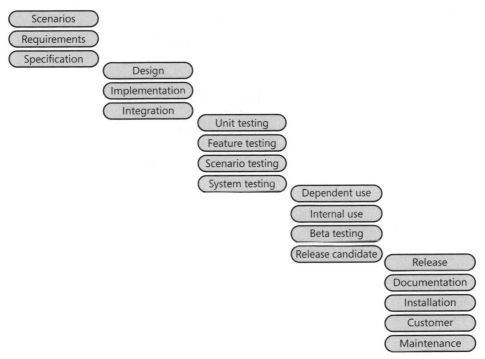

Figure 10-1   Phases of the product cycle

Occurrence Stage

The occurrence stage information describes the symptoms and extent of the defect. An occurrence is classified according to these categories:

- **Defect area**   How was the product being used when the defect occurred?

- **Defect type**   What does the defect affect?

- **Attack surface area**   What usage can cause the defect to occur?

- **Damage extent**   When the defect occurs, what functionality or class of users is affected?

You can no longer assume that a defect may be an obscure situation or application coding error. If the effect of the defect is visible outside the computer on which it occurred or if it can be caused by another computer (as happens in some types of malicious attacks), it is an exploitable security issue. You must assume malicious intent.

> **Note**   The following sections cover the four categories of occurrence stage information and use tables to provide much of this information. Note that details in a table are sometimes further described by subsequent tables.

Specifying the Defect Area

The defect area category describes how the product was being used when the defect occurred. Issues relating to construction of the product and its localization are included in this category, even though these phases take place before actual use of the product occurs.

Defect Area Information	
Construction	Synchronization and dependency issues during build (typically detected in integration or release phase)
Localization	An issue in localizing the system to a different language or locale
Installation	An issue during distribution or installation
Execution	An issue during startup or performance of an operation
Documentation	An issue in the description documents

Describing the Defect Type

The defect type category describes the effect of the defect. The top-level categories were chosen to be very distinct from each other, and as a result, security is not a top-level category but is reflected in aspects of all the categories. Only the disclosure category is purely security related.

Defect Type Information	
Reliability	An operation produces incorrect results or unexpected errors, hangs, or crashes.
Performance	An operation takes more than the expected time to complete.
Corruption	Individual data elements or data management has been damaged.
Disclosure	Information is disclosed to unauthorized parties, or deception can be used to gain information.
Functionality	An operation is complicated (includes extraneous steps/information) or not possible to perform (a critical element is missing).
Documentation	Missing or misleading content and technical inaccuracies inhibit users from using features or scenarios.
Localization	Gross errors in translation mislead the end user; translated text is not completely visible; keyboard functionality is broken such that native input is not possible; and so forth.
Geopolitical/Legal	An operation includes an issue that could create legal liability, damage the product image or hurt sales.

Reliability   *Reliability* indicates whether the operation completes successfully. Reliability issues can range from completion with incorrect results to no completion because of errors.

Reliability Detail	
Incorrect result	The operation completes without an indicated error, but the results are incorrect.
Ignored failure	A suboperation unexpectedly fails, but the operation succeeds anyway (often results in incomplete performance of operation).
Unexpected failure	The operation completes, indicating an error that should not have occurred. Often results in a crash (an unhandled exception).
Unexpected success	The operation should have failed but instead completes without an indicated error.
Incomplete	The operation does not complete because of a crash, hang, or error message, for instance.

An operation can be incomplete for a number of reasons, from crashes and error messages to just hanging.

Incomplete Subdetail	
Crash	Bugcheck* or unhandled exception, for instance.
Assert	Assert failed dialog box.
Shutdown/reboot	Shutdown or restart of application or system without any indication as to cause.
Hang	Operation loops waiting for a condition that is never satisfied (includes resource deadly embrace, lost connections, and asynchronous operations completing too fast) or is retrying a failed operation.
User intervention	A modal dialog box (typically an error message) is displayed to the user.

* A *bugcheck* is a serious error detected by Windows, also known as a "blue screen."

Performance   Performance issues indicate inadequate speed to accomplish an operation. They may be caused by resource starvation as a result of a resource leak, a calculation that does not scale to actual usage, a timing problem with independent operations, or a deliberate attack. Although adequate speed for the operation may also be considered slow, it is the best that current knowledge and technology can provide.

Performance Detail	
Memory leak	Degradation caused by memory pressure from not freeing unused data.
Resource leak	Degradation caused by exhaustion of a nonmemory resource.
Algorithm	A chosen means of calculation is too computationally expensive. Typically shows up as a scalability problem.
Inherent	The performance problem is fundamental (for example, bandwidth limitation, can't avoid scaling problem).

Performance Detail	
Excessive inputs	Inputs to the operation are of excessive size, causing resource exhaustion (typically memory). Some denial-of-service attacks use this method.
Synchronization	The operation has asynchronous parts and there is a problem with communication, resulting in excessive retries or timeouts.

Corruption   Corruption is unintended damage. A particular item or the system that organizes the items can be corrupted (for instance, unexpectedly setting a property of an object as opposed to corrupting the heap). Items may also be persistent (such as files on a disk) or not (such as run-time objects). Damage to unrelated objects (not self), other objects/organization, or persistent objects/organization can cause secondary or persistent failures.

Corruption Detail	
Self	Damage is only to the object the method immediately deals with.
Objects	Damage is to additional objects beyond self.
Object organization	Damage is to organization of objects (heap or stack damage, for instance).
Persistent	Damage is to persistent item(s) such as files, resources, or registry keys. Restarting application or system does not remove problem.
Persistent organization	Damage to the organization of persistent items, such as the file system or registry. Unrelated items may be damaged or inaccessible.

Disclosure   *Disclosure* is the unintended access to information. This does not include modification or destruction of information, which is covered by the corruption category. Three classes of information are considered:

- Internal information that does not concern a particular user or users
- Information about a particular user (getting the current user's MSN account password)
- Information about any or all users (getting the credit card numbers of all MSN users)

Additionally, disclosure can occur as a result of deception, when the user is deceived into providing information or a server is deceived by an impersonated user.

Disclosure Detail	
Internal data	Disclosure of internal information but not about any user.
Stored user data	Disclosure of a particular user's data.
Stored users data	Disclosure of any user's data, for example, e-mail account names or credit card information.
Deception	Deception is used to get a user to disclose data (spoofing, reputability), or false credentials are used to get a server to disclose data.

Functionality   The functionality category describes defects that make a desired operation difficult or impossible. If the operation is possible but does not work correctly or completely, it has a reliability problem. Functionality defects typically indicate errors early in the development process or mistakes of omission in implementing a design.

Functionality Detail	
Missing part	Element (file, resource) is missing.
Accessibility	There is a problem that will affect people with disabilities.
Complex	Operation is possible but complicated to perform.
Missing functionality	A method is missing for a given scenario.
Missing scenario	An entire usage scenario is missing.

Accessibility Subdetail	
Programmatic access	Issues that affect the ability for assistive technology products to access the application user interface and the client area information, such as missing, incomplete, wrong, or inconsistent programmatic interface support.
User settings	Issues that are caused by ignoring user settings and the profile (system settings). For instance, color should not be hard coded unless it is absolutely necessary.
Visual UI design	Issues that affect a user's visual operation; typically, problems caused by confusing, inconsistent, illogical, too small, or inconvenient visual user interface (UI) designs.
Navigation	User interface design issues that affect user navigation, such as missing, poor, inconsistent, illogical keyboard tab order.
Multimodal output	UI design issues that are conveyed by only one mode; for example, sound or color is used alone to indicate information.
Compatibility	Failure of programmatic compatibility with assistive technology devices and software, such as device-dependent scripting or information-pass-though failure.
Documentation	Insufficient or incomplete documentation regarding accessibility of the product, such as missing shortcut keys list in the documentation.
Needs to be determined	Any bug with this option selected should not be resolved until the component accessibility triage team has determined the impact of the bug.

Determining the Attack Surface Area and Damage Extent

The attack surface area and damage extent fields were chosen to directly reflect a concern for security defects. They surface the factors needed to determine the security risk of a defect and drive investigation as to whether a defect has an exploitation.

Attack Surface Information (Choose Most General)	
Internal	The issue can be caused only using nonpublic functionality.
Extensibility	The issue can be caused by independent extensibility code (device drivers, plug-ins, Component Object Model [COM], Microsoft ActiveX).
Client	The issue is in a public application programming interface (API) that is accessible only on the client computer.
Network	The issue is in a public API that can be accessed over the network (exploitable).

Damage Extent Information (Choose Widest)	
Function	Affects only the function.
Object	Affects the object.
Process	Affects the process.
Compatibility	Something that worked previously no longer works.
Application	Affects the application.
Machine	Affects the entire computer.
Server	Affects a server.
Clients	Affects clients of the server.
Net	Affects the entire network.

Contributing Cause(s) Stage

The purpose of cause information is to provide indications of the root cause of a defect. Contributing cause information falls into two broad categories based on James Reason's model of human cognition (see the sidebar titled "Cognitive error model," which follows):

- **Human factors** An individual made a mistake of some kind.

- **Systemic factors** The available systemic information (guidelines and procedures; company culture; domain-specific information, such as documentation, code, tools, and so on; organization) caused the error.

All humans are capable of error, but many human errors really indicate failures in the environment in which people work. Data about human failings should be used to investigate environmental means of reducing or preventing such failings.

Cognitive error model

The model of human cognition used to define the broad category of human factors in the contributing cause(s) stage is based on James Reason's model of human error.[1] This model divides human cognition into four parts:

- **Selection**   Gathering the information needed to decide on a plan of action to solve the defect

- **Analysis**   Determining the nature of the situation to formulate a plan

- **Solution**   Actually formulating the plan

- **Execution**   Implementing the plan

At each one of these stages, errors can be made. The selection phase is the main area where problems with systemic information can occur—information is missed or misapplied. There is a limit to how much information someone can memorize and apply. The scale of the Microsoft Windows operating system, for instance, is so large that this point was passed a long time ago. The possibility of selection phase errors increases the importance of knowledge access—being able to find the needed information without information overload.

When an action is performed again and again, a person's response becomes more automatic, the selection phase of cognition may be short-circuited, and analysis may be skipped in favor of the often-used solution. The same kind of short-circuiting may occur in deciding what information is relevant, whether a guideline should apply, where to find information, or whether information even exists. The positive value of skill is the ability to more quickly arrive at a correct decision as a result of experience and talent. The negative value of skill becomes evident when conditions change, causing rote behavior to become incorrect.

For example, decree that red means go and green means stop, and see a huge increase in accidents (errors). The skill you acquired in recognizing green as go and red as stop may become rote (automatic) behavior so that when the meaning is reversed you have to consciously correct yourself from following the acquired habit. Naturally, when new conditions are at odds with experience, there is a higher probability of making a mistake by relying on experience.

Human reasoning and systemic factors have an associated quality measure that describes any shortcomings that contributed to the error.

---

1   James Reason, *Human Error* (Cambridge, England: Cambridge University Press, 1990).

Human Factors

The human factors section of the taxonomy is divided into four phases: selection, analysis, solution, and execution. The first three phases are aspects of reasoning, and the last is a skill of transcription (that is, putting the solution into another form).

Selection Information	
Misapplication	Choice of a procedure/guideline or knowledge that doesn't apply to the issue (found but shouldn't use).
Omission	Exclusion of a relevant procedure/guideline or knowledge (found but decided not to use).
Unfamiliar	The area is not familiar or externally created, so assumed domain information was not known (someone else's code).
Didn't look	Person didn't look for relevant procedure/guideline or domain knowledge (may not have known it even exists, just winged it).
Didn't find	Looked for relevant information but couldn't find it (it does exist out there somewhere).
Blindness	Prejudgment of solution results in either not looking at or ignoring contrary information.

Analysis Information	
Superficial	The analysis identified a problem that may contribute to the issue but that is not the entire cause of the issue (broad but not deep).
Incomplete	The analysis does not solve the entire problem (deep but not broad).
Incorrect	The analysis of the issue does not identify any aspect of the problem that caused the issue.

Solution Information	
Symptom treatment	The solution corrects the effect of the issue but not the cause.
Unforeseen side effects	The solution corrects the issue but in doing so creates other issues.
Omitted side effect	Missing synchronization, notification, modification of an object property, or other side effect occurs.
Unstable	Solution is prone to failure under various circumstances.
Destabilizing	Solution changes functionality that causes failures in other code that previously worked.
Misuse	Solution uses other functionality incorrectly.
Partial	The solution does not entirely correct the problem or does so only in some of the failure scenarios.
Verification	Solution is missing verification steps to ensure that it functions correctly.
Other instances	Same problem exists elsewhere but is not fixed.

Execution Information	
Omission	A step was omitted in the solution.
Transcription	The correct step was incorrectly performed (typos, for instance).
Repetition	A step was repeated (typically, forgot where one was in a procedure).
Ordering	A step was performed in the wrong order.
Habit	Applying a rule, a procedure, or knowledge that has been used often in the past when it no longer applies. It includes "knowing" if a class of information exists and how to find it.
Extraneous	An extra step not in the original solution was performed.

Systemic Factors

Systemic knowledge is broken down into rules (procedures and guidelines), domain knowledge (guides, code, specifications, designs, and so on), and organization (how the information is accessed and the degree to which it is consistent).

Systemic knowledge is mostly created by humans, so it includes the possibility of error: human error in deciding which part of the systemic knowledge is applicable to the problem at hand, as well as problems relating to accessing the set of applicable systemic knowledge.

Systemic factors encompass the context in which a person performs work. The factors are determined by what we can reasonably control and their effect on the selection phase (finding the needed information), which is one of the main human factors causing wider impact and defects that are harder to find. Many types of execution errors can be caught by tools or reviews. Many solution and analysis errors can be caught by reviews. Training can also have a positive effect on catching execution and analysis errors. Selection errors are the most difficult to catch because everyone doing a review is using the same systemic knowledge and can make the same mistakes (which is why having domain experts in reviews can help).

Rules: Procedures and Guidelines   Procedures and guidelines have conditions to specify when they should be applied and then which action(s) to apply. There may be problems with either or both parts of a procedure or guideline.

Rules: Procedures and Guidelines Conditions Information	
Missing indication	A relevant condition is omitted from the rule.
Assumed context	A relevant condition is missing as a result of assuming context knowledge on the part of the user.
Missing exclusion	Relevant conditions on when not to use a rule are omitted.
Irrelevant condition	A condition is not germane to deciding whether the rule can be applied.
Time-consuming	The rule tends to be avoided because of the time required to evaluate its conditions.
False positives	The rule conditions are met when they shouldn't be. (This makes the rule less likely to be used in practice.)
Too complex	Evaluating the rule's conditions is prone to error.

Rules: Procedures and Guidelines Action Information	
Missing	A relevant action is omitted from the rule.
Assumed context	A relevant action is missing as a result of assuming context knowledge on the part of the user.
Ordering	The actions are in the wrong order.
Extraneous action	An action is not germane to the function of the rule (may be redundant or possibly damaging).
Fragile	Performance of the actions often results in errors—that is, the actions are correctly expressed but often fail (build scripts, for instance).
Time-consuming	Although the rule is valid, the time it takes to execute it limits its usefulness, leading to ad hoc shortcuts (running a subset of tests because a change "couldn't possibly affect" other areas, for example).
Too complex	Expressing actions is prone to error.
Incorrect	The actions are just wrong.

Domain Knowledge   Domain knowledge is not so much rules or guidelines but descriptive information about the domain. In the domain of code, this would include the code itself and the various documents describing it, such as specifications and design documents. Additional areas may include the bugs reported in an area of the code, knowledge of the subject domain independent of the code, and customer knowledge about applications or scenarios in the domain.

Domain Knowledge Information	
Scenarios	The scenarios for the domain
Requirements	The requirements for the domain
Architecture	The implementation architecture
Interfaces/classes	The interfaces and/or classes
External	Code, interfaces, classes, or standards that are not under direct control
Constraints	Constraints of the requirements and/or architecture
Side effect	The side effects of actions
Dependencies	Dependencies of this domain on others and vice versa
Tests	The tests for the domain and their coverage

Organization   The organization classification captures how accessible and useful domain knowledge and rules are.

Organization Information	
Priority/ordering simplification	Order or priority of information is used to determine validity rather than more exactly describing the conditions under which information is applicable.
Conflicting	Multiple conditions are satisfied and their conclusions (actions) conflict, or information from different sources is contradictory.

Organization Information	
Difficult to locate	The information exists but is hard to find. For instance, a correction for a temporary build problem may be mentioned only in an e-mail message and stated nowhere else (it's out there somewhere).
Missing	Information should exist but doesn't (it's not out there).
False positives	A search for the information returns irrelevant information (such as a Google search returning hundreds of hits).
Scattered	The information exists but is in multiple pieces (multiple places)
Notification	A change in knowledge (such as becoming obsolete or out of sync) is not communicated.
Overload	A flood of information is returned, and significant effort is required to wade through it.

Quality   The quality category captures any issues with using systemic information or human reasoning. Issues with the combination of domain knowledge, procedures, and guidelines are captured in the organization category.

Quality Information	
Incomplete	The information is missing important aspects.
Obsolete	The information is out of date and should be removed.
Misleading	The information, on reading, is prone to misinterpretation.
Out of sync	The information is partially incorrect as a result of not being updated from a change made elsewhere.
Incorrect	The information was never correct.
Too complex	The information is hard to understand, and its usage is prone to error.
Extraneous	The information contains a significant amount of nongermane information.
Verbose	The information is not concise.

Change Stage

Change stage information describes the correction area (part of method, class structure, design, domain knowledge, and others), the type of change made, and the extent of the effect of the change.

The location of a change can indicate defects in the process that generated it. The most obvious case is changes in classes or interfaces (as opposed to inside methods) that indicate that the original design of the class or interface missed something. This particular case is one of the most useful indicators of the Orthogonal Defect Classification (ODC) system, as described in the sidebar titled "Orthogonal Defect Classification" earlier in this chapter.

Correction Area

The correction area is similar to the defect type in ODC but provides a bit more fine-grained classification as well as includes intramethod classification and systemic knowledge. Intramethod information may drive improvements to code analysis tools or training methods. Systemic knowledge information may drive improvements in organization, ease of use, or quality of knowledge that everyone is using.

Correction Area Information	
Method code	Changes limited to the body of existing methods
Private class structure	Addition, deletion, or signature change of methods local to a class
Nonprivate class/ interface	Addition or signature change of methods visible outside the class
New classes/interfaces	Addition of classes or interfaces, often nonpublic to avoid being considered a design change
Design change	Reexamination of the design of classes/interfaces. Typically indicated by deletion or replacement of key interfaces, classes, or methods
Specification change	Functional specification corrected
Scenario change	Usage scenarios corrected
Process	A change in the process followed
Rule	A change in the rules followed
Domain knowledge	A change in the domain knowledge used
Knowledge organization	A change in organization or consistency of knowledge

Method Code   A *method* consists of a main (or common) code path that has tests that branch into alternatives or error-handling code paths. A high-level description of a change is whether it is a missing code path or some kind of correction to an existing code path. Error code paths are distinguished from normal code paths by their infrequent execution during testing, and any errors in them tend to cause corruption or other errors.

Method Code: Change Extent Detail	
Single method	Changes are limited to a single existing method.
Methods in same class	Changes span multiple methods but in the same class.
Methods in multiple classes	Changes span methods in multiple classes.

Method Code: Change Branch Detail	
Common code path	Code that is always executed (typically prefix/suffix code).
Alternative code path	Code that executes only under certain conditions (typically *switch* or *if*).
Error code path	Code that only executes when an error occurs (special case of alternative code path).
Method(s) added	Change involves addition of methods.

Method Code: Change Part Detail	
Initialization	Variable or property initialization (assignment).
Checking	Validation of parameters and checking for errors.
Side effects	Cross-method/object communication by assignment (setting an object property, for instance).
Notification	An event or calling a method/delegate to inform it of a change (cross-method/object communication by call).
Iteration	The tests used to limit the extent of iteration and/or the object being iterated.
Interaction	The use of an existing type, interface, class, or design pattern.
Step	Any other statement (typos, reversed logic, off by 1).

Change Type

The change type describes the nature of the change made from source documentation to code changes relating to common human errors.

Change Type Information	
Verification	Verification of correct result is added.
Documentation	Details about usage or common errors/dependencies are added.
Addition	An addition is made.
Removal	A removal is made.
Correction	A correction is made.
Order	The order of operations is changed.

Change Extent

The change extent describes how visible the change is to other code, including external applications. This information can be used to gauge the extent of testing needed for the change and if other groups need to be notified.

Change Extent Information	
Intraclass	Changes are local to a class (private).
Derived class	Changes are visible to derived classes (protected).
Internal	Changes are visible to a class's assembly or dynamic-link library (DLL) (internal).
Extensibility	Changes are visible to independent extensibility code (device drivers, plug-ins, COM, ActiveX).
Public	Changes are to a public API.
Compatibility	Changes affect application compatibility (change in public API entry points or behavior).

Detection Stage

The detection stage describes how the defect should be detected. There are a few basic cases of defect detection:

- A test detected the defect in the optimal phase of the product cycle, and the defect was reported: a success story.

- A test detected the defect but not in the optimal phase: test should be pushed upstream.

- A test detected the defect but a defect was not reported: You must find out why not.

- The test has an error, so it didn't detect the defect.

- There was no test for the defect.

- There is no way to measure an occurrence of the defect.

The defect detection categories are captured in the result category.

Test Result Information	
Detected	The issue was detected by the correct test (generated this defect).
Detected but not recognized	The issue was detected but not recognized (rolled off screen, buried in mass of output, misread).
Detected but ignored	The issue was detected, and the failure was recognized but ignored (there's no way my change caused that failure).
Test error	Test was designed to detect the issue or to replicate the failure conditions, but there was an error in the test implementation.
Unreliable	The test generates false positives or false negatives inconsistently (a failure may often be ignored).
Skipped	The test exists but was removed from the verification step or not manually run.
Too expensive	The test takes so long to run or requires such a large amount of manual effort that it is used infrequently.
Complex conditions	The necessary conditions to trigger the issue are complex to reproduce.
Intermittent	The test detects the issue, but the issue appears intermittently (not a solid failure).
Missing test	It is possible to test for the issue, but the test has not been written.
Missing measurement	It is not possible to detect the issue because there is no way to measure its occurrence. However, an existing test may already be creating the issue's contributing factors but can't measure the failure.

A test, existing or needed to detect a defect, is described in terms of its process (how it is run), type (what level of code it tests), parameters (what condition it exercises), and what it measures to determine success or failure.

These categories are useful to indicate the types of tests that are detecting defects as well as the types of test that are missing.

Test Process Information	
Automatic	The test is run and evaluated automatically.
Manual evaluation	The results of the test must be evaluated manually.
Manual script	The test is manually performed using a described procedure.
Ad hoc	It is not a formal test; tried something and it failed.

Test Type Information	
Unit	A single unit (method or function)
Class	An entire class
Interface	An interface
Design pattern	A design pattern (may be cross-class and cross-object)
Scenario	A usage scenario
End to end	A test of a complete user task that may encompass multiple scenarios
System	A mix of scenario, end-to-end, and other tests

Parameters Information	
Valid	Valid parameters are used.
Extreme	Valid but extreme values are used, typically to detect performance or leakage problems. For instance, use a 20-MB path string to an API whose implementation copies the path into other objects.
Invalid	Invalid values or state is used to detect the presence of parameter validation code and exercise some error branches.
Error injection	Even though the parameters are valid, errors are forced into execution to find problems with error-handling code paths.
Scalability	Multiple simultaneous operations, using large numbers of items, are run.
Resource starvation	Resources such as memory or disk space are artificially limited.

Measurement Information	
Static analysis	Validation is done without running code. Compiler error detection is a classic example.
Output values	Output values are compared against known good values.
Error occurrence	Tracking whether an error occurred or didn't occur, depending on whether the inputs or state was valid.
Performance	The time or resources used in an operation.
Side effect	Verifying execution has the correct side effects on other objects.
Corruption	Detecting undesired side effect from execution.
Memory leak	Whether memory is being accumulated.
Resource leak	Whether other resources are not being released.
Code coverage	The percentage of code paths that have been executed.
Race conditions	Whether behavior is time dependent because of asynchronous operations.

Mitigation Stage

Mitigations are suggestions to reduce or eliminate the root cause (or at least a more root cause) of the defect that was corrected. *Prevention* is when the defect cannot be produced, or at least when the defect is detected in the same phase in which it was created. Prevention is the best mitigation—a defect is made impossible to introduce rather than merely unlikely.

Compilers are a simple example of preventing defects by detecting them in the same phase as their introduction: with a compiler, you can enter bad syntax but can't produce a binary to advance to the next step. Code analysis tools are other examples. However, if run manually, they provide only a reduction in the number of defects introduced unless you implement an automatic verification system that can detect whether the tools have been run. If they are run in a later phase such as integration, they are a detection method, not mitigation. Similarly, although a tool may run automatically, if it can't detect every instance of a defect, it is a reduction or detection, not prevention (mitigation).

If a defect can't be prevented, it can be reduced. Reduction typically involves manual processes; for example, you can have a checklist of defects to look for but can't guarantee there will be no errors. The checklist immensely reduces the possibility that defects will slip through (if it is short and clear), but it can't eliminate them entirely.

Mitigations are described in terms of their extent (how much they reduce the possibility of future defects) and their method (what kind of change is used to implement them).

Mitigation Extent Information	
No change	No suggested change to improve mitigation.
Reduce	The change will reduce but not eliminate the issue.
Detect	The change will detect the issue in the same phase of development.
Prevent	The change will prevent the expression of the issue.

Mitigation Type Information	
Staffing	Depends on the skill, reasoning, and knowledge of the people chosen.
Training/education	Directly spread knowledge (implement security training, for instance).
Culture	Company culture (value of quality, for instance).
Central knowledge	Add/change central knowledge (answer only in e-mail message, for instance).
Knowledge access	Make particular knowledge more accessible (knowledge somewhere but hard to find or there is information overload).
Process change	Change a process (includes automating, reordering, deleting).
Tool change	Change a tool (add a new static text rule, for instance).
New tool	Needs a new tool.
Communication	Communication between groups/individuals needs to be improved.
Hardware	Additional or more powerful hardware could reduce the issue.

Example of a Classified Defect

A defect taxonomy is a fairly detailed way to collect information about a defect from different points of view, so an example classification may help clarify its usage.

Recently at Microsoft there was a security bug involving animated cursors. It was reported externally and turned out to be caused by using a size in the animated cursor structure that specified the size of a following structure. The code did not check whether the size was valid, so an invalid value could be passed in, and that could cause a buffer overflow error. The following is an explanation of the bug from Determina.com:[1]

> The ANI file format [a graphics file format for animated items] is used for storing animated cursors. The format is based on the RIFF [Resource Interchange File Format] multimedia file format and consists of a series of tagged chunks containing variable sized data. Each chunk starts with a 4 byte ASCII tag, followed by a dword specifying the size of the data contained in the chunk.

---

1   Determina Security Research, "Windows Animated Cursor Stack Overflow Vulnerability," *www.determina.com/ security.research/vulnerabilities/ani-header.html.*

```
struct ANIChunk
{
    char  tag[4];       // ASCII tag
    DWORD size;         // length of data in bytes
    char  data[size];   // variable sized data
}
```

One of the chunks in an ANI file is the anih chunk, which contains a 36-byte animation header structure. The buffer overflow fixed in MS05-002 was in the LoadCursorIconFromFileMap function. The vulnerable code did not validate the length of the anih chunk before reading the chunk data into fixed size buffer on the stack. The pseudo code of the vulnerable function is given below:

```
int LoadCursorIconFromFileMap(struct MappedFile* file, ...)
{
    struct ANIChunk  chunk;
    struct ANIHeader header;        // 36 byte structure

    ...

    // read the first 8 bytes of the chunk
    ReadTag(file, &chunk);

    if (chunk.tag == 'anih') {

+       if (chunk.size != 36)       // added in MS05-002
+           return 0;

        // read chunk.size bytes of data into the header struct
        ReadChunk(file, &chunk, &header);
    ...
}
```

The defect is an execution problem that corrupts object organization, which includes the stack frame. In the worst case, it can be generated remotely by downloading an animated cursor and it damages the operating system (machine). If the problem had been reported with an exploit, the classification may have been corruption or disclosure instead of reliability.

The contributing cause is a guess. Most likely, the check for a valid size was just forgotten, although the defect could have been caused by a knowledge issue: communicating the requirement of the security domain that any structure supplied externally should not be trusted to be correct. Note that the attributes for human and systemic failure are not filled out in the taxonomy shown in Table 10-1; the failure may center on only certain aspects rather than all of them.

Table 10-1   **A Classified Defect**

Defect Taxonomy Item	Value
Occurrence stage	
Discovery product phase	**Customer**
Defect area	**Execution**
Defect type: Corruption	**Object organization**
Attack surface area	**Network**
Damage extent	**Machine**
Contributing causes stage	
Cause product phase	**Implementation**
Human factors: Execution	**Omission**
Change stage	
Correction phase	**Maintenance**
Correction area: Method code	
Change branch	**Single branch**
Change part	**Checking**
Change type	**Addition**
Change extent	**Compatibility**
Detection stage	
Detection product phase	**Implementation**
Test result	**Missing test**
Test process	**Automatic**
Test type	**Unit**
Parameters	**Invalid**
Measurement	**Static analysis**
Mitigation stage	
Mitigation product phase	**Implementation**
Extent	**Prevent**
Type	**Tool change**

The change that was made was to add to the checking part of the method (function) a check for the correct structure size. The change was in a single branch and affects compatibility because previously valid (though dangerous) animated cursors will not be invalid. An argument could be made that the effect should be internal instead of compatibility because we don't mind breaking exploits.

This defect should have been caught when the code was written. There was no test that detected this issue because it escaped to customers (although actually there were tests that caught other cases of this problem but not this particular one).

At first, you may think the mitigation would be to make this kind of problem (using untrusted size information) an issue in code reviews. But code reviews are an error-prone process because they are manual, and there would be a vast number of such rules to check in a code review. Searching source text for occurrences may pick up some instances, but the name of the structure field (*dwSize*) may be very common, resulting in a large number of false positives. In any case, there are more structures for files that may be downloaded from the Internet than animated cursors.

The best mitigation would be one that detects and prevents all instances of using untrusted sizes. At Microsoft, we use static code analysis tools to detect classes of defects, such as many buffer overruns. By adding annotations to every structure field that may contain an untrusted size, static analysis can detect all cases.

A complete description for a defect in a defect taxonomy includes detail text fields, but these aren't included here because they can't be mined like the attributes can be. There may also be multiple answers to many of the stages, and sometimes there are multiple causes, detections, or mitigations. Deeper analysis of a set of defects may reveal more general detections and mitigations. In this example, we short-circuited the preventions to jump to a code analysis mitigation, but this may have been a solution arrived at after later examination of a number of defects involving untrusted sizes in different structures.

Conclusion

The example taxonomy is fairly broad, and it has attributes addressing many assumptions of behavior and dimensions of how to look at a defect. Peaks in various attributes or combinations of attributes may validate assumptions of the kind of error developers are making or may target subsets of defects for more in-depth analysis. Comparing frequencies by team may identify both good and bad results. These results can then be analyzed to discover local best practices or to correct local bad practices. In large software projects, you can't afford to perform in-depth analysis of every bug, communicate the results to every developer, and expect every developer to remember everything. Defect taxonomies are lower overhead than in-depth analysis of each bug, and then frequency analysis can highlight areas of concern with much less effort than reading the details of every bug.

Chapter 11
Root Cause Analysis

Some people see things that are and ask, Why? Some people dream of things that never were and ask, Why not? Some people have to go to work and don't have time for all that.
—George Carlin

The most likely way for the world to be destroyed, most experts agree, is by accident. That's where we come in; we're computer professionals. We cause accidents.
—Nathaniel Borenstein

The growing recognition of the complexity of software development, diverse customer usage scenarios, hardware and networked environments, and the corresponding requirements for complex test environments continues to drive the incidence of adverse events higher than ever before and is supporting the movement of many software development organizations toward formal root cause analysis (RCA) programs.

Root cause analysis is a structured defect prevention technique that analyzes the cause-and-effect relationships of an event in pursuit of a corrective action that eliminates the cause(s) of problems. The biggest advantage of root cause analysis as a defect prevention technique is its ability to identify the lowest-level problems rather than just immediate symptoms. For example, studying a class of defects using root cause analysis may conclude with a recommendation that code reviews should include a check for uninitialized variables. This chapter covers a series of steps illustrating how to perform an effective root cause analysis study.

Understanding How a Root Cause Analysis Study Helps Prevent Defects

Successful software development in today's complex and dynamic world absolutely requires a process of ongoing improvement. The only certainty is that as the Internet evolves, bandwidth increases, hardware gets more powerful, and users get more dependent on software solutions to run their lives, there are uncertain times ahead for software. Without making an effort to learn and improve, software development organizations will find it impossible to keep up. The root cause analysis process can yield huge quality and efficiency gains.

The goal of conducting a root cause analysis study is to identify one or more actions to take to ensure that the undesirable event does not recur. As the number of studies increases, the findings should start to enhance the causality model, building a complete taxonomy that accelerates classification of issues addressed in future studies. See Chapter 10, "Defect Taxonomies," for more details on using this classification technique to augment the RCA process.

Right away, however, it is important to emphasize that there are many levels of causality, each with its own preventions, cures, and contributing factors. Unfortunately, human activities do not fit nicely and cleanly into an analytical model, which is why a root cause analysis study is an effective technique. It would be nice to have it work out that problem A was caused by B, B caused by C, and so on, down to cause K, where a corrective action eliminates A, but it is not that simple. More likely, there is a recommendation at B, a preventive action at D, a form of detection at F, and perhaps nothing to do at C or even at K.

A huge benefit of root cause analysis as a defect prevention technique is its ability to identify deeper-level problems rather than just immediate symptoms. The structured methodology of root cause analysis covered in this chapter can help guide the effort through layers of cause and effect to identify the lowest-level causes.

A root cause analysis study or program has a few simple objectives:

- To learn from mistakes
- To systematically identify areas for improvement
- To prevent repetition of mistakes

The result of a root cause analysis is one or more corrective action recommendations—changes in the development process to eliminate the cause of errors. These may be simple solutions, or they may be complex process changes. In software, the implementation of a code review process and even a tool or automated test that can eradicate the cause of the problems is an example of a corrective action. The following sections cover who, when, what, where, and how to perform a successful study.

When to Do an RCA Study

An RCA study can be performed at any time during the software development cycle, although the requirements of a class of defects for input into the process may dictate when a study is appropriate. These defects, also known as *sentinel events*, dictate the timing of the study.

RCA is an expensive process, so a deliberate approach that includes establishing a set of criteria for cost-effectiveness should be established before the study is begun. Therefore, the most effective approach is to apply structure to the event selection process to ensure that the largest return on investment is realized for the resources that are applied. For example, if one very expensive defect is discovered by several customers, it may be effective to initiate an RCA study on just the single defect. Another study may begin when automated tests expose dozens of similar crashing memory leak defects. Early beta feedback may expose design defects that warrant an RCA study. In each case, the timing is slightly different, but the criteria—these are big, nasty, and expensive problems—are very similar.

Staffing for Success

Staffing a root cause analysis effort can include a number of different people and teams, including those named in Figure 11-2 (later). Each party plays a different role in the RCA study process, as mentioned throughout this chapter. Although the specific makeup of the RCA team may vary dramatically, from a single engineer or researcher to an entire team, the role of an RCA analyst is critical to success, regardless of how the effort is organized.

The Role of the RCA Study Analyst

The use of an analyst or team of analysts conducting an RCA study can be implemented a number of different ways. In some cases, the organization may dedicate a formal, full-time team to administer a study and implement the corrective actions. In other cases, people may be assigned temporarily to a single root cause analysis study or to a team. Often, the study is completed as part of a postmortem exercise at the conclusion of a milestone or project cycle. In any case, a number of skills are required for successful analysis. A good RCA analyst has the following skills and characteristics:

- Has a good understanding of a wide range of the development process and modes of failure
- Is familiar with, or capable of understanding, the engineering practices
- Is able to investigate failures at component and system levels
- Uses a logical and technical approach to failure analysis
- Assesses and understands process limitations
- Involves developers, testers, program managers, support technicians, and perhaps marketing and field personnel throughout the investigation and analysis phases
- Has a depth of internal and external resources available to analyze various types of failures

The analyst or analysis team should be capable of performing the following tasks:

- Defect and low-level code analysis
- Process infrastructure characterization
- Operating and maintenance procedure or process analysis
- Operating efficiency diagnosis
- Root cause analysis for event understanding
- Root cause analysis for problem diagnostics and operating optimization
- Algorithm and metric development for system condition monitoring
- Data acquisition system development

- Data presentation and interpretation

- Diagnostic computational architecture

- Results presentation and education, instruction, training

- Ongoing instrumentation and monitoring

The specific tasks of an RCA analyst or team can vary significantly depending on the nature of the project. A person or team with the preceding capabilities can react to the dynamic nature of the study. Without knowing what cause is "around the corner," sometimes an analyst with limited experience or skills may find it difficult to maneuver successfully through a study. A more experienced, senior person with a broad set of skills can help shepherd the study toward successful results.

Phases of an RCA Study

An RCA study is an effort to find preventive techniques to eradicate a single defect or an entire class of defects. A root cause analysis can be performed in a number of different ways, but RCA studies typically map to six distinct steps or phases (see Figure 11-1):

1. Event identification

2. Data collection

3. Data analysis and assessment

4. Corrective actions

5. Inform and apply

6. Follow-up, measurement, and reporting

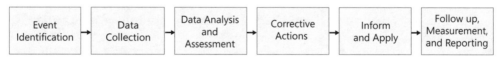

Figure 11-1   Phases of a root cause analysis study

A formal root cause study includes the six distinct phases; however, less-formal studies are still effective and may contain fewer phases or smaller tasks in a phase. The scope of the effort can span from a single engineer performing a study on his or her own defects all the way to a highly structured team of experts studying defects across the features of a product. Figures 11-2 through 11-7 depict the six phases of the RCA process in detail and include information on which members of the RCA team perform which activities during specific phases.

In general, a study usually begins with the identification of a significant or sentinel "event" to analyze. Data is collected into a defect report or bug report that describes the sentinel event. Sufficient data must be available with which to analyze the event. Then the RCA analyst or analysts review and analyze the defect and related data to identify one or more "corrective actions" designed to prevent that event or that class of defect from recurring. The analysts next present these corrective actions, grouped in categories, to those affected by the recommendations, and the corrective actions are then applied as necessary. After this is completed, the newly implemented processes are measured, monitored, and reported to ensure success.

Phase I: Event Identification

In the typical software development process, a customer-reported issue is a good place to start an RCA study; however, the RCA process does not require a *software* defect—the methodology supports the investigation of *any* undesirable event. The sentinel event is the defect or defects that are being studied. The significance and impact of the sentinel or initiating event should determine the scale and effort of the RCA study. (See Figure 11-2.)

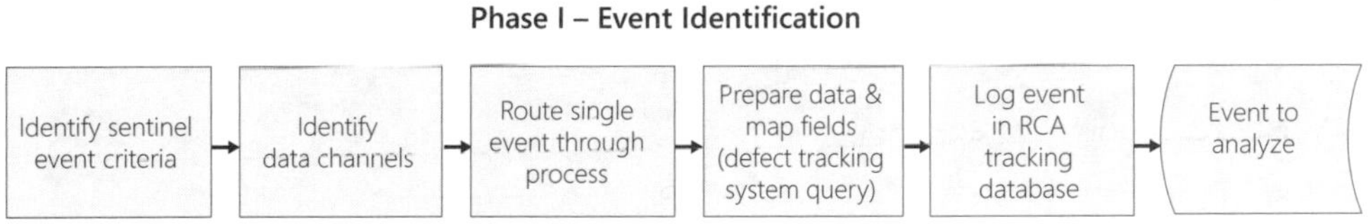

Phase I – Event Identification

Figure 11-2   The root cause analysis process: phase I

Identify Sentinel Event Criteria

It is unusual for a software project to have a shortage of "undesirable events" to study. It is also unusual for resources to fund a root cause analysis project to be available. And there is no guarantee that any analysis will yield a true "root" cause. It is important to gather a statistically valid sample of defects and conduct preliminary analysis and screening to improve the odds of selecting the most important sentinel events.

Typically, an RCA study focuses on the most severe or most undesirable events. Cost of repair, cost of discovery, risk to or impact on the user, press coverage, support costs, language or maintenance costs, and the like are all factors in determining the level of undesirability. Analyzing the most severe defects usually returns the greatest yield.

Use Risk Assessment in the Selection Process

It is important to use a structured approach in the selection of RCA sentinel events for investigation. Selection should be based on an assessment of risk (of severity and of recurrence) and of cost (actual cost of repair versus opportunity cost of recurrence). In addition, selection may be based on any broad category of defects, including impact, development language, customer environments, or other commonalities across defect types.

An evaluation and measurement of risk may be used to prioritize and select undesired events or issues for root cause analysis and to define the recommended actions. As time goes on and the number of studies increases, it is likely that many different selection criteria will be used to select study targets. See Chapter 8, "Risk Analysis," for more details on using a risk-based approach to select defects for an RCA study.

Identify Data Channels

After the events have been selected for analysis, the next step is to identify and evaluate the sources of additional data. These sources can supplement the analysis and may vary depending on the nature of the project and on the types of defects being studied. Additional data sources that can be used to track why the event occurred include the following:

- Defect tracking system
- Individual surveys and interviews
- Source code repository
- Test case management systems
- Test code coverage data
- Product support
- Customer or marketing data
- Findings from previous RCA studies

The data will exist in a variety of forms and should be copied and/or consolidated in a central location for the purpose of the RCA study.

List Sentinel Events

At this stage, the team creates a formal list of the sentinel events and corresponding descriptions. This list may be a list of bug reports, customer issues, support calls, maintenance requests, or any combination. By keeping the event list relatively fixed throughout the study, the team can better manage the data inflow. Although there may be instances when items are added to or deleted from the list, the more static the list, the more likely the data can be analyzed in a structured way.

A good pilot program for a formal study studies every customer issue that resulted in a maintenance release or update. Defects that result in a maintenance release are typically the most costly type of defect. The issues are described in customer-reported bugs, and hence, the initial collateral for an RCA study is a set of customer-reported defects and their corresponding reports. It is important, however, to note that over the long term, the sentinel events may differ from a list of defects. The process may easily expand to analyze other customer events that were brought to the surface through channels other than the defect tracking system. Using customer-reported issues as sentinel events for an RCA study is a great first step—they are easy to see, have lots of supporting data, and can illustrate the cost-effectiveness of an RCA study. RCA studies are a common practice for maintenance releases at Microsoft, and successful RCA efforts in software development often begin with high cost customer reported defects as the sentinel events for the study.

Gather and Prepare the Preliminary Data

The next step is to gather the easily accessible data. Some data is very expensive to gather (for example, surveys or personal interviews) and can be done later in the process. But some data, such as a defect reports and customer issues queries, is easy to retrieve. This preliminary data-gathering activity helps validate the sample by illustrating how representative the sample is of the class of defects being studied, exposing holes or missing data, and highlighting areas where additional data gathering may be necessary. It can also help to provide some grouping and additional context for entry of the information in the RCA database.

It is usually a good idea to set some guidelines for data accuracy and to review the preliminary data to ensure that the expectations are reasonable. After the preliminary data is gathered, review the data to make sure that the data sources are legitimate and provide valuable data, and look for holes or missing data.

Route a Single Event Through the Process

It is a good idea, especially for a larger-scale RCA study, to run a brief pilot of the process. For example, the type of data required, the proximity of experts, number of participants, and other related factors can influence the choice between using interviews or surveys to gather data. A test of the process identifies these types of decisions early—before the full study begins. Obviously, on smaller-scale studies, a pilot is not as necessary or certainly does not have to be as formal, but it is always a good idea to think about first. As mentioned earlier, using defects or events that result in a maintenance release make a great pilot program.

Create the RCA Tracking Database

One of the main goals of a root cause analysis study is to learn from mistakes. It is in the best interest of the organization to create or identify a location where the learning will be stored. In addition to storing the results, the RCA tracking database contains copies of or links to supporting data for analysis, expert names, survey results, interview notes, test results, conclusions, and corrective action recommendations. This database becomes the repository in which the organization can house its learning. Following are the items to store in an RCA tracking database:

- Sentinel event or study ID, title, and dates
- Related defects—links to defects in the bug tracking system
- Failure areas and source code links/examples
- Team contacts and owners
- RCA analysts and contacts
- Expert groups and contacts

- Causes of defect and corrective action recommendations (these can be associated with the prevention tab database discussed in Chapter 14, "Prevention Tab")

- Survey data and results

Phase II: Data Collection

After the sentinel events have been identified and validated through an early look at easy-to-gather data, the formal data collection phase can begin. It is important to begin the data collection process (see Figure 11-3) as soon as possible after the identification of events to minimize the loss of data. The information collected helps shed light on conditions surrounding the introduction of the defect. Information is collected from testers, developers, program managers, and perhaps product support or field personnel to help describe as much as possible about the issue.

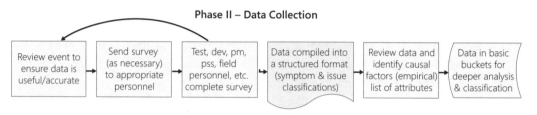

Phase II – Data Collection

Review event to ensure data is useful/accurate → Send survey (as necessary) to appropriate personnel → Test, dev, pm, pss, field personnel, etc. complete survey → Data compiled into a structured format (symptom & issue classifications) → Review data and identify causal factors (empirical) list of attributes → Data in basic buckets for deeper analysis & classification

Survey supplements: Bug reports, source changes, binaries, repros, interviews, emails, studies, logs, minutes, design docs, etc.

Figure 11-3   The root cause analysis process: phase II

Use Common Sense and Trust Gut Feel

It is quite common for the RCA analyst to have a "feel" for the problem—ideas about what may be the source of the defects under study. It is a tricky balance because it is important for the reviewer to remain unbiased and be open to alternatives, but a gut feel can go a long way toward sniffing out the right path for the study and expediting the identification of one or more root causes. The time to acknowledge a gut feel is during the data collection phase. All of the preliminary data may point in one direction, but if the analyst has a feeling that other things may be relevant, the team should spend the effort to collect that additional data.

Create a Survey and Gather Survey Data

If the size or scope of the study is large enough, it is wise to use a survey to get information from experts and/or participants in the discovery or repair of the defect. If the team is using a defect classification process, such as the defect taxonomy covered in Chapter 10, the survey process is an excellent place in which to gather taxonomical information. In addition, survey questions could cover topics that answer questions such as follows:

- Are there any additional details on failure areas?

- How could this bug have been prevented (see Chapter 14)?

- If this is an old bug, would static detection tools or process improvements have caught the problem if the code were written today?

- Was the problem noticed and ignored?

- Is this a common type of error?

- What interruptions or diversions may have contributed to this code being erroneous?

- What are the suspected causes of this problem?

- If you could change things to prevent this bug, what would they be?

These are useful questions to ask, even independent of a survey.

Compile Data in a Structured Format

After the data is collected, it should be compiled in a structured format. The type of structured format may vary depending on the type of data. Look for common denominators in the data to help categorize and link sets together. For example, a defect is found and fixed in a certain area of the code, and so the function name, file name, or binary name may be relevant to other data sets, such as test cases or product support calls. An investment in organizing the data can help provide insight into why events may have happened.

Methods of Data Collection

Data about the issues may be collected in a number of different ways and from a wide variety of sources. Ideally, the cost of data collection is minimized, so the primary source of data will be the bug report in the defect tracking system. However, after a set of bugs has been identified, additional data is collected by using an automated survey. There may be cases where survey data is supplemented with source changes, binaries, repro scenarios, individual interviews, e-mail conversations, studies, logs, meeting minutes, design documents, and other sources. The goal is to ensure that the analysis team has all relevant data on the problem. Data is prepared and classified to best route the problem to the correct set of experts, to make optimal use of the experts' time, and to eliminate redundant conclusions.

Over time, it is reasonable to assume that many of the standard conclusions, descriptions, basic classifications, corrective actions, and additional learning can be pushed upstream into the data collection phase to speed the resolution and minimize the reuse of experts. The output from this phase is a set or sets of structured data, ready for detailed analysis.

Phase III: Data Analysis and Assessment

The data analysis phase (see Figure 11-4) is performed by the RCA team, the research team, and related experts. The first step in data analysis is to identify the causal factors and categorize the findings in cause categories. To identify the causal factors, a number of different root cause methods can be used, but essentially, the basic steps are the following:

1. Ensure that the problem/defect/sentinel event is identified.

2. Organize all related data.

3. Evaluate the significance of the problem/defect/sentinel event.

4. Identify the causes immediately preceding or surrounding the problem (the reason for the problem).

5. Identify the reasons why these causes existed, and continue to work backward to the root cause using Five Whys and other techniques.

6. Classify all causes identified in this phase.

Phase III – Data Analysis and Assessment

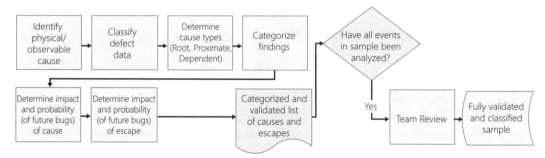

Figure 11-4   The root cause analysis process: phase III

Overview of the Five Whys

Five Whys is a very simple concept that stemmed from the early work in the Toyota production system and is a popular Six Sigma technique. The purpose of the technique is to get past the initial cause of a problem and look at the bigger picture to find the root cause. This technique is the heart of the root cause process: Take the problem and ask why it might have occurred. List all possible answers, and then for each of those causes, ask why it could have occurred. Then do the same thing five times.

It is important to note that despite the name of the technique, the number five is just a guideline—in some cases, the situation may call for just a couple of "why" questions, and other times it may require seven or eight whys. The main point is to ask "why" until the causes start to become irrelevant or unsolvable. For example, asking why back to the point where single-cell amoebae split in two or why silicon was chosen as a viable material in making computer chips does not help prevent future defects. Asking why is useful to a point, and then further analysis can begin. Five is a good guideline and can really help identify causes at a deeper level.

It is sometimes helpful to chart out the five whys using a fishbone chart, also called a cause-and-effect diagram, or another graphic to help you think visually. An example is shown in Figure 11-5.

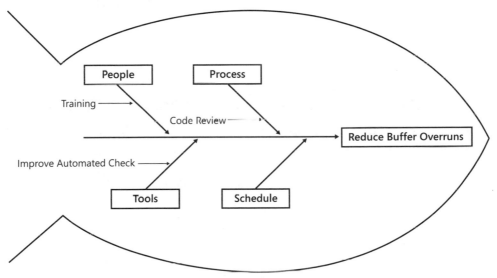

Figure 11-5   Simple fishbone or cause-and-effect diagram

Typically, in a root cause analysis study for software defects, the "why" focus can be on the defect itself, resulting in code or architectural design recommendations, or on process techniques, resulting in coding habit or organizational policy recommendations. In some cases, it is beneficial to do both. Start by asking, "Why did this defect occur?" and "Why did this defect make it into the code?" These two slightly different questions will yield very different conclusions.

Example:

- Why did this defect make it into the code?

  - Answer: Because the code review and unit tests didn't catch it.

- Why didn't the code review catch it?

  - Answer: Junior team members had to substitute for the usual reviewers.

- Why were the substitutes doing the review?

  - Answer: The usual team was frantically coding and couldn't break.

- Why were they so busy coding?

    ❑ Answer: Schedule pressure to get late changes in.

- Why was there so much schedule pressure?

    ❑ Answer: Two key dependencies underestimated dates and forced late changes.

Although this is a simplified and abbreviated example, it is clear that the root cause may lie in a much different area than originally suspected. Although the original defect may have slipped through code reviews and unit tests, the real root cause of this defect making it into the code is the inability of a couple teams to estimate accurately. The Five Whys technique helps the analyst to think at a different level and uncover areas of concern that may not otherwise be discovered.

Review Data, Identify Causal Factors, and Map Data to Causes

After the supporting data has been gathered and analyzed, it should be mapped to the causes identified through the Five Whys process. In many cases, the data can support or help answer "why" questions, but many times, the answers to "why" are easy, and a secondary step of mapping the supporting data to the answers is necessary. This is helpful because when suggestions for corrective actions are evaluated, the supporting data can often add details that are not obvious.

> **Best Practices**   It is generally a good idea to include events just prior to and immediately following the cause of the defect to ensure that any related events are captured.

Identify Physical or Observable Causes

Some of the causes identified through the Five Whys analysis or through other data analysis may be physical or observable causes. It's important to identify and flag these because they are typically easier to find solutions for and may have broader impact and more significant repercussions than other types of causes. For example, a developer may be unable to submit his local changes in the product because he is physically denied access to the room that contains the build computer. This problem is easier to solve than the problem of the developer who requires training on the process used to submit her local changes to the build computer. A more likely example is that code dependencies may require one developer to make changes in an area that is not her own, and she does not have the appropriate permissions to make the change.

Identify Root Causes

The root cause or causes will be a set of causes, at the lowest level of focus, that will be surrounded by the glowing halo to indicate that they are indeed the root of all defects. All kidding aside, there is usually a cognitive snap or "aha!" with a few of the causes that will indicate the need for obvious action. These are the starting points for corrective actions and should be labeled the root causes for the purpose of the study. The scope and impact of these causes will vary—not every study will result in a single, all-encompassing root cause that solves all the world's problems—but in many cases, there are some great, easily identifiable, actionable areas where corrections can improve the environment and prevent defects.

Determine Cause Types

The identification or classification of causes will help with corrective action recommendations. Each organization must decide the degree to which causes should be classified. This can be as simple as a three-category classification: Human Error, Physical Error, or Organizational/Process Error—or can go into tremendous detail and cover specific types or subcategories of these classifications. For example, human error caused by oversight, interruption, or development process error versus design process error. Be careful because some of this can muddy the water and get into different types of causes—is a "design process error" classification really a cause? To avoid this problem, the team should decide on a classification schema before beginning the study. The classifications can help tremendously with generating the recommendations for corrective actions, so targeting the same audience that will receive the correction action recommendations is a good way to help define an appropriate level of classification.

Determine Impact and Probability (of Future Bugs) of Cause and Escape

As the causes are classified and analyzed, the team should review the impact of bugs arising from this cause. It is critical to look at the impact and probability or likelihood of the bugs as they are caught or if they are not caught. One of the risks of root cause analysis is that the prevention costs more than the symptom. This is the phase where those types of tradeoffs are evaluated and understood. Can the team afford to incur bugs of this type or is the cost of fixing the cause justified by the severity or scope of impact of the defects?

Conduct a Component Team Review

After defects have been appropriately categorized and evaluated, the findings should be reviewed with the affected teams. This step is important because gaining agreement with a team on the cause of the problems helps ensure that the team will adopt the corrective actions later. If the RCA team dismisses this step and waits until corrective actions are finished before contacting the teams, the likelihood of their adopting the corrective actions diminishes greatly. An agreement on the cause(s) of the problems builds a level of trust and a relationship between the RCA analysts and the component teams that really helps the success rate of the study.

During this review, the component team will often find holes or problems with the results, as well as provide additional information that didn't come out during the first round of data gathering. A presentation by the RCA team often results in comments like, "Oh, yeah, that's right, we did this extra step during that phase—I forgot about that," and may result in a reset or new round of data gathering.

Compile a Categorized List of Causes

After the analysis and team review are complete, the next step is to compile the complete list of causes, categorized by area, level, and classification. The classification may flag one or more "root" causes. A *root cause* is *the* cause of the undesired event or defect. A *proximate cause* is a root-level cause discovered through the analysis, but it is not the root cause of the event under study. A *corollary cause* is a cause that follows the root cause but precedes the undesired event. For example, a root cause of buffer overruns in the code may be the lack of specific developer training on how buffer overruns occur. Another root cause may be the unwillingness or inability of a developer to compile with switches designed to catch buffer overruns (*/GS*). A proximate cause may be a lack of developer training on numerous security vulnerabilities, such as buffer overruns. A corollary cause, in this example, may be a missing item that covers buffer overruns in a code review checklist.

The classification taxonomy should support each type of cause, and there may be cases where preventive or corrective actions are prescribed for proximate or corollary causes. Identifying causes this way helps prioritize the corrective action recommendations.

Examples of Common Areas to Investigate

The following are common high-level areas where defects may be caused. As the RCA study is under way, review this list for suggestions of places to look. As the analysis team gains experience, they can add to this list from their specific expertise.

- Training
- Procedures
- Process
- Accountability
- Lack of vision or mission
- Recognition and awareness
- Inspection and supervision
- Pressure or stress

Phase IV: Corrective Actions

The corrective actions phase (see Figure 11-6) is where solutions to the problems are identified, written up, and recommended to the affected team. In some studies, this phase is very easy because the solutions are obvious and fall naturally out of the data gathering and causal analysis phase, whereas in other studies, the majority of the work must be done in the corrective action phase.

The RCA study may or may not be staffed and funded to implement corrective actions. Some organizations look to the RCA team for a full-scale eradication of causal factors, including tool development, process change, and training. In other cases, the RCA team is a study team that returns to management with a set of prioritized recommendations, which are evaluated and funded as a separate step.

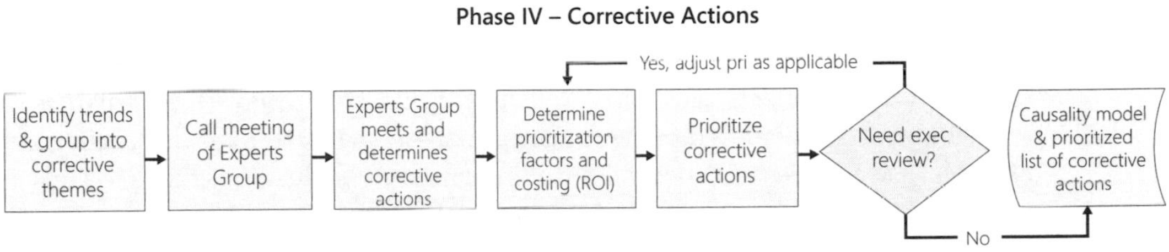

Phase IV – Corrective Actions

Figure 11-6   The root cause analysis process: phase IV

Identify Trends and Group Them in Corrective Themes

The first step in the identification and development of corrective action recommendations is to look for trends in the causes. The categorization efforts done in the preceding phase should help with identifying any trends that may exist. Grouping the causes into "themes" or broad areas will help. Again, the gut feel of the analysis team is OK to go with here. For example, causes that look to be related to time or schedule pressure could be grouped together, while other causes that may be related to outdated processes, inadequate training, lack of detection or prevention tools, and other problem types can all be grouped separately. Some causes may appear in multiple groups. This grouping can provide tremendous insight into what actions can be taken.

Call a Meeting of the Experts Group

After the causes have been grouped together into theme areas, notify the set of experts and others contributing to the study to review. If possible, this should be a discussion or debate, not an e-mail conversation. A brainstorming review of the corrective "themes" with the experts and other participants flushes out any holes in the data or in the thinking about recommendations.

Many times, the experts group will agree with the majority of the ideas and be able to add a few more suggestions or insights to firm up the quality of the recommendations. In this meeting or discussion, the themes can be narrowed down to specific corrective actions. For example, the training theme can be narrowed to "Security training on coding to prevent denial-of-service attacks" or the process theme can be distilled to "Automate the developer build process."

These corrective actions should be compiled for as many of the causes as possible. Although the overall goal of the root cause study may be to identify one or more low-level root causes and eliminate them, if the opportunity exists to eradicate the causes of other problems, it makes sense to follow through with the experts during this phase. Even if the recommendations are not adopted for nonroot causes, the data is still valuable for future changes or improvements, as well as future studies.

Determine Prioritization Factors and Costing (ROI)

When the study has come this far, the RCA team is confident about what needs to be done to fix the problems. The final steps relate to gathering data to ensure that deployment and adoption of corrective actions take place. Many studies can fizzle out with corrective action recommendations never deployed because management is unable to fund their deployment. For example, if a set of security defects is studied, and the conclusion is that a tool can be written to detect them prior to developer check-in, but that tool costs $200,000 to create, management may not see the payoff or return on that tool development investment. That's the goal of this step—to show the return on investment (ROI) by costing out the corrective actions and mapping them back to impact costs of the defects. These impact costs can include the cost of finding defects plus the cost of missing them—letting them escape to customers.

This ROI analysis should be done on all corrective action recommendations, and the actions should be prioritized accordingly. No organization has an unlimited budget, so showing the return on investment is a good way to prioritize actions for the management reports. The data should be available from earlier phases of the study, and typically, the returns are significant. In fact, the average return on investment for RCA studies ranges between 600 and 1,000 percent.[1] This includes the costs related to the study as well.

Conduct a Longitudinal Analysis

The RCA team may be staffed and organized a number of different ways. However it is staffed, the study team should spend some time looking at progress over time. A *longitudinal analysis* is a review of the results of multiple studies over time and yields findings in trends, behavioral similarities, and culture tendencies that won't be visible after a single study. Longitudinal analysis is a study in which behavior is analyzed over time, and it can allow the RCA team to review the results of one study in comparison with another. The advantages of an investment in a longitudinal analysis include the following:

- It has a credibility impact of repeated observations on individual study results.

- Change over time can be studied directly.

- Defects and corresponding corrective actions are measured repeatedly.

---

1   Robert J. Latino, Reliability Center, Inc. See *www.reliability.com*

- Repeated observations can be correlated.

- Sequential measurement highlights correlations between studies.

- Cross-study data can provide conclusions outside the scope of an individual study.

The longitudinal analysis encompasses the last two phases of the RCA study process.

Phase V: Inform and Apply

At this point, the RCA team must present the corrective actions to those affected by the recommendations. Then the corrective actions are applied. (See Figure 11-7.)

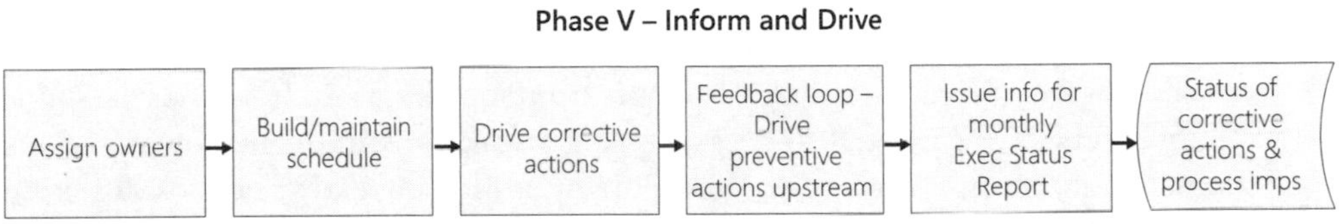

Phase V – Inform and Drive

Figure 11-7   The root cause analysis process: phase V

Host a Management Review

After all the recommendations for corrective actions have been gathered, reviewed, and prioritized and returns assessed, it is time to schedule a review with management. For larger organizations, this can be a big event, and in other cases, it may be a nonevent. The goal of the management review is to get approval for any additional spending or investment in corrective action implementation, as well as get support for process or procedural change recommendations.

The management review should start with a reiteration of the problem or sentinel events, walk through an overview of the RCA process, and conclude with the recommendations and specific action items or management requests. In smaller organizations, any independent associate can perform this review and provide a second opinion. The second opinion can help determine the reasonableness of the corrective actions.

Assign Owners

After the management review has been completed, and assuming approval has been granted, the next step is to assign owners to the corrective actions. These owners may or may not be part of the RCA team—preferably not—and are responsible for driving the recommended changes into the organization. If possible, these owners should report back to the RCA team on a regular basis on their progress. In some organizations, a "corrective action team" may be funded to fully staff the efforts to implement the corrective action implementation. These dedicated teams help accelerate the changes and ensure that ownership and implementation are top priorities.

Build and Maintain Schedule

The owners are responsible for creating the schedule on which the recommended corrective actions will be implemented. Typically, this schedule aligns with the project schedule, but that isn't a requirement. Each organization must manage the schedule in a way that best suits its own priorities.

Create a Feedback Loop

It's important for the RCA team to gather feedback on its recommendations. Although the goal is for the analysts to have a good understanding of the processes and behavior of the organization, there is never a complete guarantee that the corrective action will be the right one. As recommendations are deployed through the organization, the RCA team should ensure that they monitor feedback from the team members and from those responsible for deploying the changes. In some cases, a small change early in the deployment can save a recommendation from being a complete failure by addressing early feedback. It's critical for the RCA team to ensure that these communication mechanisms are in place as recommendations are rolled out.

Establish a Monthly Status Report

Management that is funding the RCA effort will need to be kept up to date on how things are going. If the goal of the RCA study is to find ways to prevent a class of defects, at the conclusion of the corrective action deployment, the monthly report should be able to show a drop in the frequency of that class of defects, or explain why things have not changed. The RCA team also wants to monitor progress, and the creation of this report will help connect the various data sources to monitor activity and perhaps help refine the recommendations.

Track Status of Corrective Actions and Process Improvements

Beyond the monthly management reports, the RCA team should regularly monitor the status of the corrective action implementation and process improvements. Particularly if the team has moved on to a new study, the status of the defect prevention efforts is important to monitor.

Phase VI: Follow-up, Measurement, and Recommendations

This part of the longitudinal analysis provides an opportunity for the organization to invest in understanding the relationships and findings across multiple root cause analysis studies, to follow up on the learning acquired by measuring success applying recommended actions, and to report the results to stakeholders. (See Figure 11-8.)

Phase VI – Longitudinal Analysis

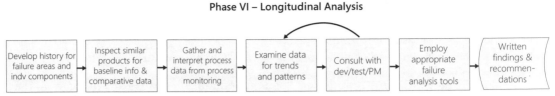

Figure 11-8   The root cause analysis process: phase VI

Know the Areas of Interest for Longitudinal Analysis

The following is a partial list of subjects for longitudinal analysis. The most import element of a multiple-study analysis is the identification of trending or tendency information to demonstrate how corrective action recommendations relate.

- **Develop history for failure types and component areas**   For most projects, it should be a straightforward process to review the types of defects and problematic areas over time. Defect tracking systems should hold enough detail in the problem reports to analyze defect trends. However, as root cause studies are performed on various subsets of the defects, an analysis of the root cause findings along with the traditional defect trends may yield additional insight. For example, defect reports may indicate that a certain component area, perhaps the user interface, is the most problematic area. However, a series of root cause studies may reveal that interlocking dependencies beneath the user interface are responsible for the problems and a change in coding practices or component architecture for a memory management component, for instance, will reduce the defects in the user interface. Similarly, the user interface coding may change to account for potential low-memory conditions that had previously been handled by the memory manager—in most cases.

- **Inspect similar products/areas for baseline and comparative data**   A root cause analysis study of two different areas may result in similar conclusions. For example, a study of two components may indicate a prevalence of buffer overrun bugs. The corrective action recommendations may be deployed differently in the two teams, with one working better than the other does. Monitoring the study results over time and going back to perform a longitudinal analysis across studies can show how teams have performed following the study results. These results can also be used as baselines for future results. If one team reduces buffer overrun bugs by 50 percent using a new process, the RCA team can help propagate some of the best practices throughout the organization.

- **Gather and interpret process data from process monitoring**   A longitudinal analysis will benefit from data-gathering efforts across studies. Remember that one of the goals of RCA is to enable the team to learn from mistakes, and by measuring process changes and gathering data on corrective action deployment and defects prevented, the RCA team can hone their skills over time. Monitoring key processes and gathering data on improvements are tremendously beneficial to future studies and improve the RCA effort with each successive study.

- **Examine data for trends or patterns**   As detailed data arrives from each successive study, the RCA team is responsible for analysis and understanding the trends and indications. Patterns in the data and repetitive behaviors can point to major cultural tendencies that can expedite the efforts of future analysts.

Present Written Findings and Recommendations   Periodically throughout the series of RCA studies, the team should spend time writing up and publishing the current findings. These reports serve a couple of purposes. First, the team members and those who have been surveyed, interviewed, and studied can see the results of the effort. This helps assure them that their time was not wasted. Second, managers who are funding the studies are able to see the results regularly, encouraging and confirming future investments. Finally, other teams who are making similar errors can evaluate corrective actions.

Benefits of Root Cause Analysis

The structured methodology of root cause analysis helps guide the effort through layers of cause and effect to identify the lowest-level causes. An ordinary investigation of a defect does not typically lead to the discovery of lower-level causes. One of the advantages of addressing problems at a lower level is the breadth and scope of the impact. Following are other important benefits an organization can realize from conducting an RCA study.

- **Can start as small pilots and grow accordingly**   A root cause analysis program can start small. A single engineer can perform his or her own root cause analysis on a single defect. The ability to scale the size of the study makes this method of defect prevention very flexible. By starting small with minimal investment, the organization or individual can experiment and grow the program only after measurable success. Because many different types of defects occur, and the amount of supporting data that can be analyzed may vary, not every study will be successful in identifying corrective actions that can be deployed to prevent recurrence. Different organizations will see different results from root cause analysis programs, and the ability to scale up the level of investment is a great benefit of this technique.

- **Uses an identical process regardless of type, age, or scope of defect**   Any undesirable event can benefit from a well-defined and structured root cause analysis process. The technique is an effective prevention technique for use with all types of defect without much change to the methodology. The first step—selection of the sentinel events or defects to study—does not dictate the subsequent steps in the process. Although the defects under analysis may influence the amount of data available, or the availability of experts to interview, the steps remain the same. For example, if the defect sample is very old or obscure, there may not be much data available for analysis. However, that would not remove the data collection phase from the study.

The fact that the process does not change dramatically based on the selection is a benefit because as more studies are completed, patterns can emerge to improve the efficiency of the study. Over the course of many studies, the analyst will learn what types of information can be gathered from interviews and surveys versus those gathered by raw data collection. The types of defects under study will not directly influence the applicability or value of the results.

- **Avoids repeat failures**   As mentioned, a successful root cause analysis study will yield corrective actions that avoid or eliminate repeated mistakes.

- **Can be the shortest path to determining and correcting causes of failure**   A root cause analysis study may often be the fastest and least expensive way to find sources of defects. The study can begin simply by asking why the defect may have occurred. As mentioned previously, a root cause analysis study can begin with a single engineer and grow accordingly. In many cases, an engineer can look at his or her own work and identify defect prevention techniques immediately. If, for example, I see a series of logic errors reported against my code, I can perform a small root cause analysis study against my code. I may find that in times of high stress, perhaps I forget semicolons or use the assignment equal sign (=) instead of the double equal sign (==). I can learn from this study to add specific checks in my code inspection for these types of errors, especially when I know I am under duress. When there is schedule pressure, I can remind the code reviewer or pair programmer with whom I'm working to look out for these types of errors, and I can encourage anyone testing my code to beware of these classes of defects.

- **Improves operating efficiencies and maintenance procedures to expedite defect discovery**   Root cause analysis studies result in recommendations for corrective actions that address the cause of defects. The deeper the analysis can go into the causes of the defect, the more effective the corrective actions can be. In many cases, these recommendations can introduce operating efficiencies and process changes that result in earlier defect discovery. A good example is a code review or formal code inspection. A root cause analysis of a given defect may find that the best technique to discover this class of defect is a code review. Upon implementing a code review policy, the team may see other classes of defects discovered regularly in code reviews that may otherwise escape to later in the product development life cycle.

- **Lowers maintenance costs**   Recommendations from a root cause analysis study can lower maintenance costs by preventing recurring defects. A root cause analysis study yields a set of recommendations for corrective actions to eradicate a class of defects. Eliminating recurring defects lowers the maintenance costs and sets the stage for ongoing cost reduction. A root cause analysis study is a particularly cost-effective technique because the recommendations typically address an entire class of defects rather than a single error.

Risks of Root Cause Analysis

There are some potential pitfalls with the RCA strategy. For example, without a careful selection of sentinel events, the RCA effort can become a series of glamorized case studies that never yield corrective recommendations or result in any changes. Early RCA pilot programs should focus on high-profile defects—those that directly affect customers—to increase credbility and avoid the "glamorized case study" label.

Another potential risk is bias. RCA findings can be biased in a number of different ways, including hindsight, current tools or process refinements, and unrelated peripheral causes such as management or staffing issues. These can contribute to a bias by influencing the results in a given way. For example, if there is a heavy investment in static analysis tools, the study team might be biased towards those tools as a potential corrective action. If developer coding skills has been a problem in past releases, a hindsight bias might contribute to a similar finding. If it's hard to staff testing operations, a bias might lead to a conclusion that includes the need for more testing. The point is to be careful to avoid becoming biased by the current state of affairs.

To avoid these biases, the process should be independent and rely heavily on the detailed analysis of the events, using data from a wide variety of sources to determine the corrective actions. This removes product or management-related biases and legitimizes the process by focusing just on the analysis and corresponding recommendations.

The following sections detail other more specific risks involved in using root cause analysis.

- **Draws the incorrect conclusion or makes invalid recommendations**   The biggest risk is that of being wrong. An inaccurate conclusion or recommendations that do not address the problem can potentially lead to more damage than that caused by the original defect. For example, a study of buffer overruns may recommend an investment in automated tools to catch buffer overrun errors but may incorrectly assume the development team has training on how not to write code that leads to buffer overruns. The study may stop short of the root cause and make a recommendation that will help but not eradicate the cause of the defects.

  The goal is to follow a process for completing the study and involve others at many levels to avoid an incorrect problem set selection or invalid recommendations. Mistakes can happen, and errors can occur in the study. This risk brings up the humorous possibility of implementing a root cause analysis of the problems in performing a root cause analysis study. Seriously, though, if any errors occur in the root cause analysis study, it is important to learn from them and use that information to improve the process because root cause analysis study capabilities are valuable to an organization.

- **Focuses on the wrong set of defects**   One of the dangers of a root cause analysis study can occur before the study even begins. If management or the RCA team selects the wrong set of "undesirable events"—or software defects—as the target of the study, the conclusions drawn from the analysis will be less relevant than conclusions drawn if a good set is chosen. For example, if customer feedback indicates that software security is a big issue, and the team decides to do a root cause analysis of performance-related defects, the study results may be valuable but are not relevant to the most important area of the product.

■   **Begins too long after the event to have good data**   It is natural to think about process or quality improvements at a milestone event. A root cause analysis study can benefit from an abundance of data, and the longer the team waits to begin a study, the less data is available. Limited or irrelevant data hurts the success rate of an RCA study.

■   **Ends at the wrong level—too early or late**   As the analyst walks through levels of cause and effect, there is a risk of halting the study too early or too late. As the study team identifies the causes, it is important to monitor the level of relevance, viability, and like-lihood of addressing defects through corrective actions. Going too far can render correc-tive actions irrelevant or impossible to achieve. Stopping too early will not address broader issues and will solve only local problems. Although either case is still a net positive for the team, the best way to ensure that RCA studies are successful is to care-fully monitor the level of relevance of the causes to the undesired event that prompted the study.

Conclusion

Root cause analysis is a popular and successful technique for identifying ways to prevent defects. There are a variety of approaches to study unfortunate events in an effort to under-stand the low-level causes. Root cause analysis is an effective technique that can improve the software development process for an individual, a small team, or a large organization. Anyone can perform a root cause analysis, although the results will improve with the level of experi-ence of the analyst.

Although there is typically no shortage of sentinel events—usually defects—to initiate a study, root cause analysis is not a technique that is a predictable investment in every software project. Some defects are more "important" than others are—whether they are found by customers, are expensive to repair, require a maintenance release, or cause data loss or security holes—and therefore the investment in a root cause study may vary from project to project. However, for an analyst or a team staffed to perform the studies, the work is always interesting and therefore easily sustained.

One of the big advantages to having root cause capabilities in an organization's arsenal of defect prevention techniques is that these studies will lead to the discovery of deeper, more fundamental problems in the way the code is developed; these problems are not usually exposed by other techniques. Although RCA can be an expensive and time-consuming process, often it yields results that are not achievable using any other method.

Part IV
Defect Prevention Techniques

Chapter 12
Adopting Processes

It must be remembered that there is nothing more difficult to plan, more doubtful of success nor more dangerous to manage than the creation of a new order of things.
—Niccolò di Bernardo dei Machiavelli

A man who carries a cat by the tail learns something he can learn in no other way.
—Mark Twain

Dans les champs de l'observation le hasard ne favorise que les esprits préparés.
—Louis Pasteur

Humphrey (2003) compares getting software developers to follow a process to herding cats.[1] If that is the case, implementing the process requires you to pick up the cat by the tail and carry it around until an understanding is reached. As Twain envisioned, it results in learning something that can only be learned by doing. It also requires a bit of luck. But luck is the by-product of good engineering.

Volumes have been written on change management, with more still on software methods. This chapter does not rehash change management philosophies except for pointing out two seemingly contradicting ideas that must be considered when implementing process. First, deploying a new process requires senior management direction. Second, people cannot be forced to do that which they do not want to do.

An organization will make no progress unless senior management drives the initiative and pays attention to the improvements. This is often thought to mean that a mandate from the senior executive will force the organization to use a certain practice or set of practices. As the old adage goes, "You can lead a horse to water," but you might have to hold its head under to make it to drink. Unfortunately, that style of leadership doesn't work with the types of improvement described in this book. If it were as easy as writing a memo, an organization would need only to define a coding standard that states, "*Do not write bugs!*" and all code would be defect free. Instead, management must lead and motivate the organization and trust the data to guide implementation, as is described in other chapters.

Senior management cannot mandate improvement, and people cannot be told to implement a process. The result of attempting to force a solution is that people will treat process improvement as a game and the metrics will become almost meaningless. Software engineering is knowledge work that requires best practice as part of the daily routine. The individual doing the work must own the process. This seems to contradict the need for management to drive

---

1 W. S. Humphrey, *Winning with Software: An Executive Strategy* (Boston: Addison-Wesley, 2002).

the initiative. However, senior leadership must reward quality and have the processes in place to recognize it when they get it.

This chapter is devoted to describing concepts of various well-known methodologies as they related to process improvement. Because, as Pasteur pointed out, "in the fields of observation chance favors only the prepared mind," the purpose of this chapter is to help you have a process prepared to use the techniques described throughout the book. The intent is to dispel a variety of process myths so that a quality practice is recognizable by those who set organizational strategy. The chapter begins with a discussion of traditional thinking and its merits. Next, agile methods are described using the Capabilities Maturity Model (CMM) framework from Chapter 2, "Defect Prevention Frameworks." Finally, the Personal Software Process (PSP) is described as an implementation of the CMM framework to expand the concepts of a data model.

Understanding the Traditional Development Process

Software development is a process of producing mathematically rigorous interpretations of imprecise ideas. All software projects begin with an idea, or system requirement. No one begins a project by randomly writing code and then figuring out what it does. The code originates from a requirement, which is transformed into a high-level concept for implementing a more detailed understanding of the implementation, and which is ultimately transformed into the final source code. Some may say that code is not mathematically rigorous. However, a microprocessor is essentially a very fast adding machine augmented with the ability to jump between equations. It understands only math. A development process bridges the gap between the product concept and the sequential instructions executable on the modern processor.

The extremes of the creative process explain the debates associated with using various methodologies. On the one hand, the process must allow the developer to think conceptually to solve a real-world problem. On the other hand, it must be disciplined enough to translate a possibly ill-conceived problem statement into a sequence of computer statements that completely and fully define operation under all possible conditions.

The examples used throughout this book rely on a traditional conceptual process often termed the "waterfall method" of software development. A common misconception of the waterfall method is that requirements precede design, which in turn precedes coding, and so on.[1] The problem lies in the fact that the sequence of events is not enforced in the manufacture of the software product. As a result, a developer can simply sit down at the computer and start hacking out code.

---

1 Winston Royce, author of the original work on the waterfall method, did not assume a one-way flow, although this has become the modern interpretation of his work. See W. W. Royce, "Managing the Development of Large Software Systems: Concepts and Techniques," in *Technical Papers of Western Electronic Show and Convention (WesCon)*, August 25–28, 1970, Los Angeles, CA.

The traditional view contends that first requirements are documented, then design specs of some sort are produced, and finally code is written because this mirrors the natural information flow created over time. Test cases are required, but their exact placement in the process is not fixed. This traditional view is the most common method of implementing a process using a framework such as the CMM possibly because of the fact that progress against a schedule can be clearly gauged by the existence of various work products. However, the CMM framework must work equally well with alternative methods because it indicates what needs producing, not how it is to be produced. The traditional flow of work products from requirements to working code needs rethinking, but the framework of what needs producing need not change.

As the project progresses in time, the developers will learn more about the problem and implement more of the solution. Royce conceived of various work products, requirements statements, designs, code, test cases, and so on, being transformed at each stage, with each providing more detail about the problem. As developers learn more, they may rework prior items. All processes will produce information flow in this manner simply because every activity in the development process continues to modify prior knowledge. Of course, not all processes require the effort of creating formal requirements specifications or designs. But even in the case when an engineer simply sits down and writes code, more is learned about the requirements as the code is written, resulting in changes to the requirements.

Implementing Agile Processes

A myth around the so-called agile methods is that they are not rigorous process methodologies. Agile processes, when implemented correctly, are actually quite rigorous, perhaps among the most disciplined of methods. Of course, the phrase "implemented correctly" has many possible interpretations. For purposes of discussion, *correctly* means according to the authors' original goals.

This section describes one of the popular agile methods, eXtreme Programming (XP), in the light of some of the CMM key practice areas. Additionally, it examines process measurements as they relate to organizational scorecards and stochastic modeling.

Kent Beck is credited with the invention of XP in the mid-1990s, although mention is often made of Ron Jeffries and Ward Cunningham as contributing to the effort. Undoubtedly, by this time, a myriad of individuals have contributed to the effort. For purposes of this discussion, Kent Beck's book *eXtreme Programming eXplained*[1] (and the *HBR* article by Takeeuchi and Nonaka on Scrum) is the original work and serves as the standard of correctness. For those unfamiliar with these processes, see the original works.

CMM level 2 key practices (KPAs) include requirements management, project planning, project tracking and oversight, software quality assurance, and software configuration

---

1 K. Beck, *Extreme Programming Explained: Embrace Change* (Reading, MA: Addison-Wesley, 2000).

management.[1] Typical first-time process assessments focus on the level 2 practices, so we give a brief critique against many of the activities of level 2.

XP defines a three-phase process for development: exploration, commitment, and steering. The exploration phase provides "an appreciation of what all the system should eventually do."[2] The outputs of this phase are a series of stories that document system functionality from the business perspective and rough estimates of the effort required for the story. The commitment phase prioritizes the stories, assigns risk, determines productivity (known as velocity in XP), and sets the project scope. The steering phase or phases result in the implementation of the stories and changes to them based on new information. Because the process is tightly integrated, there is not a one-for-one mapping to the traditional flow of requirements, design, code, and test. Therefore, the assessment requires considering whether the alternative practice fulfills the goals of the KPA. For each KPA, several, but not all, of the activities are considered, and a representative sample is given of the total activities possible.

Requirements Management

Requirements management (RM) has two goals: to baseline the software requirements, and to keep plans consistent with the requirements. As stated in Chapter 2, KPAs have associated activities. RM has three:

Activity 1: The software engineering group reviews the requirements before they are incorporated into the software project.

Because the software developers are part of the exploration phase, they must be reviewing the requirements. The purpose of this activity is to ensure feasibility, consistency, testability, and so forth; the fact that developers are part of the creation process seems to ensure the purpose. Additionally, this activity ensures that commitments made on the part of the engineering team are negotiated with the team. Because the team members are responsible for sizing the stories, they are part of the negotiation.

Activity 2: The software group uses the requirements for planning.

Planning and requirements are tightly bound in XP. The requirements do not precede the plan in a formal specification. Because planning is integrated with the creation of the stories, the plans must come from the stories. Additionally, the engineers are expected to break stories into tasks. The CMM uses the phrase "managed and controlled" to indicate that some form of version control system is put in place. The history of change is not explicitly addressed in XP, but it is unclear whether such a measure is necessary in the XP method; gathering team data can identify whether this is an area for potential process improvement.

---

1 The practice of subcontractor management is excluded because it is not germane to team practice.

2 K. Beck, *Extreme Programming Explained: Embrace Change* (Reading, MA: Addison-Wesley, 2000).

Activity 3: Changes to the requirements are reviewed and incorporated into the project.

During the steering phase, new stories can be created. A new story can result in either an existing equivalent story being removed from the plan or possibly a reestimation of the plan. The description provided by Beck indicates that the impact of changes is assessed and commitments are updated. It is unclear whether the impact to existing stories is determined, although it seems likely. Also, the CMM defines the need to review changes with senior management. Once again, the framework does provide potential improvement opportunities, and examining team data can determine whether the improvement would be beneficial in your organization.

Project Planning

The project planning (PP) KPA has three goals, namely, document the estimates in project plans, document the activities, and have those affected by the plans agree to the commitments.

Activity 1: The software group participates on the proposal team.

Because the planning game involves members of the team, and in fact requires their participation, the software group is part of the proposal. The CMM is written in such a way that the business may create the project proposal at a separate point in the project life cycle before any software planning occurs. XP does not separate the business and development functions, instead requiring that they work together.

Activity 9: Estimates for the size of the product are made according to a documented procedure.

Activity 10: Estimates for the effort and cost are made according to a documented procedure.

XP has a well-defined practice for creating the plans. The process is one of continual integration and update. The number of stories is the size measure, and the velocity is the measure of productivity. Assuming the project team is not new to XP, historical data for stories per week are known. Those involved with traditional development may be uncomfortable with the fact that little reference is made to formal documentation, such as pert or Gantt charts.

The biggest issue in the XP style of planning is the inability to determine the source of a misestimate. When your team reflects on the project after delivery of the software, it is beneficial to return to the planning information to look for improvement opportunities. Stories are likely to have a large variance of effort because they are not precise. This is probably the biggest problem in XP-style planning and could be a good first improvement. The PSP implementation for proxy-based estimation can merge very well with the story-planning process and address the issue.[1]

---

1 See W. S. Humphrey, *PSP: A Self-Improvement Process for Software Engineers* (Upper Saddle River, NJ: Addison-Wesley, 2005).

Activity 13: Risks associated with cost, resources, schedule, and so forth are identified and documented.

In the planning game, a process step calls out the need for a risk assessment of the stories based on the ability to plan using them. The impact on the schedule is not called out explicitly, but it is reasonable to assume an experienced manager would do so.

Activity 15. Planning data are recorded.

XP makes use of charts, such as velocity per week, which are available to all team members. The only problem with such data is the inability to maintain a historical database for significant lengths of time.

Project Tracking and Oversight

There are 13 activities associated with project tracking and oversight (PTO) in the CMM. The goals of PTO are to track actual results against the plan, to take corrective actions when the plan differs from the actual result, and to add changes to the project to the team plans.

Activity 1: A documented plan is used for tracking activities.

XP uses the plan to determine the tasks required of the engineer. The stories are broken down into individual tasks, which then become items to track against. The progress against tasks is recorded on a periodic basis. If the progress shows that an engineer is overcommitted, tasks are redistributed to other team members or stories are deferred to later cycles.

Activity 5: The sizes of the products are tracked and corrective actions taken as necessary.

Activity 6: The project's effort and costs are tracked and corrective actions taken as necessary.

The number of stories completed is an important measure of progress. Additionally, cost is tracked in the form of weeks of work, which leads to the productivity measure of velocity (stories per unit of time).

Activity 11: Actual measurement data and replanning data for the project are recorded.

Beck describes the need for tracking data, saying, "You can make all the estimates you want, but if you don't measure what really happens against what you predicted would happen, you won't ever learn."[1] Obviously, the commitment to tracking data exists in XP. A team role known as tracker must "keep an eye on the big picture." The data tracked includes such items as velocity, functional test coverage, and defects logged. The tracker role actually fills multiple CMM roles. Not only does the tracker assist in project tracking, he or she also acts in a quality assurance role.

---

1 K. Beck, *Extreme Programming Explained: Embrace Change* (Reading, MA: Addison-Wesley, 2000).

Software Quality Assurance

The software quality assurance (SQA) practice has four goals: Planning for SQA, verification of adherence to the workgroup standards, communicating the SQA activities, and addressing issues with the conformances.

Activity 2: The SQA activities are performed according to plan.

The CMM definition of SQA activities includes not only assessing product quality but also assessing process conformance. In XP, product quality is assessed by using code reviews during pair programming and exhaustive testing. Process adherence is not mentioned. The implication is that professionalism determines behavior of XP team members, so members of the team will adhere to such requirements as coding standards as a matter of course. For test coverage, metrics determine whether such standards as 100 percent test coverage are met.

Activity 5: The SQA group audits the product to verify compliance.

It is unlikely that the concept of audit would sit well with an XP team. The intent of the CMM is that independent verification provides a check step to catch unintentional mistakes. XP uses the concept of pair programming, which can be viewed as continuous verification. Additionally, the role of tracker previously mentioned can be viewed as an SQA role. XP also includes a process coach role, which has responsibility for the process. The coach is another form of SQA.

Software Configuration Management

Software configuration management (SCM) practices are not explicitly called out in XP, possibly because so many tools exist to address this area. The philosophy that "anyone can change any code anywhere in the system at any time"[1] is diametrically opposed to the SCM goal of "changes to identified software work products are controlled."[2] However, XP attempts to minimize the risk of uncontrolled change though alternative practices. The activities of SCM attempt to create a version control system such that the product can be rebuilt at any point in the future, and that errant changes can be removed. It is unlikely that the philosophy of collective ownership would work when the collective is the size of the Microsoft Windows operating system product team. This KPA is probably the weakest of the framework for XP. However, changing to meet CMM requirements would possibly have system impacts that eliminate the benefits of XP.[3] Someone attempting to adhere to the CMM framework would need to take great care to guarantee that the improvements did not have unintentional side effects.

---

1 K. Beck, *Extreme Programming Explained: Embrace Change* (Reading, MA: Addison-Wesley, 2000).

2 M. C. Paulk, C. V. Weber, B. Curtis, and M. B. Chrissis, *The Capability Maturity Model: Guidelines for Improving the Software Process* (Reading, MA: Addison-Wesley, 1994).

3 See chapter 9 for a discussion of system impacts when making process changes.

Scrum

The Scrum method dates back to a *Harvard Business Review* article from the mid-1980s.[1] It was applied to software by many individuals, including Ken Schwaber, Jeff Sutherland, John Scumniotales, and Jeff McKenna. Takeuchi and Nonaka define a set of process philosophies by using an analogy to rugby. Many of the activities described for XP also apply to a Scrum team. Like XP, Scrum teams will time-box coding activities, that is, set a fixed development cycle and fit as much functionality as possible into the time quantum. The process defined by Takeuchi and Nonaka includes size characteristics: Built-in stability, self-organizing teams, overlapping phases, "multilearning," subtle control, and organizational transfer of learning. The original concept focuses on the organizational aspects of product development.

Scrum adds to XP by advocating daily team meetings to track the project status. The daily meeting is designed to be of a short duration, typically 15 minutes, during which team members describe current status and garner any required assistance. Each team member answers the questions, "What have I done since yesterday?" "What am I planning to do by tomorrow?" and "What problems will prevent me from accomplishing my goals?" One criticism of XP is that it does not scale. By adding the Scrum concepts to those of XP, teams can grow bigger.

Personal Software Process

The Personal Software Process (PSP) is often categorized as a religion by those who first hear of it. In a sense, it is a religion in exactly the same way that the scientific method is a religion. Theories are proposed and rigorously tested using an accepted method. The belief in the theory continues only so long as the data are not available. The data becomes the ultimate arbitrator, and opinion is dismissed.

The PSP was created by Watts Humphrey at the Software Engineering Institute of Carnegie-Mellon University.[2] The basic hypothesis is that the individual engineer must do the work; therefore, it is the individual engineer who must own the process. Like the agile methods, the individual is valued over the organizational process. Such a philosophy has a significant problem, though, in that software products are built by teams and, in some cases, the team can be very large. The premise of having an individual owning her or his own process is directly opposed to the fact that teams, not individuals, build products.

The brilliance of the PSP is that it turns traditional process improvement concepts upside down. Typical methods are conceptualized from the top down. That is, an organizational set of best practices is documented, and all engineers conform to those practices. As was indi-

---

1   H. Takeuchi and I. Nonaka, "The New New Product Development Game," *Harvard Business Review* 64, no. 1 (1986): 137–146.

2   See W. S. Humphrey, *A Discipline for Software Engineering* (Upper Saddle River, NJ: Addison-Wesley, 1995); or W. S. Humphrey, *PSP: A Self-Improvement Process for Software Engineers* (Upper Saddle River, NJ: Addison-Wesley, 2005).

cated in Chapter 2, the CMM includes such a practice explicitly for level 3 companies. It is expected that all engineers will use a standard set of practices. The CMM expects teams to "tailor" the organizational processes to the needs of the team, requiring coordination "at the organizational level." The organizational focus implies that the team processes will be a proper subset of the organizational practice. The PSP instead expects each engineer to develop his or her own process based on the practices that work best for the individual, and then team processes consolidate the individual practices..

One of the most serious problems associated with the basic principle of the PSP is the realization that two individuals working in adjacent offices could have wildly disparate processes. In theory, one engineer may choose to use XP-like techniques[1] while the second may attempt a "pure" waterfall implementation. The PSP makes such variation possible, albeit somewhat unlikely.

The PSP framework is relatively simple. The most fundamental process consists of three steps: plan, develop, and postmortem. The possible differences between two very different engineers are shown in Table 12-1. The XP engineer jumps between creating test code, coding, compiling, testing, and refactoring, whereas the waterfall engineer is designing, coding, compiling, and testing. The only synchronization points occur when the engineers release their respective work products. The only difficulty occurs in determining who will create which parts of the product (more on this problem later in the discussion of the Team Software Process).

Table 12-1   Processes for Two Different PSP Engineers

PSP Process	XP-like	Waterfall-like
Plan	Plan	Plan
Develop	Create test code	Design
	Test	Code
	Code	Compile
	Compile	Test
	Refactor	
Postmortem	Postmortem	Postmortem

Note: Of course, there is no real order to the tasks other than that already specified in the agile discussion.

Notice that the PSP simply began with a planning phase and appended a postmortem, that is, a reflection, phase at the end. There appears to be no difference between this and the agile discussion earlier. However, the difference lies in the data framework.

The PSP assumes a framework as shown in Figure 12-1. The idea is that the size of the work product drives the effort associated with creating it, or, in other words, the size correlates to the effort. Also, the size correlates to the number of defects. The effort required for the project drives the schedule for the project based on the number of hours an engineer works per unit

---

1 Ignoring, of course, the pair programming technique.

of time, for example, 40 hours per week. This data model is not used just to collect the data; it actually determines the data that team members may collect for the process.

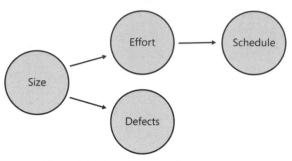

Figure 12-1   PSP data framework

Data that does not correlate according to the simple rules just described is not considered good data. For example, lines of code correlate well with number of defects[1]–not all lines of code, but only lines of code that change correlate well with system defects. A similar relationship exists between new and modified lines of code and effort[2] but, once again, not under all conditions. When a developer does a bug fix to a defect found in the field, the relationship between changed lines of code and effort is not likely to exist. The idea of the framework is to define the criteria under which a metric is usable. The PSP data framework provides the following set of criteria in addition to the required correlations:

- Data must be precise.
- Data must be specific.
- Data must be obtainable.

For data to be precise, there must be no subjectivity in the collection method. That is, every time someone measures the same thing, the same answer is obtained. In addition, if two different people measure the same thing, the same result is obtained. Second, specificity means that the measure is based on a property of the measured item. Finally, an obtainable measure is one that can be made. This sounds intuitively obvious, but consider trying to measure the entire Windows code base without an automated means to do so. In fact, any reasonably large software product cannot be measured by hand. Also, there are size measures that are not countable, such as function points.[3]

If the criteria for the data are met, the data are acceptable. Acceptability is important because of the ways in which processes are allowed to fit together and the use of the data from the processes. The PSP is a bottom-up method: process is driven from the bottom, as is data

---

1 N. Nagappan and T. Ball, "Use of Relative Code Churn Measures to Predict System Defect Density," *ICSE 2005 Conference Proceedings* (2005): 284–292.

2 W. S. Humphrey, *A Discipline for Software Engineering* (Upper Saddle River, NJ: Addison-Wesley, 1995).

3 *Function points* are a means for estimating the effort required to build a product and are popular in some software segments. Although there are ways to determine the number of function points, such means usually violate the criterion of precision.

collection and hence project tracking. To determine the project status, the data from individuals must be collected and data items of similar types consolidated.

In the previous example of the XP engineer and the waterfall engineer, the size data may be stories and lines of code, respectively. When the plan is created, the XP engineer states that he needs to build 10 stories, whereas the waterfall engineer states she needs to build 1,000 lines of code. When tracking the project, the XP engineer and the waterfall engineer report progress against the plan. Additionally, to determine schedule, productivity is defined by the two engineers as stories per unit time and as lines of code per unit time. Thus, the schedule can be determined. The overall project reports all of the size metrics and merges those into a consolidated estimate of the completion date, perhaps using a stochastic model. Finally, engineers may also use complex size measures that are combinations reflecting their individual processes. For example, the waterfall engineer may measure not only lines of code but also objects in a formal design. Then, using multiple regression techniques, she can create complex productivity measures (see Humphrey[1]).

The main point to remember about the PSP is that implementing it requires understanding how the data are to be used and adhering to the data model. The process is secondary, and the implementation supports any underlying method, even one of the agile methods.[2] However, the process must belong to the individual engineer and not to a central authority, often referred to as the Software Engineer Process Group (SEPG). The central group can own the data model, but not the individual processes.

Understanding the data model and realizing that the data are the important aspect of the process and not the actual process steps is the first step to implementing the PSP. Unfortunately, it is not intuitively obvious how you go about merging process data from individual engineers. For this reason, the Team Software Process was created.

Team Software Process

The Team Software Process (TSP) is designed to allow those using the PSP to collaborate even though their individual practices may vary. Like the PSP, the process used by the team is not specified but is instead agreed on by the team members during team planning. The planning process is well defined, designed to bring together the individual processes in such a way that meaningful data are generated.

Using the TSP, team members define a team process that allows data from various phases to be combined. Typically, team members use similar processes, that is, team members use a process with comparable process steps, so the data are similar enough to be directly combined. Then, during planning, the size of the software is described using the various measurables per phase. For example, to define the features, the team can measure requirements and

---

1 W. S. Humphrey, *PSP: A Self-Improvement Process for Software Engineers* (Upper Saddle River, NJ: Addison-Wesley, 2005).

2 See L. Williams, "The Collaborative Software Process," Ph.D. dissertation, Department of Computer Science, University of Utah, Salt Lake City, 2005.

architecture elements such as classes. To define designs, the team can count pages of functional specs or classes, or both. During coding, the team will likely count lines of code. When the project is completed, the team reports the total size of each type of deliverable: requirements, designs, code, tests, and so forth. They also report defects and effort against each type of deliverable. This becomes the historical data such as that reported in Chapter 9, "Using Simulation and Modeling for Organizational Innovation."

The purpose of the TSP is to develop a means to bring together varied processes—processes from different team members as well as different processes from each individual. The TSP contains the elements of the CMM required of teams but that are lacking in the PSP, such as configuration management practices, training plans, and team inspections. Like agile methods, the PSP lacks certain elements of scalability, which are addressed by the TSP. Thus, the TSP is not designed to stand by itself.

Encouraging Adoption of Innovative Practices

Everett Rogers provides guidance on the adoption of innovation. Adopters are placed in five categories with an explicit time ordering: Innovators, Early Adopters, Early Majority, Late Majority, and Laggards.[1] The categorizations define a number of properties about adopters that help in deciding how and why different types of people adopt innovative technologies and processes.

Innovators adopt the latest new ideas simply because the technology is daring and risky. Innovators do not mind occasional problems with the new technologies. The opinions of the Innovator do not influence the other four adopter categories. However, because Innovators are the first adopters, they are the gatekeepers to the remaining adopters. Because Innovators are willing to adopt risky methods, they provide a necessary pilot group for new processes.

The Early Adopters tend to be only slightly ahead of the average as far as the degree of innovation that they will adopt. Early Adopters are the opinion leaders of the majority of users of new technologies and make judicious recommendations as a result. New technologies must not be too risky and must solve specific problems. Of course, the Early Adopters seek to remain an opinion leader, so they must balance innovation with risk. Only after the Early Adopters approve innovations will the majority adopt them.

Early Majority are those who adopt only slightly ahead of the average. They compose about one-third of users and will make deliberate decisions only after the Early Adopters have approved the innovation; this makes them followers but not leaders in the organization. Because of the large number of Early Majority, they are an important step in the adoption curve.

Late Majority are behind the average adoption time. Rogers classifies them as skeptical and cautious. The data must clearly point to a beneficial system impact before this group will

---

1   E. M. Rogers, *The Diffusion of Innovations* (New York: Free Press, 2003).

adopt a new technology or process. Peer pressure is required before this group will be motivated to adopt. Finally, there must be little, if any, remaining risk.

The last category is known as the Laggards. As the name implies, they are far behind the average adoption rate, preferring to base decision on events that have happened in the past. Risk must be completely removed from the new technology and enough historical data proving the benefits of the technology must exist before Laggards adopt.

Along with the categorization for the types of adopters, Rogers provides a five-stage model for the decision process used to adopt. The model stages are knowledge stage, persuasion stage, decision stage, implementation stage, and confirmation stage. During the knowledge stage, the adopter is becoming aware of the innovation. As the innovation becomes more desirable to the individual, he or she enters the persuasion stage and communicates with others to learn more and garner support. If the innovation has a positive image and enough support exists, the adopter enters the decision stage. In this stage, adopters seek more information and make the decision to try the innovation. During the implementation stage, the adopter gathers still more information and begins to use the innovation on a regular basis. Finally, in the confirmation stage, the adopter recognizes the benefits of the innovation, integrates it into daily routine, and espouses the benefits to others.

The information on the type of adopter and the phases of deployment is useful in developing a strategy for deploying defect prevention technologies. Rogers provides information on the methods by which different types of innovations are adopted. Innovations described as *preventive innovations* are those that are adopted now to prevent a possible future event. Preventive innovations have a particularly slow rate of adoption because of the difficulty people have in perceiving the relative advantages of the innovation. The problem lies in the separation in time of cause and effect. Additionally, it is difficult to realize something that does not happen. Connecting a nonevent to a prevention activity is difficult for most people. In contrast, an *incremental innovation* is adopted relatively quickly because it is built on an existing practice.

Deploying a Coherent Process

To deploy the practices in this chapter, the information from Rogers needs to be fitted into a coherent strategy. A practice such as XP has some areas that can be augmented by either the CMM or the PSP. XP has a reputation for not scaling and being less rigorous than CMM is. However, it has a "coolness" factor with the Innovators; therefore, it will be readily adopted. This jumps the hurdle defined by Rogers that the Innovators are the gatekeepers. Once adopted, the areas that require augmenting become incremental improvements rather than preventive innovations. Additionally, the Innovators will be willing to discover the areas that require improvement for a particular organization, making for a customized solution. The areas that require improvement, for example, the need for permanent designs, are easily covered by practices such as the TSP, and the data to convince the Late Majority and Laggards to adopt is easily obtained by practices such as the PSP. Additionally, the data of the PSP can help provide proof during the implementation phase of deployment. A multiparadigm approach, that is, CMM, XP, PSP, and TSP, also helps to reduce the risk associated with a single technology and should appeal to the risk aversion of the Majority and Laggard populations.

Conclusion

The processes discussed in this chapter are not orthogonal to one another. The practices for data collection made possible by the PSP can easily be merged with the methodology used in XP, as was shown by Laurie Williams at the University of Utah.[1] Rigorous methods, such as XP and Scrum, can be combined with process frameworks, such as the CMM, or data frameworks, such as the PSP, to provide thorough methods and measurements.

The typical problem you may find is the misperception that the methods are at odds or somehow designed for specific situations and organizations. The CMM is not only for what Mintzberg called Machine Bureaucracies,[2] and neither are agile methods undisciplined practices. Processes such as XP implement many of the elements of the CMM, and processes defined using the CMM, such as the PSP, are very flexible. The framework of the CMM and even the PSP define what must happen, and when merged with a method that defines how to develop, the organization has a baseline practice on which to build and also the metrics necessary to understand where to change.

As discussed in Chapter 2, "Defect Prevention Frameworks," the processes must be compatible with the constraints of the business. A business that operates in a highly complex and dynamic industry, such as Internet companies, cannot hope to implement a top-down centralized control structure and expect to be competitive. However, that does not mean that a CMM framework is not useful. Agile processes are generally considered to be highly responsive, hence the name. As shown, agile process are compatible with the CMM and are also measurable.

By combining different types of processes judiciously and using the technology adoption curve, you can overcome organizational resistance. The challenge for deploying improved practices comes not in perceived incompatibilities of the methods but rather in the incompatibilities of the individual and organizational goals. Individuals require the freedom to work using a method that makes them comfortable, whereas organizations require controlled schedules and predictability. The two goals seem to imply a "Tyranny of Or" situation: either the process is controlled or it is flexible. An understanding of the needs of the organization, using a framework such as the CMM, and the needs of the individual, using a philosophy such as that espoused by XP, Scrum, or the PSP, provides the means to break the Tyranny of Or, yielding flexibility and predictability.

---

1 See Williams, L. (2000). The Collaborative Software Process. PhD Dissertation, Department of Computer Science. Salt Lake City, UT: University of Utah.

2 Mintzberg, H. (1980). Structure in 5's: A synthesis of the Research on Organizational Design. *Management Science, 26*(3), pp 322-341.

Chapter 13
FMEA, FTA, and Failure Modeling

> *Anything that is caused can be prevented.*
> *–Philip B. Crosby*

Nobody really intends to create defective software. However, somewhere between concept, design, and implementation, defects are often introduced. This is true for all software as well as other types of products and services. Over the years, companies such as Microsoft have come to realize that the only acceptable defects are those that are never introduced in the first place. If a defect can be designed out of the software, it never needs to be found and fixed later in the product cycle. Not only does this save time and money, but it allows the development team to focus more on building great new features rather than diagnosing and fixing defects in the poorly implemented ones. Unfortunately, the prevention of defects has become a constant battle in product development. To help combat this situation, many techniques have been developed to anticipate and avoid the potential defects that can occur. This chapter describes several of these techniques that are applicable early in the software development cycle and that can be used effectively to avoid defects in the product design stage.

The first defect prevention technique that is covered is failure modes and effects analysis (FMEA). This technique helps product teams anticipate product failure modes and assess their associated risks. Prioritized by potential risk, the riskiest failure modes can then be targeted to design them out of the software or at least mitigate their effects. The second defect prevention technique described is fault tree analysis (FTA). Unlike failure modes and effects analysis, which focuses on potential failure modes and does not drill deeply into the potential causes, fault tree analysis starts with an "unintended event" (for example, a defect or failure mode) and then drills into all the potential causal events. This makes it a natural complement to FMEA. Taking a broader view, FMEA and FTA can be combined into a more general "failure model" that takes advantage of the benefits of both techniques. In some respects, this is a similar approach to threat modeling,[1] which Microsoft has used extensively to assess security risks and identify vulnerabilities in software products. This chapter concludes with a brief illustration of one potential failure modeling technique.

Failure Modes and Effects Analysis

Failure modes and effects analysis (FMEA) is a defect prevention technique used to identify potential failure modes[2] in a product design, assess the risk of each potential failure, and then

---

1 Michael Howard, *Writing Secure Code*, 2nd ed. (Redmond, WA: Microsoft Press, 2002); Frank Swiderski and Window Snyder, *Threat Modeling* (Redmond, WA: Microsoft Press, 2004).

2 A *failure mode* is a type of failure that can occur in a product.

implement appropriate actions to eliminate or mitigate those failure modes. Once identified, this information can be persisted and used in future projects to help avoid defects.

After describing the origin of FMEA and its application in other industries, the focus of this section is on FMEA and its use in software development. In this context, software FMEA focuses on software systems, components, and functions.

History of FMEA

In 1949, the U.S. military created a Military Procedure (MIL-P-1629) titled "Procedure for Performing a Failure Mode, Effects and Criticality Analysis."[1] This procedure established an evaluation technique for assessing the effects of system and equipment failures. In the early 1960s, the U.S. military established this technique as a Military Standard (MIL-STD-1629a) with the same title. As described in the standard, the scope of MIL-STD-1629a was to establish the requirements and procedures for systematically evaluating the potential impact of functional or hardware failures on mission success, personnel and system safety, system performance, maintainability, and maintenance requirements.

The aerospace industry adopted FMEA in the 1960s, and it was used in the Apollo space program. In the late 1970s, the concept of using software failure modes and effects analysis (SFMEA) was introduced. In the early 1980s, the automotive industry began to incorporate FMEA into the product development process and the QS 9000 standard was developed by an industry task force to standardize supplier quality systems. These efforts led to an automotive industry FMEA standard (SAE J-1739) in the early 1990s.

Although the idea of using FMEA to improve software reliability was introduced in the late 1970s, it did not really appear in software literature and development processes until the mid-1980s. Traditionally, SFMEA has been used in safety and hazard analysis efforts in industries such as aerospace, automotive, and nuclear. Because industries such as these face potential risk to life and limb when their products fail, there has been strong motivation to use tools that could help proactively eliminate or mitigate those risks. This was the purpose for the original development of FMEA by the military and its subsequent evolution in the automotive and aerospace industries. Although the early use of FMEA was focused on hardware systems, it was just a matter of time before people tried to use FMEA for software and automated systems.

Implementing FMEA

What does it take to implement FMEA effectively? As with any defect prevention technique, the benefits achieved are usually commensurate with the effort expended. In terms of FMEA, this also holds true.

---

1 Information and documents presented here are works of the U.S. government and are not subject to copyright protection in the United States. These may be reproduced or used without permission. The U.S. Department of Defense should be acknowledged as the source (U.S. Department of Defense, U.S. Government Work [17 USC §105]). Foreign copyrights may apply.

Prerequisites

Based on Microsoft Engineering Excellence practice guidelines, consider the following prerequisites for completing an efficient and effective FMEA.

- A skilled FMEA facilitator

  - ❏ The FMEA facilitator should have a good understanding of the FMEA procedure and the ability to guide the discussion and keep it on track. This role is often supported by a team manager or lead, but it may also be an independent facilitator if warranted by the FMEA focus area or team dynamics.

- The right participants

  - ❏ Participants that represent a variety of skills, knowledge, and experience.

  - ❏ Participants that feel comfortable contributing to the FMEA discussion.

  - ❏ FMEA can be performed by a single individual, but usually it is most effectively performed as a team activity. There are great benefits in receiving a variety of inputs.

- A clear understanding of the FMEA focus area

  - ❏ All participants know what the focus area will be.

  - ❏ Effective documentation and diagrams are available to help participants understand the focus area details.

Procedure

Traditionally, FMEA starts with choosing a focus area in a product, brainstorming potential failure modes, and then for each failure mode, estimating and ranking the impact[1] of the effect, the likelihood of potential causes, and the detectability of existing controls. These ranks are then multiplied, resulting in a risk priority number that indicates the highest-risk failure modes to eliminate or mitigate in the design.

The following procedure describes the steps for completing an FMEA in more detail. Use it as a general guideline and not as a specific sequence of steps that must be followed. As the team becomes more familiar with the procedure, they may identify some opportunities to consolidate the steps. The key is to understand what is being accomplished in each step and then make sure this is being achieved regardless of the actual steps performed. A basic software example is used to help illustrate the procedure.

---

1 The common FMEA ranking terms for effect (degree of severity), cause (frequency of occurrence), and control (chance of detection) have been shortened, respectively, to impact, likelihood, and detectability for conciseness and simplicity.

Example: E2EMan Software Setup Logging FMEA

The E2EMan[1] software team is starting to plan and design the next version of their popular service management software product. Users really like the features and ease of use, but based on support call volumes for the previous version, the team knows that the software setup process has been failure prone and causing customer dissatisfaction. This has been particularly true for the setup logging part of the process. The team is determined to make this more reliable in the new version, but first they need to determine what could go wrong so that they can determine what to fix or mitigate.

At the suggestion of Mary, their team lead, they decide to use FMEA to identify the possible setup logging failure modes proactively. The team sees the value of identifying the possible failures early, and they are motivated to eliminate as many as they can. Because Mary has completed FMEAs in her previous job, she offers to facilitate the FMEA session.

Partial FMEA

Before jumping into the steps to complete an FMEA, it can be helpful to first see a portion of the final result to know what will be achieved. Figure 13-1 is a partial FMEA that illustrates the basic result format that becomes the primary output of the FMEA procedure.

Figure 13-1   Partial software setup logging FMEA

---

1   E2EMan is a hypothetical product, but the FMEA is based on a real Microsoft example.

> **Note**   In describing the FMEA procedure, each step is described in generic terms and then related to the E2EMan setup logging example to make it more tangible.

Step 1: Identify and Describe the Target Product Focus Area

The first step is to choose the focus area for the FMEA session. For a software product, example focus areas could be installation and setup, networking, and product-specific feature areas.[1] Ideally, the focus area chosen will have complete documentation and diagrams available from previous tasks. Unfortunately, this is often not the case. If documentation and diagrams do not exist or are not complete enough, an additional step is needed to improve the information and make sure it can be effectively used in the FMEA session. This information will provide reference material to give each FMEA participant a common view and understanding of the focus area.

Compile Details About the Focus Area   Details about the focus area should include information such as:

- How the product will be used by external and internal customers (for example, scenarios)
- Description of what the product should do and how it should perform (for example, specs)
- How the product is architected
    - Physical system diagrams
    - Logical system flow diagrams
    - Data flow diagrams
    - Interface diagrams
- Which technologies are used

The more details known about the focus area, the easier it is to identify potential failure modes.

---

1   Although this chapter describes a software product FMEA, FMEA works equally well when analyzing processes and services.

Example: Software Setup Logging FMEA

Mary asks the team to gather information about the E2EMan Setup Logging area in preparation for the FMEA sessions. The team was able to produce one logical flow diagram (see Figure 13-2) but had to spend some time compiling the other information to support the FMEA effort. Ideally, all the necessary information would just be available, but Mary knows this is often not the case and that the FMEA can be a forcing function to help make that happen.

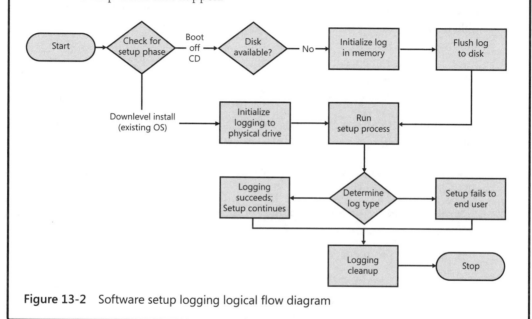

Figure 13-2   Software setup logging logical flow diagram

Step 2: Create an FMEA Worksheet and Enter Initial Data

As originally described in Military Procedure MIL-P-1629, a table has traditionally been used as an FMEA worksheet. Although there are special-purpose software packages that support very large FMEAs, typically an FMEA worksheet is implemented using a spreadsheet program that supports the automatic calculation of the risk priority number for each failure mode (see Figure 13-3).

Process Step, Function or Task	Potential Failure Mode	Potential Effect(s) of Failure	Impact Rank	Potential Causes	Likelihood Rank	Current Controls	Detectability Rank	Risk Priority	Improvement	Owner
								0		
								0		
								0		
								0		
								0		

FMEA Worksheet
Project: <project name>

Figure 13-3   Typical FMEA worksheet implemented using Microsoft Office Excel

The purpose of each column is defined as part of describing the FMEA process. The software setup logging example is used to help illustrate the steps of completing the FMEA worksheet.

Example: Software Setup Logging FMEA

Mary has available an FMEA worksheet based on Microsoft Office Excel and decides to use it for the upcoming Software Setup Logging FMEA session. After creating a copy of the worksheet, she enters "E2EMan–Setup Logging" as the project name.

Decompose the Focus Area and Identify Focus Area Targets   To facilitate the FMEA, decompose the focus area by functionality, scenarios, logical flow, technology, components, interfaces, and so forth. As an analogy, if the focus area is a process, during the decomposition individual process steps are identified. This breakdown can help identify *focus area targets* that will structure the analysis and help identify potential failure modes.

Example: Software Setup Logging FMEA

Because the focus area of this FMEA is the software setup logging logic, Mary reviews the setup flow diagram and identifies the key logging steps and decides to use those to focus the FMEA analysis. She adds those to the FMEA worksheet in logical order and one per row (see Figure 13-4).

FMEA Worksheet
Project: E2EMan - Setup Logging

Process Step, Function or Task	Potential Failure Mode	Potential Effect(s) of Failure	Impact Rank	Potential Causes	Likelihood Rank	Current Controls	Detectability Rank	Risk Priority	Improvement	Owner
Check for Setup Phase								0		
Downlevel Install								0		
Boot off CD								0		
Initialize setup logging to physical drive								0		
Setup Logging								0		
Setup Logging clean up								0		

Figure 13-4   Partial FMEA worksheet with focus area targets

Step 3: Determine Failure Modes and Add to FMEA Worksheet

A *failure mode* is a type of failure that could occur. In software systems, this is evidenced by symptoms such as a blue screen, system hang, incorrect output, and data corruption.

For each focus area target, determine all the potential failure modes and add them to the FMEA worksheet. The goal is to be as complete as possible. Later in the FMEA process, the risk priority number and the data to calculate it will be used to identify the failure modes that represent significant risks that must be addressed. Failure modes with few or no risks may become lower priority and addressed only as time and resources allow.

Identifying Failure Modes   Potential failure modes can be identified from many different sources:

- Brainstorming
- Root cause analysis
- Defect taxonomy
- Security vulnerabilities and threat models
- Bug and triage data
- Sustained engineering fixes
- Support issues and fixes
- Customer feedback
- Static analysis tools

In some cases, failure modes will come from previous product versions and feedback data gathered from customers. In other cases, failure modes are most efficiently identified using group techniques such as brainstorming and root cause analysis that take advantage of the knowledge and experience of the team.

To help determine which technique to use, consider the following brief descriptions of each source listed above.

Brainstorming   Brainstorming is probably the most common technique and the easiest to implement. All it takes is to get the right people into a meeting focused on identifying potential failure modes. A facilitator or someone experienced with running brainstorming sessions can be helpful but is not required. In a typical FMEA work session, brainstorming is the primary method used to identify potential failure modes.

Root Cause Analysis   The purpose of root cause analysis is to drill into the root causes of some defect or failure. (See Chapter 11, "Root Cause Analysis," for a more detailed description of the process.) In doing so, information often is uncovered that can be interpreted to identify potential failure modes.

Defect Taxonomy   A good defect taxonomy such as the one described in Chapter 10, "Defect Taxonomies," can provide a thorough list of possible defects that can be generalized into potential failure modes. Because the defect taxonomy addresses all types of system defects, it can be used to help analyze all aspects of the software product.

Security Vulnerabilities and Threat Models   A security vulnerability is a specific kind of failure, and threat models are used to enumerate them along with their causes. This information can be used to identify security-related failure modes.

Bug and Triage Data   Analyzing bugs and other product issues can increase awareness of potential failure modes. A *triage* occurs when people from the product team get together to discuss and analyze bugs. The results of these discussions can highlight potential failure modes.

Sustained Engineering Fixes   The work done to investigate and fix issues after a product has been released can also help identify potential failure modes.

Support Issues and Fixes   A wealth of information about product failures is available as a byproduct of the product support process. If a product failure has occurred once, there is often the possibility that it can occur again. The types of failures that can recur represent possible failure modes.

Customer Feedback   Customer feedback gathered through newsgroups, surveys, chats, and focus groups can also highlight failure modes. These are particularly useful because they come directly from customers and are based on unmet expectations.

Static Analysis Tools   Static analysis tools are used to automatically identify defects in software source code. The rules used by these tools can represent specific software errors that can be aggregated and transformed into possible failure modes. Using static analysis tools may be most appropriate when the FMEA focus area is a lower-level part of the software product.

Example: Software Setup Logging FMEA

As part of the FMEA session invitation, Mary asks specific people to bring in failure mode source information related to software setup logging. This information will be used by the team to help identify potential failure modes.

At the FMEA session, Mary first describes the purpose of the meeting, what FMEA is, and the process that will be followed. She also makes all of the failure mode source information available to everyone in the meeting. After they review the information, Mary leads the team through a structured brainstorming session to identify the failure modes for each focus area target. They start with "Check for Setup Phase." (See Figure 13-5.)

FMEA Worksheet											
Project: E2EMan - Setup Logging											
Process Step, Function or Task	Potential Failure Mode	Potential Effect(s) of Failure	Impact Rank	Potential Causes	Likelihood Rank	Current Controls	Detectability Rank	Risk Priority	Improvement		Owner
Check for Setup Phase	Incorrectly determine phase							0			
Check for Setup Phase	Indeterminate setup phase							0			
Check for Setup Phase	Fail to create log file directory							0			
Downlevel Install								0			
Boot off CD								0			
Initialize setup logging to physical drive								0			
Setup Logging								0			
Setup Logging clean up								0			

Figure 13-5   Partial FMEA worksheet with initial failure modes

Note   Figure 13-5 shows the focus area target name replicated for each failure mode. Although this is not required, it can help maintain context when sorting the rows by the risk priority number to identify the highest-risk failure modes.

Step 4: Rate Failure Mode Impact, Likelihood, and Detectability

Each failure mode represents potential product failures that could occur. If one of these product failures were to occur, it would generate one or more effects that would affect the product or its usage. Each effect can be rated with an estimated severity, and the severity rating can be used to help prioritize risk based on potential impact. Each product failure also has one or more causes. These causes can be rated based on the likelihood of occurrence. Finally, the product design can incorporate various kinds of controls that can be used to detect or even prevent potential causes. Each of these controls can be rated based on its ability to detect those causes.

In this step, each failure mode is analyzed to determine the worst-case *impact* of the effects, the *likelihood* of the causes, and the *detectability* of current controls. It is generally easier to take each failure mode and think about all the effects, causes, and controls before moving to the next failure mode in the list. Since each failure mode has a context, it can be more efficient to continue thinking within that context rather than constantly changing focus.

Determining Effects and Assessing Potential Impact   For each failure mode effect, the potential impact is estimated and quantified using a scale such as the impact ranking scale shown in Table 13-1. Traditionally, FMEA impact ranking has been on a 1 to 10 scale. Although this is still an option, it can be a challenge to make such a fine-grained impact rating for software-related failures. Consequently, a 1 to 5 scale is used in this example.

Note   Use these impact rankings as examples, and create new definitions as necessary for your specific FMEA. There are no universal guidelines for these ranking levels, except that level 5 represents an impact with the highest possible magnitude. You may also want to redefine the ranking definitions in other terms such as the impact on the user or even the overall system executing the software.

Table 13-1   Impact Ranking Scale

Impact Ranking		
Impact	**Criterion**	**Rank**
Catastrophic	The entire software product or system stops working properly (for example, it crashes, hangs).	5
Critical	A specific area of the software product (for example, networking) stops working properly.	4
Moderate	A specific part of the software product (for example, a networking feature) stops working properly.	3
Minor	The software product works properly but has minor issues with fit and finish, usability, and so forth.	2
None	No impact.	1

Evaluate the impact of each failure mode effect, and add it to the FMEA worksheet.

Example: Software Setup Logging FMEA

Starting with the "Incorrectly determine phase" failure mode, Mary leads the team through a discussion to determine the possible effects of this type of failure. The team identifies three possible effects and adds them to the FMEA worksheet. For each effect, the team uses the impact ranking table to estimate the worst-case impact. (See Figure 13-6.)

Note   Although the team will likely choose to complete the analysis of the "Incorrectly determine phase" failure mode before moving to the next one, to make this example more complete, the other two "Check for Setup Phase" failure modes are also being analyzed at the same time.

FMEA Worksheet
Project: E2EMan - Setup Logging

Process Step, Function or Task	Potential Failure Mode	Potential Effect(s) of Failure	Impact Rank	Potential Causes	Likelihood Rank	Current Controls	Detectability Rank	Risk Priority	Improvement	Owner
Check for Setup Phase	Incorrectly determine phase	Might proceed when shouldn't	4					0		
Check for Setup Phase	Incorrectly determine phase	Try to reinitialize drive	5					0		
Check for Setup Phase	Incorrectly determine phase	Unpredictable errors are generated	3					0		
Check for Setup Phase	Indeterminate phase of setup	When to initialize logging unknown	4					0		
Check for Setup Phase	Fail to create log file directory	Fatal error that stops setup	5					0		
Downlevel Install								0		
Boot off CD								0		
Initialize setup logging to physical drive								0		
Setup Logging								0		
Setup Logging clean up								0		

Figure 13-6   Partial FMEA worksheet with failure modes, potential effects, and impact ranking

Determining Potential Causes and Assessing Likelihood   Each failure mode can have one or more potential causes. For each potential cause, the likelihood is estimated and quantified using a scale such as the likelihood ranking scale shown in Table 13-2. As with the impact ranking scale, traditionally the likelihood ranking has been a 1 to 10 scale. If more precise likelihood ranking is required, use that option and simply adjust the scale. In this example, the 1 to 5 scale is used.

Table 13-2   Likelihood Ranking Scale

Likelihood Ranking		
Likelihood	**Criterion**	**Rank**
Very High	> 1 in 2 (50%)	5
High	1 in 10 (10%)	4
Moderate	1 in 100 (1%)	3
Low	1 in 1,000 (0.1%)	2
Very Low	< 1 in 10,000 (0.01%)	1

Evaluate the likelihood of each failure mode cause, and add it to the FMEA worksheet.

Example: Software Setup Logging FMEA

After determining the effects of the "Incorrectly determine phase" failure mode, Mary has the team brainstorm potential causes of the failure mode and use the likelihood ranking table to assign a likelihood rank to each cause (see Figure 13-7).

Note   Each failure mode can have multiple causes. If that is the case, each cause should be listed on a separate row and ranked individually.

FMEA Worksheet
Project: E2EMan - Setup Logging

Process Step, Function or Task	Potential Failure Mode	Potential Effect(s) of Failure	Impact Rank	Potential Causes	Likelihood Rank	Current Controls	Detectability Rank	Risk Priority	Improvement	Owner
Check for Setup Phase	Incorrectly determine phase	Might proceed when shouldn't	4	Hardware failure	1			0		
Check for Setup Phase	Incorrectly determine phase	Try to reinitialize drive	5	API failure	2			0		
Check for Setup Phase	Incorrectly determine phase	Unpredictable errors are generated	3	Incorrect use of API	3			0		
Check for Setup Phase	Indeterminate phase of setup	When to initialize logging unknown	4	API failure	2			0		
Check for Setup Phase	Fail to create log file directory	Fatal error that stops setup	5	Dev oversight	3			0		
Check for Setup Phase	Fail to create log file directory	Fatal error that stops setup	5	API failure	2			0		
Check for Setup Phase	Fail to create log file directory	Fatal error that stops setup	5	No disk space	2			0		
Downlevel Install								0		
Boot off CD								0		
Initialize setup logging to physical drive								0		
Setup Logging								0		
Setup Logging clean up								0		

Figure 13-7   Partial FMEA worksheet with failure modes, potential causes, and likelihood ranking

Determining Current Controls and Assessing Detectability   In terms of risk, a failure mode that cannot be detected can present a greater overall risk than those that can be detected. If a failure mode can be detected, there is at least the opportunity to eliminate or mitigate it before the product or service is affected. The worst case is for a failure mode with significant potential impact to occur undetected. Consequently, in calculating an overall risk priority for a failure mode, it is important to also factor in the chance of detection. The detectability of each failure mode cause is estimated and quantified using a scale such as the detectability ranking scale shown in Table 13-3. As with the other ranking scales, the detectability ranking has traditionally been a 1 to 10 scale. If more precise detectability ranking is required, use that option and adjust the scale. In this example, the 1 to 5 scale is again used.

Table 13-3   Detectability Ranking Scale

Detectability Ranking		
Detectability	**Criterion**	**Rank**
Very Low	Very low probability (0–19%) that current controls will detect the cause	5
Low	Low probability (20–39%) that current controls will detect the cause	4
Medium	Medium probability (40–59%) that current controls will detect the cause	3
High	High probability (60–79%) that current controls will detect the cause	2
Very High	Very high probability (80–100%) that current controls will detect the cause	1

There is a difference between the detectability ranking scale and the other ranking scales. In the case of the impact and likelihood ranking scales, more effect impact and cause likelihood result in more risk and are ranked higher. In contrast, in the detectability ranking scale, less detectability results in more overall risk and is therefore ranked higher.

Evaluate the detectability of each failure mode cause, and add it to the FMEA worksheet.

Example: Software Setup Logging FMEA

As a final step in determining the overall risk of the "Incorrectly determine phase" failure mode, Mary has the team identify potential controls in the product design that could detect the occurrence of the failure mode causes. She knows that the worst-case situation would be if the team were unable to identify any controls that could detect the failure mode. Similarly, if controls do exist, but they are potentially unable to detect the failure mode, Mary knows that an increased overall risk will also occur. After describing the importance of this step to the team, she instructs them to identify the controls that can detect each failure mode cause and use the detectability ranking table to assign a detectability rank to each of them (see Figure 13-8).

Note   As with causes, multiple controls can detect each failure mode. If that is the case, each control should be listed and ranked individually.

FMEA Worksheet
Project: E2EMan - Setup Logging

Process Step, Function or Task	Potential Failure Mode	Potential Effect(s) of Failure	Impact Rank	Potential Causes	Likelihood Rank	Current Controls	Detectability Rank	Risk Priority	Improvement	Owner
Check for Setup Phase	Incorrectly determine phase	Might proceed when shouldn't	4	Hardware failure	1	Msg box - "Failed to determine phase of setup..."	2	8		
Check for Setup Phase	Incorrectly determine phase	Try to reinitialize drive	5	API failure	2	Stop (exit) setup	1	10		
Check for Setup Phase	Incorrectly determine phase	Unpredictable errors are generated	3	Incorrect use of API	3	Error message	2	18		
Check for Setup Phase	Indeterminate phase of setup	When to initialize logging unknown	4	API failure	2	Stop (exit) setup	1	8		
Check for Setup Phase	Indeterminate phase of setup	When to initialize logging unknown	4	API failure	2	Error message	2	16		
Check for Setup Phase	Fail to create log file directory	Fatal error that stops setup	5	Dev oversight	3	Code review	2	30		
Check for Setup Phase	Fail to create log file directory	Fatal error that stops setup	5	API failure	2	Error message; Stop setup	2	20		
Check for Setup Phase	Fail to create log file directory	Fatal error that stops setup	5	No disk space	2	Error message; Stop setup	2	20		
Downlevel Install								0		
Boot off CD								0		
Initialize setup logging to physical drive								0		
Setup Logging								0		
Setup Logging clean up								0		

Figure 13-8   Partial FMEA worksheet with failure modes, current controls, and detectability ranking

Step 5: Calculate the Risk Priority Number for Each Failure Mode

The *risk priority number (RPN)* is a very straightforward calculation. It is simply the product of the impact rank, likelihood rank, and detectability rank:

RPN = Impact Rank * Likelihood Rank * Detectability Rank

Using an Excel FMEA worksheet, it is very easy to construct a formula to perform the calculation automatically. See Figure 13-8 to view the calculated risk priority numbers.

Example: Software Setup Logging FMEA

After Mary enters the control detectability rank, the Excel FMEA worksheet that she is using automatically calculates the risk priority number for each row where an impact, likelihood, and detectability rank has been entered.

After working through these initial failure modes, the team understands that the tool and process are very straightforward. Armed with this new knowledge, the team is able to more rapidly complete the rest of the FMEA worksheet.

Step 6: Identify the Failure Modes with the Highest Potential Risk

After the FMEA worksheet is complete, simply sort the worksheet rows in descending order based on the calculated risk priority number. The failure modes with the highest risk priority numbers usually represent a priority for the team (see Figure 13-9).

FMEA Worksheet
Project: E2EMan - Setup Logging

Process Step, Function or Task	Potential Failure Mode	Potential Effect(s) of Failure	Impact Rank	Potential Causes	Likelihood Rank	Current Controls	Detectability Rank	Risk Priority	Improvement	Owner
Check for Setup Phase	Fail to create log file directory	Fatal error that stops setup	5	Dev oversight	3	Code review	2	30		
Check for Setup Phase	Fail to create log file directory	Fatal error that stops setup	5	API failure	2	Error message; Stop setup	2	20		
Check for Setup Phase	Fail to create log file directory	Fatal error that stops setup	5	No disk space	2	Error message; Stop setup	2	20		
Check for Setup Phase	Incorrectly determine phase	Unpredictable errors are generated	3	Incorrect use of API	3	Error message	2	18		
Check for Setup Phase	Indeterminate phase of setup	When to initialize logging unknown	4	API failure	2	Error message	2	16		
Check for Setup Phase	Incorrectly determine phase	Try to reinitialize drive	5	API failure	2	Stop (exit) setup	1	10		
Check for Setup Phase	Incorrectly determine phase	Might proceed when shouldn't	4	Hardware failure	1	Msg box - "Failed to determine phase of setup..."	2	8		
Check for Setup Phase	Indeterminate phase of setup	When to initialize logging unknown	4	API failure	2	Stop (exit) setup	1	8		
Downlevel Install								0		
Boot off CD								0		
Initialize setup logging to physical drive								0		
Setup Logging								0		
Setup Logging clean up								0		

Figure 13-9   Partial FMEA worksheet sorted by risk priority number in descending order

> **Note**   A good practice is to copy the completed FMEA worksheet to create a separate worksheet and then sort the copy. By doing so, the team can adjust the primary worksheet without needing to re-sort it back into the original order.

One potential optimization of the analysis is to perform the primary sort on the risk priority number and a secondary sort on the likelihood rank. By doing so, the team can focus its resources on eliminating frequent causes of high-risk failure modes.

Step 7: Define an Action Plan to Eliminate or Mitigate the Causes

Starting with the highest-risk failure modes, define action plans to eliminate or mitigate the causes. Assign action owners and target dates for each action. Most FMEA worksheets provide the opportunity to document the action and assigned owner. After the actions are identified, they can be managed just like any other project. The FMEA worksheet enables the action to be traced back to the failure mode and the analysis used to justify it. (See Figure 13-10.)

FMEA Worksheet
Project: E2EMan - Setup Logging

Process Step, Function or Task	Potential Failure Mode	Potential Effect(s) of Failure	Impact Rank	Potential Causes	Likelihood Rank	Current Controls	Detectability Rank	Risk Priority	Improvement	Owner
Check for Setup Phase	Fail to create log file directory	Fatal error that stops setup	5	Dev oversight	3	Code review	2	30	Add to code review list	Dan
Check for Setup Phase	Fail to create log file directory	Fatal error that stops setup	5	API failure	2	Error message; Stop setup	2	20	Improve the API spec	John
Check for Setup Phase	Fail to create log file directory	Fatal error that stops setup	5	No disk space	2	Error message; Stop setup	2	20	Add disk space check	Sam
Check for Setup Phase	Incorrectly determine phase	Unpredictable errors are generated	3	Incorrect use of API	3	Error message	2	18	Create more detailed API doc	Mary
Check for Setup Phase	Indeterminate phase of setup	When to initialize logging unknown	4	API failure	2	Error message	2	16	Improve the API spec	John
Check for Setup Phase	Incorrectly determine phase	Try to reinitialize drive	5	API failure	2	Stop (exit) setup	1	10	Improve the API spec	John
Check for Setup Phase	Incorrectly determine phase	Might proceed when shouldn't	4	Hardware failure	1	Msg box - "Failed to determine phase of setup..."	2	8		
Check for Setup Phase	Indeterminate phase of setup	When to initialize logging unknown	4	API failure	2	Stop (exit) setup	1	8	Improve the API spec	John
Downlevel Install								0		
Boot off CD								0		
Initialize setup logging to physical drive								0		
Setup Logging								0		
Setup Logging clean up								0		

Figure 13-10   Partial FMEA worksheet with proposed improvements

---

Example: Software Setup Logging FMEA

After sorting the failure modes in descending order based on their risk priority number, it became clear to the team that a few failure modes had high risk. After some discussion, the team identified actions that could be taken to eliminate or mitigate the causes of those failure modes. Owners were assigned to each action to manage their implementation.

Step 8: Reassess the Risk Priority After the Actions Are Implemented

After the actions are implemented, the risk associated with those failure modes should decrease, causing other failure modes to become higher priorities. To determine these changes in priority, the team should meet to review the improvements and then reassess the impact, likelihood, and detectability ranks for the failure modes. Assuming that the actions actually mitigate the impact, reduce the likelihood of a cause, or increase the detectability, the rankings might change and result in a reduced risk priority number for the failure mode.

After these changes are made, re-sort the FMEA worksheet into descending order based on the risk priority number to identify the new failure modes with the highest potential risk. Repeated execution of this cycle can help the team continuously improve the product. By focusing on the highest risks first, the team can use resources more effectively.

Step 9: Ongoing FMEA Maintenance

The FMEA worksheet should be viewed as a living document and updated on a regular basis as changes and enhancements are made to the product. The final FMEA results should also be persisted to capture software engineering knowledge for use in future product cycles. In software development, the same failures are often introduced repeatedly. To increase awareness, the FMEA worksheet provides insight into the types of failure that can occur. Also, the actions taken to address those failure modes can guide future work and help the team avoid repeating known mistakes that can cause failures. To support testing, the FMEA results can provide initial input into test planning and test case development.

FMEA Summary

Failure modes and effects analysis is a procedure for proactively identifying potential failures and assessing their risks. In software development, this provides benefits such as the following:

- Improved software quality and reliability result in an improved customer experience and greater customer satisfaction.

- Focus on defect prevention by identifying and eliminating defects in the software design stage helps to drive quality upstream.

- Proactive identification and elimination of software defects saves time and money. If a defect cannot occur, there will be no need to fix it.

- Prioritization of potential failures based on risk helps support the most effective allocation of people and resources to prevent them.

- Engineering knowledge is persisted for use in future software development projects and iterations. This helps an organization avoid relearning what is already known.

- FMEA can be a catalyst for increased product team interaction and group analysis. Different team members will have different knowledge, experience, and viewpoints that can help increase the breadth and value of the analysis.

In addition to the benefits, there are also some risks that could affect adoption and successful implementation:

- The potential time commitment can discourage participation.

- Focus area documentation does not exist prior to the FMEA session and needs to be created, adding to the time commitment.

- Generally, the more knowledgeable and experienced the session participants are, the better the FMEA results. A risk is that key individuals are often very busy and therefore unable or unwilling to participate.

Industries such as the automotive and aerospace industries have adopted FMEA to increase the reliability of their product designs. Because failure in products produced by these industries can result in the loss of life and limb, these organizations are willing to invest in FMEA to reap the reliability benefits. Although most instances of software failure have less impact, there is still a desire to improve software product reliability to improve customer satisfaction and increase product sales. FMEA provides an effective technique to help you achieve those goals.

Fault Tree Analysis

Fault tree analysis (FTA) is a technique that uses Boolean logic to describe the combinations of intermediate causal events that can initiate a failure ("unintended event").[1] Where failure modes and effects analysis (FMEA) strives to enumerate all failure modes for a product and then estimate their risk, fault tree analysis starts with a specific failure and strives to enumerate all the causes of that event and their relationships. The overall goal is to identify specific opportunities to eliminate or mitigate the causes that can ultimately result in product failure. A fully constructed fault tree represents a failure and all its potential causes (see Figure 13-11).

> **Note**   FMEA and FTA are complementary techniques that can be combined into a more comprehensive defect prevention technique. In effect, FMEA is used to identify potential failures, and FTA is then used to discover the causes of those failures.

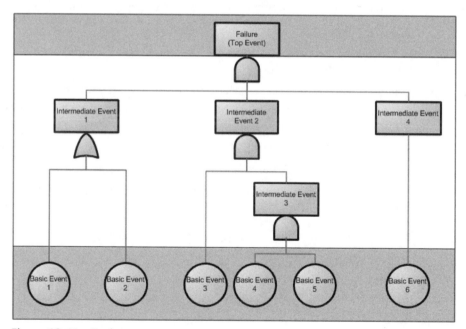

Figure 13-11   Fault tree structure

From a qualitative perspective, the tree represents a logic diagram that depicts a set of causal event sequences. Ultimately, this diagram can be used to identify *cut sets* that are unique combinations of *basic* causal events for which, if each event occurs, the failure will occur. A cut set can potentially be reduced by removing basic events and still cause the failure. Ultimately, this reduction results in a minimal cut set of basic events that cannot be reduced further.

---

1 Traditionally, in fault tree analysis, the root node of a fault tree has represented the generic unintended event being analyzed. Because a failure can also be considered an unintended event, in the context of this chapter the root node represents a failure.

These minimal cut sets can help software development teams identify the combinations of basic causal events that will result in product failure. Targeting and eliminating these basic events can prevent one or more failure opportunities and improve the overall reliability of the product.

From a quantitative perspective, if the probability of occurrence for each causal event can be estimated, this information can be used to calculate the overall probability that the failure will occur. This is useful for software reliability analysis and can provide valuable input into failure modes and effects analysis, which depends on accurate estimates of cause likelihoods.

After describing the origin of FTA, the primary focus of this section is on the application of FTA in software development. Software FTA focuses on the causes originating not only in the software system but also in the software operating environment, including human error. As a result, it can encompass a more systemic view of a failure and its potential causes.

History

In the early 1960s, the U.S. Air Force was concerned about an inadvertent launch of a Minuteman Missile that was being developed by the Boeing Company and Bell Laboratories. To evaluate this concern, H. A. Watson of Bell Telephone Laboratories developed fault tree analysis as a way to analyze all aspects of the weapons system. The goal of this approach was to identify all potential causes and event sequences that could result in an inadvertent missile launch by incorporating Boolean logic concepts.

The fault tree analysis method was later adopted and extended by the Boeing Company and has now become a standard hazard analysis technique in many industries. In the software industry, FTA was sporadically adopted for reliability analysis starting in the early 1970s. As the awareness of software safety increased in the 1980s, FTA became a reliability analysis technique often referenced in software hazard and safety analysis. Since then, the use of FTA has increased especially in regard to safety-critical software systems that demand very high reliability.

Implementing FTA

To implement FTA effectively, consider these prerequisites and use the following procedure.

Prerequisites

Based on Microsoft Engineering Excellence practice guidelines, consider the following prerequisites for completing an efficient and effective FTA.

- A skilled FTA facilitator
  - The FTA facilitator should have a good understanding of fault tree analysis concepts and the procedure for generating a fault tree. Although a facilitator may not be absolutely required if the meeting participants are very familiar with FTA, an advantage of having one is the person's ability to guide the discussion and keep it on track. This role often is supported by a team manager or lead, but it may also be an independent facilitator if warranted by the FTA focus area or team dynamics.

- The right participants
  - Participants that represent a variety of skills, knowledge, and experience.
  - Participants that feel comfortable contributing to the FTA discussion.
  - FTA is generally most effectively performed as a team activity. Because FTA encompasses any potential causal event, it is important to get input from a variety of participants with different perspectives.

- A clear understanding of the failure and the system and operating environment in which it can occur
  - All participants thoroughly understand the failure.
  - Effective documentation and diagrams are available to help participants understand details of the system and operating environment.

- Available causal event probability data
  - Although not an absolute prerequisite, if the fault tree is to be used to assess overall failure probability quantitatively, information about causal event probabilities must be available or feasible to calculate.

- Access to specialized fault tree analysis software
  - Although not required to benefit from the fault tree analysis and qualitative analysis of the results, using specialized fault tree analysis software can help the team quickly determine minimal cut sets and calculate the failure probability.

Procedure

Fault tree analysis is a deductive analysis technique that starts with a failure and focuses on deducing all the potential causes and their relationships. Therefore, FTA starts with choosing a target failure, possibly identified in FMEA, and then using the standard FTA event and Boolean gate symbols to create the logic diagram of possible causal event sequences. After it is constructed, the fault tree can be analyzed manually to identify the key causal events that can lead to the failure. Alternatively, specialized FTA software can be used to quickly perform an automated analysis of the fault tree.

The following procedure describes the steps for completing an FTA in more detail. Building off the FMEA example, a software setup logging failure is used as an example to help illustrate the steps.

Example: Software Setup Logging FTA

As a result of the Software Setup Logging FMEA, a number of potential failure modes were identified. Mary, the team lead, decides to facilitate a fault tree analysis session with the team to show them how a failure mode can be analyzed to identify potential causes. Although a cause of the failure mode was identified during the FMEA process and used to estimate the likelihood rank, Mary knows it didn't represent all possible causes. Consequently, she wants to introduce the team to a logical technique for diagramming a more thorough analysis of potential causes.

Use the following procedure as a general guideline and not as a specific sequence of steps that must be followed. As the team becomes more familiar with the steps, they may identify some opportunities to consolidate the steps. The key is to understand what is being accomplished in each step and then make sure this is being achieved regardless of the actual steps performed.

Step 1: Select and Define the Failure to Analyze

Fault tree analysis is a deductive technique, so the first step is to select and define a specific failure to analyze. Because a fault tree also reflects the current state of a software system and surrounding environment, it is important to understand the software system and environment to provide the right context for the discussion. Likewise, in addition to context, the participants need to understand the scope of the investigation to establish boundaries and keep the discussion focused.

To help all participants identify the causal events, it is very helpful to have available diagrams and documentation that fully describe the software system and the environment in which it will operate. If this information is not available, input will come solely from participant knowledge and experience. Although this can provide a wealth of information, it may also limit the conclusions to what is known (or thought to be known) and not help in discovering previously unknown causal events.

At times, excessive time and effort are devoted to constructing an elaborate fault tree with more breadth and depth than is necessary to investigate the target failure. Although this can be a useful discussion, it can initiate a loss of focus on the problem at hand. Consequently, to manage the discussion and keep it focused, it is also helpful to preestablish the fault tree parameters to scope the analysis and make sure all participants understand what is in scope and what is not.

Compile Details About the Software System and Environment   After the FTA target failure has been identified, complete information about the software system and operating environment should be compiled. This could include information such as:

- Who will manage, operate, and support the software system
- Which environmental factors will influence the operation or use of the software system
- How the product will be used by external and internal customers (for example, scenarios)
- Description of what the product should do and how it should perform (for example, specs)
- How the product is architected
  - Physical system diagrams
  - Logical system flow diagrams
  - Data flow diagrams
  - Interface diagrams
- Which technologies are used

The more details known about the software system and operating environment, the easier it will be to identify potential causal events.

Step 2: Create the Fault Tree

Conceptually, the basic construct of a fault tree is very straightforward. As shown in Figure 13-12, one or more causal events provide input into a Boolean logic gate that defines their relationship and the conditions that must be met for the output event to occur.

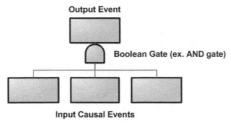

Figure 13-12   Basic fault tree construct

In this input→gate→output construct, the input conditions are formed by three causal events that can potentially occur. The Boolean symbol defines the logical relationship between the input events, and the output event represents what will occur if that relationship is met. A fault tree is formed when the output event of one construct becomes an input condition to another.

As a more concrete example, Figure 13-13 depicts a partial software fault tree.

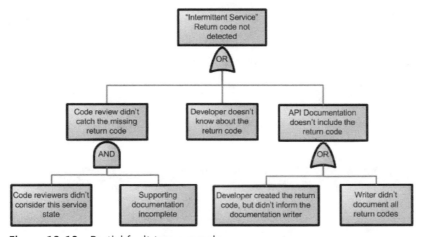

Figure 13-13   Partial fault tree example

In the example in Figure 13-13, two basic input→gate→output constructs have been created and joined to create a partial fault tree. Specifically, the "Code review didn't catch the missing return code" event is an output of the AND gate and the "API documentation doesn't include the return code" event is an output of the OR gate. Both of these events are inputs into another OR gate that specifies when the target failure event " 'Intermittent Service' Return Code not detected" will occur. By joining these basic fault tree constructs, complex causal event sequences can be formed. This is one of the key strengths of fault tree analysis.

Over the years, standard symbols have been defined to represent different events and Boolean logic gates. This makes it much easier for people to understand and visually analyze a fault tree. Microsoft Office Visio contains a Fault Tree Analysis stencil that includes standard event and Boolean logic symbols. These symbols are used to form the fault tree examples in this chapter.

Event Symbols   Figure 13-14 lists the symbols used to represent events.

Event Symbols	Description
Undesired Event	The failure mode under investigation. As the root node in a fault tree. It is sometimes called the "top event." In this chapter, it is simply referred to as the target failure. The goal of FTA is to identify and diagram all the causal event sequences that can lead to this event.
Intermediate Event	An event that is both the output of one Boolean gate and an input into another Boolean gate.
Basic Event	A basic causal event that can initiate an event sequence leading to the undesired failure event. Depending on the fault tree scope, basic events often represent component failures or human error.
Undeveloped Event	A basic event that could be expanded into additional causal events but that will not be broken down further in this fault tree. Sometimes undeveloped events are used to represent human errors.
House Event	A binary event that can be set to occur (a fixed probability of 1 or 0). In most situations, this event is expected to occur. A house event can represent an event with the ability to turn an event sequence on or off.
Conditional Event	A condition that can be applied to any gate, but often is used with an inhibit gate to specify a condition that must be satisfied for the output event to occur.

Figure 13-14   Fault Tree Event symbols. Source: Microsoft Visio Fault Tree Analysis Stencil

Boolean Logic Symbols   Gates represent the logical relationship between input events that must be satisfied to generate the output event. These gates act as basic building blocks for constructing the fault tree. Each gate is represented by a distinct Boolean logic symbol (see Figure 13-15).

Boolean Logic Symbols	Description
AND gate	Specifies that all input causal events must occur for the output event to occur. If any input event does not occur, the output event will not occur. By default, the order in which the input events occurs does not matter. However, in some cases the event sequence is important (see Priority AND gate).
Priority AND gate	Specifies that all input causal events must occur in a specific sequence for the output event to occur.
OR gate	Specifies that one or more input causal events must occur for the output event to occur.
Exclusive OR gate	Specifies that exactly one input causal event must occur for the output event to occur. If zero or two or more input events occur, the output event will not occur.
Inhibit gate	Specifies that all input causal events plus a specific conditional event must occur for the output event to occur. Basically, an inhibit gate is an AND gate with an additional conditional event that must be met. See the description of "Conditional Event."
m:0:0	Specifies that a specific number (k) of more of all the input causal events (n) must occur for the output event to occur. If less than k input events occur, the output event will not occur.
Transfer symbol	Specifies a transfer point to or from another fault tree. It has been typically used to reflect a continuance to a fault tree described on another page or even in another file.

Figure 13-15   Fault tree Boolean logic symbols. Source: Microsoft Visio Fault Tree Analysis Stencil

Final Note About Fault Tree Symbols   These symbols are based on the Visio Fault Tree Analysis stencil and should be used as examples of the traditional fault tree symbols. Other fault tree tools or methods can use similar, but potentially different, symbols. Typically, the core fault tree symbols are standard. However, some tools and methods define special-purpose symbols to address specific event logic situations that are difficult to depict using only the traditional symbols.

Fault Tree Development Process

To construct the fault tree, first start with the failure and identify all the immediate causal events. After these events have been identified, determine how they relate and which gate best represents that relationship. Start the fault tree by diagramming the failure and first row of causal events.

Example: Software Setup Logging FTA

Because fault tree construction is new to the team, Mary decides to start with a failure mode that is easy to analyze: "Fail to create log file directory." For clarity, Mary translates the failure mode to the failure event "Setup log file directory not created." After explaining the basic fault tree analysis process and the meaning of the various event and gate symbols, Mary asks the team to first identify all the causes of why the log file directory may not be created. After some brainstorming, the team comes up with a list of three potential causes and determines the relationship between them that would result in the failure event. Mary uses this information to construct the initial fault tree. (See Figure 13-16.).

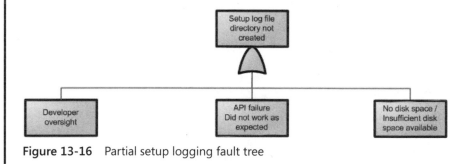

Figure 13-16   Partial setup logging fault tree

Recursively perform the same analysis approach for each intermediate causal event. In many cases, the intermediate event will require further breakdown to identify the additional events that can cause it. In some cases, the team may find that the intermediate event is really a basic event that will not be analyzed further. In this case, simply change the symbol to a basic event and stop analyzing that event sequence.

The team needs to decide when to stop the analysis of each event sequence. The fault tree boundaries that were defined can help determine when to stop. Another criterion to consider is when the event is no longer reasonably actionable. For example, if an event involves a software component failure that can be fixed, that is reasonably actionable. Similarly, if the event involves a lack of knowledge on the part of someone, that is also reasonably actionable. However, going further than this last event to identify "Incomplete computer science curricula in training institutions" as a cause is not generally actionable and would not be necessary in most cases.

Example: Software Setup Logging FTA

With the first level of causal events diagrammed, the team now understands the process of analyzing the events and constructing the fault tree, so the rest of the process goes much quicker. Before analysis begins on the first level of causal events, Mary explains that the team could either analyze all of these events before proceeding on to the next level or analyze each event until the basic events are identified. The team thinks that analyzing each event fully before proceeding to the next event would allow the team members to stay in context and that would make the analysis faster. Mary agrees with that approach, so the analysis starts with the "Developer oversight" event and fully enumerates all underlying intermediate and basic events. (See Figure 13-17.)

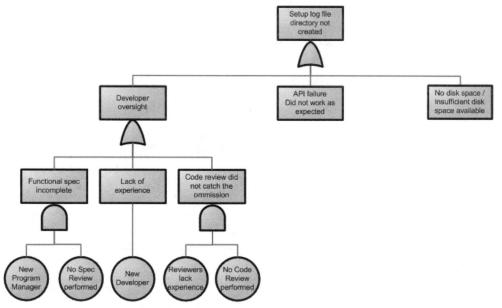

Figure 13-17   Partial setup logging fault tree with "Developer oversight" analysis

Encouraged by the results, the team continues the analysis until the complete fault tree is constructed. (See Figure 13-18.) Mary congratulates the team and informs them that the next step is to analyze the fault tree to identify the combinations of basic events that will cause the failure. These are the events they need to prevent in the setup logging software to make sure this failure cannot occur and affect customers.

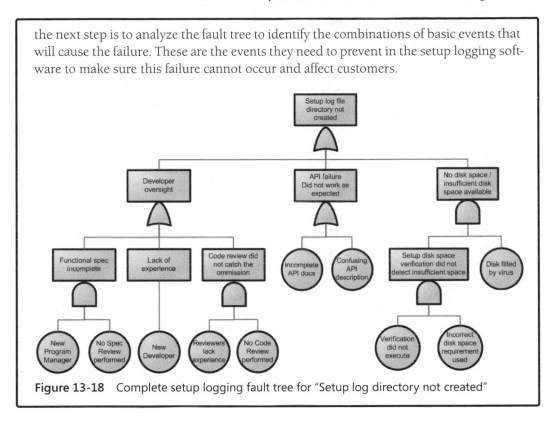

Figure 13-18   Complete setup logging fault tree for "Setup log directory not created"

Step 3: Analyze the Fault Tree

The process of creating a fault tree is beneficial to participants because it helps create a shared understanding of a specific failure or undesired event and its possible causes. The biggest benefit, however, is that after the fault tree is created it can be thoroughly analyzed to identify all the possible ways basic events can cause the failure. Initially, the fault tree can simply be discussed and visually analyzed to identify obvious causes of failure. Although this method can be quick and requires minimal effort, as a fault tree becomes larger and more complex, it will be difficult to identify all the possible causal event combinations. Therefore, a more formal and scalable method is required for analyzing larger fault trees.

The mathematical concept of cut sets originated in graph theory and has been used in the context of fault trees to mean the unique combinations of basic events that, should they all occur, will cause the failure or undesired event. Therefore, the purpose of this formal method is to identify all cut sets in a fault tree and then reduce them to minimal cut sets if necessary. In this context, a *minimal* cut set means that no events in the cut set can be removed and still cause the failure *if they all occur at the same time*.

In the early 1970s, algorithms for computing minimal cut sets in fault trees were developed. For example, the Method of Obtaining Cut Sets (MOCUS) computer algorithm was developed and proposed by J. B. Fussell and W. E. Vesely.[1] This algorithm for identifying minimal cut sets in fault trees is still in use in fault tree analysis software packages. Over the years, other qualitative methods for determining minimal cut sets have been developed based on the MOCUS algorithm. In one such method, a matrix is used to translate a fault tree into minimal cut sets.[2]

Example: Software Setup Logging FTA

To help illustrate a method for identifying minimal cut sets, Mary walks the team through an approach advocated by P. L. Clemens of Jacobs Sverdrup and referenced in the NASA Systems Engineering Toolbox for Design-Oriented Engineers.[3] Mary assumes that if the method is good enough for NASA, it is good enough for her team. Using the "Setup log directory not created" fault tree, Mary walks through this procedure with the team to identify the minimal cut sets.

Jacobs Sverdrup Method for Manually Determining Minimal Cut Sets

Step 1: Ignore All Fault Tree Elements Except for the Top-Level Failure and All Basic Events
The key is to focus on the basic events and top-level failure, not on the intermediate causal events. However, the Boolean gates are also important because those define the logical relationships between the basic events and the failure.

Step 2: Assign Unique Letters to Each Gate and Unique Numbers to Each Basic Event
Starting with the level immediately below the failure event, assign the letters and numbers. Typically, the gate letters start with A and the basic event numbers start with 1. If the fault tree is large enough to extend beyond Z, start the next sequence with AA or some other logical nomenclature.

---

1 J. B. Fussell and W. E. Vesely, "A New Methodology for Obtaining Cut Sets for Fault Trees," *Transactions of the American Nuclear Society* 15, no. 1 (1972): 262–263.

2 P. L. Clemens, *Fault Tree Analysis*, 4th ed. (lecture, Jacobs Sverdrup, Inc., May 1993).

3 B. E. Goldberg, K. Everhart, R. Stevens, N. Babbitt III, P. Clemens, and L. Stout, "System Engineering 'Toolbox' for Design-Oriented Engineers," NASA Reference Publication 1358, December 1994, *www.hq.nasa.gov/office/codeq/doctree/rp1358.pdf.*

Example: Software Setup Logging FTA

Using the Jacobs Sverdrup method instructions, Mary helps the team go through the fault tree analysis. First, the team systematically analyzes the fault tree and assigns unique letters to each gate and unique numbers to each event. (See Figure 13-19.) Then the team goes through the procedure for identifying minimal cut sets.

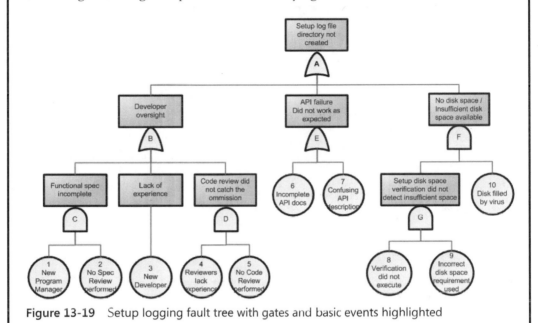

Figure 13-19   Setup logging fault tree with gates and basic events highlighted

After the gates and basic events have been labeled, you are ready to use a matrix and a series of recursive steps to identify cut sets for the "Setup log directory not created" fault tree. (See Figure 13-20.)

Step 3.3 Start the matrix by placing the letter of the failure event gate in the upper-left (0, 0) cell. *Typically, this step will place the letter A in the upper-left corner of the matrix.*	A matrix with **A** in the upper-left cell
Step 3.4 Recursively replace each gate letter with the letters or numbers of the next lower level gates or basic events. For OR gates, replace the gate letters vertically; for AND gates, replace the gate letters horizontally. *The following example steps are based on the Setup Logging fault tree. (See Figure 13-19.)*	
A is an OR gate, so it is replaced vertically with B, E, and F	Matrix column: **B**, **E**, **F**
B is an OR gate, so it is replaced vertically with gate C, basic event 3, and gate D	Matrix column: **C**, **3**, **D**, **E**, **F**
C is an AND gate, so it is replaced horizontally with basic events 1 and 2 D is an AND gate, so it is replaced horizontally with basic events 4 and 5	Matrix: **1 2**, **3**, **4 5**, **E**, **F**
E is an OR gate, so it is replaced vertically with basic events 6 and 7	Matrix: **1 2**, **3**, **4 5**, **6**, **7**, **F**
F is an AND gate, so it is replaced horizontally with gate G and basic event 10	Matrix: **1 2**, **3**, **4 5**, **6**, **7**, **G 10**
G is an AND gate, so it is replaced horizontally with basic events 8 and 9	Matrix: **1 2**, **3**, **4 5**, **6**, **7**, **8 9 10**

Figure 13-20   Cut set matrix with transformation sequence

The rows in the final matrix represent the cut sets of the fault tree. The next step is to determine whether any of these rows need to be reduced to form minimal cut sets.

Step 4: Review the Matrix Rows to Identify Minimal Cut Sets

As a reminder, a minimal cut set is a cut set where no events can be removed and still cause the failure *if they all occur at the same time*. It just so happens that all of the cut sets identified in the example are also minimal cut sets. However, if a basic event can be removed from a row and the remaining events exactly match another cut set, the row is not minimal.

For example, assume there is a matrix with two cut sets of basic events identified: {1,1,3,5} and {1,5}. Are they minimal? No, the redundant basic event 1 can be consolidated. The remaining cut sets are {1,3,5} and {1,5}. Are they now minimal? No, if basic event 3 is removed from cut set {1,3,5}, the remaining basic events 1 and 5 exactly match another defined cut set, which means those basic events will cause the failure event. Therefore, cut set {1,3,5} is not minimal and can actually be replaced with the minimal cut set {1,5} (see Figure 13-21).

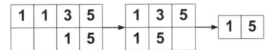

Figure 13-21   Identifying minimal cut sets from a list of cut sets

Alternative Methods for Identifying Minimal Cut Sets   The Jacobs Sverdrup method is visual and relatively straightforward. Consequently, it is a good initial method to try. An alternative method for identifying minimal cut sets is based on Boolean algebra. In this approach, a fault tree is translated into a set of Boolean equations that is then evaluated to determine minimal cut sets. Although we do not describe this method, a full treatment can be found in the NASA *Fault Tree Handbook with Aerospace Applications*.[1]

When using either method, after analyzing anything more than a small fault tree, it quickly becomes apparent that larger fault trees are very tedious and time consuming. Fortunately, because fault trees are based on Boolean logic, they are also very well suited for automated analysis using specialized FTA software. In fact, analyzing moderate to large fault trees is really practical only with FTA software. Many good applications exist and can be found by searching for "fault tree software" using the Internet.

Step 5: Interpret the Results

After the list of minimal cut sets is determined for a fault tree, this information can be used to identify opportunities for defect prevention. Because the minimal cut sets represent the combinations of basic events that can result in a failure, any minimal cut set with either a single or very small number of events can represent a serious risk. Fortunately, to eliminate these defect

1   NASA, *Fault Tree Handbook with Aerospace Applications*, Appendix A (Washington, DC: NASA, August 2002), www.hq.nasa.gov/office/codeq/doctree/fthb.pdf.

opportunities, only one basic event out of each minimal cut set must be prevented. Assuming the original analysis is accurate, the actual basic event to try and prevent can be chosen based on criteria such as speed of implementation and return on investment.

> ### Example: Software Setup Logging FTA
>
> Reviewing the FTA results with the team, it became apparent to Mary and everyone else that a number of individual basic events would be easy and quick to address. By addressing these basic events, whole groups of failure opportunities could be prevented. The team was excited and impressed with the results. Mary helped them formulate a few virtual teams to start looking at these basic events and what could be done to prevent them.

Step 6: Ongoing Maintenance of the Fault Tree and Analysis Results

The fault tree and the minimal cut set results should be updated periodically as changes and enhancements are made to the product. Use of a good fault tree software package can make this much easier and encourage more frequent updates. The final results should be persisted to capture software engineering knowledge for use in future product cycles.

Fault Tree Summary

Fault tree analysis is a deductive analysis technique that starts with a failure and focuses on deducing all the potential causes and their relationships. In software development, this provides benefits such as the following:

- Improved software quality and reliability result in an improved customer experience and greater customer satisfaction.

- FTA includes the capability of diagramming any pertinent causal events that can lead to failure, including software and hardware errors, human errors, and operational or environmental events.

- The ability to represent complex relationships between causal events supports more systemic analysis.

- FTA can be used proactively to understand and identify the causes that can lead to failure. This information can be used to prevent these causes.

- FTA can be used reactively to diagnose and learn from a failure that has occurred, whether in testing or as part of final product usage.

- Engineering knowledge is persisted for use in future development projects.

- FTA complements FMEA by supporting qualitative and quantitative analysis of a failure mode.

In addition to the benefits, there are also some risks that could affect adoption and successful implementation:

- It can be difficult to represent all possible relationships between causal events.

- Large fault trees can be daunting to analyze without the aid of specialized FTA software.

- It may be difficult to find participants that have the knowledge and experience to cover all potential causal events.

- The time commitment involved in creating a complete fault tree for each potential failure could discourage participation.

Like FMEA, FTA has been used in industry for years to improve product reliability, especially in conjunction with safety and hazard analysis. Because it is based on Boolean logic, the FTA procedure is generally straightforward and intuitive to software development teams. Completing the FTA helps provide deeper insight into product failures and the events or sequence of events that must occur to cause it. This makes it a natural complement to FMEA and a valuable defect prevention technique available to software development teams.

Failure Modeling: Combining FMEA and FTA

As noted earlier in this chapter, FMEA and FTA are complementary because the failure modes identified in FMEA can become top failure events in FTA. Combining the use of FMEA and FTA into a unified "failure model" has conceptual similarities with the threat models used in security threat modeling.[1]

In 2002, Michael Howard introduced threat modeling as a way to proactively identify potential security vulnerabilities in software. In 2003, Microsoft started experimenting with ways to combine FMEA and FTA. Recognizing that FMEA and FTA can analyze a broader notion of failure beyond just security vulnerabilities, the combined method was referred to as "failure modeling." See the upcoming section titled "Comparing Threat Modeling with Failure Modeling" for a brief description of the differences.

Failure Modeling

Figure 13-22 depicts a partial failure model based on the Setup Logging example used in this chapter. It is included to illustrate one approach for combining the FMEA and FTA techniques into one tool. More information on this approach is available at *www.defectprevention.org*.

---

1   Michael Howard, *Writing Secure Code*, 2nd ed. (Redmond, WA: Microsoft Press, 2002); Frank Swiderski and Window Snyder, *Threat Modeling* (Redmond, WA: Microsoft Press, 2004).

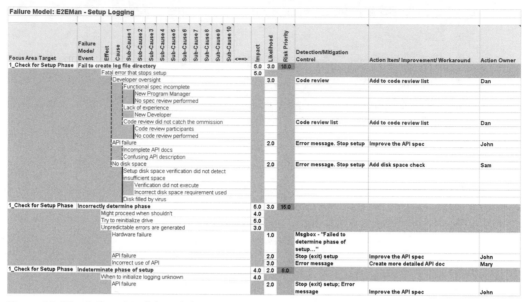

Failure Model: E2EMan - Setup Logging

Focus Area Target	Failure Model/ Event	Effect / Cause / Sub-Cause	Impact	Likelihood	Risk Priority	Detection/Mitigation Control	Action Item/ Improvement/ Workaround	Action Owner
1_Check for Setup Phase	Fail to create log file directory		5.0	3.0	15.0			
		Fatal error that stops setup	5.0					
		Developer oversight		3.0		Code review	Add to code review list	Dan
		Functional spec incomplete						
		New Program Manager						
		No spec review performed						
		Lack of experience						
		New Developer						
		Code review did not catch the ommission				Code review list	Add to code review list	Dan
		Code review participants						
		No code review performed						
		API failure		2.0		Error message. Stop setup	Improve the API spec	John
		Incomplete API docs						
		Confusing API description						
		No disk space		2.0		Error message. Stop setup	Add disk space check	Sam
		Setup disk space verification did not detect insufficient space						
		Verification did not execute						
		Incorrect disk space requirement used						
		Disk filled by virus						
1_Check for Setup Phase	Incorrectly determine phase		5.0	3.0	15.0			
		Might proceed when shouldn't	4.0					
		Try to reinitialize drive	5.0					
		Unpredictable errors are generated	3.0					
		Hardware failure		1.0		Msgbox - "Failed to determine phase of setup..."		
		API failure		2.0		Stop (exit) setup	Improve the API spec	John
		Incorrect use of API		3.0		Error message	Create more detailed API doc	Mary
1_Check for Setup Phase	Indeterminate phase of setup		4.0	2.0	8.0			
		When to initialize logging unknown	4.0					
		API failure		2.0		Stop (exit) setup; Error message	Improve the API spec	John

Figure 13-22   Failure Model worksheet with controls and action items

> **Note**   To avoid the need for a separate Microsoft Office Visio–based FTA diagram, the FTA relationships between subcauses are represented by a solid bold line to represent a Boolean AND relationship and a dashed bold line to represent Boolean OR. If no solid or dashed line is used, the default is a Boolean OR between the causes at the same level.

Comparing Threat Modeling with Failure Modeling

How does threat modeling compare with and relate to failure modeling? In some ways, threat modeling can be considered a subset of failure modeling. As shown in this comparison, there are some basic similarities in approach and some important differences. For example, out of necessity threat modeling enumerates and analyzes all types of potential security threats, while failure modeling tries to first determine and focus on the highest-risk failure modes.

- Threat modeling (security "failures" only)
  - Determine the threat targets from functional decomposition.
  - Determine the types of threats to each component using STRIDE.[1]
  - Use threat trees to determine how the threat can become a vulnerability.

---

1 STRIDE: A classification system that describes the effect of a threat: Spoofing, Tampering, Repudiation, Denial of service, and Elevation of privilege–in other words, what the adversary will attain if the threat is exploited as a vulnerability. (Frank Swiderski and Window Snyder, *Threat Modeling*, page 27 [Redmond, WA: Microsoft Press, 2004])

❑ Apply a ranking mechanism, such as DREAD,[1] to each threat.

■ Failure modeling (all failures)

❑ Determine the focus area targets using scenarios, specifications, and functional decomposition.

❑ Determine possible failure modes for each target focus area.

❑ Calculate a risk for each failure mode based on overall impact and likelihood.

❑ For the highest-risk failure modes, detail intermediate subcauses, if needed, to identify underlying root causes (faults/defects).

❑ Describe the relationships between the intermediate subcauses using fault tree concepts.

❑ Identify actions to eliminate or mitigate the root causes of the highest-risk failure modes.

Conclusion

Over the years, engineering disciplines have used a variety of techniques to improve products and product reliability. A couple of the commonly used techniques in industries such as aerospace and transportation are failure modes and effects analysis (FMEA) and fault tree analysis (FTA). These techniques are used to proactively determine potential product failure modes and the causes of unintended events. The purpose is to identify potential defects early in the product development process so that they can be eliminated or mitigated during product design.

These same techniques can also be used in software development to help prevent software defects. As in other applications, the goal is to identify potential defects proactively so that they can be designed out of the software product or mitigated by design, if the former is not possible. Because a failure mode identified in FMEA can viewed as the unintended event being analyzed in FTA, these are complementary techniques. This alludes to the potential of combining them into a failure model.

Like the phrase "pay me now or pay me later," the resources and time allocated to perform FMEA and FTA early in the product cycle can help avoid the costly need to fix software defects found later during testing. Not only does this reduce software development costs, but it also reduces the potential for defects to remain undetected and eventually affect customers.

---

1 DREAD: A ranking of the risk associated wit a condition or vulnerability: Damage potential, Reproducibility, Exploitability, Affected users, and Discoverability. (Frank Swiderski and Window Snyder, *Threat Modeling*, page 27 [Redmond, WA: Microsoft Press, 2004])

Chapter 14
Prevention Tab

Efforts and methods for improvement of quality are . . . fragmented, with no overall competent guidance, no integrated system for continual improvement. Everyone, regardless of his job, needs a chance to learn and develop. In a climate of fragmentation, people go off in different directions, unaware of what other people are doing.
—W. Edwards Deming

Prevention is any action that stops something from happening: an action or actions taken to stop somebody from doing something or to stop something from happening.[1]

In this defect prevention technique, a *prevention* is a noun and is defined as an entry in a defect tracking system describing a preventive technique that can help eliminate a defect or class of defects. The *prevention tab* is a tool used to gather defect prevention techniques in real time when the defect is discovered or repaired.

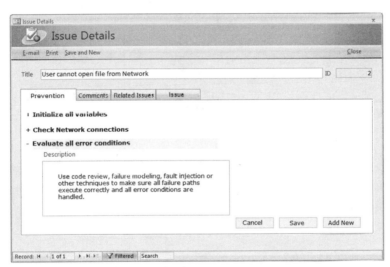

Figure 14-1   Sample issues database

The *tab* is an area in the issues or defect tracking system in which preventive techniques are collected. The prevention tab is designed to help capture defect prevention information so that it can be used to improve the quality of the software by helping the team learn from its mistakes.

---

1 Microsoft® Encarta® 2007.

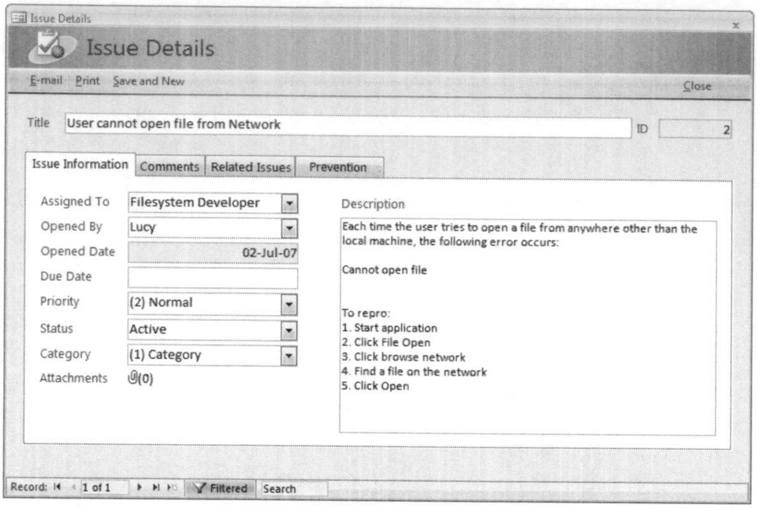

Figure 14-2   Prevention tab in sample issues database

Example preventions would include:

- Use of dynamic verification tools for heap and pool corruption.
- Code reviews.
- Removal of dead code.
- Unit testing.
- Early usability testing.
- More detailed specification and design reviews.
- Fault injection.
- Leak testing.
- Search for unitialized variables.
- Validating input data.
- Improving schedule accuracy.
- Performance analysis and testing.
- Early beta testing.

The examples above are relatively simple ideas and practices that are well known to most software developers. However, people are not perfect. They take shortcuts, they optimize for what they think is correct, and they make mistakes. The prevention tab is a place to capture the simple learning that occurs when a mistake is found. The prevention tab has its roots in root cause analysis, as described more fully in Chapter 11, "Root Cause Analysis." Typically, root cause analysis studies are performed by senior-level analysts who meet with and survey developers in a postmortem effort—usually weeks, sometimes months or years, after the particular issue first surfaces. Even with a root cause analysis study that begins immediately, the process requires an analyst to get up to speed on the issue at hand and make the connection across a diverse set of defects. In many cases, even with a significant investment in deep analysis, those closest to the action know best what needs to be done. As a result, even formal studies have shown that the best information typically comes from people actually working on the defects.

A formal root cause analysis study is a good method to analyze in detail and learn from mistakes, but it is formal and requires training and effort. In comparison, the prevention tab can, in many cases, jump right to a well-known solution and can provide a strong return on investment in terms of time and the number of defects that can be addressed. Just as important, the prevention tab can ask the questions at the *point of experience*—the time when the level of knowledge is the highest—when the defect is found or being repaired. The point of experience, when the developer or other product team member is working on the defect—is the richest point at which to gather prevention knowledge, and the prevention tab provides that opportunity.

How the Prevention Tab Works

The prevention tab helps prevent defects by providing a place where preventive information can be gathered at a point in time when knowledge of the defect is greatest and storing the information for future use. In other words, the prevention tab helps the organization learn from its mistakes. By capturing information throughout all phases of the development process about how to prevent defects, the product team can alter processes, build tools, and train people to improve quality and avert defects.

"Galloping Gertie": A History Lesson in Defect Prevention

In 1940, the Tacoma Narrows Bridge, also known as "Galloping Gertie," collapsed and fell into Puget Sound. A detailed history of the design and construction of the bridge shows that engineers on the project knew the design was flawed, but financial pressure and politics allowed the bridge to be built anyway.

Clark Eldridge, the State Highway Department's lead engineer for the project, developed the bridge's original design. But federal authorities footed 45 percent of the bill and required Washington State to hire an outside, and more prominent, consultant. Leon Moisseiff promised that his design would cut the bridge's estimated cost in half.

Similar structures built around the same time were expensive. At $59 million and $35 million respectively, the George Washington and Golden Gate bridges had a span similar to that of the Tacoma Narrows. Moisseiff's new design cost a bit over $6m, clearly a huge savings.

Except it fell down 4 months after opening day.

Moisseiff and others claimed that the wind-induced torsional flutter that led to the collapse was a new phenomenon, one never seen in civil engineering before. They seem to have forgotten the Dryburgh Abbey Bridge in Scotland, which collapsed in 1818 for the

---

same reason. Or the 1850 failure of the Basse-Chaine Bridge, a similar loss in 1854 of the Wheeling Suspension Bridge, and many others. All due to torsional flutter.

Then there was the 1939 Bronx-Whitestone Bridge, a sister design to Tacoma Narrows, which suffered the same problem but was stiffened by plate girders before a collapse.

And who designed the Bronx-Whitestone? Leon Moisseiff.

Lessons had been learned but criminally forgotten. Today the legacy of the Tacoma Narrows failure lives on in regulations that require all federally funded bridges to pass wind tunnel tests designed to detect torsional flutter.[1]

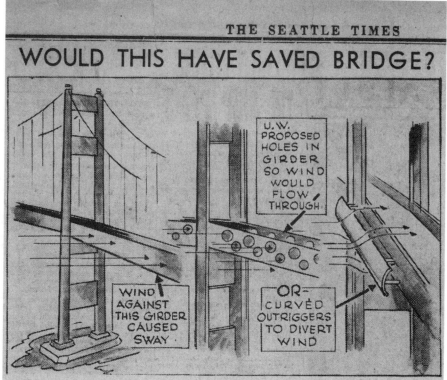

Figure 14-3 Galloping Gertie cartoon from The Seattle Times, November 8, 1940. University of Washington Special Collections, negative number UW27089z

The goal of the prevention tab is to give members of the product team a way to pass along knowledge about defects and how to prevent them—not to allow "lessons to be criminally forgotten."

1 http://www.ganssle.com/articles/Firmwaredisasters1.htm

Using the Prevention Tab Throughout the Product Cycle

Prevention data can be gathered in any phase of the product cycle. The length of time between the introduction of a defect, its discovery, and its repair may vary dramatically depending on the phase in which the defect is introduced. Defects introduced in the design phase may not be discovered until the product is released to users and may not be repaired until a future release. Therefore, prevention data gathering may lag defect introduction significantly. However, there should be no lag time between repairing defects and gathering prevention data. It is important to the success of the defect prevention activity that this data be gathered at the point of experience—the point at which the defect is repaired.

Writing High-Quality Preventions

The goal of the prevention tab is to provide a place to capture knowledge about a defect when a defect is found or repaired. This knowledge must be described in a way that is useful to those who want to apply it. In many cases, the preventive technique described in a prevention will be applied generically to similar types of problems and will usually be applied over one or more project cycles, so the importance of high-quality preventions cannot be overemphasized. It is important to write high-quality preventions because the knowledge captured in the prevention tab will persist throughout the product cycle and beyond and will be available to many other team members and organizations.

Clear and concise descriptions of prevention techniques have the following characteristics:

- Good preventions stem from a solid understanding of the defect.
- Prevention authors should think about the big picture and write the prevention to apply broadly, yet provide specific details.
- Clearly written preventions are more actionable.

Spending the time to create and write high-quality preventions is a long-term investment that pays dividends throughout one or more product cycles.

Who Can Contribute Preventive Techniques?

Anyone with relevant knowledge can contribute a prevention. Depending on the phase of the product cycle, different members of the product team may have different levels of prevention contributions. In early design phases of the product cycle, the types of defects that are introduced and repaired are dramatically different from the types of defects encountered later during the coding phase. Therefore, it is reasonable to assume that the type of preventions will be different, as well as the contributors.

There may be many different viewpoints on preventive techniques for any given defect. In some cases, the test team may offer a prevention related to the discovery of the defect, while the development team may offer suggestions to prevent the introduction of the same defect.

Each suggestion is valid because the goal is to capture organizational learning and improve organizational behavior. There may be an opportunity later to categorize or weight the preventions depending on the source of the recommendation. In other words, the ability to report on preventive techniques offered by the test team or those suggested by the developer is important because the audience for the report may be different from the audience doing the implementation work.

The big difference between the prevention tab and other defect prevention techniques is that the prevention tab uses the community or the wisdom of the crowd to develop the preventions. There is no single authority or expert who determines what and how the organization will learn. The other big advantage of the prevention tab is that the data is gathered at the point of experience in real-time while the defect is being analyzed. This takes advantage of the fact that local experts have the knowledge and familiarity with the defect at hand while they are making suggestions for prevention. Project management can decide whether prevention suggestions are required to be entered for each defect or whether the use of the prevention tab is optional. Another option is to require preventions only for high-priority or severe defects.

Understanding Who Benefits from Writing Preventions

In the short term, it is very difficult to show how the prevention tab work benefits those who contribute. The fact is, writing a quality prevention is additional work for team members to document the team's learning for the future. It's rare for people to consistently have the foresight to think preventively. For example, how many times does someone lock the keys in the car before stashing a spare? After the first time, or sometimes second, the benefit of a spare key is easy to see. The same is true for the product team investing time to write preventions. After a pattern or second instance of a problem is recognized, the benefit of a prevention is easy to quantify. However, the trick is to prevent that second occurrence by learning from the first.

When given a choice, most people are lazy and will take the path of least resistance. In other words, two or three similar mistakes will occur before they will invest in a prevention activity. The unfortunate result is that it is very difficult to encourage developers or other members of the product team to invest up front in creating or documenting preventive techniques. The benefit is for the team, not necessarily for the individual–a volunteer's dilemma. See Chapter 11 on Game Theory.

Encouraging Participation

The product team must actively participate in creating and reviewing preventions. The documentation of preventive techniques is a long-term investment and may not have an immediate payoff for the immediate code change, the current phase, or perhaps even the current product cycle. There is a risk that individual developers do not see the long-term value of the time investment required to create applicable preventions. Another danger is that the team does not invest the requisite time to produce quality preventions.

It is typical in the software industry for teams to be focused on the immediate need to ship the code with little regard for long-term investments and ongoing learning. The pliable nature of software encourages rapid development, quick adjustments, and "crunch mode" to get products out the door. However, a small investment in documenting how the team has learned from its mistakes can pay huge dividends in subsequent releases. Project management may want to allow scheduled time for the product team to document the learning and prevention information to help encourage or require participation.

A number of different options address the effort required to gather prevention information. The team may decide that this work is critical and mandate all users to provide detailed information when applicable. It's also possible to scale the effort back a little bit and require prevention information for certain distinct classes of defects. Another option is to allow individuals to make their own decisions as to whether they want to participate. This may lead to inconsistent results, but it is an effective way to get started.

That next important step in obtaining preventions is to make sure that data is reviewed and that preventions are applied whenever and wherever possible. A visible effort to incorporate the learning from the prevention information back into the product cycle will lead more team members to add their information. If the team members feel that the information is not being looked at, or that the information does not lead to a change, it is less likely that people will participate. The application of prevention data is critical to the success of any prevention program. Showcasing how the data is used encourages participation more than any other technique does.

A few different options can ensure that the data is used. Some organizations dedicate full-time staff to the implementation of prevention techniques. This model has the benefit of stability and a reasonable guarantee that prevention information will be reviewed and implemented where applicable. The downside is that quality and quantity of preventions adopted are directly related to the team size and effort.

Another approach is to cycle employees through a program or team responsible for the prevention information. This model has the benefit of varying the skill set, discipline, and makeup of the prevention team. For example, prevention information that must be dealt with during the release phase may take advantage of slack time for the planning team. This effort must be balanced across skill sets but can lead to a more efficient and successful implementation.

A third method is to gather preventions throughout the product cycle, and then as planning begins for the next product, the prevention information is reviewed and the learning is applied and designed into the process for the next product. This model has the benefit of limited resource investment during the current product cycle and allows the full set of preventions to be prioritized and weighed against one another to ensure that the most beneficial preventions are implemented. The disadvantage of this approach is that good preventions are not implemented immediately.

Another way to implement preventions is to encourage volunteer efforts as resources allow. This is probably the least effective model because there is a lack of consistency in the prioritization process, and preventions may be implemented based on individual rather than product team priorities. In some cases, the all-volunteer method may be the only option available to get started with a pilot program. Any effort to learn from mistakes and apply that learning more broadly is worthwhile, even if it is not the optimal approach.

Applying any of these models to implement preventions improves the likelihood that product team members will participate in documenting their learning. The individual or team responsible for reviewing and implementing prevention information should publish a regular report and distribute it broadly across the organization. This report helps show progress, as well as helps justify the individual investment in the creation of prevention data.

In large organizations, the team applying the prevention may not be familiar with the individual or the team who created it. The prevention tab is a great way to help spread best practices and ongoing improvements across the organization. In many cases, teams across the organization will be on different schedules, different products, and different technologies and will have a different set of skills. The sharing of prevention information across this diverse population helps improve the quality of the product, as well as improves the development skills of the individual and the process by which the software is developed. The key element of the prevention program is getting knowledgeable members of the product team to participate by describing their learning in a reusable format. Because the quality of the data will be at its highest at the point of experience—the point at which the developer is repairing the defect— the most important task is to gather the data then.

Seeking Patterns of "Defect Introduction" Activity

It is very likely that the prevention information will start to coalesce over time and some common themes or patterns will start to emerge. This is a good sign and is indicative of fertile areas for improvement. If possible, the prevention data should be used in conjunction with the defect taxonomy, metrics, and modeling techniques mentioned in other chapters to provide a comprehensive view of the defect and related learning. Categorizing preventions will be very helpful in identifying these patterns. (See the section titled "Categorizing Preventions" later in this chapter.) For example, defects that could be prevented by a code review appear late in the cycle, when schedule pressure may force people to skip formal code reviews in exchange for cursory peer reviews.

Causes of errors are usually categorized as one the following:

- Inadequate training
- Communications issues
- Missing the details of the problem
- Mistakes in manual procedures
- Incorrect rules or processes

In each of these error categories, use of the prevention tab helps people who introduce errors to learn from their mistakes. They improve, they get better, they gain experience.

Implementing a Prevention Tab Program

The biggest hurdle in implementing a prevention tab methodology is addressing the culture of the organization. The product team must be committed to a process of ongoing improvement and perhaps be given some incentive to do so. People, and organizations, don't like to make mistakes. As a result, they are not typically willing to discuss errors openly. However, to spread the learning from these mistakes across the organization requires that the information be available to all. The ability to be honest about failure requires an individual to trust that the manager will not be using it as part of a performance review. The actual implementation of the prevention tab can be as simple as a suggestion box or a yellow legal pad. Try the following methods to get started:

1. Establish measurable goals for prevention activity.

2. Identify progress tracking and communication methods.

3. Establish a location to store prevention data and a method to get it.

4. Provide incentives for prevention-related work (ideally, schedule time, rewards, and so on).

5. Staff for analysis.

6. Practice regular reporting and change measurement.

Each step is discussed in more detail in the following subsections. Also, remember that anonymity may be a feature of the prevention tab that is required for the program to be a success.

Establish Goals

The first step is to establish goals for the prevention tab program. Is the objective to save money, improve reliability or performance, increase test team agility? What areas of defects are causing the most pain and need to be addressed? SMART goals and measurable objectives help justify the effort and improve the likelihood of success. See Chapter 7 for a detailed discussion of SMART goals.

Identify Progress Tracking and Communication Methods

How will results be communicated to the product team? What measurements can be used to track progress? The type of investment made in analyzing, implementing, and deploying preventions will have an effect on how progress is made and communicated. (See the upcoming section titled "Staff for Analysis.")

Establish a Location to Store Prevention Data

Prevention data should be stored in a central location where all team members can find and review it. This could be a centralized database or a shared worksheet. Ideally, access to this data is open and the data is easy to find when people are working on defects. A developer repairing a defect is going to know more about preventing it at that time than any other time in that bug's lifetime, so links to the prevention data should be easy to find. The invitation, or requirement, to enter data should be obvious to the developer at that time.

Provide Incentives for Prevention-Related Work

The prevention work does not come for free. It's important to ensure that there is time in the schedule or even compensation or other rewards for doing prevention work. The long-term benefit is measurable, particularly with good tracking in place, so a positive return should justify investment in prevention work. Anonymous suggestions may be worth considering, although they can contribute to a "platform for blame" stigma for the prevention tab.

Ensure Sufficient Staff for Analysis

As mentioned earlier, the prevention data can be inconsistent and hard (or easy) to act on, so staffing for the analysis phase is important. Senior members of the team should review and aggregate the prevention data and make formal recommendations for change.

Practice Regular Reporting and Change Measurement

Regular reporting demonstrates and showcases the value in prevention activity. If team members can see visible results from this data, it's more likely they will invest time in preventing defects. Upper management will benefit from reports on measured changes and, if possible, cost savings associated with the activity. In many cases, the individuals will know what needs to happen, and the prevention tab gives them the forum to explain it.

Taking Action on Prevention Tab Data

In today's typical development environment, the learning of the individual is not distributed beyond that person or that person's immediate group. There is no standard methodology to capture knowledge and take advantage of learning experiences. The prevention tab is a methodology that can be used for these purposes. The prevention information collected is designed to help product teams eliminate defects during any stage of the development process, increase the amount of prevention information available to all who need it, propagate the use of good tools, and eliminate human errors.

The type and corresponding detail of prevention data gathered by the prevention tab may vary dramatically depending on the type of defect, the skill of the developer, the context of the discovery or fix, and the scope of the prevention. In some cases, the prevention information may be so detailed that it applies only to the single defect on which it was gathered. In other cases, the prevention information may be so broad or so high level that it is impossible to take any action on it. Preventions submitted at either end of this spectrum can be irrelevant.

If the information is too detailed or describes something that is unlikely to happen again, it may be difficult for anyone to apply the learning forward to other defects. If the information is too broad, there may be no obvious or suitable change that can be made. It is also possible for the issues, complaints, or gripes of individual team members to show up as recommended preventions. The composition of the prevention team can help discourage or reconcile these types of issues. As team members add more preventions and understand the use and application of the technique, the quality of the prevention data will improve.

Over time, as the prevention information starts to accumulate, the team can start to take action and start to implement the suggestions. These corrective actions are the same type of corrective actions that come from a root cause analysis study. (See Chapter 11, "Root Cause Analysis," for more information on conducting a root cause analysis study.) The prevention tab is very similar to a root cause analysis study but is much faster and lighter weight. For example, a prevention might be to inspect the code for buffer overruns.

Categorizing Preventions

Every defect is different. It may be difficult for an expert on a single defect to understand how the prevention for his or her defect applies to other defects. It may be challenging to apply the techniques from one defect to another. However, by grouping the preventions into categories, it becomes easier to project the relevance and usefulness of one technique to another category of defect, even if the specific technique cannot be applied directly. High-level categories, such as static analysis tools, can help users discover the relevant techniques.

The preventions typically fall into one of the following high-level categories:

- Training opportunities
- Process change recommendations
- Process automation opportunities
- Detection tool creation
- Prevention tool creation
- Focus change opportunities
- Recommendations for more study and measurement

Training Opportunities

One of the most obvious defect prevention techniques is to improve through training. The prevention tab can yield a number of suggestions for training opportunities on techniques that may be well known to one individual, yet not popular or understood by the rest of the team. For example, one of the most successful and viable prevention techniques is the code review or code inspection. Many experienced developers and testers are experts at looking at the code. Agile methods such as pair programming involve a second set of eyes on the code to look for defects that the author may overlook. However, new employees or someone starting in a new job may not be familiar with how a code review is done. Training is a way to propagate the learning across the organization on a scale that can be successful. Tying training classes to prevention techniques is also a good way to focus training efforts in areas where the reward is high and to track adoption of the preventions. In other words, the organization can offer training in areas where prevention data is focused. If a number defects could have been prevented through a code review, training on how to perform better code reviews might make sense.

Process Change Recommendations

Another common corrective action that stems from the prevention tab data collection effort is a recommendation for a process change. Again, using the code review example, the team may decide that a formal code review is required for all code changes in a certain area or of a certain type. This new process can prevent the type of defects identified through the prevention tab. The process change recommendation may remove or eliminate a step. For example, schedule pressure may preclude a developer from scheduling a formal code review that would find a certain class of defect and prevent it from being added to the code base. To accommodate the need for a formal code review, the check-in process can be modified and the requirement to test the code on an old platform may be deemed optional in lieu of a formal code review, or a schedule adjustment may be allowed to accommodate a formal code review.

Process Automation Opportunities

One of the best ways to prevent defects is to use a machine to automate a task that is error prone for humans to do. If mistakes are repeatedly made during a certain phase of performing a certain manual activity, automation is an incredibly effective technique to remove the chance of error. For example, if a developer is required to copy files to a certain location to perform a series of tests, there is a chance of error in choosing the set of files, finding the right location, or choosing the tests. If this activity can be scripted for a computer to do automatically, the developer must remember only to run the script—and even that can be automated as part of the process. The results are now far more consistent, and the likelihood of an oversight that may cause an error disappears. Another example is to require a developer to run a set of automated tests prior to submitting new code to the product.

Detection Tool Creation

As prevention techniques are identified and accumulate through the product cycle, there may be an opportunity to create supporting tools to help detect or prevent defects. For example, static analysis tools can be run against the code to detect certain types of errors, enforce certain coding standards, or measure properties of the code. Other examples of detection tools include test and quality assurance tools to create low memory conditions, low disk space, or user privilege environments to help detect problems in those situations. Early detection of a defect or potential defect is often equivalent to preventing the defect completely. The fewer people affected by a defect, the less costly the defect in terms of schedule and impact. A product planner can detect a potential problem in the design before any code is written. A developer may detect a buffer overrun by running an analysis tool on the code before it makes it into the product. The test team may run a set of detection tools prior to release and find language translation issues before the product goes to market. All of these detection tool examples illustrate how effective detection is as significant and cost effective as is prevention.

Prevention Tool Creation

Prevention tools are a step above detection tools. Think of them as guardrails that help an individual, a product team, or the product itself stay on track. The best example of a software defect prevention tool is the compiler. The compiler prevents defective source code from being run by disallowing the creation of an executable program. The feedback from a prevention tool can be immediate or the tool may be completely silent, capably preventing problems in the background. A good example of a silent prevention tool is a firewall. With a good firewall in place as a prevention technique, attackers are prevented from getting to a computer, and typically the user never realizes that someone was trying to attack.

Focus Change Opportunities

Another common type of prevention is one that results in a focus change. A focus change is similar to a process change but will look at the time and task allocation of members of the team. An example might be a series of defects that arise because of double-byte characters that could be prevented if the product team focused more on international configurations. Product planners and designers can adjust their focus to consider how localized versions of the product should look, architects can alter the way the product is built, developers can adjust their data structures, and testers can broaden their test matrix—everyone can adjust their behavior and change their focus to account for these issues.

Recommendations for More Study and Measurement

Another likely result of the prevention information is that no definitive conclusion can be drawn. The prevention data may be inconsistent or may vary enough to indicate that there is a problem, but further study may be required to identify the best corrective action. In many cases, a single prevention may introduce a new way of looking at things that will require a variety of research activities.

In-Depth Analysis

After a series of preventions has been gathered, an analysis can be performed to understand where to make investments. This deeper focus on the data is usually done in a structured fashion. The first step is to take stock of the preventions to ensure that a representative set has been gathered. After the team is confident that there is a significant number of preventions, the next step is to evaluate the preventions based on the scope or severity of the defect. Because the preventions will usually come from many different sources, the data will likely be inconsistent in its level of detail and clarity. Evaluating the prevention data based on the severity, type, class, priority, and area of the defect will help the team understand where to make investments in prevention techniques. For example, a prevention may apply only to a specific instance, a specific developer, or a specific defect. Other preventions may be written so broadly that it is impossible to take any action.

It may also be valuable to analyze how the defect was discovered, the phase of the product cycle where the defect was introduced, the severity or impact of the defect, and the priority for getting the defect fixed. Using the prevention tab in conjunction with some of the other techniques in this book will yield the best results. All this data, and perhaps other information related to the defect, should be part of the defect tracking. The defect taxonomy is another effective prevention technique. (See Chapter 10, "Defect Taxonomies.")

Benefits of Using the Prevention Tab

There are many advantages to gathering prevention data during product development. The most significant benefit is the contribution to the ongoing learning process of the organization. It is a fact that people learn from their mistakes. People are also capable of learning from the mistakes of others. The goal of the prevention tab is to capture that learning and offer it to the organization. Anyone reviewing defect data can now see suggestions for how to prevent the defect as well. The prevention tab is not rocket science—it is an easy way to gather information that might otherwise be lost in the rush to ship the project. A real-world metaphor for the prevention tab is the pad of paper on which you write a note to remind yourself to stash a spare key—while the locksmith is unlocking your car for you.

Helps to Shift Individual Thinking to the Big Picture

Defect prevention efforts can often change the frame of mind of the individual from thinking specifically about a given defect to thinking about the broader lessons that can be learned. This mindset change happens because the value in prevention information increases the more relevant the lessons can be to multiple defects, so product team members will often think about the big picture in describing prevention techniques and lessons learned from a given bug. This thinking helps the quality of the prevention and may help team members identify other mistakes on their own.

Preventive Techniques and Knowledge Are Easily Shared

It can be very difficult to share or reuse prevention information, even for small product teams. The amount of learning that happens throughout a product cycle makes it difficult to track efficiently. A small product team may go for months between similar defects, or a large product team may have similar defects repaired by different people, and in either case, having a system to organize and track prevention data helps team members share the learning. The product team can benefit from reports and statistics about the prevention data the same way they benefit from defect reports and statistics. In some cases, it may make sense to staff a team to do a detailed analysis of the prevention techniques and look for patterns and make formal recommendations.

Prevention Data Is Stored with Discovery and Repair Data

Storing the prevention data alongside the rest of the information about the defect makes it easy to find. Also, team members who work with similar defects can search on a variety of defect-related data and find the prevention information easily.

Provides Feedback Mechanism for Process Improvement

The prevention tab institutionalizes process improvement by giving product team members an easy way to give feedback and to capture their learning about a defect at the point of experience—when they are fixing the bug. Typically, bug analysis projects such as root cause analysis start long after the defect is fixed, and the prevention tab provides an opportunity to provide immediate feedback on the defect.

Eases Data Collection

The point of experience—the time at which the developer or other product team member is working on the defect—is the richest point at which to gather prevention knowledge. Adding a place to collect defect prevention information makes it convenient to collect the data.

Is Applicable in All Phases

Unfortunately, mistakes can happen at all phases of the software development cycle. However, so does learning from those mistakes, and with the prevention tab team members from all disciplines at all phases of the product cycle can catalog their prevention techniques as they learn from their mistakes.

Risks of Using the Prevention Tab

Becomes a Platform for Blame

Without the right guidance, product team members can use the prevention tab as a platform to push their own personal agenda. Developers can suggest that the test team should work harder, and the testers can say that developers should write better code. Monitoring and maintaining the quality of the prevention suggestions help keep this from happening, but it is important to address the possibility of personal attacks or agendas making their way into the data. It is also important not to overreact to any given suggestion, especially when it involves team member behavior.

Subject to Skewed Data

It is virtually impossible to ensure that data collected through the prevention tab will be consistent. The amount of information about a defect, the skill of the developer or team member adding the prevention data, the phase of the product cycle, the type of defect, and the impact are all examples of variables that contribute to the quality of the prevention. In many cases, prevention details may be sparse and therefore not required. The data about preventive techniques, therefore, may be skewed and should be treated accordingly. Over time, as more preventions are gathered, the best suggestions will bubble to the top, but it is important to understand all the variables involved.

Easy to Overweight or Overreact

The prevention tab may capture some gems—prevention ideas of pure genius. Some of the more obvious preventions, such as a formal code review, are easy to relate to and deploy. It is also possible to get a prevention that details a very specific type of coding error, for example, one that can be caught in a code review, and the temptation may be to include that small detail in *every* code review simply because it was a good suggestion and despite the fact that the likelihood of the error is very small. The appearance of clearly actionable data may cause the team to overreact. This type of cognitive bias is known as the *availability heuristic*.

> *The availability heuristic is based on an assessment of accessibility, in which frequencies or probabilities are judged by the ease with which instances come to mind.*[1]

It is important to take all prevention suggestions in context and to review them using standard procedures.

---

1 Tversky, A., and Kahneman, D. (1973). *Availability: A Heuristic for Judging Frequency and Probability.* Cognitive Pscyhology 5, 207-232

Requires Compilation and Analysis

The prevention tab data must be compiled and analyzed to be used effectively. Sometimes, individual developers or testers will review the data about the defects they work on to look for patterns. In other cases, a central team can be staffed to review–similar to the root cause analysis process. There are other virtual team or temporary case study or project postmortem options to address the prevention data. Because the data comes in at varying times, with varying levels of detail and quality, it is important to examine the data and compile recommendations for corrective actions. Although there may be some cases where corrective actions are obvious from the prevention data, to provide some consistency and ensure that the recommendations are high quality the team should review and summarize the preventions regularly.

Preventions May Be Too General or Too Specific

Mistakes can be prevented in a number of different ways. Coding errors can be prevented by modifying coding behavior, deploying smarter editors or compilers, or simply by having a developer take a day off. Each prevention is valid and has varying degrees of impact on the probability of a recurring error and on the productivity of the team. The goal of the prevention tab is to provide a place to gather the data at all levels, and as a result, it's likely that suggestions may come in at all levels. In some cases, as in the developer taking a day off, the recommendation may be too broad–or it may be too specific, such as a developer not editing a given file when another specific file is being worked on. General recommendations can be derived from either of these cases, but there is a risk that the prevention data is out of scope in one direction or the other.

Conclusion

The prevention tab is a simple addition to a defect tracking system that enables the team to gather defect prevention data from the developer working on the defect at the point of experience. The most knowledgeable person on an expert team for a root cause analysis study or failure modeling exercise is the developer working on the defects under study, so it makes perfect sense that their knowledge of the preventive techniques is the richest. The prevention tab provides a place for this information to be recorded. The "tab" can be implemented as an addition to the defect tracking system, or it can be as simple as a small process change to enable developers and testers to add more prevention information directly to the defect report.

Part V
A Culture of Prevention

Chapter 15
Scenario Voting

> *Before beginning a Hunt, it is wise to ask someone what you are looking for before you begin looking for it.*
>
> —Winnie the Pooh

Software development can be a lucrative business, but it is complex. Typically, a successful software application contains a variety of features and functionality that empowers the user. As software applications and the environments in which they run continue to become more and more complex, it's difficult to gather comprehensive user feedback. It takes effort for users to give feedback, and many times this effort is discounted or ignored. Scenario voting offers the opportunity to gather lightweight data across a broad set of scenarios. The goal of scenario voting is to make it easy for the user to provide simple feedback quickly, perhaps in as little as two or three clicks of the mouse. As the feedback starts to come in, the product team can begin to put together a plan to take action on the data.

A *scenario* is a user task or activity in a software application, and the *scenario voting process* presents a description of these activities to users and asks them to provide a rating or opinion of the scenario. Users can offer an opinion on their satisfaction with the scenario, as well as the relative importance. A software development team can use scenario voting to capture the perception of the user base on various aspects of the software application in a roughly prioritized fashion. The development team can use the results to quickly identify areas where users are having difficulty, which scenarios users view negatively, or tasks that are easy for users and working well. Scenario voting can prevent costly design or customer-reported defects by improving product team communication with customers throughout the product cycle.

Applying the Law of Large Numbers

The Law of Large Numbers guides the design of the scenario voting process. By providing an easy, lightweight way for users to give feedback, a development team increases the likelihook that users will vote and will subsequently vote on more scenarios. Wikipedia defines the Law of Large Numbers as follows (at least for now):

> *The law of large numbers (LLN) is a theorem in probability that describes the long-term stability of a random variable. Given a sample of independent and identically distributed random variables with a finite population mean and variance, the average of these observations will eventually approach and stay close to the population mean.*[1]

---

1 Wikipedia, "Law of Large Numbers," *http://en.wikipedia.org/wiki/Law_of_large_numbers.*

In other words, it may not be possible to predict the outcome of a single coin toss, but flipping numerous times helps increase the accuracy of the aggregate prediction. Likewise, a statistically significant number of users voting on a scenario can provide a more accurate assessment of that scenario that can help guide product changes and identify problems earlier in the development cycle. As James Surowiecki says in *The Wisdom of Crowds*, "Under the right circumstances, groups are remarkably intelligent, and are often smarter than the smartest people in them." And he continues, "We feel the need to 'chase the expert'—we should stop hunting and ask the crowd instead."[1] Although any individual voting on a scenario may not represent exactly how all users view it, the average across a large number of voters (users) can provide a good indication of user sentiment. It can be subject to "the squeaky wheel getting the grease," but careful participant selection can eliminate that risk.

> *I hate to be a kicker [complainer],*
> *I always long for peace,*
> *But the wheel that does the squeaking*
> *Is the one that gets the grease.*[2]

Without a statistically significant sample size, the program can run the risk of attracting only the complainers.

Using Scenario Voting to Help Prevent Defects

Scenario voting prevents defects by helping the product team assess customer requirements, needs, and wants early in the product development cycle. The team can use the scenario voting process to monitor progress toward achieving customer satisfaction throughout the product cycle. By allowing end users to participate in the development of the software application in this way throughout the entire development process, the product team can more easily understand and track the requirements that must be met to ship the product.

Closely monitoring customer requirements helps prevent the wrong features from being built or the wrong designs from being implemented. By getting early customer feedback, the product team can tailor the feature set to the exact needs of the customer as the code is being written. Learning earlier what's important to the user base helps focus the development effort. Understanding the mindset of the user, the makeup of the user environment, and the details of user configurations can help steer quality efforts throughout the project.

Although scenario voting can provide feedback on the feature design and end user experience, it cannot replace the compiler. As a defect prevention technique, it will not find missing semicolons or other code-based defects, but it can provide detailed information on the user experience. Also, because scenario voting is a fairly lightweight process, it easily scales to thousands or millions of end users or potential customers. The larger the voting population, the more likely the nuances of individual users will be rendered insignificant. If the tendency of

---

1   James Surowiecki, *The Wisdom of Crowds* (New York: Anchor, 2005).

2   Josh Billings, "The Kicker," 1870, *http://en.wikipedia.org/wiki/Josh_Billings*.

10,000 people is to vote a particular scenario as low in satisfaction, it's fairly likely that this is an area that warrants more detailed investigation. Although the scenario voting process may not be able to identify the details of the differences between two similarly ranked scenarios, it makes it easy to identify the outliers quickly: the underperformers and the delighters. In addition, the opportunity is available to address every individual piece of user feedback.

Knowing When to Apply Scenario Voting

Scenario voting can be applied in all three phases of the project cycle, from design through implementation to release. For example, the product team can ask the user, "how satisfied are you with the experience of printing a document?" and "How important is it to you?" while the feature is being designed, while the code is being written, and/or when the code is complete and being verified.

The goals and implementation of the scenario voting process may differ depending on the phase, but the basic concept is the same: present a scenario to the user, and ask for an opinion or rating on it.

- **Design phase**   In the design phase, scenario voting can provide critical, early feedback on the viability and relevance of user scenarios. At this stage, the scenarios may be only textual descriptions, mockups, or even video renderings. As long as users are able to assess the intent, rough implementation, and general goals of the scenario, they are capable of providing feedback. It is particularly useful to get feedback on the relative importance of the proposed feature set at this stage of the project.

- **Implementation phase**   During the implementation phase, scenario voting can provide the product team with a broader quality assessment framework. A wide set of users can give feedback on the implementation and on the relative stability of the scenarios. The voting population can help bridge the design and release phases by giving feedback on the importance of the scenarios, as well as how satisfied they are with the implementation.

- **Release phase**   The final phase before release is a critical time in the project. Scenario voting can be used to involve the users in the release process. The analysis of voting feedback during this final phase can also help assess whether changes made based on feedback throughout the project have made a difference in the user opinions.

Introducing scenario voting early in the project cycle can establish customer behavioral trends early as well as provide trend data on customer perception of scenario improvements through the entire project cycle. This feedback is important for a couple of reasons. First, everyone on the project team is working toward building a useful feature set that the end user will enjoy. Tracking progress toward an end user satisfaction goal and showing measurable improvement through the product cycle are important. Second, users are more likely to be satisfied with the end result by knowing that the team listened to and acted on their feedback.

Scenario voting techniques can also be easily used on existing products already in the market. Although the results data cannot be used to direct and design the product because the product has already shipped, the product team can use customer feedback on existing versions as a baseline to direct the focus for the next generation, or for maintenance release or updates. For example, if certain features generate high technical support costs, an analysis of those cost generators can yield a list of features or scenarios in which customers have difficulty or require assistance. A product team can directly affect the product's bottom line by addressing those cost generators in future versions of the product.

Figure 15-1 is a high-level illustration of the scenario voting solution process and current tools used in this methodology. Note that a Suppliers Inputs Process Outputs Customers (SIPOC) diagram is a process-mapping tool that highlights relevant elements of a process. It expands on a high-level process map by showing who supplies inputs to a process step and who receives the output from that step. (Note: ISV is Independent Software Vendor, and OEM is Original Equipment Manufacturer.)

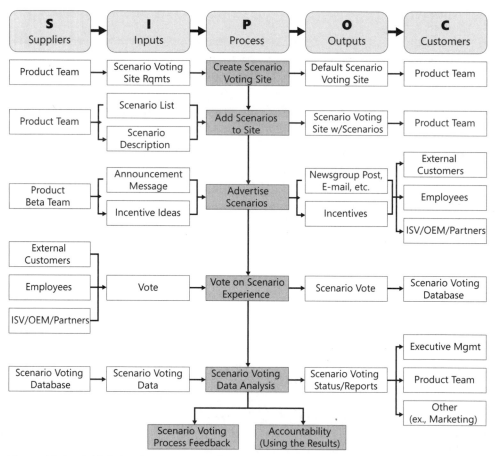

Figure 15-1   A high-level process map for scenario voting

Understanding the Scenario Voting Process

The definition of tasks, features, use cases, user activities, and scenarios differs from organization to organization. For the purpose of clarity, the focus here is on the user and how users manipulate the software application. Although it can encompass one or more features or use cases, the user activity dictates the start and finish of a scenario. A certain feature may provide a range of functionality to the user, but a scenario links specific functionalities together to accomplish a task. For example, a feature of the operating system may allow sound to be played from the PC speaker, but the scenario is "play music on your PC" or "adjust the volume of the PC speaker."

Well-designed scenarios describe the software in a way that makes sense to users. It's important to note that users come in many types and varieties, so the definition of the scenario, even across the same set of features, may differ. For example, a scenario description for a technical user may be "download a podcast and rip it to CD," and that same scenario may be described to a novice user in much more detailed steps, such as "go to a Web site, find a digital recording, and copy it to a blank CD." The feedback in each scenario may be different and targeted at a different audience. For example, feedback on the ease of use may be directed to the design team, whereas slow performance issues are directed to the development team. A scenario should be defined in a way so that the resulting feedback is usable by the product team.

Operational Profiling

An *operational profile* is a specific technical description of how the product will be exercised by a given user. In the case of software, the operational profile is the set of code functions exercised as the user proceeds through the scenario. Creating the operational profile—the function list—requires the following steps:

1. Understand the scenario.
2. Instrument a build or run with the debugger on.
3. Exercise or step through the scenario.
4. Analyze and record the code-based data output.
5. Store the mapping between the scenario and the code functions in reusable form.

Operational profiling represents the mapping of the high-level textual description of the scenario to the path through the code that the user takes when performing the scenario. This type of profiling not only helps define the risk and coverage of the product but also can help guide test activities during the verification phase of the project cycle. Operational profiling can be done a few different ways but always requires an in-depth understanding of the underlying code.

Ideally, users are given "debug" builds instrumented so that they are capable of detecting function-level usage. That is, the user can perform a scenario, and the code required to perform that scenario is listed in a separate log file. The log file can be analyzed later to understand the mapping between the code and the scenario. Operational profiling is a more costly extension of the scenario voting process, but the benefits over the life of the product cycle and beyond are huge. For example, the product team can use a function-level profile of a single scenario to understand the following:

- Relationship between code changes and customer impact
- Most important (most widely used) code in the product
- Where test investments have greatest impact
- Interaction of the product with underlying or dependent code
- Code usage by a particular profile
- Feature-based scheduling and project management
- How internal users should use the features to help emulate external users
- Code complexity and risk of late changes to user base
- Code optimization, refactoring, dependency management, and code-sharing opportunities
- Support and maintenance impact

Data-mapping scenarios have other uses for coding, but as the list shows, they can be an invaluable resource for understanding users' actions.

> *The benefit-to-cost ratio in developing and applying the operational profile is typically 10 or greater.*[1]

Writing High-Quality Scenarios

Creating and writing high-quality end user scenarios is a long-term investment that pays dividends throughout the product cycle by providing a focus point for all development efforts. The development team, management, product support, and marketing can all rally behind clear and concise scenarios.

Spending time creating solid, high-quality scenarios has many benefits:

- Scenarios require an understanding of the product, and the development of the scenarios forces the understanding to happen.
- Scenario authors must think of the product from the user perspective.
- Clearly written scenarios can generate better, more actionable feedback.

---

1 John Musa, *Software Reliability Engineering: More Reliable Software Faster and Cheaper*, 2nd ed. (Bloomington, IN: AuthorHouse, 2004).

- Scenarios invite users to explore areas of the product they are not familiar with.
- Well-written scenarios are the first step toward help and marketing documentation.

Categorizing Scenarios

Grouping scenarios can also improve the efficiency of the voter (user) because the voter can complete similar scenarios together. For example, when all music-related scenarios are grouped together, the user can focus and complete related scenarios, judging them in context and comparing against one another. This also increases the likelihood of a user to vote. If similar activities are grouped together, users exploring that area of the product are more likely to try a variety of actions than if the set of scenarios presented to the user is for features scattered across the functionality of the product.

How to Categorize Scenarios

No single correct way to categorize or classify scenarios exists. Much of the decision about how to categorize will depend on the types of users as well as how the scenario voting results will be used. From a user perspective, categorization should follow a logical pattern that matches the application or process where voters are providing feedback. If the application has three or four major types of tasks, categorization should fall along those lines.

It may make sense to provide alternative views of the voting results for different members of the product team. Often, the organization of the product team spans user functionality, so an alternative view that aligns with the responsibilities and organizational structure of the product team may make sense.

Therefore, there should be at least two distinct steps in analyzing how to categorize the scenarios. One should be from the point of view of the user who is doing the voting and the other for the product team, who are expected to view and act on the data. Ultimately, aligning these categories with a single view is a useful exercise in encouraging the product team to think like the user, but initially, the scenarios may span multiple product teams. Also, architectural constraints, shared code, and other organizational optimizations may preclude a simple, single view of the scenarios.

Understanding Who the Voters Are

Voters are people who provide feedback on scenarios. Anyone who is willing to provide feedback can be added to the pool of voters, but it's important to use good judgment in selecting voters.

Importance of Voter Selection

Successful selection of voters is imperative because it influences the relevance, applicability, and usability of the feedback. In essence, the voters are a sample of the broader user population. As in statistical sampling, the sample should represent the target population well enough so that the researcher is able to infer things about the full set by observing only the sample. A random voter selection process that avoids or minimizes any bias will help the quality of the results.

What is most important about selecting a voting population is knowledge of the type of user, or voter, chosen. There are many different types of users, and for scenario voting to be effective, each type or class of user should be represented in the voting population. This is yet another case where the Law of Large Numbers can apply. The larger the size of the population, the more likely that all types of users will be represented.

Five stages of the sampling process apply to voter selection:[1]

- **Identify the target population**   Typically, the target population is made up of existing or potential users, but it could be expanded to include partners, sales personnel, and so on.

- **Select the sampling frame**   The *sampling frame* is a list of sampling entities that represent the population. In most cases, the sampling frame is composed of different types of users stratified by user type.[2]

- **Choose a sampling method**   Usually the best choice is to use a stratified simple random sample for which you choose randomly from various user types and demographics.

- **Perform data collection and effective sampling**   Quality data collection involves marking notable events, keeping data in time order, and recording nonresponses.

- **Review the sampling process**   After selecting the sample and getting the voting results, review the sample selection process to assess the validity of the sample.

The makeup of the sample is important because the voting population determines the type of feedback that the team will receive through a scenario voting effort. "Garbage in, garbage out" does apply. If the makeup of the voting population poorly represents the set of users, the conclusions drawn from the results are meaningless.

Knowing What Voters Want

Voters want the opportunity to be heard. People are happy to provide feedback if they know that someone is listening and willing to do something with the feedback. If voters believe that the product team is acting on their feedback, they will be willing to invest more time in providing quality feedback than they would if they don't believe anyone is listening. What the voters want is simple, yet it takes some investment from the product team to provide it.

---

1   Wikipedia, "Sampling (Statistics)," *http://en.wikipedia.org/wiki/Sampling_%28statistics%29*.

2   G. David Garson, "Sampling," PA 765 Web site, *http://www2.chass.ncsu.edu/garson/pa765/sampling.htm*.

Implementing a Privacy Policy

Users may want to give feedback anonymously. The product team must make a decision and perhaps a tradeoff early on: Although it's great to understand exactly who is giving feedback so that the team can check specifically whether the issue is addressed, users may be more likely to give honest feedback if they can do so anonymously. Therefore, the team should develop a privacy policy early on and respect it throughout the voting process. Users should be given clear descriptions of exactly what data is being collected about them, how it will be used, and who will have access to it.

Implementing a Scenario Voting Program

There are some basic steps to get scenario voting up and running successfully. Although the steps should be done in order, the order can vary depending on the nature of the project. In some cases, the type of development process dictates which elements of scenario voting make sense for the team to implement.

Understand the Appropriate Project Phase

This may sound obvious, but the first step to implementing scenario voting is to understand in which phase of the project the feedback will be most useful. In many cases, the early design phase is the best place to understand how changes will affect the user because code has not been written and changes are less costly. However, in many cases, at these early stages simply not enough is known about the product to ask the user important questions. Therefore, the implementation phase may be a better place to use scenario voting to gather user feedback.

Know the Product

Again, this sounds very simple, but knowing the product and knowing the usage of the product are two very different things—and for scenario voting to be successful, it's important to know both. The user's view of the product can be very different from the developer view of the product. Scenario voting techniques can be applied to fill in some holes in the knowledge of the product team about how users employ the product, but the user should be giving feedback on the product he or she understands, not the product the design or development team thinks they have built. In other words, present the scenarios in a way that makes sense to the user, not to the product team.

Develop an Experience Tree

An *experience tree* is a layered view that maps a high-level user experience to an individual feature, or even to a function in the source code (see Figure 15-2). The detail level of an experience tree can vary, depending on the size and complexity of the product. In some cases, the experience tree can include persona information in the hierarchy, and in other cases, the experience may be unique to a persona. (Personas are explained in the section titled

"Personas" later in this chapter.) Again, the nature of the process varies depending on the project.

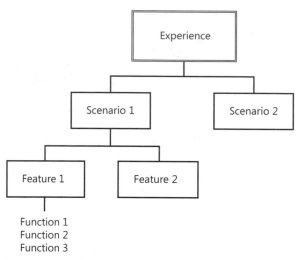

Figure 15-2   An experience tree

It is important to develop an experience tree to understand how the various levels of the application fit together. Here is an example for a word processor experience.

Experience: Create a Newsletter

Scenario 1: Find a photo and place it in a document

Feature 1: Insert a JPG in a document

Function 1: *File_Open(name, ...)*

Mapping the product by using an experience tree can help identify how all the pieces fit together. Because users will be giving feedback at the scenario level, the effort to map scenarios to an experience helps identify areas where scenarios are missing. In the preceding Creating a Newsletter example, for instance, it might be easy to forget to include a scenario that addresses printing color copies or multiple copies, but if the thinking is done at the experience level, it's easy to see where the holes in scenario coverage may be.

Note that it may not be possible to complete the entire tree from top to bottom at design time. The function-level documentation of the experience tree may have to be done after scenarios are identified and the code is written. The experience tree can be very helpful in the development of the operational profile.

Set Clear Goals for Feedback

The product team should set some goals for feedback prior to beginning the scenario voting project. Along with identifying the voting population, it is important to set targets for participation, voting totals, feedback and comments, and follow-up requirements for the team ahead of time and then monitor through the exercise. Creating goals for the use of feedback also helps the product team communicate results back to the voters more frequently by clearly explaining what changes have been made as a result of user participation.

Document and Develop the Scenarios

The next step is to develop the scenarios on which users will vote. Often, the product specifications and early design documents will contain the basic scenarios, or perhaps the scenarios are being developed at the same time as the feature specifications. In either case, the scenarios should be written so that users understand them, and then the team should invest time and effort into understanding how the scenarios cover the product, both from the broad, cross-product, perspective and the deep, code-level, perspective.

How to Write a Good Scenario

A well-written scenario leads to useful voting results, which leads to a more successful product. When writing scenarios, start with an assumption that the user has a limited amount of time to try it out and give feedback. The user can probably answer a small number of questions about a given scenario. With that in mind, consider how user answers will be used in improving the product. If, for example, users are asked if they felt that performance was slow, and results data indicates a perceived slow performance, ignoring the results or blaming them on network latency or some other factor outside the control of the feature owner is a waste of valuable feedback. If network performance issues are a real possibility and could skew the results, think about how to ask the question in a way that returns useful data to the feature owner. Careful selection of questions involves careful analysis of the resulting data and an understanding or forecast of what behavior will change or how the product will be altered based on the voting results.

Use these tips to write good scenarios:

- Set a goal or an experience for the scenario.
    - Involve all stakeholders early.
- Categorize product areas to help structure.
- Think like the user.
- Do not lead the user.
- Consider alternative ways to describe sensitive steps in a scenario.

- Note that there may be differences in types of users—include each/all of them in this thinking.

- If you don't understand the users, study them, invite them in, or find a real user to help.

- Choose scenarios most relevant to user activity.

  - Don't write feature-based scenarios—think about the user.

  - Be thorough—capture important scenarios, and don't leave holes.

- Decide on a level of detail most appropriate for the product.

  - Guiding the user step by step can have some pros and cons.

  - The level of detail may vary based on the phase of the project.

  - It's important to establish the setting or context required to perform the scenario.

  - Provide setup instructions if necessary.

  - Avoid simply giving instructions to the user—consider describing what to do, not how to do it.

- Use the active voice and short sentences.

  - When the subject of a sentence performs the action of the verb, the sentence is said to be in active voice: "The dog bit the mailman."

  - If the subject is being acted on, the sentence is said to be in passive voice: "The mailman was bitten by the dog." The mailman has become the subject of this sentence, but he isn't performing the action; the dog is the one doing the biting.

  - Active sentences tend to be more dynamic and easier to read and understand.

- Write for a single user.

- Don't use acronyms or technical terms that might not be familiar.

- Check carefully for spelling and vocabulary errors.

- Provide a description of the verification steps or other checks where appropriate. How does the user verify that the scenario is complete and successful?

- Perform scenario evaluations.

  - Identify and understand operational profiles and experience trees: How do the scenarios travel through the code? What code has changed, what code is new, or is the code buggy?

- Work with stakeholders and users to iterate and get it right.

- Understand how results will be used.

  - If voters rate the scenario poorly, is it easy for feature owners to know where to focus and what to do?

- Evaluate, review, rank, and weight the scenarios with all stakeholders to understand how to incorporate this feedback.

Figure 15-3 shows a sample voting dialog box that demonstrates good scenario-writing form.

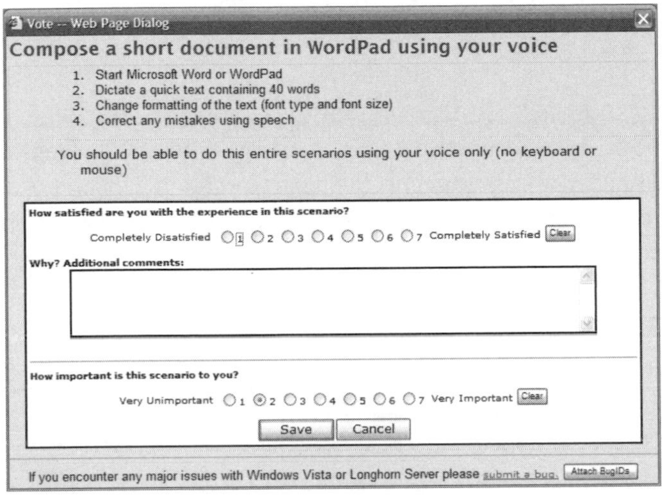

Figure 15-3   Sample voting dialog box

Solicit User-Developed Scenarios

On many projects, it is unlikely that the product team will know exactly how every user interacts with the product. Lead-user innovation—ideas that come from heavy users of the product—can be a key driver of successful product development by empowering the users to fill in the gaps left by the design team. Scenario voting provides an opportunity for the team to gather scenarios from the users to help round out the product offering.

External Voters

Gathering product design and marketing ideas from the community is becoming a very popular notion. From the Blair Witch Project to YouTube to MySpace to music sampling, community-based design is driving the rise of the creative class. For scenario voting, providing the community the opportunity to contribute to the scenario base helps the product team learn about how the application is being used. Often, more advanced users, called *lead users*, can contribute to the scenario-building effort.

> *Lead users are users whose present strong needs will become general in a marketplace months or years in the future. Since lead users are familiar with conditions which lie in the future for most others, they can serve as a need-forecasting laboratory for marketing research. Moreover, since lead users often attempt to fill the need they experience, they can provide new product concept and design data as well.*[1]

---

1   Eric von Hippel, "Lead Users: An Important Source of Novel Product Concepts," *Management Science* 32, no. 7 (July 1986): 791–805.

These lead users can identify holes in the existing scenarios as well as present new and unique ways in which the product may be used.

Internal Voters

The product team is usually intimately familiar with the application and hopefully is knowledgeable enough about the users and how they use the product to develop scenarios. By using internal pilots, other members of the product team can fill in gaps in the scenarios to be presented to the user for voting. If the team is large enough, consider swapping areas of the product and validate the scenarios across the team first.

Understand the User Base

It is important to understand the user base. The user is the customer and the reason for the existence of the application. To design and build great software, it is imperative to know and understand the types of users and their behavior.

Personas

If there are different types or classes of users, the product team may benefit by clearly identifying user classes and creating representative users, called *personas*. "A persona, in the word's everyday usage, is a social role, or a character played by an actor. The word derives from the Latin for 'mask' or 'character,' derived from the Etruscan word 'phersu,' with the same meaning."[1] In software development, personas are fictitious people with characteristics representative of users or potential users. Personas are a proxy for a class of user, created to ensure that all types of users are represented in the design of the product.

By using personas, the product team can design features that are more likely to meet the needs of the users by enabling the team to learn about general user characteristics without each developer having to go through extensive interviews or user case studies. The marketing or planning team can do the research to develop a persona that captures the salient traits of the average user types. In some cases, an application may have many different types of users, each of whom uses the product in a different way. With careful development of accurate personas, the product team can represent these user types through all phases of the development cycle.

The best way to develop accurate personas is to understand as much as possible about each type of user. This understanding can come from interviews, surveys, observations, product support, and firsthand use. The goal is not to develop a persona for each and every user, but personas should be fairly general to represent classes of users who behave differently. Examples of personas might include the home user and the IT professional. It's useful to give names to the personas and sometimes even provide a generic photograph to help the product team visualize the user. A short back story about the persona can contribute to better understanding: Mary, the home user, bought her first computer last year.

---

1   Wikipedia, "Persona," *http://en.wikipedia.org/wiki/Persona*.

After a representative persona or set of personas has been developed, it is prudent to validate it with a subset of real users to verify that the statements and descriptions are accurate. For example, if a user persona describes a novice user as "not familiar with what an Internet service provider does," gathering a small set of users of that type and obtaining their opinions on that statement can help verify that the personas are accurate. Making an effort to quantify the accuracy of these representations pays off throughout the design and development processes. By taking these steps to represent the users early in the process, all members of the development team can become familiar with their target users.

After the personas have been developed and the team is fairly comfortable with their accuracy, the personas can be used to help develop and categorize end user scenarios. After the voting process begins and results or feedback is gathered, the personas can be used to segment the data for reporting. The scenarios should be developed by members of the team who are intimately familiar with the personas and how the personas represent real users, as well as how these people will use the application. Even for applications with only one type of user, a representative persona will increase the likelihood of developing scenarios that resonate with the real user.

Get Feedback

When authoring a scenario or trying to get useful customer feedback, less is usually more. It's easy to overengineer the feedback process. Any good designer or product planner, with a customer willing to provide feedback, will want to ask a thousand questions. Although a large amount of data about a given scenario can help the product team with decisions about that feature, customers typically have a budgeted amount of time to invest in giving feedback. If each scenario requires a lengthy, detailed response, users will not be able to spend their time on many different scenarios. A goal of the scenario voting process is to minimize the time that the voter must invest so that the voter can vote on many scenarios.

The overall goal of scenario voting is to get votes across many different features and end user scenarios as a way to assess the entire product. Even something as simple as a five-question survey becomes tedious by the second or third scenario. But users typically are more willing to invest significant amounts of time if they know their feedback is being heard, so it is important to be sensitive not only to how much is being asked but also how the results are used.

The purpose of scenario voting is to identify areas of the product where detailed investigation is required. Even asking a simple question on satisfaction gets things started in this direction. If the voting process is lightweight, quick, and easy, the user is more likely to participate on a large or broad scale. An area for freeform comments or attachments offers those users who would like to provide additional feedback a way to do so. It's also prudent to offer an opt-in mechanism that customers can use to make themselves available for additional questioning by the feature owners. Surveys, site visits, or detailed customer behavioral studies are other great forums to learn about customer behavior, and this opt-in mechanism can help to identify those customers who are willing to participate in these types of events.

The Survey Scale

There are many schools of thought on how to appropriately ask survey or satisfaction questions. The Likert scale, defined by Microsoft Encarta as "a scale measuring the degree to which people agree or disagree with a statement, usually on a 3-, 5-, or 7-point scale," is one of the most common scales used to get feedback on user satisfaction. A tremendous amount of research has been done on how to ask questions using a rating scale, and there is little consensus among researchers on the best approach. Some recommend a 4-point scale; others suggest a simple Yes-No. A 9-point scale is also an option, as is almost everything in between.

The size of the scale can become an intense debate, but the evidence suggests that the scale has little or no impact on the success of the project or the usability of the results. Don't let it become an issue.

> **Tip**   Don't let a debate over the survey scale overwhelm or derail the design of the feedback program.

No specific method will work for everyone; however, you should follow (or at least consider) certain guidelines when selecting a rating mechanism. Some research seems to indicate that a higher-point scale is effective with a more highly educated survey population and that a 5-point scale is most effective when the audience is unknown. Given that you will likely be dealing with software users and the prior research the product team has done on the application's end users, a 7-point scale seems to be a good compromise, but it's best to consider other user or marketing data gathering efforts before finalizing the decision. For example, if the marketing or customer satisfaction team is surveying using a 5-point scale, using a 5-point scale in scenario voting as well may be the best decision.

If the voting population is international, cultural characteristics can influence which type of rating scale is effective. For example, some cultures tend to exaggerate their answers or focus only on the positive. A good understanding of the voting population can help the product team decide how to set the rating scale.

Initiate Pilot Programs

A pilot program allows for systematic testing of the scenarios and evaluation of the feedback process and overall satisfaction with the methodology. The advantage of using a pilot program is that the feedback can come from "friendlies"—typically members of the product team or other stakeholders—who can give constructive feedback on a program that is still evolving.

Internal Trials

After the scenarios have been defined and categorized and a mechanism has been developed to gather votes, it is time to deploy a pilot voting project to a small set of friendly users. Typically, this set of people is the development team—a set of voters who are "internal" to the project. This population should be fairly familiar with the personas and with the scenarios in the application. This familiarity allows the voting population to simulate the behavior of real users to find any holes in the voting process or missing scenarios. In many cases, because the application is developed over a period of time, this internal voting process can help augment the traditional test activity.

If the internal population is large enough and some of these customer attributes can be quantified, a "user IQ" could be developed and administered to internal voters to help categorize them and improve the stratification of the internal data. A *user IQ* is a test that is administered to internal voters—members of the project team—that challenges them to think like a user. The questions are based on real user experiences, comments, and behavior. The following set of True/False/Don't Know questions is an example user IQ test for a novice user for word processing software:

1. Clicking the small square "computer disk" saves the file.
2. Using the File menu and choosing Open does the same thing as clicking the small square "computer disk."
3. I can select text in a box by using the mouse, but not the keyboard.
4. I can copy and paste from one sentence to another using the keyboard.
5. I can find and change my user name.
6. I know the commands to print a copy of my document if I have a printer.
7. I am able to create a table.
8. I am able to draw a diagram.
9. I am able to change the color of the text using the menu.
10. I am able to change the color of the text using the buttons.
11. I am able to send a document by e-mail.
12. I am able to post a document on the Internet.

The product team members answer the questions as if they were that persona or that user type, and their test score assesses how well team members can put themselves in the frame of mind of the user type. These user IQ ratings can be used to further calibrate the internal results with results coming from real users. For example, asking, "What is your IP address used for?" will get very different answers from an IT professional than it would from a home user.

If the correlation between a subset of internal voters and real customers can be identified or achieved, it's reasonable to use internal data as an early predictor of customer behavior. Therefore, it's feasible to accelerate the design, planning, and development cycle to prevent early design defects from reaching the market or perhaps even being coded at all.

External Trials

After the internal pilot is complete, scheduling one or more external pilot programs is the next step. The point of an external—outside the product team—pilot is to get additional feedback on the program from a perspective other than that of the product team.

Deploy the Voting Program

After the pilot programs have been completed and feedback analyzed, it's time to deploy the real thing. The basic steps to deployment are the following:

1. Ensure that feedback tools are in place. These could be paper-based surveys, a Web site, or an interview. A Web site is the most effective.

2. Validate that the scenarios are accurately described.

3. Verify that the scenarios work in the application software being evaluated, if applicable.

4. If the software is a beta or prerelease version, release it to the users.

5. Announce the voting program.

6. Instruct voters on how to assess scenarios and give feedback.

It's important to note how quickly the planning team can come together and respond to this type of customer connection. It takes customers just seconds to vote and give feedback, and therefore the process can be used far and wide. Even for complex and complicated features requiring large setup investments, the voting technique can be quite enlightening. Ratings can be captured on all parts of the scenario, including setup, documentation, user assistance, support, and maintenance.

Keep the Program Lively

To keep the program alive and fresh, make an effort to add new scenarios, documentation, surveys, games, and design team "chats." Voters have only so much time for and interest in giving feedback, so be sure to give them a reason to come back to vote. If the development process involves sending out multiple prerelease versions of the application for feedback, be sure to differentiate the scenarios that are available in the new version when it goes out. Schedule frequent interactions with the design team and the users to help encourage the users to try out the new scenarios and give feedback. Many times, bug bashes, design ideas, or other contests can help to stimulate interest.

Report Results

After voters start giving feedback, the team's attention must immediately turn to reviewing the results. The value of the reports is built on the earlier investments in writing good scenarios, building a quality application, and selecting a representative voting population. A breakdown in any of these areas detracts from or eliminates the usefulness of the reports.

Reporting can take on a number of different flavors, depending on the audience, the goals and/or stage of the project, and the type of application. Typically, a scenario has an "owner" on the product team—someone who is responsible for the success or viability of that scenario. The owner should be able to see voting results for the scenario, along with any user comments or other feedback, support calls, defect reports, trend information, and relation to other scenarios in the product. This data can help the scenario owner understand the details of the user feedback relative to other scenarios so that he or she can participate with the rest of the product team in making the appropriate changes.

The best bet is to provide the team access to the raw user data and let them experiment with various types of reports. It's important to understand the privacy issues of the users because not all data is necessarily appropriate to provide to the product team. As mentioned earlier, a privacy policy should be implemented before voting begins and should be honored in the reporting phase.

Tip   Provide the team access to the raw user data, but make sure to respect voter privacy issues.

Depending on the makeup of the product team, it may be more efficient to distribute ownership of the results investigation and track progress to ensure that all feedback is understood and addressed. Tools can support the tracking process, but most important, users must be confident that their voices are being heard.

How to Weight Votes

Depending on the makeup of the software application, and the breadth of the scenarios, applying different weights to the votes may make sense. These weightings can be applied to voters, if known, to scenarios, or even to individual votes. For example, votes from a large, important customer might have more influence than do those from a noncustomer. If the list of scenarios includes various prototype scenarios and then a couple of key upgrade scenarios, results in the prototype area may be underweighted to ensure that the right focus is given to the results while maintaining the ability to collect data. Votes that occur at a given time, perhaps during a Web site trial run, may be viewed differently. The decision to weight the results, as well as how they should be weighted, should be made as the scenarios are developed. Typically, the voter will not see anything about the weighting; those values will be applied to the voting results as they are reported.

Analyze the Results

Start with simple chart of all scenarios and all feedback. If possible, look across all scenarios and understand relative ratings, and be sure to understand vote totals—scenarios with limited feedback may show up as extremes. Look for extreme differences, and then look at specific voting trends, raw comments, user personas, and demographics. Understand potential global issues—is performance or code quality particularly poor in a given area?

Figure 15-4 shows a sample voting results chart. You can use the following scheme to analyze and categorize voting results:

- Favorable: Rating of 6, 7
    - Strength—67 percent to 80 percent favorable
    - Real Strength—80 percent favorable
- Neutral: 3, 4, 5
    - Opportunity to Move to Favorable—may not take as much work as Unfavorable rating
    - Greater than 30 percent neutral should be paired with importance rating—may not view as important
    - Build-over-build shifts in neutral ratings could indicate trends
- Unfavorable: Rating of 1, 2
    - Area for Improvement—25 percent to 35 percent unfavorable
    - Area for Immediate Attention—greater than 35 percent unfavorable

Very Satisfied (6, 7)	Neutral (3, 4, 5)	Very Dissatisfied (1, 2)

Application Voting Results

	Favorable	Unfavorable	Votes
Bld 8	88%	2%	134 votes
Bld 7	74%	4%	1017 votes
Bld 6	65%	8%	2654 votes
Bld 5	58%	11%	7129 votes
Bld 4	63%	9%	5104 votes
Bld 3	61%	7%	4135 votes
Bld 2	61%	2%	297 votes
Bld 1	63%	4%	354 votes

Figure 15-4   Sample voting results chart

Quality of Results Data

The validity of the data depends on the validity of the sample selection, the clarity of the written scenarios, and the diligence of the voters. The product team must first analyze results to understand the validity of the data. Tracking and analyzing vote times, user or scenario distribution, and so forth can identify trends and patterns that can help assess the quality of the data. If users vote multiple times in a period of seconds, team members may question the quality of the results. Similarly, if they vote on disparate parts of the product, it may be worth a follow-up e-mail query to clarify the results.

The Importance of Trend Information

If the project plan is to deliver multiple prerelease versions to the users for feedback and to make changes or improvements based on user feedback, it is important to watch trends in voting results. The goal, obviously, is to see improvements in user perception based on changes made in the product. If the first build is released and users are dissatisfied with it, and then changes are made to the product and the next version is released with no change in user perception, there is a bigger problem in the process.

Trend data, therefore, is very helpful in tracking progress in customer satisfaction using the scenario voting results. Voting results can be aggregated at the product level, by persona, in a given category or subcategory, or even at the individual scenario level. Typically, many different views are required to get an accurate picture of how things are going and where the team should focus.

Encourage Ongoing Voter Participation

The product team can foster continuous voter participation by using some of the following methods:

- Get the support and sponsorship of the feature or scenario owners.
- Explain the purpose of the voting and how the data will be used.
- Use influential persons to introduce the program to voters.
- Tell voters in advance when new builds or new scenarios are coming.
- Keep the scenario votes short—1 to 3 questions to vote on with optional comments.
- Respect voter privacy if necessary.
- Give flexible time for voting—don't expect immediate results.
- Put the coolest scenarios on top to intrigue voters.
- Share data with voters whenever possible—if data can't be shared, explain why.
- Follow up with voters during the program.
- Continue to improve the feedback mechanism/voting application by fixing bugs and responding to user suggestions.
- Set up contests and competitions. (See Chapter 5, "Using Productivity Games to Prevent Defects.")
- Offer prizes, free copies—but be careful here so as not to influence voting results.

Give Results to the Support Team

User feedback provided through a scenario voting program can be a great leading indicator for the product support team, field consultants, deployment and installation professionals, and maintenance release developers. Particularly if voting is done during one or more prerelease phases, it is imperative to involve these other teams. Ideally, the support team can be involved early enough in the development cycle to give product design feedback before release, thereby reducing or eliminating product support and other postrelease costs.

High-Level Summary Data

Scenario voting returns a limited amount of data from any one voter on any one scenario. This is by design. When the data is aggregated, either across a given voter or across a given set of scenarios, the conclusions that can be drawn are more interesting. For a given voter, the pattern will tend to indicate preferences regarding the product: people are more likely to vote on things that are important or interesting to them. For a given scenario, ratings across all voters or a class of voters can provide an interesting view of where to take action. Scenario voting results should be used as a launching point for further study, as shown in Figure 15-5.

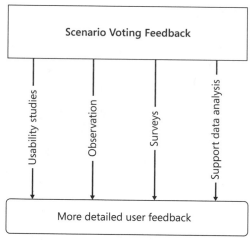

Figure 15-5   Using the results of scenario voting to begin other studies

The Normal Distribution Curve

To some degree, everyone is familiar with the normal distribution curve shown in Figure 15-6: the bell curve, grading on a curve, Gaussian distribution, Laplacian distribution, the Central Limit Theorem, the Error Curve, and so on.

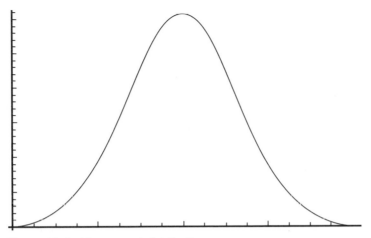

Figure 15-6 The normal distribution curve

This distribution is a fundamental part of scenario voting, for it provides a framework for taking action on the data. As the sample set of voters becomes large enough, a distribution curve will form. In Figure 15-7, the full distribution of average satisfaction rankings is charted. A team looking at this can focus on the shaded outlying areas and drill in for more details. The right-hand shaded area, the highly rated scenarios, can be mined for marketing and sales opportunities, while the left-hand area can be investigated for design problems, defects, and usability and support issues.

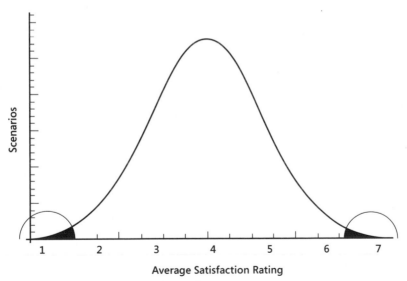

Figure 15-7   Sample scenario results

Voting Patterns

As more customer research is performed and voting patterns are assessed, it should be fairly straightforward to determine classes, categories, or types of customers in the voting population. It's likely that user classification has already been done as part of the design effort, and these results should be reconciled against that classification to improve the accuracy and help better understand the results. This data should be correlated to other types of market research or user classification to further understand the customer base and its preferences.

For scenario voting, and in particular the internal deployment of scenario voting as described in the section titled "Ease of Data Collection" later in this chapter, the product team can reasonably expect to quantify user results based on the voting patterns in the data. After these patterns have been established by a sufficient volume of voting data, the product team can simulate these customers either programmatically or by using sophisticated internal voters. If, for example, one customer type is a computer administrator who votes on existing scenarios with a given pattern, an educated product planner should know this customer well enough to be able to project this voting pattern.

Take Action

Because scenario voting is designed to be lightweight, rarely can the feature or scenario owner look at scenario voting results and then make direct changes to the product. As mentioned earlier, scenario voting results should be used as a launching point for further study. Scenario voting results are useful leading indicators of customer satisfaction and can help the product team decide where to gather more detailed customer feedback. The product team can use more detailed surveys, user observation or interviews, or more thorough operational profiling to understand more about how customers feel about the software.

The intersection of importance and satisfaction data, an example of which is shown in Figure 15-8, can also provide a different view of the results and help identify which scenarios to investigate further. A rating of high importance and low satisfaction is the best indicator and will show up in the bottom right of the chart. A high satisfaction and low importance rating will be in the upper left and could be categorized as, "Who cares—we did a great job on something that wasn't important to the user."

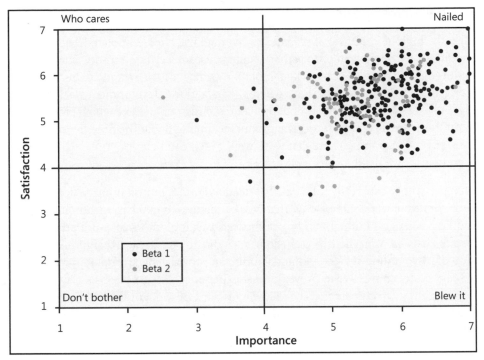

Figure 15-8   Comparing satisfaction with importance

In approaching the feedback process in this staged manner, the overall feedback loop is tighter and more effective. Scenario voting data can easily provide a high-level view of the product, the user environment, the class of users, and the overall perception of user scenarios in the product. This high-level view is typically not available through any other low-cost feedback mechanism. Scenario voting is a process that's low cost to the user and low cost to the product team.

After a statistically significant volume of data has been received for a scenario or a given set of scenarios, the product team can begin the next step of obtaining from users additional information on which to base specific product changes. In many cases, the scenario voting data and the supplemental comments that tag along with the votes are indicative of the changes that may need to be made after more research is completed.

In many cases, the product team will already know the trouble spots in the user experience and will have ideas on how to improve them. Scenario voting data can support and justify previous decisions to focus on those areas. However, it's important for the team to be diligent and to analyze the broad set of scenario voting data so as to ensure that their suspicions are confirmed. Take the time to read any detailed comments about the troublesome areas to make sure that those are indeed the highest-priority problems.

Deeper Investigation

After the high-level review of scenario voting data has been completed, the product team should begin the next steps to gather detailed customer data on troublesome areas and areas at the edges of the bell curve. The temptation will be for the team to focus on the problem areas, and for the most part, that's where the bulk of the development work will lie. But building on success and understanding from a marketing perspective which scenarios users are happy with are also important. The product team must take the time to understand the elements of the user experience that work well, which can help identify attributes that can be used to improve troublesome areas.

Scenario voting can highlight areas that need attention, but often more detailed feedback is necessary to understand exactly what type of changes to make in a feature. The product team should have a good understanding of the feedback tools at its disposal prior to beginning results analysis. Whether the team employs a direct, face-to-face, technique or uses a more cost-effective online survey, additional tools can provide specific data on where and how to make product changes to improve the user experience. Many options are available to get more information from customers. The following is a list of some of the techniques the product team can use to get detailed customer feedback on a given scenario:

- Surveys
- Case studies
- Observation
- Interviews
- Focus groups
- Online chats

Benefits of Scenario Voting

Scenario voting provides a number of advantages to the product team. In the design phase, scenario voting data can be applied as part of the planning and design phase to understand how customers feel about the software and its features. Scenario voting provides significant benefits, such as the following:

- Ease of data collection
- Ability to gather a large volume of data across a wide range of features and users
- Applicability in all phases of the project cycle

Each of these benefits is described further in the following subsections.

Ease of Data Collection

One of the benefits of a broad-based scenario voting approach to gathering customer feedback is the ease with which the data can be gathered. Because the process is fairly lightweight and flexible, internal users—users of the product that work in the company producing the software such as software developers, designers, members of the product planning team, and even managers and executives—can all vote on their preferences as well. Data gathered internally can then be compared with actual customer data and used to determine areas that may require more thorough testing or verification, or where internal biases or blind spots may exist.

By deploying scenario voting techniques internally, the product planning team can also publish trial versions of different scenarios without any impact on the voting population. After internal users' preferences and behavioral patterns are well known, it's fairly easy to predict the viability of a feature change from internal data alone. This is not to say that internal data is sufficient for the release of a scenario or feature in the product, but to suggest that the internal beta can be used to determine whether to ask external users or customers for additional feedback through scenario voting.

Ability to Gather a Large Volume of Data Across a Wide Range of Features and Users

Scenario voting is an easy way for users to give feedback. For software that has users already, user feedback is one of the most useful tools available to build great (greater) software. For software that doesn't yet have users, connecting early to get feedback from potential users is a critical step on the road to release. Most users are more than willing to give feedback. It's a part of human nature to want to influence your environment. However, software developers must demonstrate the ability to listen and incorporate feedback, and reassure the users that their time in giving feedback is invested wisely.

As mentioned earlier, users have a limited amount of time they are willing to invest and will indicate when products aren't ready to ship, or that something they tried didn't work. But because their time is precious, they will rarely go out of their way to send good news, kudos, and compliments, and they usually do not have the time or willingness to comment on every feature. However, because scenario voting techniques are intentionally lightweight, it's easier for users to give feedback on a variety of features and tasks. For each scenario, as little as four mouse clicks can provide a rating on satisfaction and importance. The belief is that if the user has enough emotion to give feedback on something, keeping the incremental steps required to give additional feedback small can encourage more user participation. Extensive user surveys are not the goal for scenario voting. That part comes in phase 2, when interesting areas have been identified.

Making scenario voting easy for the user, therefore, is geared to one goal—get more feedback. Ensuring that scenario voting methods are quick and easy to use can help the product team obtain a large volume of data across a broad set of scenarios and environments.

Applicability in All Phases of the Project Cycle

Scenario voting can be used in all phases of the product development cycle. In the early design phases, a text description, a mockup, or screen shots of a potential feature can be used to convey the scenario to potential users. At this stage, a broad set of users can rate conceptual ideas only and the feedback is as legitimate as if they had used real software.

After prototypes have been built—preferably based on the early design decisions and user feedback—customers can be involved in a new round of voting to give feedback on the specific implementation decisions, and the ratings can be compared against their early design phase ratings.

After the users have weighed in on the prototypes and feedback has been incorporated through several iterations of mockups, specifications can be written and the development team can start to code the real thing. Then, as early versions of the software become available, customers can weigh in again using the voting technique, and again the results can be compared with results from earlier stages. This process can continue through alpha and multiple versions of beta releases before the final product is ready. The trend comparisons can illustrate the customer view or opinion of a given feature or scenario throughout the lifetime of the project.

Upon final release, scenario voting techniques can be used in conjunction with product support data to evaluate and improve the development process. Scenario voting results gathered prior to release can be compared with those gathered after to establish whether the early results are a good predictor of postrelease satisfaction. If so, they lend credibility to prerelease voting results.

Eric von Hippel provides an example of how noticing and responding to customer needs can lead to incredible results:

> In the early 1970s, store owners and salesmen in southern California began to notice that youngsters were fixing up their bikes to look like motorcycles, complete with imitation tailpipes and "chopper-type" handlebars. Sporting crash helmets and Honda motorcycle T-shirts, the youngsters raced their fancy 20-inches on dirt tracks.
>
> Obviously on to a good thing, the manufacturers came out with a whole new line of "motocross" models. By 1974 the motorcycle-style units accounted for 8 percent of all 20-inch bicycles shipped. Two years later half of the 3.7 million new juvenile bikes sold were of the motocross model.[1]

Trend and comparative data across all scenarios in the product can also help determine how to focus resources as the product nears completion. Although scenario voting data can be used to improve and accelerate the response to early customer feedback, it's also useful at the end of the project cycle to help determine whether the product is ready to ship. It can help answer the question, Has the team made the necessary adjustments to satisfy the entire voting population?

Risks of Scenario Voting

Scenario voting comes with four main risks:

- Results are subject to the makeup of the voting population.
- Results provide only a summary view of user opinions.
- Incomplete scenario selection can skew results.
- Poorly authored scenarios can skew results.

Results Are Subject to the Makeup of the Voting Population

The biggest risk of scenario voting is reacting to the views of a voting population with unknown demographics. A decision maker taking action on data without understanding the makeup of the voting population is making decisions based on inaccurate information. It is therefore important to qualify the voters prior to allowing them to vote and certainly before using the voting results. This qualification, in many cases, should be done at the individual scenario level. If a feature requires a certain set of knowledge, specific hardware, or other environmental conditions, its voters must be qualified to give feedback on that scenario. Laptop users voting on server scenarios or small business owners voting on enterprise features can render the data invalid. Restricting the voting population to qualified users improves the quality of the data and helps the product team make the right decisions.

Results Provide Only a Summary View of User Opinions

One of the benefits of scenario voting can evolve into its biggest risk. The goal of scenario voting is to get feedback from a large volume of users across a large set of user scenarios. To achieve this goal requires a lightweight, user-optimized method of gathering feedback. As a result, the data gathered is limited. For example, the feedback from a given user may be limited to two rating numbers—one for satisfaction and one for importance. Therefore, scenario voting results can indicate only *where further research is desirable*. Scenario voting results, by themselves, do not indicate what to do to fix a broken scenario or how to optimize the user experience. Raw comments provided by hundreds of users can paint a pretty clear picture, but certainty requires gathering additional data.

---

1 Eric von Hippel, "Lead Users: A Source of Novel Product Concepts," *Management Science* 32, no. 7 (July 1986): 791–805.

More Analysis Is Required to Fully Understand the User View

Scenario voting is intended to build the bell curve across users and across scenarios to help the product development team understand the best and the worst areas of the product. The best areas, to the right of the Gaussian curve, can be handed to the marketing and sales department, and the areas to the left need to be fixed or pointed out to product support. There are plenty of other techniques to gather detailed customer feedback, from user studies to surveys, newsgroups to user meetings, and so on. Scenario voting can identify the areas of the product where those techniques should be employed.

It's Easy to Overreact!

Again, one of the benefits of scenario voting is that it provides quick feedback on a large scale. However, without an in-depth understanding of the product, of the user base, and of the technology, it can be easy to misinterpret the data and overreact. The fact that user data is coming in—and coming in early—is typically new for the feature and design teams. As discussed in earlier chapters and in the work of James Reason,[1] people will pay more attention to what's in front of them simply because it's there. This can result in an overweighting of the importance of the early data. Again, the Law of Large Numbers and the wisdom of crowds will eventually lead to the average, but the initial data makes it easy for team members to overreact and make a mistake.

Incomplete Scenario Selection Can Skew Results

It's important for the feature owners who create the scenarios on which users will vote to consider the entire product and ensure that user tasks are represented consistently across the breadth of the voting. In many cases, the people using the voting data as feedback to improve their features will not see the entire picture. If scenarios are missing or an area is overemphasized, voting feedback may vary across features and suggest a different feeling than is really there. The Law of Large Numbers applies to scenario selection as well: the more scenarios available, the more likely any individual voter will pick an accurate set to vote on. If there are huge blocks of product features or user tasks that are not available in the list of scenarios on which a user can vote, the results data will be skewed and inaccurate.

Poorly Authored Scenarios Can Skew Results

Writing a good scenario takes some work. There are many steps, many options, and many opportunities for error. The goal of scenario voting is to get a large volume of feedback, and a scenario that is written poorly, or one that misses its goal for feedback, runs the risk of introducing bad data and defects back into the product. If, for example, the goal is to get an

---

1   James Reason, *Human Error* (Cambridge, UK: Cambridge University Press, 1990).

understanding of the intuitiveness of a feature, and the scenario is written with specific steps and instructions, the user will vote on those steps specifically and may not give any feedback on how nonintuitive the scenario is. By the same token, users may completely avoid a complicated scenario that requires extensive setup if they are left to figure out the setup procedure on their own. Understanding the phase of the project, the product, the goals for feedback, and how the data should be used can help the author write effective scenarios that provide the user a way to give feedback that is clear, concise, and useful to the feature owner.

In addition, there are several risk factors that can influence the success of the program itself:

- Lack of clear objectives for voting effort
- Poor job understanding user type, sample set, persona, voter demographics
- Lack of stakeholder and management involvement
- Unclear or ambiguous scenarios
- Disruptive current events (for example, a security hole, bad press)
- Reckless use of prizes and rewards
- Excessive length or complexity of scenarios
- Voting application or feedback mechanism that is hard to use
- Insufficient time to execute scenarios and give feedback
- Lack of trust in how results will be used
- Unclear or lacking policy on privacy, confidentiality, anonymity
- Poor communication to support the program

Conclusion

Scenario voting is a fairly straightforward way to improve software development and prevent early defects by getting feedback from users. The feedback program should be designed carefully, ensuring that the voting population is well understood and that the scenarios they are asked to try are clearly defined and functional. This feedback can provide tremendous insight to the product team, often before the software is even written. Using the "Wisdom of Crowds" and the Law of Large Numbers enables the product development team to employ scenario voting as an effective technique to prevent defects from reaching customers.

Suggested Readings

Garson, G. David. "Sampling." *www2.chass.ncsu.edu/garson/pa765/sampling.htm.*

Koerner, Brendan I. "Geeks in Toyland." Wired, January 4, 2006. *www.wired.com/culture/lifestyle/news/2006/01/69946.*

McNamara, Carter. "Basic Methods to Get Feedback from Customers." Authenticity Consulting. *www.managementhelp.org/mrktng/mk_rsrch/needs.htm.*

von Hippel, Eric. *Democratizing Innovation. http://web.mit.edu/evhippel/www/books.htm.*

von Hippel, Eric. "Downloadable Papers." *http://web.mit.edu/evhippel/www/papers.htm.*

Wikipedia. "Sampling and Data Collection." *http://en.wikipedia.org/wiki/Sampling_%28statistics%29#Sampling_and_data_collection.*

Chapter 16
Creating a Quality Culture

Defect prevention in an organization that has a quality culture shifts the emphasis from "Who caused the defect?" "Why did this happen?" and "What fixes the problem?" to "How can we prevent it?" The basis of a quality culture is learning from defects and making corrections upstream in the development process to reduce or eliminate defects downstream. A quality culture has the following attributes:

- **It is customer focused.** Product teams obtain feedback on proposed designs before implementing them.

- **It is design focused.** Developers spend the time to understand the customer models for functionality, the scenarios derived from the model, and the technical challenges to implement the functionality. These are the precursors to specifications and designs that have a much lower chance of late-surfacing design errors.

- **It fosters openness.** People feel free to report honestly the details of why defects occurred and any design issues that occur.

- **It is failure tolerant.** New designs are expected to be learning experiences.

- **It promotes learning.** Defects are viewed as opportunities to improve existing processes or tools.

- **It is quality focused.** It promotes the idea that quality is everyone's job.

These attributes may be quite different from the attitudes and processes in place in your current culture. The first step to achieving a quality culture is to evaluate your organization honestly to see where it differs from the preceding attributes. Beyond reducing the indirect disincentives in your current culture, there are methods to improve your culture that are discussed in this chapter.

Evaluating Your Current Culture

Achieving a quality culture is not just about adopting new values and implementing effective processes but also removing the negative effects of the typical software development process. Many of the values in your organization can have a negative effect on quality. This isn't surprising because it is not easy to measure the attributes of quality—it's easy to measure the lack of quality, but such metrics typically become negative factors that inhibit surfacing the issues that can improve quality. Testing, at best, can indicate only a lack of quality.

Reexamine the metrics used to evaluate people in your organization, management priorities, and processes in terms of their effect on the attributes of a quality culture. Determine which are positive, negative, or neutral in relation to a quality culture. The easiest changes you can make are removing negative incentives that inhibit employees from adopting a quality culture.

To quickly assess whether your organization has a quality culture, ask yourself how many of the following attitudes are pervasive:

- The *real* work of development is implementation.
- Quality is achieved by testing.
- Fixing defects takes time away from implementing features.
- Software can be completely tested.
- There are few processes in place to learn from defects (at best ad hoc conversations, postmortems).
- Developers are primarily valued for completing coding tasks.
- Failure (that requires redesigning and reimplementing functionality) is a negative for a developer rather than a likely occurrence for new functionality and a learning experience.
- Quality is achieved by molding software into shape by correcting defects.

If people subscribe to the preceding attitudes, quality is not overtly valued in your organization. You can use the information in this chapter to help your organization achieve a quality culture.

Common Cultural Pitfalls

The primary obstacle to implementing a quality culture in an organization is the existing culture that has been created by the organization's processes, measurements, and management attitudes. There is a tendency for organizations to gravitate to the measurable, such as number of lines of code, but in doing so, perverse incentives can be created that in turn can create a culture that works against creating quality. Much of the effort to achieve a quality culture is getting rid of such perverse incentives.

On the other hand, important attributes and behaviors that generate quality are less measurable, such as customer testing, workable design, and use of robust coding techniques. It's easy to count defects, but it's hard to count the number of defects avoided by a culture of quality. The invisible nature of quality makes it all too easy to use absence-of-quality measures instead. Failure is a measurable attribute but is typically valued in a counterproductive way.

Typically, organizations have management and measurement systems that work insidiously against a quality culture; removing these impediments is a necessary catalyst for change. Trust between employees and managers—which takes time to build—is required so that people can learn from defects and know that they are allowed to spend time doing the upfront work that creates quality but that isn't writing code.

Creating a quality culture takes time, but it can be done. Just as it is possible personally to change behavior and get rid of bad habits, it is possible for an organization to move to a quality culture. Over a period of time, people will make the effort to change the culture of an organization to place an emphasis on quality.

Assessing Blame Prevents Learning

Everyone makes mistakes; it's human nature. However, for the most part, we are all taught that mistakes are bad. In life and in work, emphasis is placed on being correct, not necessarily on the reasoning behind procedures. When a mistake is made, rarely is it used as an opportunity to learn not to make the same kind of mistake again. Prevalent in code development organizations these days is negative reinforcement where people are blamed each time they make a mistake (they introduce a defect into the code) and are given no reasoning about why the mistake may have occurred or any information on how to correct the underlying cause. Training by punishment for repeated mistakes is not tenable given the myriad opportunities for defects to occur in software. Mistakes will happen in complex software.

This training by blame eventually will permeate your culture, creating in people a reticence to describe the mistake made, how it occurred, and how it can be reduced or prevented—working against the basis of defect prevention.

The indirect effect of the "defects are bad" attitude can actually result in more defects! The alternative of "learn from defects to improve quality" still considers defects undesirable but recognizes that they will occur and that by analyzing them future quality can be improved.

Defect prevention requires an organization to learn from its mistakes rather than blame the person or team who made the mistake. However, it is very easy for the processes of defect detection and correction to create a culture of blame; such a culture breeds defensiveness about how defects are caused. For example, measuring developer performance in terms of number of defects found in code can reinforce this counterproductive attitude.

Avoid Using Defect Metrics for Evaluation

Openness and honesty are required for many defect prevention techniques[1] that involve information provided by developers, such as the defect taxonomy, Team or Personal Software Processes (TSP/PSP), or root cause analysis (RCA) studies. Risk analysis techniques[2] that involve source churn or defect data may generate developer metrics. Without openness and honesty, developers may not report defect or risk information accurately, and then it is difficult to use this data to learn and improve processes to prevent defects in the future. Defect information and metrics must be used purely for learning about how defects are caused rather than for judging developers individually or against each other.

---

1   See Chapter 10, "Defect Taxonomies," and Chapter 11, "Root Cause Analysis."

2   See Chapter 8, "Risk Analysis."

Because of the wide variances in code complexity, defect prevention metrics can't be normalized to make them useful for evaluating the performance of developers. The use of a bad metric is worse than using no metric at all—you will only get more of what you measure. Not only that, you will poison the atmosphere of openness that is necessary for optimal defect prevention.

On the other hand, consider negative, indirect incentives of the common metric of rating developers on the basis of the amount of code they write. Remember that time spent on design doesn't produce a single line of code but can yield higher-quality results. Also, duplicating code rather than writing common methods results in more lines of code; concise and efficient methods produce fewer lines of code. Therefore, high-quality, performant code can take longer to design and write and may not result in more lines of code. Code that is written to support effective diagnosis of future defects takes longer to write than does code that assumes there will be no defects or need to debug later.

Allow Developers to Spend Time on Design

If your manager asks how much code you've written and you say, "None," the next question often is, "Why?" followed by, "When will you start coding?" So you start writing code as soon as possible, short-changing the specification and design processes. Design errors often show up after you've invested enough time to get the code to a testable level; after all, the scenarios, specification, and design weren't well understood when you started because their description was shortchanged.

Because the development schedule is time-driven typically adequate time is not allocated to correct design defects. Even though design errors are fairly common late in the implementation phase, schedules rarely account for it—instead, the optimistic assumption that only defects that require minor localized changes will occur is implicitly made. Often, developers are pressured to correct design defects by using local corrections because other teams may depend on the existing design and their schedules would be affected by a redesign.

More often, the basic frailty of a design goes unreported and ideas on how the system should be designed go undocumented. After spending a considerable amount of time on implementation, few developers will admit that the original design is inherently flawed—to do so would not look good on their performance reviews. The specialization of roles in the development process can reinforce this behavior: developers push testing off to testers, and customer-reported defects are handled by a support team.

These behaviors inhibit a team from generating a quality product, but they are the unforeseen effects of the processes and metrics currently used to evaluate people. Not only is the quality of the product lower but the honesty needed to learn and improve is lost.

Metrics for Detecting Insufficient Designs

The larger your organization is, the more difficult performance evaluation can be. Indirect indications of performance can be taken from your existing defect tracking system and development schedules.

A few indicators of performance in the defect tracking system are the distribution of stages in which defects are detected, the number of regressions, and the frequency of design/architectural errors. For example, a majority of defects detected in late stages, particularly during customer testing and release, can indicate a lack of concern about quality. Frequent design or architectural errors, particularly those discovered late in the development cycle, can indicate a shortchanging of initial design and analysis of usage scenarios. An Orthogonal Defect Classification[1] system can directly indicate these performance factors, but they can also be approximated from your existing defect system.

Performance against the schedule, such as delays and their reason, as well as the relative sizes of design, implementation, and test efforts against schedule accuracy can also be useful measures of organizational health. Delays in the testing phase can indicate a lack of concern about quality during implementation. Delays in implementation can indicate a shortchanging of the design process if design elaboration is being done during development or major architectural issues are discovered.

"Schedule chicken" is an example of a schedule-oriented metric you can track to determine whether management is second-guessing original estimates. Schedule chicken occurs when you cut time estimates for completing tasks when you are under pressure from higher management. Quite often, upfront design time is the first thing that is cut, followed by implementation time, and then overly optimistic testing estimates are made. You must record initial estimates so that you can detect when estimates are cut to meet a schedule—sacrificing quality.

The typical results of schedule chicken are late products even though the goal was to produce the product quicker. In addition, the heavy load caused by schedule compression tends to make people rush and take a short-term view. Lower-quality code is produced, and ideas that would help in the longer term or help other groups are not pursued in favor of getting the immediate tasks finished. The view that schedule dates or features are more important than quality easily becomes part of the organizational culture, and the result is that features are cut and the product is delayed as a result of the lack of quality and upfront work. Companies get paid when their products ship—customers want and pay for features and just assume quality is inherent in a product, so the optimization is usually toward features.

If the performance indicators from the defect tracking system and schedule correlate, they add weight to the importance of the problem. The worst case—all too typical in software development—occurs when delays happen as a result of fixing the defects found in testing and from significant design changes being made late in the development process.

---

1   Chapter 10 includes a sidebar that describes Orthogonal Defect Classification systems.

Improving Your Culture

Organizational culture is the result of the experiences of workers before they joined the organization and their experience working in the organization. Training by repetition has a slow effect on changing culture; over time, the organization tends to reward (or not punish) habit. As you know, when habits are established, they can take a long time to change. Some of the major means available to influence culture are as follows:

- **Tools**   Applications to automate procedures, simplify expression, or verify results
- **Procedures**   Standardized instructions for common operations
- **Organization**   How people work together, management, and how deep the organization is
- **Metrics**   What you measure about results
- **Valuation/rewards**   What qualities the organization values and rewards
- **Communication**   How information is transferred across the organization
- **Learning**   Adding to the experience of employees

To be effective, changes you make in any of these categories must be consistent with each other—mixed messages are ineffective. For example, a value in your organization may be that quality is important, but if metrics, organization, procedures, learning, and in particular valuation and rewards don't follow through, little will change. All too often, good results occur despite the system, not because of it.

Influence Your Culture Toward Quality

It takes time to achieve a quality culture, and it may be difficult to measure progress toward this goal until a tipping point is reached and quality becomes a habit. People don't change overnight, but when they do change, the changes can reap huge rewards. However, no endpoint or metric can say, "Yes, we now have a culture of quality." Some metrics can indicate that you are moving to higher quality, but measuring achievement of this goal is like trying to determine that there are no defects by testing the code.

You can't order people to focus on quality because the result typically is that people will meet goals minimally rather than exceed them.[1] A quality culture allows ideas on improving quality to emerge spontaneously rather than by edict. If people in your organization offer suggestions on how to change processes or create tools to improve the product development cycle, it is another sign that your culture is shifting toward quality.

A good gauge is the kind of decisions made between quality and schedule—a quality culture tips the scale toward quality over schedule and features. If, for example, significant defects are

---

1   See Chapter 18, "Rewards, Motivation, and Incentives."

not fixed and a tight schedule is used as the excuse, or hard reproduction procedures are required for intermittent defects without a failure analysis of possible causes, your organization will still have quality problems.

Changing culture is slow and hard but necessary. Honesty and removing the culture of blame are precursors to cultural change for quality. To gain trust, you need to demonstrate a commitment to learning from defects and failures. You can influence your culture in a number of ways:

- Showcase successes and failures.
- Discover local best and worst practices.
- Institute defect prevention practices.
- Experiment with different processes, organizations, and valuations.
- Practice ongoing learning about the costs of lack of quality.
- Practice ongoing learning about the value of customer focus.
- Practice ongoing learning about the value of moving quality upstream. (See Chapter 17, "Moving Quality Upstream.")

Showcase Successes and Failures

Showcasing local (team or individual) quality successes can educate your employees about desired behavior and also show that management is on board with the idea of improving quality. To showcase failures, the culture of blame must be replaced with a culture of learning; otherwise, employees will be less than honest about quality failures. Rewarding exceptional quality can reinforce the fact that quality is important.

Discover Local Best and Worst Practices

Performance typically varies across an organization: some teams consistently deliver higher or lower quality than others do. It's hard to normalize such results because there are so many variables involved, such as the complexity of the code, the dependencies of the code, and how frequently the code is executed by customers.

Team performance can be examined by using root cause analysis (Chapter 11), the prevention tab, (Chapter 14, "Prevention Tab"), or a defect taxonomy (Chapter 10) to see if they are doing something that other teams aren't that contributes to their results. Both the positive and negative findings are useful in improving quality. Look at failure as an opportunity to learn and improve; quite often, mistakes being made by one team are the same mistakes other teams may make.

Institute Defect Prevention Practices

Defect prevention practices provide at least three main benefits:

- They allow you to measure aspects of quality to identify areas of high or low quality for further investigation.

- They provide other means of estimating the quality of a product and its stage of development.

- They bring the issues of quality to the everyday processes of employees.

Initially, it may be difficult to get accurate data for a few reasons. First, employees may fear the data will be used against them. Second, reporting may be considered added overhead, and so accuracy of the data will be of little concern. Third, if employees perceive that no one is using the data, little importance will be placed on providing it accurately. These problems can be reduced by making quality reports from the data very visible to everyone.

Try Different Processes, Organizations, and Valuations

Software development is quite different from most other industries. Developers are intelligent, and their job responsibilities vary widely. This is why it is difficult to create useful metrics (ones that contribute positively to company goals) to measure productivity. Using metrics from other industries with more homogeneous employee roles often is counterproductive.

If your organization is large enough, you can experiment with different management styles, processes, and metrics to find out what works well for you. Small pilot programs or skunk-works[1] projects are a great place to experiment with quality techniques. These pilot programs should have a few attributes to help ensure success. Any good scientific experiment shares many of these same attributes. The first consideration in establishing a good pilot program is to ensure that the work is observable. A small group with well-known behavior will be easy to observe and will notice any cultural change. The more representative the pilot program is of the larger organization, the more effective it will be.

When trying to identify a pilot program for software quality improvement, analyze and understand the type of code, the experience of the team, the existing quality and complexity, and other software metrics that will help frame the measurements of success. Performing this type of research and documentation up front lays the foundation for successful comparisons after the various quality improvement techniques are undertaken by the pilot team.

Quality can be measured any number of different ways, the choice of which can often spark controversy. It is critical that everyone involved agree on the type of measures that will be used to assess the success or failure of the pilot project. Without this agreement up front, it is very

---

1 *Skunkworks* refers to Lockheed Martin's Advanced Development Projects Unit. It has become a term for experimental projects that have a high degree of freedom from existing bureaucracy and processes.

easy to waste time and undermine any success of the pilot program. It is far more efficient to have quality measurement debates before the experiment begins. If no agreement can be reached and a compromise using multiple measures is adopted, a larger investment in the analysis of the results may be necessary. However, these decisions should be made before the experiment begins. If not, the debate is sure to happen at some point on the road to cultural change, and waiting to come to an agreement may inhibit or negatively alter the type of pilot programs necessary to affect cultural change.

After the measurements of success have been defined, a variety of quality improvement–related initiatives should be evaluated. There is no shortage of methods, practices, studies, books, and other documentation on how to improve quality. Although a complete list of quality improvement programs is outside the scope of this book, the key to cultural change is to experiment, learn, and adapt the best of these practices to fit the people, the history, and the culture of your organization.

During the process, it is important to evaluate motivation rewards (see Chapter 18 for more information) as a factor of success. The most effective quality improvement effort may require additional incentives. The return on these incentives should be measured against the overall quality improvement measures to understand whether the program is worthwhile. For example, doubling employee pay for a 25 percent gain in quality may result in a 100 percent increase in revenue, whereas keeping employee pay the same may result in a 3 percent improvement in quality with no measurable increase in sales.

Practice Ongoing Learning About the Costs of Lack of Quality

The specialization that can occur in a large organization can isolate most employees from the cost of the lack of quality. This is particularly true when customer support has been differentiated from development—the developers can lose sight of the cost of their mistakes. Some methods of bringing this point home include the following:

- Scenario voting to report raw satisfaction and customer comments.
- Publicized customer-reported defect counts.
- Publicized reviews and customer feedback.
- Publicized cost of support both in total and per call.
- Publicized cost per team of customer-reported defects.
- Publicized customer satisfaction numbers.
- Making it personal—putting developers tightly into the loop of customer support for some period of time such as by letting them listen in on calls, field calls, or participate in customer online chats. Microsoft developers who have spent just a few days in product support have found the experience eye-opening.

Avoid using examples of the cost of low quality as blame. Your organization must get beyond the culture of blame to learn from negative examples without blaming the individuals involved. People must realize that they can cause the same failure next week and that it's better to learn from mistakes than it is to repeat them.

Practice Ongoing Learning About the Value of Customer Focus

Software is becoming more and more a consumer item—many customers are not computer technical. It is all too easy for developers, or other employees, to substitute their views for their customers' views. When this happens, functionality is often difficult for your customers to use; "read the manual" is not a valid response to the perception of complexities in an application or Web page. Some customers may be knowledgeable in the domain your product addresses—your product will be easier to use if it reflects the concepts of the domain rather than an engineer's interpretation of them.

Donald Norman (*www.jnd.org*) has written extensively on the suitability of products to their function as well as software design and errors. He has edited an out-of-print book (*User-Centered System Design: New Perspectives on Human-Computer Interaction*[1]) that introduces two important concepts:

- A means of thinking about how a user interacts with a system—gulfs of execution (how to express what you want to do) and interpretation (how to determine if it was done correctly).

- A user interface can be designed to eliminate the expression of error rather than detecting incorrect expressions and reporting them to a user.

The series of books starting with *The Psychology of Everyday Things*[2] describes various physical products and describes how well or poorly they are designed. Although the products are physical, not software, many of the examples are good, tangible analogs of problems in software user interface and programming interface design. They can help developers understand the value of customer-oriented design.

---

1 D. A. Norman and S. Draper (Eds.), *User-Centered System Design: New Perspectives on Human-Computer Interaction* (Hillsdale, NJ: Lawrence Erlbaum Associates, 1986).

2 D. A. Norman, *The Psychology of Everyday Things* (New York: Basic Books, 1988); D. A. Norman, *Turn Signals Are the Facial Expressions of Automobiles* (Reading, MA: Addison-Wesley, 1992); D. A. Norman, *Things That Make Us Smart* (Reading, MA: Addison-Wesley, 1993).

Practice Ongoing Learning About the Value of Moving Quality Upstream

The earlier in the development process a defect is discovered, the cheaper it is to correct.[1] This is a result of many factors, including the following:

- The time wasted implementing something incorrectly

- The time wasted testing to discover the problem

- The ripple effect on teams that depend on flawed functionality

- The inability to make the best correction because of late discovery of the issue

- The cost in customer satisfaction of defects

- The cost of delivering a correction to the field

One major part of moving quality upstream is to focus on doing due diligence work before implementation, including understanding the customer scenarios for functionality in detail and producing a detailed design reflecting them. Testing the customer-level scenarios with customers and the revised scenarios after design is also an important step to verify that you are still meeting customer expectations at the design level before implementation.

This preimplementation due diligence serves a similar purpose to preproduction work in other industries. A point to consider is risk and due diligence: doing the up front work better informs decisions on the cost of production. Other industries, such as automobile design and movie production, also have large costs associated with defects and missing schedules. Bill Buxton (*www.billbuxton.com*) gives an informative talk on the comparison of software development with these two other industries.[2] It is well worth viewing to see the details of how these industries describe a project before they commit the large sums of money required to implement it.

Conclusion

A culture of quality pays dividends beyond the various specific techniques and measurements described elsewhere in this book. After quality becomes a central tenet in an organization, ideas for improvement will surface throughout the organization and the initial quality of the code will rise.

---

1   See Chapter 1y, "Moving Quality Upstream," and Chapter 3, "The Economics of Defect Prevention."

2   Bill Buxton, "The Role of Design in Software Product Development," ePresence Webcast presentation, *http://epresence.tv/mediaContent/archives/2004_apr22/?archiveID=65.*

Often, the key obstacles to establishing a culture of quality in your organization are the values of your current culture that were created by the indirect effects of the metrics used to evaluate people. Because positive metrics for quality are not nearly so easy to determine and measure as are metrics for the lack of quality, this is not surprising. Two common issues are a culture of blame for defects and measuring development by amount of code written, which short-changes understanding the customer's view of the functionality, design, and robustness.

Moving from a culture of blame to a culture of learning from defects is vital for improving your culture. This chapter discusses the methods you can use to improve your organization's culture.

These methods typically consist of two parts, a value and a process. The adoption of the value in terms of a positive metric for personnel evaluation is key—if there is no recognition or reward, participation will be minimal rather than transforming. Edicts typically result in just enough participation to meet minimal requirements. A rewarded cultural value results in exceeding expectations.

Chapter 17
Moving Quality Upstream

Everyone needs to be concerned with quality from initial conception to implementation. The lack of quality of inputs to each stage in the software development cycle is amplified in each succeeding stage. Moving quality upstream means defects are detected or prevented at their source rather than much later in the development process. Few people would disagree with the value of this process in theory but in practice tend not to follow through to make it happen. In your organization, look at the distribution of defect reporting to see if you are detecting problems upstream—are there significant bugs reported by internal or external self-testing? If the latter, your organization can improve your processes to move quality upstream.

Beyond detecting defects earlier through learning from defects, changing your processes to provide early focus on customer needs and organization-wide focus on quality can pay significant dividends. A major part of software quality is customer perception. To a customer there is little difference between a defect and difficult-to-use functionality. Quality is not something that you sprinkle across your development processes; your organization's culture needs to focus on quality as a central tenet. (See Chapter 16, "Creating a Quality Culture.")

Earlier chapters discuss means of uncovering more defects, measuring defects, improving processes to reduce defects, and some techniques that uncover defects more proactively. Applying these techniques to your existing development practices and changing your practices based on the learning will improve quality: Your organization will detect more defects earlier. This chapter discusses development practices designed around the goals of high initial quality.

Quality and Customer Focus Are Intertwined

Quality and customer focus go hand in hand—you can't have one without the other. For example, a feature can be implemented perfectly according to a specification yet be a total failure if your customers don't understand how to use it. It may be high quality in terms of having no technical defects but may be useless to your customers. When a customer calls support, it doesn't matter whether the issue is a technical defect or a usability issue—both reflect the quality of your product.

Functionality must be customer oriented. Customers must readily understand the concepts involved and knowledge and steps required to use a feature. Users form a naïve view of how they think some functionality works based on their experience and knowledge (if any) of the domain. If this view matches what actually happens, the user is satisfied. If it doesn't, the user is frustrated and blames the software. Donald Norman has written extensively in this area concerning software[1] and product design.[2]

Functionality should be designed to meet customer scenarios and requirements; it should not be a toolkit of all the myriad parts that could be used to assemble an implementation of a scenario. The former approach typically results in less code and a smaller application programming interface (API) surface.

Developers like to add features, yet how many new features are customer vetted before they are implemented? Often, your developers are not the same kind of users as your customers are, and implementing developer-generated features does not guarantee that your customers will be pleased with the result. Having a multitude of features creates unnecessary complexity for customers, who typically use only a small part of an application's functionality.

If a customer-desired functionality can somehow be constructed from the functionality implemented, developers may consider it adequate—no matter if customers cannot figure out how to use that functionality. If the customer doesn't understand it, a feature is useless baggage—and the customer pays the bill.

Feedback on the customer approachability of functionality should be given at design time and confirmed during development, not late in the cycle or in beta releases. This moves quality upstream. This feedback can come by involving key customers early in the design process, including verification of detailed scenarios with customers before design and implementation. Executable code is not required; if functionality is so complex that it can't be storyboarded or mocked up, it is probably a priori too complex for your customers.

Understanding Development as a Series of Translations

When you consider the development process as a series of translations,[3] you can see the costliness of late-cycle defects and other defects. Figure 17-1 shows the typical development process. The first few stages are documentary; there are no executable artifacts. Because the artifacts aren't executable (verified by people), they inherently have a possibility of error.

Later, these artifacts are verified as executable expressions or by customers, as shown in Figure 17-2. The time delay from when scenarios are documented to when their implementation is finally presented to customers is the basic cause of late-cycle design defects: if there's a mistake in an early translation, the subsequent translations tend to reproduce the mistake.

---

1   In particular, see Chapter 3 of *User Centered System Design*, by Donald Norman and Stephen Draper (Hillsdale, NJ: Lawrence Erlbaum Associates, 1986).

2   *The Psychology of Everyday Things* (New York: Basic Books, 1988); *Turn Signals Are the Facial Expressions of Automobiles* (New York: Basic Books, 1993); *Design of Everyday Things* (New York: Basic Books, 2002); and others.

3   As described in Chapter 4, "Quality and the Development Process."

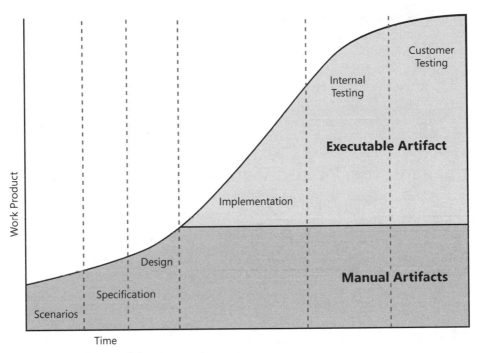

Figure 17-1   Stages of development

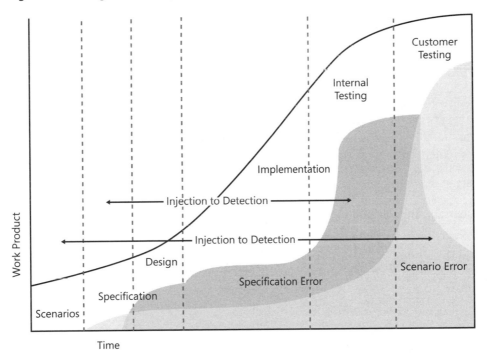

Figure 17-2   Time of likely detection of a type of defect and its injection

Late detection of scenario-oriented defects is the worst of all cases: the error occurred at a very early stage and propagated forward in the form of all kinds of dependent errors. The correction may involve design-level changes that can require large changes and that run the risk of introducing further defects. The correction may take significant time to implement because of all the dependencies on the previous expression. Finally, because the issue was discovered late in the development cycle there may not be enough time to implement the correct solution, much less test and correct any defects introduced by the solution. As time passes in development, the ability to make major changes declines.

Transformations from Product Vision to Code

Each stage of development that produces an artifact ("work product" in Figures 17-1 and 17-2) has some kind of verification process, and the next stage primarily uses that artifact as its source material. Of course, there is still occasional reference to prior artifacts (such as checking scenarios in design), but the primary source is the output of the previous stage. Certainly, when the verification process is manual there is a possibility of error, and additionally, errors can be made in interpreting the prior-stage artifacts.

One naïve assumption about the nature of defects is that they are primarily localized. Each stage translation has a different gap of expression, or how foreign the concepts of the destination are from the source. Particularly large gaps exist between design and code as well as specification and design. When there is a large gap, the translation isn't simple. It doesn't just add detail but often maps concepts nonlinearly. A concept represented in one place in the source may be represented in many places in the destination, each with slight differences. This results in more representations and the possibility of error in each place a central concept is replicated.

Figure 17-3 shows how a single concept (the star) at one stage can be represented by multiple concepts in latter stages and finally is represented by a range of code (the shadowed triangles). Additionally, the implementation of initially separate concepts may overlap in actual implementation.

Part of this fanning out of concepts can be caused by developers not completely understanding the concepts behind the customer scenarios. It is better to represent scenario concepts directly in the design to maintain a 1:1 mapping. Even the translation from a good design to code tends to fan out because of the large conceptual differences—programming languages and class libraries are designed for general purposes, not to reflect the concepts of a particular set of scenarios. Programming languages are conceptually closely related to the processor.

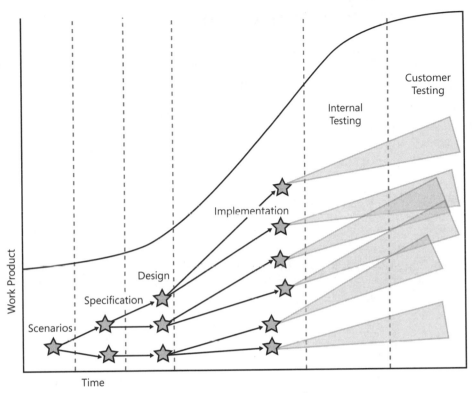

Figure 17-3   Concept mapping between stages and code coverage

A simple example is the type system of languages such as C, C++, and C#. Conceptually, you can have a type that is an even integer but that can't be expressed, so everywhere you use even integers you have to add code to check whether the integer is even. Without specialized static checking tools, it can be difficult to find places where the even integer check is missing or incorrectly specified. In C or C++, macros are sometimes used to get around the incorrect specification problem, but the omission problem remains.

A more complex example is user interface state. Activating various controls or menu items may depend on the state of multiple related items. The model of user interfaces typically decomposes into events for the user interface interactions such as clicks, selection, and properties, including checking and enabling. To help with the enabling problem, before and after events are provided for primary events. This kind of organization spreads a simple concept, such as when a toolbar item or menu item is activated, across a number of events, each using slightly different code. Even Web pages written in JavaScript or Java have this same problem with user interface expression. Look at how your specification of screen shots and interaction behaviors is spread out in the code. The possibility of error is large, and if the user interface specification is changed, it can be difficult to uproot the previous implementation.

Avoiding Obstacles to Upstream Quality

A number of the issues with upstream quality are similar to issues with quality in general. Your organization, metrics, valuations, and rewards may have formed a culture where quality is not a high priority and the wrong tradeoffs occur.

Many issues with quality involve incentives that on the surface seem fine but indirectly reward not taking steps to improve quality. As in medicine, the rule is *first do no harm*—eliminating negative incentives works wonders. The obstacles described in this section are addressed in the section titled "A Model of Future Product Development" later in this chapter.

Testing Does Not Create Quality

Quality is not a result of testing. Testing can only indicate an absence of quality, not its presence. It is far more expensive to test and detect a bug than it is not to introduce a defect in the first place. For example, incomplete customer scenarios easily lead to incorrect designs, which lead to implementations with design defects that are detected only when scenario tests are finally run. A defect checked in is magnified in its effect—every user of the functionality may be affected.

Quality Is Invisible

Often, quality is not a high concern to developers or managers unless it degrades or disappears. Improving infrastructure, from the tools used in the development process to the supporting applications (such as installation), holds little appeal to developers because work in such areas is not highly visible. In some organizations, even, there is an attitude that work that does not ship to customers (infrastructure) is less glamorous, regardless of its impact or scope of influence.

Both quality and functional infrastructure are *invisible* when they are present and glaringly *obvious* when they are not. A single fault in either area is a splash of red wine on a white tablecloth; it doesn't matter if 99.99 percent of the cloth is unspoiled—the defect stands out.

For instance, if installation works successfully, it isn't noticed; but if it is broken, the application doesn't run—and the customer can't reach those cool new features no matter how great they are. Yet, in the development culture of many organizations, ensuring that installation is smooth and functional is often considered a secondary task. Features, on the other hand, are visible and create impact by their very nature—they are selling points for a product. Working on features is exciting for developers because their work is very visible.

But consider the risks and rewards of focusing on features instead of quality and infrastructure. For example, implementing a new feature that has already been determined valuable to the customer is a winning situation; even if the feature contains a few bugs, it can make the product seem like a success. Lack of quality (the defect that made it into the finished product) can remain invisible for a long time; often, the customer discovers the defect much later. In the meantime, however, the feature has been completed and the developer rewarded.

Cleaning up legacy code, on the other hand, includes the risk of regression and destabilization. If the cleanup is successful, the effort isn't visible to the customer—it just simplifies maintenance and future work in any area in which defects were corrected. Therefore, success has little positive exposure for a developer, but the slightest failure is glaring. Your organization needs to value maintaining legacy code and accept the inherent risks.

Features Are Valued over Quality

Quality is often sacrificed for features or schedule. This sacrifice surfaces in a number of ways.

- A smoke-and-mirrors prototype is molded into a product feature without attention to the design—code is just added and changed until it "works." The result is often difficult-to-maintain code and a lower-quality product because prototypes by their nature typically contain ad hoc design and may not be fully fleshed out. As details are added in filling out the prototype, issues with the original design can arise, but because the prototype is often considered "close" to a final product, there is not enough time allotted for design issues.

- The developer does not adequately test prior to check-in, and testing of the feature by the test team occurs significantly later in the development process. It is a bad idea for a developer to depend on testing to find bugs unless the code has no customers, that is, no one is dependent on it. Unfortunately, almost by definition, someone does depend on the code, and by checking in the code, the developer has given that customer the false expectation that the feature works.

- The implementation of a feature is 90 percent complete, and the code is checked in to reach code complete or because of a dependency on the code. There is an implicit promise to finish the implementation later, yet there is no time as a result of code slip. The result is either

    - The incomplete functionality ships.

    - The schedule slips but management decides there's time to add more features, so the last 10 percent is not completed; if there is another code slip, the process repeats.

    - The code finally ships, and the organization must support it forever. A large customer base is an advantage for revenue but also entails a requirement for compatibility. Shipping code that is not correctly designed or implemented often freezes the functionality to ensure compatibility.

Engineering Attitude Blocks the Quality Mindset

"Being first to market with features is more important than quality." This assumption may have been true years ago when there was no Internet and the applications and market were smaller; your current development culture may have been formed by this experience. These days, the size of the market makes compatibility more important, which means that if badly designed or implemented features are released, it is difficult to correct them in the future. Often, new features are prioritized over quality and improving existing code and infrastructure.[1] This assumption is still widespread; culture changes slowly, and there are many expressions of this root cause.

Market demographics have changed the business. In the past, you could rely on technically savvy "early adopters" of technology to use your products. Now we deal with computers as commodities or appliances used by less technically savvy users—"typical consumers"—who are far less technical and forgiving of quality issues. Also, the ubiquity of the Internet has opened a world of malicious attacks that can cause great monetary damage and bad press. Quality, security, and customer focus are keys to satisfying customers.

When developing code, it is common to have an engineering-focused rather than a customer-focused perspective. Features tend to be generated bottom up and defined by the teams involved rather than as top-down efforts that result from customer demand and customer testing. Customer scenarios and requirements tend to get shortchanged in the desire to get into implementation.

Task and Team Myopia Block the Big-Picture Perspective

Effort and rewards often are focused on a particular team's part in the product cycle. Effort is often further delineated by discipline. Some organizations have separate disciplines for roles such as developers, testers, and program managers as well as have a separate sustained engineering organization to maintain a product after release. Smaller organizations, in particular, typically combine roles. To some extent, the focus of effort and rewards between disciplines conflict:

- Developers implement features.

- Testers look for bugs in features that developers must fix.

- Program managers want features and track the schedule.

Each discipline focuses on its own goals. Making another team's or discipline's work easier (or even the team's own future work) is not as high a priority as meeting a task date. Concentration on particular tasks as opposed to the big picture can result in shortsighted decisions. Following are some of the results of this:

- Testability is not a priority for development.

- Maintenance is not a priority, so commenting, documentation, and clarity of code can be shortchanged.

---

1   *Infrastructure* is all the enabling technologies and tools used to produce an application, as well as the supporting applications and functionality that aren't visible features.

- Designing for diagnosing problems is not a priority, so debugging is often difficult and many crashes can't be diagnosed.

- Tests are mostly written individually instead of using one common test harness and model, so tests interfere with each other and run correctly only on certain configurations.

- Creating shared implementations is not a priority, and this results in individually duplicated implementations.

None of these are desired behaviors, but the metric of the task and measuring developers by it can lead to these short-term-oriented actions. Good developers do the right thing despite this type of myopia.

Teams Avoid Due Diligence

Due diligence is doing the required work before a project is begun. In particular, due diligence includes understanding customer needs for functionality and the customer conceptual model (see the following sidebar titled "Example of a customer conceptual model") before designing and implementing features. It means doing complete customer scenarios and requirements so that the team can avoid late-cycle design errors.[1]

It means testing concepts before the team spends time on implementation. Adding a requirement to storyboard new functionality and have it verified by representative customers or a reasonable proxy for them would catch conceptual mismatches before implementation work is done. Discovery of missing scenarios or untested scenarios should be an exception, not a common occurrence.

Part of avoiding due diligence is caused by the engineering attitude and an assumption that oversimplifies a problem into something that has been done before. Other influences are the assumption that the code can be molded into the desired functionality rather than designed for it (that is, any bugs that appear later can be fixed locally rather than involve a design change) and that the important part of development is code. Designs can be robust, but errors are more likely when the usage scenarios aren't complete. It's not surprising that when new scenarios come along an existing design may not work.

---

1 Bill Buxton (*www.billbuxton.com*) compared software design to film and autos. These industries do a large amount of upfront work to avoid surprises later. You can find a public version of the talk at *http://epresence.tv/ mediaContent/archives/2004_apr22/?archiveID=65*. In addition, look for the new book, *Sketching User Experiences: Getting the Design Right and the Right Design* (Morgan Kaufmann, 2007), for more information.

Example of a customer conceptual model

Consider a function provided for copying a file. On the surface, copying a file seems like a simple operation and the functional support for it in an application may have seemed adequate to you. It is certainly a good addition to a run-time library that previously exposed just the operating system file operations (open, create, read, write, and close). You don't have to choose a buffer size anymore and write a loop reading from one file and writing to the other.

But from a customer's point of view there is a large difference in concept, and some scenarios may not be implemented unless you think from the customer's perspective. What does *copying* mean to a customer? Very few customers would like to end up with a partially copied file if an error occurs. If the file is being copied into an existing file, the user probably prefers the original to be unchanged if the copy fails. Customers may want to know all of the copies they have made of a file. Does the copied file have the same creation time as the original file? Few users are aware of the details of a file system, so would you copy streams, security info, and file attributes?

Is making a copy optimized? Many operating systems have the concept of making a file link, a new file that refers to an original instead of being a copy of its content. Does copying in your operating system make a link and only make a copy of content when a change is made or the original can't be accessed (such as when the copy and the original are on different devices or the original is deleted)? Auditing copies and lazy copying[1] are customer scenarios that aren't satisfied.

Consider errors from a customer's point of view. Are errors classified into recoverable and nonrecoverable? If storage runs out or a network connection is broken while copying across a network, can the operation be retried, or does the user get a partial result and need to start over? Consider the source of the file: does copying using storage devices, other systems, and the Internet (FTP or HTTP copying) use the same function calls and perform equivalently?

Copying files is not first class (a concept that is directly implemented) in many operating systems. Even run-time libraries supplying copying functionality are incomplete. Retrying recoverable errors may be present for copying files in a user interface, but the command-line processor just fails the operation.

Either these deficiencies are ignored, providing a less-than-optimal user experience (partial files, canceled operations), or the implementation is uneven (copying is exposed in many ways, and not all ways are the same).

---

1 *Lazy copying* is making a reference to an original and making a physical copy only when a change is about to be made to either the original or the copy.

Values and Rewards Do Not Promote Quality

When a developer makes changes to prevent bugs or share code, positive metrics are difficult to create to capture the effort—these tasks may take more time to complete and, because "bugs avoided" can't be measured, the value of the effort isn't readily apparent. Also, a reward for this quality assurance behavior isn't guaranteed because the savings are hypothetical. If preventing defects involves changing existing code, a developer runs the risk of introducing compatibility problems and additional bugs. Yet this is the very type of behavior you want to highlight and reward!

Currently, the most visible metrics used in software development negatively value the tasks that ensure quality—the extra time it takes, possible stabilization risk, and spending time on improving invisible features (infrastructure). Also, any metric used to evaluate people can be gamed. For example, if lines of code written is used as a metric, potentially a lot of verbose and duplicative code could be written to ensure that the developer gets a good evaluation. If number of bugs is used as a metric, this is a negative metric for a developer but a positive one for a tester.

Because the valuation system can be gamed, make it a game that provides value to your company. (See Chapter 5, "Using Productivity Games to Prevent Defects," for a discussion about how to use games to promote defect prevention activities.) To promote good design, maintainable code, and high quality, the valuation system must support your goals rather than have negative unintended consequences. Tie metrics to customer satisfaction and efficiency of the entire product cycle.

A good developer makes decisions for improving quality *despite the reward system in place*. Designing rewards and offering recognition for such decisions can reinforce the behavior for the good developers and influence others to follow their example. In the absence of proactive metrics to encourage decisions improving quality, recognition of such decisions after the fact can have a positive effect.

Defects Have Different Risks

Defects aren't all the same in terms of risk, especially the cost of indirect effects (the cost of a correction in dependent code). Part of the purpose of a defect taxonomy (see Chapter 10, "Defect Taxonomies") is to capture the indirect dependencies and risks for different classes of defect. A few areas of classification are useful in determining the indirect effects of a correction:

- Symptom—malfunction or missing functionality
- Correction—simple fix to one method/function to redesign
- Dependency—few/none (leaf) or many (wide and/or deep)
- Effect—failure removed, working code fails, working code needs redesign

The type of defect with the least indirect effects is missing functionality, which has a simple correction and removes a failure—no matter what code dependencies there are, the fix should not cause any indirect failures. The type of defect with the most indirect effect requires a redesign to fix, requires a redesign in all dependent code, and causes working code to fail. This latter type of defect is often the result of a redesign resulting from missing scenarios or a serious mismatch between the feature and the features that use it.

Unfortunately, these kinds of omissions are often found late in the development cycle, when most customer testing occurs. You can gauge how often this happens if you are using a defect taxonomy or a similar technique to classify defects. The expense of these kinds of defects[1] in terms of the limited time left to market and the sunk cost of code that needs to be redesigned/rewritten is the major reason for moving quality upstream—detect and correct these expensive defects before you have made the commitment of time and effort.

Identifying the Causes of Poor Downstream Quality

To improve quality upstream, you need to know the root causes of poor quality downstream. The Five Whys[2] process is one method you can use to examine your current culture, processes, and tools. One axis of questioning is the following:

1. Why are there defects that require redesign?

    ❑ *Because scenarios are missing, incomplete, or not well understood.*

2. Why are scenarios missing, incomplete, or not well understood?

    ❑ *Because they were not known at design time.*

3. Why were they not known at design time?

    ❑ *Because design and implementation were started before they were known.*

4. Why did design and implementation start early?

    ❑ *Because code was considered measurable progress.*

    ❑ *Because we thought we knew the scenarios.*

    ❑ *Because on the surface the product is similar to something done before.*

5. Why did we think we understood scenarios?

    ❑ *Because we thought we were the customer.*

    ❑ *Because we separated understanding the customer from development.*

---

1 See Chapter 3, "The Economics of Defect Prevention."
2 See Chapter 11, "Root Cause Analysis."

The preceding example examines why the failures occur, which can generate some ideas you can use to improve the situation. Another axis of questioning is as follows:

1. Why are these defects detected so late?

   ❑ *Because they are detected by customer testing.*

2. Why is customer testing so late in the cycle?

   ❑ *Because customer testing involves the whole product.*

3. Why is customer testing performed on the whole product?

   ❑ *Because the code is the testable form of the product.*

4. Why is the code the form customers test?

   ❑ *Because it is the only interactive form.*

5. Why is code the only interactive form?

   ❑ *Because code is the final embodiment of the product; anything else is "wasted" effort.*

By relying on the executable code as the primary exposure of the product to customer testing, it is certain that this testing will occur late in the development cycle. The issue is that verification that an implementation is usable by customers is delayed until the code is mostly working (at least to developers), and at that point scenario implementation issues surface. A better approach is to make the extra effort to produce alternative descriptions of functionality that can be verified with customers to ensure that the model of implementation is correct. Simply storyboarding functionality can surface issues far less expensively than waiting until the functionality is implemented.

Habit is another reason for why software is developed using methods that do not guarantee upstream quality. This is rather strange when you consider the repeated, widespread failures of habitual methods—schedules are missed and software is released with defects. As applications become larger and more complicated, the problems become much worse, yet the development methodology changes little.

The exercise of the Five Whys process can expose the root causes of low downstream quality, which in turn can suggest changes in process to address the problem directly and improve quality.

A Model of Future Product Development

Some time back, we were asked, "What would be an ideal product development environment that focuses on the customer and quality?" We had a dozen or so points to make, including specific roles for test and development. We predicted that such a change would be years in the making, so describing it now wasn't urgent. However, the questioner's reply was illustrative, "But you have to start recruiting and training people now to have them in the future."

To know whether you are making progress, you need a vision of where you want to go. This section sets out the goals for product development in the future. You can use some of these ideas with existing processes to help your organization transition to a new development environment that focuses on upstream quality.

The model should address not only the issue of quality but also the issue of agility; client applications are becoming so large and complex that it is difficult to make improvements quickly and release a new version. Web applications are typically released on a shorter schedule, but part of this is because of their smaller size, use of server platform applications, and lesser compatibility requirements.[1]

As previously mentioned, quality and customer focus are intertwined. The development process should focus on providing functionality that customers want and implementing it in a way customers readily understand. This results in customers having a higher satisfaction with the finished product. Additionally, better understanding of what needs to be done before doing it results in fewer defects, particularly expensive design errors.

The development process should make better use of resources, use automation where possible, and result in more predictable release schedules. Part of this improvement flows from the reduction of false steps and defects through focusing on the customer.

We designed the structure of this model of future development by considering the root causes of many of the key cultural and customer issues in software development today. Rather than looking for incremental improvements in existing processes, we considered the goal to be accomplished the priority. The major pillars can be summarized as follows:

1. **Development is customer focused.**   Features are determined by customer need, not by what a team thinks is the latest "cool" feature unless that is validated by customer feedback. Some features certainly also are driven by technology and business goals, but these are just projected future customer needs and internal customer needs, respectively.

2. **Product information is executable.**   Information that was once captured in documents will be machine usable to aid consistency and static testing.

3. **Customer scenarios are moved upstream.**   Scenarios are somewhat testable early in the development cycle (before coding). Shortcomings in scenarios, requirements, and designs surface before the large cost of implementation is encountered. A key enabler is getting information previously in documents into an executable form.

4. **Testing and test generation are automated.**   Free testers from boilerplate creation of tests and manually running them. Allow testers to use and grow their domain expertise and concentrate on understanding the customer and defining scenarios. Automated tests are scenario/system/stress.

---

1   A Web page is used by people rather than through an API, and people are far more flexible at adapting to changes in the user interface.

5. **Static testing is pervasive.**   The experience with an application as massive as the Microsoft Windows operating system shows that you can't completely test dynamically—700 million customers define an immense number of unique environments. This also applies to applications that are much smaller. Malicious programming means you can't depend on Monte Carlo[1] testing to find all security problems. Dynamic testing depends on the values used to test and the branches executed (and can miss errors). Static testing analyzes the code without execution.

6. **Development process is modified.**   Development process balances rapid exploration for new functionality with later rigor in creating production code in more predictable time.

This vision of future development focuses efforts on meeting customer needs, discovering design and scenario problems very early in development when solution costs are lower, freeing a large part of the testing staff to be the voice of the customer throughout the process and yet more completely testing the product.

Development Is Customer Focused

Often, customer feedback is gained so late in the development process that it can affect only the next version of a product. Achieving customer focus includes listening to and testing with customers early in development rather than later. Customer focus has a number of aspects. You need to nail customer scenarios rather than have each team add their favorite features—complexity and a large selection of choices aren't positive aspects of an application. Scenarios flow from customer conceptual models (described in the sidebar titled "Example customer conceptual model" earlier in this chapter)—they should be simple descriptions in terms of the conceptual model. If you understand and design according to the conceptual model, any scenarios discovered later tend to be easier to implement without requiring changes to your design.

Customer-focused development can greatly reduce late-cycle design errors by attacking their causes: engineering attitude and the avoidance of due diligence. Additionally, by having customer-based justifications up front and well-described usage scenarios, the team tends to code what is needed rather than a much larger and harder-to-test broad solution.

The roles of testing and development change, although the largest effect is on testing. Testing's role evolves from writing and executing tests to defining the acceptance criteria for a feature and validating they are met—testing becomes the customer's voice in the development process.

Stage 1: Due Diligence

Before any design or implementation of a feature is done, a process of definition must occur. Customer conceptual models and scenarios should be understood. Conceptual models can

---

1 *Monte Carlo testing* is testing a system by testing a portion of the system and inferring the quality of the entire system from that part. It assumes that a significant percentage of the system is tested.

be discovered through conversations with representative customer groups. Surveys are not adequate for discovering conceptual models but can be used to verify them. People at your company or key customers may be representative customers. The process is similar to the hard part of designing an expert system—understanding the concepts of the expert. In this process, the following roles are defined:

- **Program manager**   Provides customer information, often in a coarse form, as well as business concerns.

- **Scenarioist (previously tester)**   Skilled in relevant domain areas and customer mindset. Good at filling in the details and finding holes in descriptions of scenarios and customer requirements.

- **Conceptual architect (developer)**   Skilled at gaining and understanding a customer's conceptual model for functionality as well as what it is possible to do technically. The most important characteristic is the mindset that even if a solution is technically elegant, it is useless if the customer doesn't understand it.

These roles interact to determine how the customer expects a new functionality to work and what can be implemented. Determining customer expectations may involve customer focus groups or interviewing contacts to understand the customer better or present alternative formulations to gauge customer understanding.

Specialization in these roles may be by domain knowledge or knowledge of a particular customer base. For all people concerned, *customer service* must be the byword—customers are not stupid; they pay the bills.

The result of this process is a well-defined set of scenarios and requirements that is rigorous enough to drive a quality design, create scenario tests, and focus on solving customer issues and that has been validated at its level of detail.

Stage 2: Designing Code and Scenario Tests in Parallel

The development team takes the scenario definitions and constructs a design specification for implementation. The detail and completeness of the input should result in a design that vastly lowers the chance of major design errors occurring. Before any coding takes place, the design is validated against the scenarios. Scenarios should be executable against the design, which is a form of automated design walkthrough. This is part of having a living specification—the scenario and design specifications are executable so that the ability of a design to perform a scenario can be verified before the code is written.

The customer acceptance team takes the scenarios and requirements and generates the parameters to use in execution of the scenarios to test their functionality. This involves another role, the scenario analyst, who is capable of examining scenarios and deciding which particular parameters exercise the functionality. Automatic tools that take a scenario description and parameter sets and to generate scenario tests are available.

The construction of scenario tests before code is similar to test-driven development, agile processes (see Chapter 12, "Adopting Processes"), and other methodologies.

Stage 3: Implementing the Design

The implementation stage is similar to the current implementation stage. The differences involve the validation tools available at this time and the languages available to code in. These are described in the section titled "Static Testing Is Pervasive," which follows.

The customer acceptance team may be working on automatic end-to-end scenario and stress tests. Development of these tests could also have been started in stage 2, depending on the time available. The focus of implementation testing is validation of scenarios and their interaction. Before implementation testing, unit level and static tests are performed.

Product Information Is Executable

Use specialized languages for design concepts. By making any manual artifacts machine usable, you have provided a second abstraction to verify your code against. The next step is to make a change in coding methodology—attach your code samples to the high-level description rather than interspersing the description as comments in your code. Compilation would produce the executable code from this combination. If the design no longer requires a code sample, it wouldn't be in the generated code. It is then impossible for implementation to be out of sync with design or scenario requirements because validation against these is part of the code generation process.

Instead of having written documentation about scenarios and designs, executable descriptions are used for early consistency checks. Instead of separate code files, the code is added to appropriate places in the executable descriptions. Adding to the design produces the application; adding to the scenarios produces the scenario tests. There is a continuous flow from descriptions to final product code.

This also opens the door for additional methods of reducing errors and bottlenecks, and improving productivity. In addition to languages for describing design and scenarios, define languages for various domains.[1] An implementation is the meeting of customer, design, and implementation concepts. The advantages of such domain languages are as follows:

- **Reduction of translation error**   Currently, a domain expert may describe what needs to happen, but it is translated into code by a developer who may have a different understanding.

- **Reduction of bottlenecks**   A domain expert can directly express functionality.

- **Higher quality**   Such domain languages produce code and are written by developers who are experts in the domain. Each use of the language serves as a test of its quality, and

---

1 Layout, user interface, database access, application installation, and operating system installation are a few examples.

hence it is highly tested—internal dogfooding.[1] If 20 different user interfaces that must be implemented were expressed in one language, that language would be tested far more than would 20 independent implementations each with its own errors of translation.

- **Prevention of error**   It is always best to make errors inexpressible rather than unlikely. Specific domain languages allow restriction of what can be expressed and have more freedom of underlying implementation.

- **Smaller API surface and freedom to change**   The domain language essentially limits what can be described, which results in a smaller specified vocabulary. The actual implementation of this vocabulary has much more ability to change without invalidating descriptions in the language.

The result is a knowledge base about the product of varying levels of description that can be validated against one another and used to produce code, tests, or documentation (it's just a choice of code generator).

Customer Scenarios Are Moved Upstream

Scenarios are executable from the beginning and are verified early against a design—the scenarios express the steps in terms of the conceptual model, which is described in the design. If a step can't be expressed in the model, there is an obvious problem. Scenarios and the design mutually verify each other.

Scenarios are key to the testing of the product. Scenario stress testing generates the mean time between failure (MTBF) values to measure one important aspect of quality.

Testing and Test Generation Are Automated

Ample evidence shows[2] that you can't completely test a large or complex application, even with extended test cycles and beta releases. The permutations of state, configuration, and action are just too vast. Automating testing and increasing the portability of testing improve testing quality but don't solve the problem.

Currently, teams expend significant effort writing tests, and the time it takes to run tests is a fixed overhead of development. Automating tests reduces the human resource cost of testing. When the set of tests is large, the use of code coverage information to determine what code is affected by a change and the tests that exercise those changes can provide faster results. (See Chapter 8, "Risk Analysis.") However, you need to do more than just run automated test suites. The automatic generation of test suites reduces the human resource cost of creating the automated tests.

---

1 Dogfooding is using your own product internally to discover defects before exposing it to customers.
2 See Chapter 3, "The Economics of Defect Prevention."

Executable tests focus on scenarios, end-to-end tasks, and stress. Static tests can't test everything, so executable tests can serve to catch any remaining problems. Additionally, performance is a customer requirement for most functionality, and it can be measured only dynamically. The mean time between failure (MTBF) running scenario stress provides a good measure of customer-perceived quality.

In the future, teams will make a significant effort in the construction of shared test execution systems that are driven by scenario descriptions, parameters, and expected results. This fixed cost then vastly reduces the variable cost of creating scenario tests. This can define another role for former testers.

Static Testing Is Pervasive

Complete run-time testing isn't possible because there are too many variations in input values and configuration. Complete static testing is not possible either but does not depend on choosing the right parameters to exercise a certain branch point in the code. On the other hand, what can be tested statically is currently limited.

The shortcoming of static testing tools is an artifact of the current development process—the high-level descriptions are all human-readable documents (scenarios, designs) that can't be used directly for automatic validation. Instead, a manual (human) process of review, which includes the possibility of error, is used.

The basis of validation is to compare descriptions against each other. If previously document-based descriptions were parsable, you could use them to validate against a design or code. On some occasions, a manual scenario walkthrough of a design is done to ensure that the design covers the scenario. The manual process includes a possibility of error. With machine-usable scenarios and design descriptions, an automatic complete design walkthrough could be done. Declarative descriptions are easier to use in static validation and are more natural to a significant part of scenarios and designs.

Often the comparison is not with an accurate precursor of a description but with the description itself. The phrase *the code is the spec* is the best example of this. Many tests compare against the results of a previous version—comparison with *last known good*. Code reviews often deal more with the structure of the code, examining it for bad coding patterns or mistakes in using good coding patterns, rather than whether the code accomplishes the scenarios.

Code analysis tools are valuable static tools. Code analysis tools typically look for general, small-scale instances of bad patterns or common mistakes in good patterns. Calling a function and not using the return value is an example of a common mistake a code analysis tool could detect. Using an unsafe string function that is vulnerable to buffer overrun errors is an example of a bad pattern. The patterns are typically small scale and not related to the larger design patterns of your product. False positives (issues that aren't defects) are often a problem; for example, the nonuse of a return value is not always a defect.

Validation tools work by comparing an example against a valid translation. In the case of code analysis tools, the valid translation is the patterns it recognizes. The value of code analysis can be greatly increased by adding metadata to the code to add information. A current step in this direction is the use of the Standard Annotation Language (SAL)[1] to describe more information about parameters such as associating buffers with buffer sizes and whether a pointer value may be null.

Two main improvements can make validation tools more effective:

- Change the code you write to avoid using error-prone constructs of the language, enforce it in a validation tool, and abstract concepts to a level where they can be more easily recognized by a validation tool.

- Add metadata to the code to describe design intent and constraints so that the validation tool has a second translation to verify against.

You can verify behavior constraints by making dangerous constructs or code from which it is hard for a validation tool to infer intent inexpressible (they will be rejected by the validation tool).

The added information can at least allow you to flag code for more focused review if there are still false positives and indicate the domains involved by using a section of code that can be used with a domain-oriented code review system. (See Chapter 19, "Knowledge Management and Communication.") Additionally, such information can be used where code changes have been made to focus testing and to focus on the possible sources of certain types of defects.

For example, if metadata describes any persistent effects of a function such as the effect on global variables or allocated objects, correlation could be done to find where there may be conflicts or if a defect involves such a global value pointing to the possible functions that could be the cause.

A significant effort is required to develop the description language for design and other artifacts. The scenario language will already be defined for the automatic generation of scenario tests.

Development Process Is Modified

As with most processes, it is better to have one that supports the way things really happen as opposed to one that operates as if it were in an ideal world (which never happens). The waterfall model of development has always had this problem. A development model described in *Exploiting Chaos: Cashing In on the Realities of Software Development*[2] is quite appealing because it addresses the reality of software development.

---

1 Available in some versions of Microsoft Visual Studio 2005 and the Windows Vista operating system software development kit (SDK).

2 Dave Olson, *Exploiting Chaos: Cashing In on the Realities of Software Development* (New York: Van Nostrand Reinhold, 1993).

The model shown in Figure 17-4 recognizes that software development consists of periods of stability and chaos. The periods of chaos include times of experimentation to develop new functionality. The development of new functionality goes through stages of initial development and continuation, if viable. Completion of functionality is then integrated into the core version. The result is that at all times the core is a functional version.

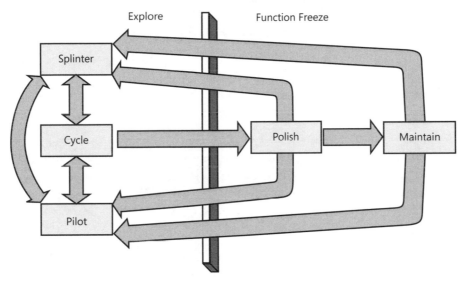

Figure 17-4   Development process from *Exploiting Chaos*

This core version is a prototype, not necessarily high-performance production-level code. The final polish phase produces the production code. The existing code is considered the source for producing production-level code. This means that the code gets a second look at a later time by different people who are very rigorous in their coding. The prototype version can be used to validate the production version. The amount of time to polish a prototype is far more predictable than the typical process is because the size and complexity of the prototype are known. Some developers are good at design, at envisioning new functionality, at rapid prototyping, at optimizing performance, or at writing solid code. This model defines roles for different developer skills.

Resulting Changes in Organization, Roles, and Career Paths

These changes can prompt organizational changes as well as changes in roles and career paths of developers and testers. The shift to customer focus opens the possibility of specialization in various knowledge domains or customer personas for both test and development. Currently, security is an example of domain specialization.

During the development process, there are different needs for different skills. People can have a choice of career path: they can specialize in an existing expertise and perhaps move to other groups when those groups need that particular set of skills, or people can expand their skills into other areas by remaining in the same group. For example, people can move between groups in response to need for their specialization, or they can change what they do to meet needs in their group.

This mobility can make better use of employees—rather than a group expanding to its maximum needed size at one point in time, duplicating effort, and needing to ramp up on new skills, it can have a core set of people and bring in additional specialists as needed.

When a team keeps a customer focus, developers and testers can specialize in understanding the customer or in understanding the final product (code or tests). Both areas need people to create and maintain the tools that generate and run the scenarios, statically validate code, and generate code from the product knowledge base.

For developers, the new process allows specialization according to their stronger skills. The splinter area values exploration and developing new ideas. The pilot area fleshes out an idea so that it can be evaluated. The cycle area integrates the results of the pilot and splinter areas. The polish area produces performant production-quality code. The maintain area supports the product. Current development processes have the equivalent of the maintain area but none of the others.

Typically, worker roles are very generic. However, career paths that focus on what employees like to do can increase worker satisfaction. Making better use of employee talents produces better results for the company. Mobility in roles can provide a means for the organization to adjust staffing dynamically according to need.

Conclusion

Some of the major causes of low quality are insufficient focus on the customer from the start, late verification of whether a design matches a conceptual model used by customers, and habits reinforced by your organization's culture and values. Metrics for quality can be difficult to determine because it is hard to measure potential number of defects averted as opposed to defects detected. Many improvements can be made by examining your metrics and rewards and how they may actually work against a quality culture.

There are two kinds of defects: customer-perceived and security. The first are important in relation to their probability of discovery by customers, and testing customer scenarios is a good means to discover them. The second are actively sought, so they should be caught by analysis rather than execution tools.

The development process can be organized around the model of development as a series of transformations from original concept to code. Instead of a series of textual documents and diagrams being used to finally produce code, these manual artifacts can be made parsable and code attached to them as development progresses. Rather than the code being separate from the design, the design is the primary organizing structure and the code is attached. This not only limits loss of information in producing code but guarantees that the information is up-to-date and allows for coarse testing such as scenario walkthroughs before implementation code is written. Scenarios are written in a scenario language that can be verified against a design. The embellishment of the design with code produces an implementation, whereas the embellishment of scenarios with parameters and details produces the scenario tests.

Another improvement to development is the chaotic model, which is organized around a central stable prototype with experimental branches that are reintegrated when they prove themselves. At any time, a decision can be made to start the polish phase, which includes using the prototype to write the production code. There are a multitude of advantages to this phase in terms of both quality and better use of personnel.

Chapter 18
Rewards, Motivation, and Incentives

If you can't make the time to do it right, when will you find the time to do it over?
—*Anonymous*

Treat people as if they were what they ought to be, and you help them to become what they are capable of being.
—*Johann Wolfgang von Goethe (1749–1832)*

It is human nature to downplay our mistakes; it is unnatural to celebrate and publicize them. Defect prevention cannot take place without first identifying defects, and that requires an individual, team, or organization to expose its flaws. Defect prevention, therefore, is an unnatural activity. Your organization can benefit by providing extra motivation or incentive for people to complete this work.

There are many years' worth of studies on employee motivation. Abraham Maslow wrote about a hierarchy of needs as a way to express human desire and motivation. Douglas MacGregor developed Theory X and Theory Y explanations of employee behavior. Business and management writers Peter Drucker, Tom Peters, Stephen Covey, and many others have written on techniques to improve motivation. All of these approaches are worth exploring when an organization is searching for a way to motivate people to spend time on preventing defects. The principles and theories of these great historical theorists and writers apply— defect prevention is just another type of work that can benefit from analysis and lessons from these experts.

Using Motivational Techniques

A wide variety of management techniques are used to motivate employees. Sports coaches use specific techniques to motivate players to perform their best. Political candidates use techniques to motivate people to vote, and to vote for them. Charities use methods to motivate people during fundraising efforts. Motivational techniques are used in many different situations. Because, as mentioned earlier, defect prevention is not a natural activity, a little boost in motivation can help improve the likelihood of implementing a successful defect prevention program. Following is a list of common, well-known techniques that can be used to motivate people to spend effective time on defect prevention, but by no means is it an exhaustive list.

- Eliminate "de-motivators."
- Set SMART goals for defect prevention work.

- Measure time and effort spent on defect prevention work.

- Ensure that leadership behavior reflects focus on defect prevention.

- Create a culture of defect prevention.

- Align organizational goals with defect prevention efforts.

- Design organizational processes with defect prevention in mind.

- Design the reward system to support worker diversity.

- Celebrate successes.

- Use competition and games.

Each item is discussed more fully in the following subsections. People, and organizations, are all different, so you must take the time to learn about them and understand them to identify the most effective motivators.

Eliminate De-motivators

Many times, a manager or an organization takes steps that are detrimental to the health and effectiveness of the workforce. Although these managers are making their best effort to improve things, their actions sometimes have the opposite effect. The following behaviors can reduce or eliminate motivation in most circumstances. Although these behaviors may not relate directly to defect prevention, someone who is not motivated will not put in extra effort to prevent defects. As an example, an employee who is turned off by repeated assignment to mundane tasks will not take time upon completion of those tasks to think about preventing errors.

- Assigning people to redundant mundane tasks

- Excessive rules or bureaucracy

- Scheduling too many/useless meetings

- Unfairness

- Politics

- Lack of clarity or direction

- Lack of vision

- Micromanagement

- No recognition of achievements

- Vague or contradicting goals

- Lack of information, withheld information, or perception of either

- Lack of management attention/concern

- Tolerance of poor performance

One of the best and most immediate ways to increase motivation is to eliminate these de-motivators.

Set SMART Goals for Defect Prevention Work

Setting solid goals for defect prevention activity helps ensure that the organization is aligned and focused on a defect prevention effort. SMART goals are goals that are specific, measurable, achievable, relevant, and time-based. (Note that the acronym *SMART* is defined many different ways with slight variations, depending on the source.) Setting SMART goals helps lay a solid foundation for successful defect prevention and ensures that individuals and teams are motivated to make consistent investments in defect prevention activity. See Chapter 7, "Software Measurement and Metrics," for more on SMART goals.

Measure Time and Effort Spent on Defect Prevention Work

After goals have been set and work begins, it is important to track the time and effort committed to defect prevention work so that you can ensure that there is an adequate return on investment. As the length of this book shows, a wide variety of techniques is available to prevent defects, and they require different levels of investment to be successful. Without tracking the level of investment, it is impossible to understand whether the efforts are worthwhile.

The return on investment of defect prevention techniques are much easier to measure when the amount of investment is known. Using methods such as the Personal Software Process (PSP), discussed in Chapter 12, "Adopting Processes," individuals can track their time investments in defect prevention–related activities, making it easier to assess the relative value of different techniques.

Ensure That Leadership Behavior Reflects Focus on Defect Prevention

Leadership is the most effective way to affect motivation. Therefore, the most effective defect prevention investment should be in leadership. If leaders can demonstrate through their actions that defect prevention is important, the organization will respond. The majority of people in the organization will emulate the behavior of organizational leadership. If the leaders visibly demonstrate the importance of defect prevention investments through their actions, individuals are likely to invest the time to prevent defects and make the program successful. Scheduling time for data analysis, encouraging the application of defect prevention techniques, and investing in the quality-related skills of the team are all ways that a leader can demonstrate a commitment to defect prevention. If the leaders ignore or dismiss defect prevention successes, the organization's defect prevention efforts will likely fall short of its goals.

Defect prevention is a long-term investment. The dividends are large but not immediate. Even if people can see the benefits of investing in preventing defects, it is unlikely they will invest heavily in preventing future defects if their leaders don't support it. This is why it is essential for leaders and upper management to focus on defect prevention, demonstrating that these efforts are worthwhile even if they don't pay immediate dividends.

Create a Culture of Defect Prevention

What is a *culture of defect prevention*? A culture of defect prevention is a significant part of a culture of quality, as discussed in Chapter 16, "Creating a Quality Culture." The goal is to create an environment that fosters the ability of individuals to see beyond the immediacy of the defect and to invest in the bigger picture or longer-term solution. In a defect prevention culture, it's OK to fail as long as the individual and/or team is able to learn from the mistakes and that knowledge persists and is shared across the organization.

Most software projects are managed in a way that focuses on completing the immediate goal of releasing the current version. Teams optimize their behavior toward the goal of getting the current version out the door. A culture of defect prevention can support these goals and coexist in a high-pressure environment of ship, ship, ship. However, it's critical that the long-term benefits of learning from the failures are not lost. For example, if a key developer must take a day to write up how to prevent buffer overruns in the code base, the team must be capable of accommodating the investment in defect prevention and schedule time must be granted to this developer. Although the payoff may not come until the next release, perhaps years down the road, the team should not be deterred from investing this valuable time.

On the other hand, the payoff may also be realized much sooner, such as when another developer makes a similar error on the current project. The rate of return for defect prevention investments is variable (See also Chapter 3, "Economics of Defect Prevention)—people make mistakes every day—and as a team goes through a project cycle, the lessons learned and the techniques to prevent mistakes will vary in their applicability and relevancy. At some point, however, it is likely that most of the lessons learned and preventive techniques documented can be applied and can help improve quality and prevent future defects. It requires a deliberate effort, and sometimes a large investment, to apply many of the techniques discussed throughout this book, but the data supports the conclusion that these efforts pay off and lead to higher-quality software.

Align Organizational Goals with Defect Prevention Efforts

The pressures of competition, ownership, Wall Street investors and shareholders, upper management, or an impatient customer typically drive the behavior of the software development organization. As the leaders of the organization establish the culture and set the goals, it's important for the immediate goals of the current project to align with the long-term goals of the organization. Assuming that one of the goals is high-quality production of useful software, the leaders of the organization should establish a vision that spans multiple releases or versions of the software and include goals for cycle-over-cycle improvements.

The aim of leadership is not merely to find and record the failures of men, but to remove the causes of failure: to help people to do a better job with less effort.[1]

When the goals of the organization include a robust defect prevention effort, the goals of the individual will follow. Typically, the individual engineer does not have the time, or perhaps the scope, to see the big picture well enough to understand why investment in defect prevention techniques is worthwhile. Engineers may not understand how defect prevention work contributes to the immediate goals of getting the current project finished. In many cases, defect prevention work does not contribute to the current project but pays its dividends in future cycles. These dividends, however, are significant, and it is the responsibility of the leaders of the organization, or of the team, to understand and track the investments and set goals to ensure that the appropriate level of investment is made. For example, the team can set a specific (SMART, see Chapter 7) goal for a certain percentage of severe defects to which formal root cause analysis (Chapter 11, "Root Cause Analysis") would be applied.

Design Organizational Processes with Defect Prevention in Mind

In addition to aligning the goals of the organization with a defect prevention strategy, it is important to make an effort to design the development processes to support preventive techniques. Typically, processes are designed or optimized to reduce expenses and cut costs. With a short-term focus, defect prevention investments are an unnecessary activity and will add to costs. However, over multiple milestones or projects, defect prevention investments can pay dividends many times over.

Competitive pressures, quality, customer satisfaction, schedules, and team morale all affect the process design, and typically, defect prevention work is one of the first to be cut. However, deliberate planning and support from the leaders helps ensure that the right level of investment in defect prevention is made. Root cause analysis studies, tools, and data-gathering activities are all examples where additional work can be integrated into the daily processes to provide long-term benefit. Individuals may not necessarily see the benefit and may complain, but a strong leadership team can drive the right solutions and provide the appropriate longer-term view of the process investments.

Design the Reward System to Support Worker Diversity

Different people are motivated by different things. The incentive system, either for the organization or for the team, should support the manager's ability to tailor the incentives to the needs of individuals. If one person wants time off, another wants a cash bonus, and a third wants dental benefits, the incentive system should allow the manager to choose the best solution for the individual. As the manager learns the techniques to motivate the team, his or her ability to enable the team to spend time on prevention techniques is much more effective.

---

1   W. Edwards Deming, *Out of the Crisis* (Cambridge, MA: MIT Press, 2000), 248.

Although no one reward or incentive system works for everyone, there are some common elements of a solid incentive program:

- Leadership supports the use of rewards and incentives.

- Incentives are distributed based on consistent, easy-to-understand criteria that support organizational goals.

- All individuals and teams are eligible for rewards.

- Rewards are distributed only to high-performing teams and individuals.

- Awards are public and are celebrations of success.

- Incentive programs are measured and evolve to match the needs of the organization.

Incentives—It's Not Just Money

From the moment we enter the world as infants, human beings look for and respond to attention. Recognition is typically the most effective motivator because it has been something people have sought since birth. Cash awards, contests, time off, and other motivators can affect the budget, but the benefit of motivating through recognition is that, for the most part, recognition does not require a budget infusion—it is available to give freely. Here are suggestions for creating incentives that provide recognition for defect prevention work:

- Recognition

- Cash bonuses

- Pay raises

- Gifts

- Swag (T-shirts, pens, coffee mugs)

- Additional training

- Extra vacation or time off

- Gift certificates

- Tickets to special events

- Parties and trips

- Contests and prizes

- "Face" time with upper management (a form of recognition)

There are many others, and it is often a great idea to ask the team or those who need motivating what incentives would be worthwhile to them. You will find there is never a shortage of suggestions.

Celebrate Successes

A big part of motivating and encouraging people to invest time in preventing defects is rewarding success. When techniques are employed successfully, or new processes or practices are created, these events should be recognized and celebrated. In particular, if the leadership of the organization can showcase successful defect prevention work as it happens, this will go a long way toward demonstrating to individuals the importance of focusing some portion of their efforts on prevention.

Leaders can showcase and draw attention to successful defect prevention efforts such as root cause analysis study results, application of failure modeling, and effective use of metrics and scorecards. By drawing attention to these investments, the leaders are implying that these are good behaviors, and smart people will get the message that if they want to be noticed by the leaders, they will do the same things. Leaders should reward and notice the things they want to encourage. Catch people doing something good.

Use Games and Competition

Games and competition are incredible motivators. People like to compete, figure out puzzles, work toward a goal. A number of activities can motivate people to put time into preventing defects. In fact, games and competition are so effective at encouraging people to work on preventing defects, we've included a whole chapter on this topic. (See Chapter 5, "Using Productivity Games to Prevent Defects.") For example, building a leader board to show prevention suggestions from the prevention tab (Chapter 14, "Prevention Tab") would be a great way to start some friendly defect prevention competition.

Understand What Motivates Individuals

People don't change their behavior unless it makes a difference for them to do so.

–Fran Tarkenton

It may not always be possible to alter organizational goals or processes. Defect prevention work may be a local team-specific activity, part of a pilot project, or performed in an area that does not warrant altering organizational behavior. In these cases, motivating individuals to spend time on defect prevention requires different techniques. There is an abundance of management information about what motivates individuals. As mentioned earlier, there is no shortage of great writings on management and motivation. Here are a couple more, and see *www.defectprevention.org* for a more detailed list.

- *Thriving on Chaos*—Tom Peters (Knopf, 1987)
- *The Enthusiastic Employee*—David Sirota, Louis Mischkind, and Michael Irwin Meltzer (Wharton School Publishing, 2005)

- *Out of the Crisis*—W. Edwards Deming (MIT Press, 2000)
- *7 Habits of Highly Effective People*—Stephen Covey (Free Press, 2004)

Methods outlined in these resources can certainly be applied to motivating individuals to spend time on defect prevention work.

For a smaller team, organizational goal and process changes may be unobtainable, which means that the motivation must come from inside the team or individual. If the organization cannot provide a stick, the team must provide a carrot. There are many ways to accomplish this, and providing individuals with a look at the big picture of the entire software development process, including insight into multiple release plans, marketing, maintenance, and support efforts, can serve them well in their careers. However, focusing some level of effort on defect prevention is a change in the way most people develop software and requires work on the part of the team leader to understand how to encourage people to participate.

Make an Ongoing Investment in Motivation

A new manager typically tries to motivate a new team by using motivational techniques to which he or she would personally respond. The new manager quickly learns that not everyone is motivated by the same things. What motivates one person may alienate or anger another. The methods must be tailored to the individual *at that point in time*. It's very likely that motivational factors will change. Unmarried employees early in their careers may be motivated by the promise of additional time off. When such an employee marries and has children, he or she may then be motivated by the opportunity to earn more or receive solid health care benefits. Perhaps the opposite is true—a married person with children would like time off to spend with children, while the unmarried person wants to work hard and make career advances. The point is that there is no magic formula that works for everyone. Motivational factors evolve over time, and the manager must evolve with them.

> *Design flexibility is important for keeping programs fresh and appealing to employees and managers alike. Adapting and refining awards programs and criteria are a natural part of an organization's ongoing use of rewards and recognition.[1]*

---

1 The Effectiveness of Federal Employee Incentive Programs—Hearing Before the Oversight of Government Management and Restructuring and the District of Columbia Subcommittee of the Committee on Governmental Affairs, United States Senate—May 2, 2000. http://frwebgate.access.gpo.gov/cgi-bin/getdoc.cgi?dbname= 106_senate_hearings&docid=f:65172.wais

Knowing What Success Looks Like

A motivated individual or team displays certain traits that are significantly different from those displayed by unmotivated individuals and teams. A highly motivated team will have the time and the desire to improve things, and that motivation can be easily applied to defect prevention. A motivated individual will be more receptive to the need for ongoing improvement through his or her optimism and energy. Motivated people typically demonstrate many of the following characteristics:

- Happy and fun to work with
- Optimistic
- Self-starters
- Full of energy
- Committed to putting in an extra effort
- Willing to follow organizational directives
- Confident thinking for themselves
- Appreciate recognition
- Able to take on new or additional challenges
- Seeking out opportunities
- Expand their capabilities
- Proactive in problem solving
- Confident in their ability and level of contribution
- Willing to set aggressive goals

There is a noticeable difference between motivated people and those who are apathetic or disgruntled. Time invested in motivating an individual or a team is worthwhile, and a positive environment is contagious.

Measuring Success

It is important to track the success rate of incentive programs. The most obvious metric is "number of defects prevented," but that gets tricky to calculate for a couple reasons: How do you count something that's not there (a mistake prevented)? If the prevention isn't deployed until the next product cycle, how does the team assess the current reward potential?

A number of methods can be used to collect data for building the incentive program. It is sometimes difficult to correlate incentive or reward and output directly, but the following steps can help you gather the data:

- Employee surveys or polls
- Interviews
- Attrition or turnover rates
- Productivity measures (specific to the job)
- Customer satisfaction surveys

Measurement of the effectiveness of rewards is difficult. There are also many external factors that may have a greater influence on motivation than specifically targeted incentives. For example, a time-off reward program may receive favorable reviews when the value of employee stock options rises with the stock price, and the same program might be severely criticized if the stock price declines. Taking the time to understand individuals and what can motivate them is the best way to ensure the success of an incentive program.

Conclusion

Defect prevention is not a natural activity. People don't like to talk about their weaknesses, mistakes and slip-ups, so leaders must take some deliberate steps to encourage people to spend time on defect prevention. In most cases, the benefits of investing in defect prevention activity outweigh the costs, but it is important for the manager to track these efforts to be sure the return on investment is positive. There are many sources of information on employee motivation, and it remains a popular topic with business writers. Many of the great business books and management theorists explore techniques in motivation, and all of these can be applied to defect prevention work.

Chapter 19
Knowledge Management and Communication

Both project complexity and specialization (decomposing the project or team members into functional areas) make knowing all pertinent aspects of a project more difficult: you can't know everything. As teams grow larger or become geographically separated, it becomes more difficult for members to communicate with one another. This difficulty occurs when functional teams are separated, and it becomes even more noticeable in large teams or at multiple sites.

Similarly, complexity increases the importance of documentation because it becomes more likely that no one person can understand all the details of the entire product. Naturally, localized expertise develops, which in turn increases the need for communication. Also, as new people are added to the team over time, they need to learn what is already known. You don't have to have a project as large and complex as development of the Microsoft Windows operating system to encounter these issues.

For example, an OpenSource[1] project can involve a number of these communication issues. Members of such a project are typically geographically isolated from each other, and each localized group is small (often a single contributor). The means of communication between members is limited compared with when team members are located just down the hall. Communicating scenarios, architecture, and design can be a challenge. Coordination of activity is another challenge for dispersed teams.

When development is outsourced or consultants are used, communication also becomes difficult and of supreme importance, particularly when there is geographical separation between in-house team members and outside help. Communication issues can be minimized in many situations by ensuring that development tasks are specified clearly and dependencies are minimized.

Problems with the communication of knowledge to those who need it and surfacing issues/improvements from individuals can both cause defects. The defect taxonomy (Chapter 10) has specific sections describing whether the quality or organization of information contributes to a defect and containing prevention suggestions to improve quality.

This chapter covers the common issues of poor communication that lead to increased defects, the typical means used to improve communication, and some techniques that use size as an advantage rather than merely trying to minimize the drawbacks of size.

---

1   See *www.opensource.org* or *www.sourceforge.net* .

Problems Associated with Poor Communication

A large, successful company has the advantages of capital, resources, and people that allow it to pursue multiple opportunities simultaneously and to work on large, complex problems.

However, ambient communication between groups, products, and levels of management typically weakens as size and stratification grow. Often, the communication methods that work for smaller, less complex products do not work well on a larger scale. The lack of effective communication causes the following issues:

- Errors resulting from information being known locally to one team but not to a team using the feature (isolated knowledge)

- Replication of learning or effort (lack of knowledge transfer)

- Local best practices remaining undiscovered (inability to discover best practices)

- Undiscovered widespread issues across teams (lack of upward communication)

Processes and tools (Web sites) have been created to ameliorate some of the problems of communicating, collaborating, and sharing knowledge across a large, stove-piped organization. However, these efforts have not eliminated the problems, and few organizations use size as an advantage rather than a disadvantage. The following subsections discuss communication issues that result from increased complexity and geographical distribution; solutions to these issues are presented later in the chapter.

Isolated Knowledge

The common knowledge that a small team on a smaller project has can be lost—no one knows the big picture in detail or what everyone is working on. If the work being done is truly independent of other projects, pursuing a large number of tasks in parallel with little shared knowledge makes sense. This often works in manufacturing; for instance, there are dependencies on the availability of component parts but not the details of their inner function. Interchangeable parts have enabled multiple and independent suppliers to manufacture parts, yet the final product can be assembled without misfits, which has reduced costs.

In reality, in a complex product there is a spider's web of dependencies about the details of how things work and localized knowledge. Each team has detailed knowledge about its area, but when there are many teams such knowledge can be hard to find when needed.

Lack of Knowledge Transfer

The limited ability to distribute knowledge from experts makes nonexperts less productive because they have to discover and learn things that the experts already know (a replication of effort). Your workforce is not homogeneous; expertise varies widely. The knowledge and experience of experts can improve the productivity of and reduce the errors made by novices. In smaller groups, experts are well distributed and expertise is transferred by intragroup communication. You can measure your distribution of expertise by the years of experience developers have, their experience with the product, and the influx of new developers.

The relative scarcity of expertise means some teams may not have highly experienced developers, and a high influx of newcomers reinforces the need to distribute expertise to less-experienced developers. The demand for expertise is high, but the supply is low. As a result of large numbers, communication tends to shift from interactive to demand based and indirect. When interaction is lost, questions can't be asked directly.

A few techniques can be used to transfer knowledge: small-group communication, documentation, presentations, training, and mentoring. Most are not well suited to use on large teams. For example, small-group (localized) communication and mentoring do not work well in large organizations. On the other hand, presentations can work in large organizations if the set of people who need the information is small. Online training and online video extend the set of people, although interaction with the speaker is lost.

Inability to Discover Best Practices

A particular team or person may get better results than are typical in the organization. This team or person may have discovered a best practice that can then be exploited by others. The problem is how to discover best practices when there is a large number of teams. If certain issues occur infrequently in a particular team but commonly across teams, best practices may not be discovered because the issue seems minor in isolation. In smaller organizations, publicizing the results outward and upward from a team can work, but it is much harder to do this on a large scale.

Lack of Upward Communication

In large organizations, upward communication is a problem. An executive can easily send an e-mail message to all employees, but handling replies from a large number of employees is quite another matter. Surveys are a mechanism you can use to get such wide feedback, but they structure and limit the replies. Upward communication through the management chain naturally loses information at each level.

Techniques of Communication

Microsoft, of course, faces the challenges of both size and complexity in developing software. At Microsoft, the following means of communication are used to address the issue of scale:

- E-mail
- Instant messaging
- Organizational mail groups and forums
- Subject mail groups and forums

- Organizational and product Web sites
- Subject Web sites
- Organizational blogs and wikis
- Subject blogs and wikis
- Online video clips of presentations and talks
- Online slide decks (on organizational, product, or subject sites)
- Online documents—designs, handbooks
- Online training
- Webcasts of meetings

When you think about it, all of these efforts try to reduce the drawbacks of size, but none of them really use size to an advantage. A subject distribution group or forum is the closest means of using size as an advantage: ask a question of an expert community and draw on its community members' knowledge for an answer. However, in practice, even these groups typically fall short of their potential.[1] The online preservation of information is good for reference purposes but falls short compared with being there in real time—you can't ask questions in the middle of a video, and a slide deck can't represent exactly what was said during the presentation.

In smaller teams, cross-pollination between members is effective. In less complex products, *pull* (seeking out knowledge) can be effective. In large, complex products, push techniques (broadcasting the knowledge) aren't effective due to the large amount of information that would need to be pushed.

Using Size as an Advantage

Size is not always a disadvantage but is often treated as one. One advantage of a large-scale project is that there are a lot of people with different experiences and expertise working on it together.

You can create a better system to reduce the communication problems that scale creates by innovating systems that support communicating information to appropriate subgroups and gathering information from large groups. Pay attention to the following aspects when creating effective communication systems:

- **Knowledge transfer**   You can form better connections between experts and novices to transfer knowledge. This also provides a learning mechanism for novices to pick up new skills and can be an adjunct to formal mentoring.

---

1 There is no guarantee of a timely answer, the group's information is not organized for reference, and the issue can get lost in volume of traffic.

- **Mining the crowd**   Use the techniques discussed in *The Wisdom of Crowds*[1] to gain useful information from internal as well as external partners.

Properties of a Good Communication Model

Three main properties of communication models address size: their overhead is distributed, they reduce the fire hose problem,[2] and they form new communication loops outside the top-down organizational hierarchy. Communication models serve a few major purposes:

- **Mining**   With models, you can gather information from a large number of people.
- **Knowledge transfer**   Models make it easier to connect expertise to those who need it.
- **Closing loops**   With models, you can connect concerns that have surfaced with those who can act on them.
- **Short-circuiting**   Models can provide out-of-band methods that bypass traditional hierarchy.

These are pull models that depend on participation. Often, including game or competitive aspects in a model increases its appeal. (See Chapter 5, "Using Productivity Games to Prevent Defects.") Using participation in such models as metrics for some of the more invisible values such as customer focus and quality can also be an incentive. You should make sure developers have time to participate in such efforts as well as have management support.

The sections that follow describe different means of addressing the issues outlined in the earlier section on communication problems. They address scale and complexity as well as geographical distribution of personnel.

Taxonomies

By using a categorization taxonomy, you can collect a large volume of information in a form amenable to statistical analysis as opposed to textual information, which requires manual introspection. (See Chapter 10, "Defect Taxonomies.") A taxonomy can help identify local good or bad practices. Taxonomies can also educate, describing areas that may not be considered otherwise.

There are several methods of generating a taxonomy, such as a folksonomy,[3] in which the set of categories is self-evolving from each individual's tagging (such as *http://del.icio.us* for social bookmarking or *wikipedia.org* for terminology), and other social networking techniques for networking information.

---

1 James Surowieki, *The Wisdom of Crowds* (New York: Anchor Books, 2005).

2 So much information you can't isolate what is important.

3 See *http://en.wikipedia.org/wiki/Folksonomy*

Organic Expertise Systems

Organic expertise systems provide a knowledge base to which self-selected groups of experts in an area can add pieces of information, which in turn are ranked by those using the knowledge. This is a combination of "Wisdom of Crowds" ranking, knowledge transfer of area experts, and lateral communication networks. Figure 19-1 shows an example of lateral advice and learning.

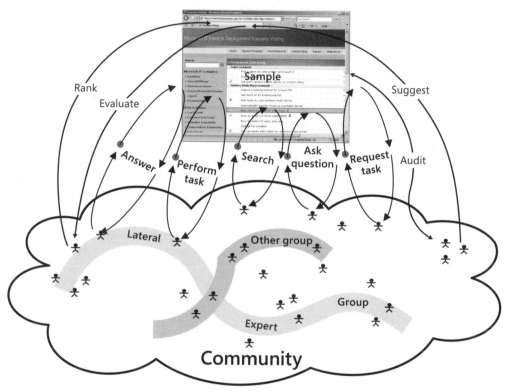

Figure 19-1 Lateral advice and learning

Quite a few useful variants of this model exist, as shown in Figure 19-1, depending on the particular need:

- The suggestion/evaluation arc can lead to action such as instituting a new best practice or improving/creating a tool—closing the loop.

- If the lateral groups are higher levels in the organizational hierarchy, rank-and-file suggestions/comments can be acted upon—short circuiting.

- Tasks can be distributed in the opposite direction, from a central group to the community to mine responses—improved self-hosting is an example.

- The community can suggest localized knowledge that may be of interest to disparate members of the community and that is edited into a useful form—community knowledge.

- The model of reviewers and critics (ranking reviewers) scales quite well on sites such as Amazon and e-Bay.

Size breaks down the communication of specialized knowledge. A Web site organized around areas of knowledge can form the needed connections across an organization to facilitate transfer of knowledge. Such a site would have a combination of features of message board and wiki sites. A site could be organized around a particular knowledge domain and have the following features:

- People can join the site as experts in the subject domain. This involves the responsibility of responding to requests from the general community.

- Members of the community can ask questions that are posted (list of current open issues), and experts are notified in some way (by e-mail or visiting the site). Members can indicate the urgency of their request.

- An expert can choose to answer the issue. Any expert may merely comment or indicate that another person is best to resolve the issue. Multiple experts may contribute to analyzing and responding to the issue.

- Other members of the community can weigh in on an open issue.

- When the issue is resolved, the initial questioner can rank the response as to its timeliness and usefulness.

- Answered issues are kept as browsable topics for members of the community to access.

- Additional topics of interest can be posted by experts and ranked by them.

- Community members can also suggest topics that the experts can evaluate. Useful topics can be added.

- Community members may choose to audit the site to be notified of issues being forwarded to experts and their responses. This can provide a means of learning about a new subject area and a means for mentoring. Experts could communicate with mentees as a group.

Some of these knowledge groups may be associated with tools or processes. Suggestions from the community can involve improvements that should be forwarded to the people working on the tool or those in charge of the process.

Participation in such groups could be measured and used as input to the review process. Answering questions, accepted suggestions, and the peer ranking of advice are possible metrics. By making participation a positive factor in performance reviews, you can encourage participation.

Measuring the extent to which the existence of the system improves quality is hard, as it is with any invisible issue. At best, you could measure indirect effects, but the indirect effects may have multiple causes. Logically, if used, communication systems should increase productivity and reduce errors caused by a lack of knowledge. Measurement of the quality and frequency of usage of the systems ends up being the best direct measure.

Legacy Code Reviews

As time goes by, code tends to grow and attention is often focused more on the code for new features than on legacy code. The people who originally wrote the code may have moved on to different areas. There are many opportunities for knowledge of legacy code, as well as domain expertise, to be lost as people move around in their careers. Finding and correcting defects in legacy code becomes more difficult and risky.

Typically, any new version of an application consists mostly of legacy code that may not take into account new customer needs, and so the code must be updated and revised. To distribute knowledge about legacy code, a variant of an organic expertise system could be created where files to be reviewed are prioritized and members of the community can sign up to review a file, make comments, and submit changes. The changes could be reviewed by the file owner. Members could indicate their areas of expertise, and files could be flagged with their expertise requirements.

Particular items to look for in a code review could be on the site associated with the issues the code involves[1] and general advice. Such items could be generated by experts in the various areas (could connect with knowledge groups). Acceptance of changes by the code owner could be reported for review purposes—the incentive to participate is that it indicates a concern for quality and collaboration on the part of the participant. You may discover great code reviewers on the basis of their ranking by the code owners who look at their changes and comments.

Prevention Tab

When a developer is correcting a defect, the knowledge of the problem, how it may have slipped through existing processes, and how it might be caught in the future may all be available for improving the process.

At Microsoft, we have added classifying and describing preventions to our defect tracking system so that developers can record the information while it is fresh in their minds and they can browse current suggestions to help them diagnose a defect. (See Chapter 14, "Prevention Tab.") The categorization of a prevention is a small subset of the detection and mitigation sections of the defect taxonomy (see Chapter 10). Adding more detail to the taxonomy reduces manual reading and interaction with the developer in the future. Popularity of a prevention may justify further investment in a tool, suggest improvements, or instigate

---

1 For example, security experts could provide a list of issues to look for in reviewing any code that involves privileged operations.

presentations/brown bags (informal presentations over lunch) to publicize the value of the tool. Improvement and increased use of a tool will reduce defects.

Closing the Loop After Release

At Microsoft, we have used the prevention tab to close a feedback loop between our sustained engineering (SE) team, which provides immediate support for defects reported in the Microsoft Windows operating system after it is released, and Windows development. Serious defects corrected by the SE team have prevention information specified. In a few months of usage, this information suggested how we should make improvements to our static code verification tools, security testing, and code review processes, among other areas.

Scenario Voting

With the Windows Vista operating system, scenario voting (see Chapter 15, "Scenario Voting") has been introduced. Prerelease users of Windows Vista can describe the quality and importance of hundreds of Windows usage scenarios. This provides invaluable early feedback to feature teams about how customers value a feature and how well it has been implemented.

Conclusion

As your organization grows in size, complexity, number of customers, number of new employees, or geographical distribution, communication problems will surface. Issues such as lack of transfer of knowledge to those who need it as well as information overload can be created. For example, most communication techniques that are used on smaller scales result in information inundation when used on a larger scale.

Some communication techniques can perform adequately at scale. One area of techniques involves abstracting information so that it can be analyzed en masse to discover problem areas or localized best practices. Another involves using domain (knowledge)–oriented sites to connect those who have the information or skill with those who need it. Domain-oriented sites are self-organizing, focus the audience to reduce its size, coordinate interaction between novices and experts, and support mentoring by auditing.

Chapter 20
Pulling It All Together

What is a system? A system is a network of interdependent components that work together to try to accomplish the aim of the system. A system must have an aim. Without an aim, there is no system. The aim of the system must be clear to everyone in the system. The aim must include plans for the future. The aim is a value judgment. (We are of course talking here about a man-made system.)
—W. Edwards Deming (1900–1993)

Software development, like other engineering or business processes, consists of smaller independent processes that together make up the overall system. Each process has different cost and resource structures, and all contribute to the success or failure of the overall system. In software development, the interdependence of individual systems affects overall system productivity and effectiveness. Because all the processes are interdependent, overemphasis on a single component or process in the system can affect the remainder of the system, leading to a net loss of efficiency through the entire system. This chapter explores techniques in defect detection, analysis, and prevention to demonstrate how to optimize a larger software development system. These techniques span disciplines and milestones in the development project, but all play a role in building quality processes, which will help you to build quality software.

The only way to achieve ideal throughput for a system is to investigate and address process issues from the perspective of the entire system. Problematic processes (that is, the slowest or least efficient components) must receive the necessary attention and investment to drive improvement and fashion them into coherent and complete processes. Changes to processes may include splitting a single larger process into several smaller ones, and staffing them appropriately. Alternatively, overall improvement may come by adding quality verification steps to an otherwise quick process. Then the team evaluates the system again and identifies and addresses any problem processes. This cycle of improvement repeats until no one process stands out as problematic and the system functions smoothly. Unfortunately, achieving this ideal throughput does not guarantee success. However, it can enable a development team to produce high-quality code at a more predictable cost.

Traditional manufacturing organizations were the first to apply these kinds of process improvement techniques, as taught by W. Edwards Deming[1] and others. However, traditional manufacturing processes differ from software significantly. Traditional manufacturing produces one object repeatedly, whereas a software project produces one product through a lengthy development process. Even with this difference, the interdependencies of individual processes in software development behave in many ways similarly to steps of traditional manufacturing processes. Analysis and improvement of the entire system can provide benefits to software projects as well.

---

1 W. E. Deming, *Out of the Crisis* (Cambridge, MA: MIT Press, 2000).

Understanding Standards and Conventions

A key part of the entire system is that all processes in the system play a role in defining the success of the system. For the entire system to function at its best, all subprocesses must share a basic set of definitions and standards. Chapter 7, "Balanced Scorecard," provides a detailed approach to creating a system of metrics for your organization. The standards and conventions you create and use will determine how successfully you are able to measure and compare different components of the system. Before any effective communication or work can take place, a set of standards and conventions must exist. The history of trains provides an illustration.

Trains, automobiles, and "PF"

In any organization, a lack of standards places huge limitations on the communications between groups and drives inefficient behaviors. Standards in your organization, especially across subprocesses, can provide better cooperation and communication, leading to higher efficiency of the entire system.

Take, for example, rail gauge used for train tracks. Undoubtedly, many factors contributed to the strength of the U.S. economy during the industrial age, but high among them were trains. Rail systems spread like a web across the country through the 19th century and into the 20th century, providing a means of transport of raw materials to manufacturers and finished goods to consumers across the nation and to seaports for distribution abroad.

The impact the rail systems had on the United States cannot be underestimated. Long before interstate highways reached across the landscape, trains were an incredibly effective method of transporting goods. Trains were so effective largely because the tracks were built using a *standard gauge* rail so that all types of boxcars and compartments could travel on all railroads. Companies doing business by rail either adapted to the common standard gauge or perished along with their own standards. In software development, a standard creates a make-or-break situation. If components of the system do not adhere to a standard, they are unable to function successfully in the system. Dictionary.com defines *standard* as

> *Something considered by an authority or by general consent as a basis of comparison.*[1]

Examples of standards include the coding language used, the code versioning and management system, and the desired hardware standards. Some teams attempting to write in a different language or work against a different hardware specification would not be successful interacting with the larger project.

On the other hand, consider the fact that the custom of driving on the right side or left side of the road differs in countries around the world. Depending on where you are, you can successfully navigate from one place to another using the right or left side of the road and, in most cases, arrive safely. Countries and peoples have chosen to apply this common practice to

---

1   Dictionary.com, "Standard," *http://dictionary.reference.com/browse/standard.*

provide safe, passable roads, though the practice varies from place to place. Whereas with trains using different rail gauges would have blocked progress, the *convention* of driving on the left or right side of the road is a seemingly arbitrary choice and the differences are inconsequential. Conventions are also vital in software development but differ from standards in that your project and project team define them as a method for working more easily together. Dictionary.com defines *convention* as

> a rule, method, or practice established by usage.[1]

A convention may define how to format code in source files to simplify the code review process. Another convention may be the communication of breaking changes between dependent component teams.

The problem, of course, occurs when separate organizations adopt different terms or concepts and apply them as a standard or convention in their own work. Inevitably, a new project forces these groups together, and they must iron out common ground. This process may take years and can lead to significant instability in shared or dependent processes. Instability can lead to reduced productivity and throughput of the entire system.

For example, not too long ago, we attended a planning meeting where a group of engineers was meeting to nail down some details of a new test automation system. The topic of the day was how to define and account for test results. In minutes, opposing camps were drawn. One favored "test case results" as the base unit for summary reports, and they defined a variation as the hardware configuration around the test case. They viewed the hardware configuration as incidental to the test case. The other group argued that "variations" were fundamental to the system and demanded that they be the fundamental base unit for results; the result must account for hardware configuration. The argument waged for a few minutes before one engineer made a suggestion: "Why not just use PFs?" A *PF* would define a single pass or fail and act as the base unit for results accounting. It would be independent from either a single test case or a single hardware configuration. This abstract label allowed both camps to have a standard measure. Additionally, to summarize a related group of results, he proposed a "PF rollup" to allow teams the ability to roll any set of results together to aid in aggregate reporting. Although simplistic, the solution met the needs of both parties because they could continue to define their test passes as they had already done in their previous systems and successfully work together on a new project.

The point is, competing groups often desire the same thing, and the terminology gets in the way of successful operation and communication. Fundamental to focusing on the development system instead of the individual processes is identifying and moving past these terminology issues. This includes setting common standards and agreeing to conventions for all different parts of the development process.

---

1   Dictionary.com, "Convention," *http://dictionary.reference.com/browse/convention.*

Common Results Criteria

Perhaps the first important standard for an organization to define is results. Differing perspectives on how results are measured and handled create rifts in the overall system and complicate the already challenging process of shipping software.

Large projects struggle when the results and tracking data from each component differ from others. Although teams must have some leeway for working in their own groups, some fundamental metrics must exist across all component teams for a coherent tracking strategy. For example, authoring specifications and design documents may have a set of results that are measurable (specifics around peer review, standard template application, threat models, and so forth), but these metrics are not all equally applicable during the development and quality assurance phases. However, teams must treat metrics consistently if they are applicable across multiple phases of the development cycle (such as the counting of lines of code, counting of features, or handling of defects).

Again, inefficiencies arise when a single piece of a larger system treats its results differently from how other teams treat their results. An example is a testing team that marks negative test cases as "expected failures" in its test system, which effectively means that a test pass completes when there are n pass results and m fail results. Aside from the dangers of attempting to hand off these tests to a new owner, this practice risks alienating other teams and other processes that expect 100 percent passing rates as their criteria for success. Another example, suggested by a colleague, points out assumptions made about the quality of testing. Some teams may erroneously choose to measure the "doneness" of the test effort by the number of tests. Whereas one team may have 10,000 test cases, another may have only 500. The team with 10,000 cases must not assume that a team with 500 cases lacks quality or has not completed its test effort. The definition of success in this example should come from another metric other than just test case quantity.

An organization must standardize on the key metrics that drive its product. Each component team in the organization must uniformly apply and report on key metrics for the larger organization to measure their status and progress effectively. For example, how lines of code are counted, or how churn is calculated. The answers to questions like these can affect some of the analysis techniques discussed in Chapter 9, "Using Simulation and Modeling for Organizational Innovation." Without standard criteria, no system can perform optimally. It wastes either time, money, or both.

Keep in mind that teams can also drive their own metrics and reporting structure if they identify metrics that are beneficial to their work. Teams are most successful working with metrics when the data falls naturally out of the work process. Teams also function better when they can modify the processes and procedures to best meet their work style. Excess or difficult-to-implement mandated policies can hinder success if the work to gather the metrics outweighs the benefits to the team. Careful planning is necessary to establish the basic metrics on which the larger project management team relies. The metrics should encompass effort, cost, and quality and must be consistent across the organization but leave space for teams to define their own work styles.

Everyone Plays a Role

After standards and conventions are in place, each part of the overall process can begin to perform and measure its function. Expectations and results should be clear, and the work of producing software can move forward with its best chances of success. Key to this is the belief that all parts of the system contribute to the quality of the product. The next few sections discuss some of the key elements surrounding different phases of the development cycle. Each role can contribute to the quality of the product, and part of that contribution may include changes in process ownership.

Quality Assurance

Project management must not expect the test team to "drive" quality into the product. If so, the remainder of the system has failed to contribute, and some of the best-quality techniques are lost. Instead of viewing the test team as resources to drive quality into a product, view it as the quality assurance team, verifying the quality of the product already in place.

Changing this perspective raises questions about many of the standard definitions in use in the industry. Many believe that the test organization creates or drives the quality of a software product. This theory implicitly assumes that the other components in the system do not contribute to the quality of the system. Because the objective is to improve the system as a whole, improving the efficiency and output quality from each process provides hope for finding bottlenecks and potential improvements. This shifts the focus of test resources from testing to quality assurance (QA). The QA group can also focus on more than just defect detection and can contribute to overall process improvement. Just the name change implies a change of role, from a single point to a system of quality in which QA plays a key role.

When shipping software, business tradeoffs must be made that often lead to concerns regarding the return on investment of quality assurance team resources. When push comes to shove, companies must balance decisions regarding best practices or ideal investments against the costs of delivering goods. This chapter cannot possibly cover every practice or technique that quality assurance engineers may employ, but some require special attention.

Portfolio Management

Clearly, more types of testing exist than can be listed here. Each has its own value proposition and cost. Most important, though, each type of testing can expose only certain types of defects. There may be overlap, but no one testing methodology will detect all classes of defects. For example, stress testing will not likely find defects that scenario testing can easily find, and vice versa. Similarly, code inspections often produce the highest yields per invested time, but they are a poor method to use to find race conditions. Your project must implement a wide-ranging number of methods to find the most defects possible and ship the highest-quality product possible.

This concept in quality assurance is similar to handling financial investments: diversification. Diversification of a portfolio reduces risk of loss. In financial terms, that means loss of money. In testing, that means defects detected by end users after the release of the product. Known for his pioneering work in modern portfolio theory, Harry Markowitz[1] describes portfolio management in terms of risk, correlation, and diversification. Understanding the correlation of specific securities to others allows a security strategist to create a portfolio that is more resilient to fluctuations in specific portions of the stock market. This analysis of the securities' past performance as well as the predictions of experienced analysts can identify good investment opportunities. Built on top of these would be a strategy to diversify across securities that do not correlate to each other because companies that correlate may compete in similar businesses or may share some other common thread, such as locale or manufacturing dependency. Dips in one company's stock often coincide with dips in companies that share correlative relationships as well. Yet the market as a whole does not often feel the impact of a dip in a single industry as greatly. Thus, diversification across differing businesses or other related data points leads to greater stability in investments.

Defect detection, analysis, and prevention techniques each succeed at identifying specific classes of defects but miss others. For a quality assurance team to be the most successful, it must analyze available techniques to understand how successful those techniques have been historically, similar to the analysis of past performance of specific investments. Understanding which techniques produced the best return on investment helps the team in planning future work. The team must then allocate investments in techniques that best detect or prevent the range of defects in the product. These techniques fit best when distributed across the different phases and roles in the product development cycle. Similar to the methodology used in investments, techniques that correlate too much (or overlap in their ability to detect or prevent defects) risk missing categories of defects going to the customer.

Diversification of quality assurance techniques not only aids in producing a quality product but also affects the management of the overall process. Identifying new and different techniques as successful, the team may need to expand or shrink existing processes and roles to incorporate the new techniques into the overall system. Work in individual processes may change, but the overall system can then produce higher-quality product.

---

1   Wikipedia, "Harry Markowitz," *http://en.wikipedia.org/wiki/Harry_Markowitz*.

Automation vs. Manual Testing

An age-old debate at Microsoft, the effectiveness of test automation versus manual testing, continues even today. Here are some additional points to consider in this argument.

Automation can benefit nearly every aspect of software testing. Automated tests can exercise great ranges of code paths that are not easily accessible to test engineers working manually. Examples including API testing, code coverage, risk analysis, stress, and long-haul testing come to mind. Beyond that, manual testing cannot replicate the scale at which a team can deploy, rerun, manage, and maintain automated tests with the same kind of return on investment. The best business sense in nearly every case prescribes automated testing tools and procedures. This perspective is easy to understand when automated tests can run repeatedly, or at night, and not require a dedicated engineer.

How Much Will You Pay to Automate?

A few years ago, we managed a few small teams whose testing area required a lot of manual plugging and unplugging of devices. A senior engineer was assigned to meet with us and our test leads to help identify methods by which we could improve our testing. Upon reviewing our test plans and procedures, he pointed out to us how little automation we were using for working with devices. We agreed, and shared our frustration about the length of time it took us to complete a test pass. His agitation was becoming apparent, and he asked what we were going to do about it. We explained that we had researched options that were available to us, but that the costs to build or acquire automatically controlled switching devices were high and had not been approved in the budget. His bellowing response sticks with me still, "If I need to go to Bill [Gates] directly and ask for $5 million, I'll do it!" His opinion on the best course of action was clear: we needed to automate.

In reality, the math was on his side. We were paying 20 engineers each about $60,000 per year. At that rate, it takes less than a year to hit the first million dollars of that $5 million investment. To a business trying to keep costs down, it always appears that automation is the best solution.

However, manual testing carries so much more context than automated testing does. Although there have been many advances in screen scraping and other techniques, there is no match for the depth of perception that can be applied by an experienced test engineer. A good engineer can quickly notice small errors in display, color shift, or text clipping even when the specific code under test does not contain the defect. Instead, engineers must actually interact with the system and must perform actions that users will perform. This kind of controlled effort yields some of the best user experience bugs, which can be resolved, thus leading to the best-quality product.

Finding the value of manual testing

The Windows Vista operating system team established a separate small team that installed the new build of Microsoft Windows each day and consistently performed a set of test cases that mapped to real user experience. The team published its results as a "self-host" score within hours of the build being released. (*Self-host* is a term that refers to individual engineers running the latest build of the product on their own workstations.) By reviewing these results, other engineers in Windows could easily ascertain whether installing the new build was advisable.

Bugs found by this small manual testing team were aggressively driven and fixed to permit the rest of the engineers to remain productive day to day. These defects were not limited to the specific cases listed in the test plan but also included other related functionality that would likely have been missed by automation. The "self-host" test team quickly became an indispensable part of the Windows Vista ship cycle, allowing more engineers to stay productive and run the product on their own workstations as much as possible. The tradeoff that was made to have a small team of manual test engineers helped prevent days of frustration on the part of thousands of other engineers across Windows because they had information on whether a build would hinder their ability to work and whether they could instead wait for another build. The team was small relative to the size of the project, but on smaller projects, perhaps one engineer fills this same role. Just a couple of hours of work may be enough to ensure that the product builds are ready for distribution to the remainder of the team.

In the end, the cost of the seemingly "inefficient" manual testers helped improve the efficiency of the whole system. The return on the small investment was huge. There is a place for manual testing, and sometimes taking a broader perspective helps to identify it.

Interoperability

In testing large-scale software systems, another large investment involves defining and executing the interoperability scenarios for your product. Now, in the era of the Internet, most software systems have many other systems with which they interact. Unfortunately, overworked managers can pressure engineers to push some aspects of interoperability testing onto the back burner, then off the stove altogether. In the end, teams perform sanity checks to ensure that one system works with another, but they are unable to do thorough and exhaustive testing.

This limited testing can be explained easily as a matter of scale: there just are not enough resources (or time) to cover all the possible interactions that could exist. This is true of third-party driver testing on new versions of Windows, just as it is true of testing every Web page on new versions of Windows Internet Explorer; there are just too many permutations and possibilities. Often, these missed cases can turn up later as security exploits or significant public relations issues.

Although there is no panacea for this problem, many creative approaches can address the key issues behind it. Often, a technology owner will invest heavily in testing that technology alone and testing it in the bounds of how customers may interact with that technology. Therein lies the problem: the defect may exist in the interaction of multiple technologies. For example, USB may function properly under most cases, but after the computer has suspended and resumed, it may lose track of a device or may lose some other functionality. The team for USB may have neglected to consider power management concerns during their original planning for the testing of USB. Moreover, the problem can be even more nuanced. Device driver samples may not actually contain properly written power management code. This, of course, results in other device driver authors suffering the same fate and more customers experiencing problems.

One solution is to step outside the bounds of the technology and identify actions that span multiple technologies that the user will undertake. This creates a kind of end-to-end scenario a user might perform using your system. Back to the USB example: A user may plug in a storage device, view the data on the device, and then suspend the system. While the system is down, a user moves the storage device elsewhere, modifies or adds data, but restores the device to the original system before the system resumes. After the system resumes, what is the expected state of the data? Does the system assume the cached data is correct because it recognizes the same storage device? Does the new data appear when browsed through the interface?

Multiple technologies are at work here, all of which must be included as methods for USB to interact with other systems, such as storage, power management, plug-and-play, system cache, and performance, among others. Identifying these scenarios requires some imagination, which takes creative people and time. Inevitably, a resource-constrained organization makes the tradeoff to get some easy work done now instead of investing in "thinking" time on the part of the engineers. This investment appears difficult to make, but time spent thinking through these complex interactions can help reduce the incidence of customers finding these issues first.

Stress and Long-Haul Testing

Caffeine has undoubtedly aided the drive to ship multiple versions of Windows over the years. However, perhaps even more addictive to the release management team has been its daily stress report. Each day, literally for years, the stress team has attended the daily "warteam" meetings and reported on the results of the stress run overnight. (The "warteam" is the group of engineers and managers who meet to discuss project status and progress. They make decisions and drive efforts to ship high-quality product on time.)

The stress process consists of dozens, perhaps hundreds, of individual test applications created to run essentially forever on a Windows-based system. The stress harness launches all these test applications on a system and runs them as long as the system can respond, or until a user reclaims the computer for other use the following day. The purpose of the stress system is to ensure that the subsystems of Windows could survive under the strain across hundreds of systems running the same types and numbers of tests. Typically, a stress run is completed in a day (or perhaps over a weekend), and the results are dutifully reported to release management. This report has been so consistent, and so reliable in its delivery, that it has become one of the key indicators of system health. It is almost unfair to mention the stress system without mentioning the heroes who come to work early every day, triage untold numbers of failures, and prepare that report. It is truly an impressive endeavor.

A suite of stress tests can be a valuable insight into the stability and reliability of any application or system when kept in perspective. Like any other approach applied toward quality assurance, stress can detect only specific categories of defects. Therein lies the challenge with any process: it can't drive all behaviors; it must be evaluated along with other inputs.

Comparatively, *long-haul* testing is another method that can add to your broader perspective. Long-haul testing differs from stress testing in intensity and in timeline. In many other ways, though, they are similar. With long-haul testing, systems are set up running a set of scenario-based or real-world test applications that exercise specific code paths but do not overly strain the system. These tests continue to execute for days or even weeks in attempts to identify memory leaks or other defects related to time. Some defects regarding counter rollovers take many days to find. In the USB area, developers assigned counters to start at high values in debug builds to identify these types of errors earlier in the testing cycle.

Both stress and long-haul testing are defect detection methods that can help identify different types of defects in the product. They may be applied to different types of projects in different ways, but they both are parts of the greater software development process that should be planned for and analyzed as part of the greater system. Each type of testing brings with it specific resource and reporting requirements. The proper scheduling and consuming of the data help drive product quality and keep the overall system in working order.

Code Development

As much as the quality assurance team, the development staff holds the reins for quality software. They must focus on both translating the needs of the customer into the software and writing the best code possible. Customer requirements can create a wide-ranging set of constraints that add difficulty, but the effort made up front to ensure that developers write quality code yields benefits to the entire development process.

A key drive in improving any business system is to evaluate and improve a single aspect of the overall process at a time, but this cannot be done at the expense of the rest of the system. Nevertheless, when metrics drive managers to improve only their own process, the overall system can suffer. The resulting decisions focus exclusively on reducing the work or effort required to meet the obvious objective: complete the code. Some experienced managers believe that developers must focus exclusively on writing code and that effort spent on noncoding efforts contributes to inefficiency. This is not true. Quality efforts performed by developers always contribute to overall code quality and system performance, which improves schedules and reduces production costs.

Unfortunately, improving only single parts of the overall process precludes many of the investments to aid in improving quality of the code during any particular phase of the development cycle. Some of the investments available in the coding phase are described in the following sections. Often, though, when development teams are challenged to implement some of these techniques, they either balk or implement the systems only partially. This resistance most likely is rooted in the teams' desire to optimize their own part of the process, sacrificing the quality and efficiency of the entire system.

Unit Tests

Often, as part of their development work, developers write small utilities that help them discover whether the code functions as expected. These utilities, or *unit tests*, validate a specific code path and are very small in scope. They provide a basis for validating the code under development, but after being completed, they are often lost or forgotten. The developer may or may not check in the unit test code with the other source code. Unfortunately, developers seldom build or run these tools again after their initial use.

As the development phase of the product cycle is ending and formal test development has begun, these unit tests can play an important role in aiding the quality assurance team's work of developing formal tests. Not only is the code itself a great example for both experienced and learning engineers of how the code should behave, it is a great starting point in the design and development of more complete test systems as well. Additionally, test resources are free to invest in additional defect detection techniques that are more complex, such as end-to-end scenario testing. Finally, these tests provide the fastest regression test possible for code changes resulting from defect repairs because of their small size and scope. Accordingly, developers and quality assurance must give unit tests a more formal status as part of the quality system. Development leads and managers should require their developers to create and run unit tests, and quality assurance engineers should incorporate them into the standard regression test suite. As mentioned earlier, the quality assurance team must manage a portfolio of test techniques, and including unit tests provides another valuable asset.

Sharing the unit tests provides numerous benefits, as described earlier, but also demonstrates a useful redistribution of work. Unit test development is a great example of how retooling processes in a system can help optimize the entire system. Moving work from one bottlenecked resource (quality assurance) onto another resource will aid in the product being higher quality, allowing the overall process to run more smoothly, and hopefully helping to reduce ship cycle lengths.

Agile Techniques

Agile techniques, although relatively new, can provide teams an added boost in productivity and quality through the development phase of the product cycle. They can also help both enhance the quality assurance organization's work and improve the quality of the output from the development phase. When evaluating the success or failure of the entire system, each part must invest in efforts that help improve the quality of the entire system.

Even more valuable than simple unit tests is a more rigorous test-driven process such as Test-Driven Development.[1] Test-Driven Development forces a more disciplined approach to development, centering on writing the unit tests for each piece of code before writing the code itself. By following the cyclical pattern of writing tests, writing code, and testing code, teams can make small steps and consistent progress. Development continues only as each test progresses from failing to passing. The wealth of up-to-date information that these functional tests provide is another valuable asset that quality assurance engineers can use in a quality portfolio.

This, among other agile development techniques, cannot fully be covered in this section but is worthy of mention. The primary difficulty that teams face in implementing agile techniques comes in the form of partial adoption. Often, teams find it easy to follow the daily meeting model of a SCRUM project but then do not apply other aspects of SCRUM such as sprints (short programming cycles) or minimal planning time. The entire process can aid in the development of some software projects but provides limited help when used in a piecemeal fashion. The same is true of Extreme Programming, where teams pick and choose the aspects of the practice they find easiest to implement (such as pair programming) but again ignore other aspects of the methodology such as short iterations or unit testing. Before attempting to claim use of agile techniques, ensure that the investment covers the full process, not just the name. Otherwise, you are not learning from or gaining from alternative approaches.

Threat Models

In 2002, Michael Howard wrote *Writing Secure Code*, which outlines a method for identifying potential security issues in a systematic way. These *threat models* became the basis of a multi-month stand-down of the development processes in Windows to drive for security of the product.

Threat models provide a schema for any organization to evaluate their product for possible security threats. This technique, among others available, creates quality in the product earlier in the development process.

---

1   K. Beck, *Test Driven Development* (Boston, MA: Addison-Wesley, 2003).

Code Inspections

Few researchers today would argue against implementing some form of code review process. Beginning with Michael Fagan,[1] the effectiveness of reviewing software as a means of removing defects is shown in study after study. You may wonder why there is continued discussion on the topic of whether to use code reviews. The answer is simple: Engineers do not use a formal process for conducting a review of the software. As a result, reviews are not effective.

The next step may be to ponder why there is no formal process. It is not a result of a lack of understanding of methodologies or dissension on the part of the research experts. With minor differences, research has provided a list of practices found to increase effectiveness, yet few engineers use such practices. For example, checklists are highly effective at focusing a process.

A likely cause for the underuse of review techniques, and often a cause of their misuse, is the intellectual challenge associated with effective techniques. Code reviews may be the single most intellectually challenging activity in software engineering. With practice, engineers can eliminate entire classes of defects from their software and release code that is orders of magnitude better than typically possible.[2] This section describes the use of several techniques to improve the performance of the inspection process.

Background   Michael Fagan is credited with creating one of the first formal software inspection techniques, but a quick search of scholarly journals indicates that the concept was not new even to him. Process descriptions include the concept of review as far back as 50 years ago. The apparent lack of penetration into daily practice may arise from the intellectual challenge, as was postulated earlier, or from the manually intensive nature of the process, or even from a lack of education. The practices described herein reflect the writings of Watts Humphrey[3] and attempt to provide a step-by-step implementation guide as well as the rationale for deploying an effective review practice rather than merely one that meets the definition. Three different terms are used to label three different processes.

The first term is *personal review*. Humphrey uses the term *code review*, but that term is overloaded and means too many things to different people. A personal review is a process of formal code inspection implemented by the author of the code in an attempt for the author to find and fix as many defects as possible. In this section, the term *review* by itself implies personal review of the code.

1   M. E. Fagan, "Design and Code Inspections to Reduce Errors in Program Development," *IBM Systems Journal* 15, no. 3 (1976): 182–211.

2   N. Davis and J. Mullaney, *The Team Software Process in Practice: A Summary of Recent Results* (Pittsburgh, PA: Software Engineering Institute, Carnegie-Mellon University, 2003).

3   W. S. Humphrey, *Managing the Software Process* (Reading, MA: Addison-Wesley, 1989); *A Discipline for Software Engineering* (Reading, MA: Addison-Wesley, 1995); *Winning with Software: An Executive Strategy* (Reading, MA: Addison-Wesley, 2003).

The next term is *peer inspection*. Again, the term used here is slightly different from the standard definition. The Capability Maturity Model (CMM) uses the term *peer review*, but the change made here is once again an attempt to avoid confusion. The term *inspection* always implies a defect discovery process that includes one or more individuals who did not author the code.

The final term is *walkthrough*. This term indicates a process not specifically designed to discover defects but rather meant to educate an audience.

Personal Reviews   The concept of a personal check of your work is not new to software. The idea is simple: find as many defects as possible early in the process. The key to this idea—and in fact all of the presented techniques—is formalization of the process. Engineers seem to believe that formal processes will somehow stifle creativity, which may or may not be true. There are some practices that do not need innovation in the execution of the process. A code review is one such process. Researchers have provided a set of techniques that result in high quality, so direct implementation will provide great benefits.

Deming[1] is often quoted as having said, "If you can't describe what you are doing as a process, you don't know what you're doing." Humphrey[2] defines one of the simplest and most effective review processes. The difficulty in implementation is caused by the apparent inefficiencies in the process. However, you must realize that the intent of a review is not to simply read the code. It is to find as many defects as possible as early as possible.

The process of a code review is simple: examine the code, correct the defects, and review the corrections. Notice that this is a three-step process, with the reviewing step separated from the repair of the code. Many people attempt to review and fix simultaneously. This is a mistake. The mindsets for defect discovery and code creation are very different. Steve McConnell provides an excellent rationale for the separation of defect discovery from code creation in his book *Code Complete*.[3] The process for creating code, or, facetiously, the process of creating defects, is antithetical to the process of finding defects. Separating the process into two different steps provides a clear mindset. It allows you to focus and get into a state of flow, as defined by psychologists. Csikszentmihalyi[4] describes the need for clear goals and focus as components of flow. Separating the defect discovery step from the defect repair step allows for the focus required for maximum effectiveness.

The process of examining the code is also somewhat counterintuitive: The idea is not to find every possible defect, but only those that are most troublesome. You review each line looking for one and only one type of defect, and you identify the existence of the defect without attempting to fix it. This is the point in the process where the use of checklists is helpful. Based on historical data of the types of errors developers make, a checklist is created that then directs the examination activities. Humphrey suggests using a one-page checklist. The Pareto

---

1 W. E. Deming, *Out of the Crisis* (Cambridge, MA: MIT Press, 2000).

2 W. S. Humphrey, *A Discipline for Software Engineering* (Reading, MA: Addison-Wesley, 1995).

3 S. McConnell, *Code Complete: A Practical Handbook of Software Construction* (Redmond, WA: Microsoft Press, 1993).

4 M. Csikszentmihalyi, *Flow: The Psychology of Optimal Experience* (New York: Harper and Row, 1990).

principle suggests that the top 20 percent of all defects will cause 80 percent of all problems. This should be the target in this step. Of course, with practice you can aspire to higher yields.

A notable difference between a formalized process and an informal practice is that the formalized process uses the concept of measurement. For example, for the code examination step the checklist is created using a historical view of all defects and is the first point in the code review process when data is required. An easy method to collect this data is simply to keep track of all defects found in any testing activity. However, there is a problem associated with this approach. Testing is a logical process designed to find systematic mistakes. For example, you may do a boundary value analysis of all program inputs and design a test to determine program response at the boundaries. This finds errors in program logic, not simple mistakes. Testing is not designed to find simple program mistakes; for example, there is no test case that finds all divide by zero errors in a program, or all null pointer de-references, and so on. Such errors are found as side effects of logical tests. As a result, the simplest and most insidious errors often go undetected. The checklist, on the other hand, is most effective when it is targeted at finding the defects not typically found in tests. Simple coding mistakes are the cause of most in-use failures and are also the easiest to find by using code reviews.

If you create a good checklist and execute the process effectively, about 200 lines of code can be reviewed in an hour.[1] This may seem like an abhorrently slow rate. If the checklist has 15 to 20 items in it, you spend only 3 to 4 minutes on each item. Two hundred lines of code, without comments, are about 4 pages, so you are working at a rate of less than a page per minute. Because a detailed understanding of the code is required, a page per minute may be too fast. The review rate becomes the second data element of the process. Measuring the rate provides instant feedback on the effectiveness of the process.

One mistake engineers often make is to try to review for multiple items at once. Although this seems like an optimization, it does hurt process flow. In addition, people typically can keep only 7, plus or minus 2, items in their heads at a time. A checklist of 15 to 20 items would require the reviewer to make multiple passes anyway, so it is best to optimize the process to look for just a single item at a time. That does not mean that reviewers should ignore defects of a different type if they happen to see one while looking for a specific item; they can instead make a quick note to document the error and then move on.

Another issue that each individual needs to address is the concept of online versus hard copy reviews. With hard copy, the reviewer can easily highlight errors without attempting to fix the problem. It forces the separation of detection and repair. However, it also requires the reviewer to use more paper than otherwise necessary. By using tools, such as those available in Microsoft Office Word, reviewers can highlight errors quickly. After all of the errors are highlighted, the repair can begin. After the errors are repaired, each repaired item is reinspected to verify correct implementation. If only a few lines of code are changed, the reviewer can invert the process to check each line for every element in the checklist. This will not significantly affect the flow because you would not expect many lines to be reinspected.

---

1   W. S. Humphrey, *A Discipline for Software Engineering* (Reading, MA: Addison-Wesley, 1995).

The process described here may seem difficult. In fact, it is probably different from the process most people use, so it will be difficult to follow at first. However, most people quickly learn the routine and get very good at reviewing the code for one and only one defect type at a time. This has a side benefit: Often when a defect of a particular type is found in test, more of the same exist in the code. When the testing process reports a defect, the engineer can quickly review the code for more instances of that type. If reviewers become proficient at reviewing 200 lines of code, taking only 3 to 4 minutes per defect type, the review rate for a single error type is 3,000 to 4,000 lines of code per hour. This makes it possible to quickly eliminate from the code repeated error types in the test process.

You may think that the preceding process is expensive. The chapter on stochastic models provides a detailed analysis of the costs and benefits. As a quick calculation, the cost is 5 hours per 1,000 lines of code (KLOC). Studies indicate that 20 to 40 defects per KLOC enter the test phases. In addition, 60 percent to 80 percent of the defects can be found by a good inspection process, so between 12 and 32 defects can be removed in 5 hours at a rate of 2.4 to 6.4 defects per hour. Unit testing is capable of finding 1 to 2 defects per hour at a yield of about 50 percent. Clearly, code reviews require less effort, and hence increase productivity, to find defects. Additionally, because reviews find the defects that are most difficult for test to find, a good review process should help to optimize the end-to-end productivity. For more details, see the stochastic models associated with code reviews.

Team Inspections   Team inspections are similar to personal reviews in that they are collections of individual reviews. The difference lies in the fact that someone else provides the service. This results in the problem of determining how many people to involve in a team inspection. Some studies show that incremental benefits accrue for each new person added to the team up to a total of 10 for such processes as requirements inspections. For most other purposes, three or four inspectors will suffice.

To determine the total number of inspectors, calculate the combined yield and work to the required level of quality. For example, if each inspector finds 50 percent of the total defects remaining, and the team desires an 80 percent yield out of the inspection process, three inspectors are required because the first inspector finds 50 percent, the second finds 50 percent of the remaining 50 percent, and the third finds 50 percent of the remaining 25 percent, for a total yield of approximately 87 percent. This assumes each inspector is independent of the others and that all are equally capable. The actual yield should be measured and compared with the theoretical yield to determine the degree to which the underlying assumptions are met.

To estimate the remaining defects after inspection, a method known as *capture–recapture* can be used. The concept behind this practice comes from the means used to estimate animal populations in the wild. Figure 20-1 shows a Venn diagram highlighting the method. The first inspector finds 50 percent of the total population of defects based on the historical yields. The second inspector independently finds 50 percent, of which 25 percent should overlap the first inspector. The third inspector finds 50 percent of the total defects, of which 37.5 percent overlap the previous two inspectors. The calculation is straightforward at this point and can be done a variety of ways as a cross-check against the estimated defects remaining.

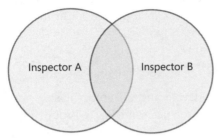

Figure 20-1 Good inspectors, functioning separately, will find some of the same defects.

The following equation is the Lincoln–Peterson method for population estimation.

$$N = \frac{n_1 n_2}{m}$$

where N is the total population count, n_1 is the amount discovered by count 1, n_2 is the amount discovered by count 2, and m is the amount discovered by both. A variety of equivalent calculations can be used depending on the number of inspectors. The degree to which different calculation methods match the actual inspection metrics determines the degree to which the stated underlying independence of inspectors is met.

Inspections should be done at some point before the test process. Test is typically the bottleneck, and Goldratt[1] points out that the way to improve process performance is to eliminate defects before the bottleneck. The question as to the exact placement in the process depends on the checklists used in the inspection process. If each individual inspector creates the checklists, doing the inspection right after the personal reviews is probably optimal. If, however, the team creates an aggregate inspection checklist based on data for the entire team, it is probably best to do the inspection just before unit test. Again, see Chapter 9 on stochastic modeling to determine the optimal placement of an inspection process.

One final note on team inspections: Unless the individual developers are disciplined enough to implement personal code reviews properly, team inspections will not likely succeed. The skills and discipline required to do team inspections include commitments from the involved team members to both do the inspections and then follow through with the changes in behavior required to improve the quality of the code.

---

1 E. Goldratt and J. Cox, *The Goal: A Process of Ongoing Improvement* (Great Barrington, MA: North River Press, 1992).

Group Walkthroughs   Group walkthroughs are very different from reviews and inspections because the process is not primarily motivated by defect discovery. Typically, the author presents a design or code section to a group for the purpose of educating the group. Feedback may be provided, but the process is not formalized. Often, a walkthrough is wrongly used in place of an inspection, and as a result, not many defects are found. Walkthroughs should be used only for educational purposes.

Program Management

Program management plays an important role in developing and shipping software, as much as development and quality assurance do. Program managers are key to producing a plan that maps the user's needs, wants, and concerns to actions to be undertaken by development. Defects in this part of the process are usually harder to find, but they are the costliest to repair if they make it into the product. As a result, improved techniques and processes early will play an important role in the quality of the final product.

Systemwide Approach

The program manager role can vary broadly, even in a single organization. These engineers often plan and help create the systems and processes by which daily development, building, and testing are performed. As a result, decisions made by program managers can affect not only the product itself but also the overall development process. In the case of the development process, the customers are the development and quality assurance teams, and the processes put into place must both meet their needs and optimize for the best work from all parties.

Optimization for all parties cannot be done correctly unless the procedures that make up the engineers' workflow are all drafted as an entire system, not as individual pieces. The same problems that afflict optimization of one segment of a system over other segments apply here as well. The processes around source code management, check-in permissions, build procedures, and defect review and approvals all affect the workflow of developers. These processes cannot be put together in a piecemeal fashion. The processes around build, build verification tests (BVTs), and release affect the workflow of quality assurance engineers. These processes, too, must be assembled with the entire system in mind. Sign-off, licensing, and many other aspects of product distribution must belong to the system as a whole. No single discipline involved in the production, testing, or shipping of a product can be left out.

Defining a Quality Product

As mentioned earlier in regard to other disciplines, not all that program managers do can be adequately discussed in this chapter. Aside from source control, build, and other project-wide process definition, program managers play the key role in defining the product.

Research has repeatedly demonstrated that defects introduced during the specification authoring phase are cheaper to fix than those found in later phases of the development process. This places significant pressure on the methods and processes that program managers use to define requirements, features, and projects. The result of this work appears in requirements specifications, feature specifications, and design specifications. Program managers can produce threat models, user interface mockups, workflow diagrams, models, and data schemas, all of which combine to describe how the product will function when complete. The value of quality in these founding documents is vital to the success of the rest of the project. Ensuring quality in these documents determines largely the quality of the product. To build quality into this phase of the project, program managers should use several techniques:

- **Use cases**   Models of users' behaviors, wants, and needs can help other engineers better understand the intent behind a given feature. Conventions for effective communication are vital here.

- **Design reviews**   Coordinate with development and test peers to review design documents. Make sure questions are answered before coding begins. Many practices from code reviews can be reused here, such as checklists.

- **User interface walkthroughs**   Prototype applications, even as paper mockups, provide insight to development and test resources associated with the product.

Still, the program manager's role does not end with the documents and processes described here. The program manager continues to be a resource throughout all development and test processes, answering questions and helping coordinate communication between dependent subsystems. Additionally, the program manager coordinates and collects data from other aspects of the community.

Community

There are many factors involved in shipping a product. Depending on the size of the product, some of the following activities may not apply to your product, but often they can provide helpful insights and experiences that aid in the quality of the product.

Self-Hosting   *Self-hosting* refers to the use of the product under development by the team developing the product. Depending on the product, self-hosting may not be appropriate, but when it is, it can provide useful insights into how the product is used by others. This makes it a valuable addition to a portfolio of quality assurance efforts. For example, in the case of the Windows operating system, development and quality assurance engineers run the latest build of Windows on their own workstations. This can be a harrowing experience because engineers may spend hours debugging issues instead of getting other work done. Inevitably, engineers have several computers to use and cycle daily between new installations.

Over the life of the product, self-hosters file mountains of bugs, which garner immediate attention from peer developers. Every self-hoster knows that his or her system could crash the next day, so helping others makes all lives better.

Usage Models   As with self-hosting, feedback may come from many sources, including beta sites, key customer relationships, or business partners. For applicable products, this community can provide key insights into usage models. The difficult part comes when comparing this feedback to the usage models for the product. Often, reported defects from beta sites or interoperability issues reported by key customers do not really define the usage model; rather, they define a specific action where a failure occurred. Aggregating these distinct actions also does not define an adequate usage model.

Instead, engineers must take a more holistic approach, where monitoring and measuring of actual usage drive analysis and review. This means spending time reviewing feedback reports to understand the intent behind a user's action. Perhaps this leads to reviewing the original requirements specification and adding or modifying use cases. As mentioned earlier, a thorough profile of user behaviors can help engineers understand how best to design, develop, and test the product. Changes to use cases may require changes to developed code and existing test processes, but almost as a bonus, engaging with customers throughout the development process can create a relationship of trust with the customer, which always makes for better business.

Usability Testing   Testing the usability of projects has become almost commonplace at Microsoft in the past few years. Teams of engineers attract customers to explore, examine, and provide feedback on products under development. Sometimes these meetings occur as interviews in a Microsoft building. These types are often video broadcast so other team members can learn directly from the feedback.

Exploration focuses on accomplishing particular tasks that users may normally perform on their own computer. The Microsoft engineers monitor the subjects' ability to accomplish a specific task but also ask questions about assumptions the users make. Users provide a valuable service to the product development team, and feedback often finds its way directly into product improvements and feature changes.

Unfortunately, only small numbers of individuals can interview and provide feedback for any given project. This kind of evaluation provides in-depth understanding of the users' preferences and assumptions but does not scale well. The lack of scale limits the product team's ability to understand the breadth of the market.

Alternatively, a small team in the Windows group began a new initiative called scenario voting. Chapter 15, "Scenario Voting," discusses this in more detail, but as compared to formal interview-based usability testing, scenario voting provides different opportunities to understand users and their preferences. With scenario voting, users can rank each feature or activity as important to them (or not). They also can rank how well the current version of the product allows them to accomplish what they want (or not).

Although it is simple feedback, the ability for this kind of solution to scale is enormous. Quickly and efficiently, feature teams can learn from broad ranges and categories. Users provide their preferences and opinions, and then feature teams see how they are meeting the needs of the customers who depend on their feature the most. When evaluating a potential market, the scenario voting approach provides better data that can be extrapolated statistically into useful information. Conversely, formal interviews can provide in-depth feedback and understanding of users' emotional reactions and assumptions.

Conclusion

Each part of the development process plays a role in defining the entire system. Focusing too much on any one component hinders the efficiency of the entire system. The only solution is to evaluate the system as a whole, identifying the least efficient or most problematic components for attention. Investing in techniques to better the problem components drives the success of the entire system. Techniques may range from diversifying the quality assurance practices to broadening and using the community.

Each discipline in the software development process plays a role in the same way that the departments function in a factory. They are dependent on each other, and quality goods must move from group to group for the final product to be its best, and every group or role must play a part in ensuring quality output. Expecting the final stage of the system to make quality appear will not work. Implementing a diverse portfolio of quality assurance techniques, deployed and implemented throughout the overall development process, makes quality products a reality.

Index

Additional Resources for Developers: Advanced Topics and Best Practices

Published and Forthcoming Titles from Microsoft Press

Code Complete, Second Edition
Steve McConnell • ISBN 0-7356-1967-0

For more than a decade, Steve McConnell, one of the premier authors and voices in the software community, has helped change the way developers write code—and produce better software. Now his classic book, *Code Complete*, has been fully updated and revised with best practices in the art and science of constructing software. Topics include design, applying good techniques to construction, eliminating errors, planning, managing construction activities, and relating personal character to superior software. This new edition features fully updated information on programming techniques, including the emergence of Web-style programming, and integrated coverage of object-oriented design. You'll also find new code examples—both good and bad—in C++, Microsoft® Visual Basic®, C#, and Java, although the focus is squarely on techniques and practices.

More About Software Requirements: Thorny Issues and Practical Advice
Karl E. Wiegers • ISBN 0-7356-2267-1

Have you ever delivered software that satisfied all of the project specifications, but failed to meet any of the customers expectations? Without formal, verifiable requirements—and a system for managing them—the result is often a gap between what developers think they're supposed to build and what customers think they're going to get. Too often, lessons about software requirements engineering processes are formal or academic, and not of value to real-world, professional development teams. In this follow-up guide to *Software Requirements*, Second Edition, you will discover even more practical techniques for gathering and managing software requirements that help you deliver software that meets project and customer specifications. Succinct and immediately useful, this book is a must-have for developers and architects.

Software Estimation: Demystifying the Black Art
Steve McConnell • ISBN 0-7356-0535-1

Often referred to as the "black art" because of its complexity and uncertainty, software estimation is not as hard or mysterious as people think. However, the art of how to create effective cost and schedule estimates has not been very well publicized. *Software Estimation* provides a proven set of procedures and heuristics that software developers, technical leads, and project managers can apply to their projects. Instead of arcane treatises and rigid modeling techniques, award-winning author Steve McConnell gives practical guidance to help organizations achieve basic estimation proficiency and lay the groundwork to continue improving project cost estimates. This book does not avoid the more complex mathematical estimation approaches, but the non-mathematical reader will find plenty of useful guidelines without getting bogged down in complex formulas.

Debugging, Tuning, and Testing Microsoft .NET 2.0 Applications
John Robbins • ISBN 0-7356-2202-7

Making an application the best it can be has long been a time-consuming task best accomplished with specialized and costly tools. With Microsoft Visual Studio® 2005, developers have available a new range of built-in functionality that enables them to debug their code quickly and efficiently, tune it to optimum performance, and test applications to ensure compatibility and trouble-free operation. In this accessible and hands-on book, debugging expert John Robbins shows developers how to use the tools and functions in Visual Studio to their full advantage to ensure high-quality applications.

The Security Development Lifecycle
Michael Howard and Steve Lipner • ISBN 0-7356-2214-0

Adapted from Microsoft's standard development process, the Security Development Lifecycle (SDL) is a methodology that helps reduce the number of security defects in code at every stage of the development process, from design to release. This book details each stage of the SDL methodology and discusses its implementation across a range of Microsoft software, including Microsoft Windows Server™ 2003, Microsoft SQL Server™ 2000 Service Pack 3, and Microsoft Exchange Server 2003 Service Pack 1, to help measurably improve security features. You get direct access to insights from Microsoft's security team and lessons that are applicable to software development processes worldwide, whether on a small scale or a large-scale. This book includes a CD featuring videos of developer training classes.

Software Requirements, Second Edition
Karl E. Wiegers • ISBN 0-7356-1879-8

Writing Secure Code, Second Edition
Michael Howard and David LeBlanc • ISBN 0-7356-1722-8

CLR via C#, Second Edition
Jeffrey Richter • ISBN 0-7356-2163-2

For more information about Microsoft Press® books and other learning products, visit: **www.microsoft.com/mspress** *and* **www.microsoft.com/learning**

Microsoft® Press

Additional Resources for C# Developers

Published and Forthcoming Titles from Microsoft Press

Microsoft® Visual C#® 2005 Express Edition: Build a Program Now!
Patrice Pelland • ISBN 0-7356-2229-9

In this lively, eye-opening, and hands-on book, all you need is a computer and the desire to learn how to program with Visual C# 2005 Express Edition. Featuring a full working edition of the software, this fun and highly visual guide walks you through a complete programming project—a desktop weather-reporting application—from start to finish. You'll get an unintimidating introduction to the Microsoft Visual Studio® development environment and learn how to put the lightweight, easy-to-use tools in Visual C# Express to work right away—creating, compiling, testing, and delivering your first, ready-to-use program. You'll get expert tips, coaching, and visual examples at each step of the way, along with pointers to additional learning resources.

Microsoft Visual C# 2005 *Step by Step*
John Sharp • ISBN 0-7356-2129-2

Visual C#, a feature of Visual Studio 2005, is a modern programming language designed to deliver a productive environment for creating business frameworks and reusable object-oriented components. Now you can teach yourself essential techniques with Visual C#—and start building components and Microsoft Windows®–based applications—one step at a time. With *Step by Step*, you work at your own pace through hands-on, learn-by-doing exercises. Whether you're a beginning programmer or new to this particular language, you'll learn how, when, and why to use specific features of Visual C# 2005. Each chapter puts you to work, building your knowledge of core capabilities and guiding you as you create your first C#-based applications for Windows, data management, and the Web.

Programming Microsoft Visual C# 2005 Framework Reference
Francesco Balena • ISBN 0-7356-2182-9

Complementing *Programming Microsoft Visual C# 2005 Core Reference*, this book covers a wide range of additional topics and information critical to Visual C# developers, including Windows Forms, working with Microsoft ADO.NET 2.0 and Microsoft ASP.NET 2.0, Web services, security, remoting, and much more. Packed with sample code and real-world examples, this book will help developers move from understanding to mastery.

Programming Microsoft Visual C# 2005 *Core Reference*
Donis Marshall • ISBN 0-7356-2181-0

Get the in-depth reference and pragmatic, real-world insights you need to exploit the enhanced language features and core capabilities in Visual C# 2005. Programming expert Donis Marshall deftly builds your proficiency with classes, structs, and other fundamentals, and advances your expertise with more advanced topics such as debugging, threading, and memory management. Combining incisive reference with hands-on coding examples and best practices, this *Core Reference* focuses on mastering the C# skills you need to build innovative solutions for smart clients and the Web.

CLR via C#, Second Edition
Jeffrey Richter • ISBN 0-7356-2163-2

In this new edition of Jeffrey Richter's popular book, you get focused, pragmatic guidance on how to exploit the common language runtime (CLR) functionality in Microsoft .NET Framework 2.0 for applications of all types— from Web Forms, Windows Forms, and Web services to solutions for Microsoft SQL Server™, Microsoft code names "Avalon" and "Indigo," consoles, Microsoft Windows NT® Service, and more. Targeted to advanced developers and software designers, this book takes you under the covers of .NET for an in-depth understanding of its structure, functions, and operational components, demonstrating the most practical ways to apply this knowledge to your own development efforts. You'll master fundamental design tenets for .NET and get hands-on insights for creating high-performance applications more easily and efficiently. The book features extensive code examples in Visual C# 2005.

Programming Microsoft Windows Forms
Charles Petzold • ISBN 0-7356-2153-5

CLR via C++
Jeffrey Richter with Stanley B. Lippman
ISBN 0-7356-2248-5

Programming Microsoft Web Forms
Douglas J. Reilly • ISBN 0-7356-2179-9

Debugging, Tuning, and Testing Microsoft .NET 2.0 Applications
John Robbins • ISBN 0-7356-2202-7

For more information about Microsoft Press® books and other learning products, visit: **www.microsoft.com/books** *and* **www.microsoft.com/learning**

Dan Bean

Dan Bean has been in the computer industry for more than 25 years and with Microsoft since 1993. Like many people with long careers in the computer field, Dan has had the opportunity to work in a variety of disciplines including system design, program management, development, test, and IT. As a member of the Microsoft Engineering Excellence Group, Dan worked on engineering practices incorporating Failure Modes and Effects Analysis and Fault Tree Analysis. In addition to earning a Bachelor of Science degree in Computer Science from Washington State University, Dan also earned a Black Belt in Six Sigma from the Juran Institute.

David Catlett

David Catlett has been developing people, tools, and techniques for testing software for more than 16 years. In his current role as Principal Test Architect in the Microsoft Windows Engineering Tools team, he is researching and implementing methods to increase the quality of software while decreasing the cost of engineering. In this role, he is focusing on risk analysis, improving testability, and improving the quality of test code itself. He holds a Bachelor of Science degree in Computer Science/Math from the University of Puget Sound, and more importantly, is husband to Erika and dad to Josh, Emilie, and Sara

Lori Ada Kilty

Lori Ada Kilty has been involved in Balanced Scorecards and metrics for software for many years. After completing her Bachelor of Science degree in Computer Science, she was hired by Microsoft to work on tools for home and entertainment software. She has 10 years of Microsoft experience and 20 years of military experience. Before retiring from the military, she was instrumental in developing and deploying an automated dashboard system for command and leadership metrics for her National Guard unit. She has worked with various teams throughout Microsoft in test, development, and program management.

Marc McDonald

Marc McDonald's career spans the 30-year personal computer industry-from Microsoft Basic on the MITS Altair to Windows Vista-and he holds six software patents. Marc is the first salaried employee of Microsoft, joining Bill Gates and Paul Allen in Albuquerque, where he designed the FAT file system used in MS-DOS and Windows. He was the first employee at Asymetrix and Design Intelligence. He pioneered the standard for free sodas and casual dress in the software industry.

Robert Musson

Robert Musson has more than 25 years of software experience as a development engineer and experience in various management positions. He spent 15 years at Teradyne, helping bring to market a variety of products for the telecommunications industry. While there, he helped deploy the Team Software Process (TSP) to the first industry site. He was vice president of business strategy at a small startup before becoming a member of the TSP Initiative at the Software Engineering Institute of Carnegie-Mellon University. He currently is a member of the Defect Prevention group in the Core OS Division of Windows and manages the department of statistical distortions. He has a Master's degree in Computer Science from Illinois Institute of Technology and a Master's degree in Business Administration from Northwestern University's Kellogg School of Management.

Ross Smith

Ross Smith has been making mistakes for more than 40 years. (See the first page of Chapter 1.) He has been in the software industry for almost 20 years, developing and testing software on everything from mainframe systems to handheld devices and PC's. He has also been a jail guard, union president, cartoonist, and graphic artist. He began his Microsoft career in Product Support in 1991 and has been a Test Lead, Test Manager, and Test Architect. He has been a long-time member of the Test Architect's Group, and has worked on every version of Windows and Office since 1995. He holds five software patents, and is currently director of the Windows Core Security Test team. He lives with his wife and four kids on a remote island in Puget Sound.

Joshua Williams

Joshua Williams has been testing releases of Windows at Microsoft for more than 12 years, working across multiple versions and architectures of the OS. He has managed teams testing globalization, drivers, and automation frameworks. He has worked as a lead, manager, evangelist, and architect in various test teams. He managed the USB test effort through the development and deployment of USB 2.0, regularly presenting at USB and industry events. Most recently, he has focused on large-scale automation systems, and group-wide process improvement strategies.

What do you think of this book?

We want to hear from you!

Do you have a few minutes to participate in a brief online survey?

Microsoft is interested in hearing your feedback so we can continually improve our books and learning resources for you.

To participate in our survey, please visit:

www.microsoft.com/learning/booksurvey/

...and enter this book's ISBN-10 number (appears above barcode on back cover*).
As a thank-you to survey participants in the United States and Canada, each month we'll randomly select five respondents to win one of five $100 gift certificates from a leading online merchant. At the conclusion of the survey, you can enter the drawing by providing your e-mail address, which will be used for prize notification only.

Thanks in advance for your input. Your opinion counts!

* Where to find the ISBN-10 on back cover

ISBN-13: 000-0-0000-00000-0
ISBN-10: 0-0000-00000-0

0 000000 000000

Example only. Each book has unique ISBN.

No purchase necessary. Void where prohibited. Open only to residents of the 50 United States (includes District of Columbia) and Canada (void in Quebec). For official rules and entry dates see:

www.microsoft.com/learning/booksurvey/